CRITICAL READING AND WRITING IN THE DIGITAL AGE

Critical Reading and Writing in the Digital Age is a fully introductory, interactive textbook that explores the power relations at work in and behind the texts we encounter in our everyday lives. Using examples from numerous genres – such as fiction, poetry, advertisements and newspapers – this textbook examines the language choices a writer must make in structuring texts, representing the world and positioning the reader. Assuming no prior knowledge of linguistics, *Critical Reading and Writing in the Digital Age* offers guidance on how to read texts critically and how to develop effective writing skills.

Extensively updated, key features of the second edition include:

- a radically revised and repackaged section that highlights the theme of discourses of power and authority and the new possibilities for resisting them;
- a revamped analysis of the art of communication which has changed due to the advent of new media including Facebook and Wikipedia;
- fresh examples, exercises and case studies including fan fiction, articles from the BBC, *Daily Mail* and *South China Morning Post*, and a selection of international ads for a variety of products;
- a brand new companion website at www.routledge.com/cw/goatly featuring projects, quizzes and activities for each chapter, a glossary and further reading.

Written by two experienced teachers, *Critical Reading and Writing in the Digital Age* is an ideal coursebook for students of English language.

Andrew Goatly has taught English Language and Linguistics in colleges and universities in the UK, Rwanda, Thailand, Singapore and Hong Kong, and is currently an Honorary Professor at Lingnan University, Hong Kong. He is the author of five books, including *The Language of Metaphors* (Routledge 1997).

Preet Hiradhar is Assistant Professor in the Department of English at Lingnan University, Hong Kong.

CRITICAL READING AND WRITING IN THE DIGITAL AGE

An introductory coursebook

Second Edition

ANDREW GOATLY AND PREET HIRADHAR

Routledge
Taylor & Francis Group

LONDON AND NEW YORK

Second edition published 2016
by Routledge
2 Park Square, Milton Park, Abingdon, Oxon OX14 4RN

and by Routledge
711 Third Avenue, New York, NY 10017

Routledge is an imprint of the Taylor & Francis Group, an informa business

First edition published by Routledge 2000

British Library Cataloguing in Publication Data
A catalogue record for this book is available from the British Library

Library of Congress Cataloging-in-Publication Data
A catalog record for this book has been requested

ISBN: 978-0-415-84261-7 (hbk)
ISBN: 978-0-415-84262-4 (pbk)
ISBN: 978-1-315-61672-8 (ebk)

Typeset in Galliard and Futura
by Wearset Ltd, Boldon, Tyne and Wear

Printed and bound in Great Britain by
TJ International Ltd, Padstow, Cornwall

CONTENTS

IMAGES

FIGURES

TABLES

ACKNOWLEDGEMENTS

This book would never have been written without the stimulus of Anne-liese Kramer-Dahl, with whom one of the authors was lucky enough to share the teaching of the courses Professional Writing at the National University of Singapore and Language and Education at Nanyang Technological University. Besides the general education she gave in Critical Discourse Analysis and Critical Literacy, she is owed a particular debt for Activity 34, for which she provided the text. Other colleagues at NTU were also good enough to read early drafts of the book and give their comments: Peter Teo, Antonia Chandrasekaran and Brendan Buxton, and we would like to express gratitude to them. The students on the module Critical Reading and Writing 1 at the National Institute of Education in Singapore were very diligent in filling in the survey feedback form which helped to make necessary revisions to the content. The students at Lingnan University in Hong Kong who used the first edition also gave invaluable feedback and pointed out some errors which have been corrected in the second edition. Most importantly, we would like to express special thanks to Gunther Kress for his invaluable insights into the reading and understanding meanings of visual texts, which forms a significant part of this second edition.

The readers recruited by Routledge were exceptionally committed and helpful. We would like to single out Thomas Huckin, David Stacey and, above all, Rob Pope for their sympathetic responses, and eminently reasonable and constructive suggestions, many of which we have been able to incorporate. The book is much better as a result. Nadia Seemungal, our commissioning editor at Routledge, and Helen Tredget, her assistant, have been as efficient as one could hope for.

Thanks are due to the following copyright owners for allowing us permission to use their texts as examples for analysis.

Extract from *Nelson Mandela death*, www.mirror.co.uk/all-about/nelson-mandela-death, reproduced with kind permission of the Mirror Group.

Extract from *Big Sur wildfire destroys 15 homes and 500 acres of national forest*, www.theguardian.com/world/2013/dec/17/big-sur-wildfire-destroys-homes-forest, Associated Press in Big Sur, 17 December 2013, reproduced with kind permission of the Press Association.

Extract from *Japan increases defence budget amid tensions with China*, www.theguardian.com/world/2013/dec/17/japan-increases-defence-budget-tensions-china, Justin McCurry, 17 December 2013, reproduced with kind permission of Guardian News and Media Ltd.

Extracts from *UK unemployment rate at lowest since 2009*, www.bbc.co.uk/news/business-25428119, 18 December 2013; *What is the appeal of Candy Crush Saga?* www.bbc.co.uk/news/magazine-25334716 18/12/2013; and *Iraqi Sunni protest clashes in Hawija leave many dead* www.bbc.co.uk/news/world-middle-east-22261422 23 December 2013, all reproduced with kind permission of the BBC.

'Where is she?', from *The Newly Born Woman* by Hélène Cixous (1986), IB Tauris: London, reproduced with kind permission of IB Tauris & Co. Ltd.

Extract from *Daily Mail Comment: Global warming and an inconvenient truth*, www.dailymail.co.uk/debate/article-2259934/DAILY-MAIL-COMMENT-Global-warming-inconvenient-truth.html, 10 January 2013, and from *Rescuers use massive strips of cloth as escape chutes after Primark factory in Bangladesh collapses killing at least 275 people*, www.dailymail.co.uk/news/article-2313974/Bangladesh-Rescuers-use-massive-strips-cloth-escape-chutes-textile-factory-collapses-killing-275-people.html #ixzz31tNPY0C0, Eleanor Harding 24 January 2013, reproduced with kind permission of Solo Syndications.

Dorma fabrics advert reproduced with kind permission of Dunelm and Graham Ford. Photograph by Graham Ford.

AGA advert reproduced with kind permission of AGA Rangemaster Group.

'Sonnet' and 'Birdsong for two voices' from *Woods etc* by Alice Oswald (2005) Faber and Faber: London, and 'Reading scheme' from *Making Cocoa for Kingsley Amis* by Wendy Cope (1986) Faber and Faber: London, all reproduced with kind permission of Faber and Faber.

'Little Red Riding Hood' from *Politically Correct Bedtime Stories* by James Finn Garner (1994) Macmillan, reproduced with kind permission of James Finn Garner.

Letter from *America needs active support from Britain and NATO in Iraq* www.telegraph.co.uk/comment/letters/11021640/America-needs-active-support-from-Britain-and-Nato-in-Iraq.html, 9 August 2014, reproduced with kind permission of Telegraph Media Group Ltd.

Extract from *#IceBucketChallenge: why you're not really helping*, www.huffingtonpost.com/ben-kosinski/icebucketchallenge-why-yo_b_5656649.html by Ben Kosinski 8 July 2014, reproduced with kind permission of Ben Kosinski, Founder at Sumpto.

Extract from *Collaborating to replenish the water we use*, reproduced with kind permission of Coca-Cola.

Extract from *Case against Coca-Cola Kerala State: India*, righttowater.info, 20 August 2010, reproduced with kind permission.

Extract from *Beijing blamed as Hong Kong's press freedom declines*, SCMP.com, 13 February 2014, reproduced with kind permission of *South China Morning Post*.

Routledge monthly highlights email, http://tandf.msgfocus.com/q/17ErBd8G4mBas9AW6V1uS7/wv, reproduced with kind permission of Taylor and Francis.

Every effort has been made to contact copyright holders. Please advise the publisher of any errors or omissions, and these will be corrected in subsequent editions.

TYPOGRAPHICAL CONVENTIONS

- The pronoun *she* is used to refer to a writer or speakers and the pronoun *he* to refer to the reader or hearer, except in cases where the sex of actual readers and writers is known.

In the main text:
- Double quotation marks are used either as scare quotes (for contested terms) or to indicate a meaning rather than a form, e.g. 'Grant deplores the "bimbos" in the White House'; '*choice* can mean "the act of choosing" or "what is chosen"'.
- Single quotation marks are used for tokens of forms cited and quotation, e.g. In line 6 we have the affective word 'great'.
- Italics are used to refer to types of words, e.g. 'the modal *can* has several different meanings'.
- Emboldened items are used for technical terms where the term is first introduced, defined and explained, e.g. 'By **ideology** I mean "knowledge in the service of power"'. These items appear in the index/glossary, where there is also a cross reference to the pages where they are defined and explained.
- Shaded areas of text include direct and useful practical hints on writing, and can be useful for revision/review purposes.
- Double-headed arrows >> mean "presupposes".
- X IS Y indicates a metaphor theme or conceptual metaphor, e.g. MONEY IS LIQUID.

In examples and boxed activities:
- In transitivity analysis the verb referring to the process is emboldened, and the participants are underlined e.g. John (actor) **smoked** (material process) a cigarette (affected).
- An asterisk * is used to indicate that it would be useful for students to bring to class a PowerPoint or multiple copies of the text to be discussed.

INTRODUCTION

0.1 WHO IS THIS BOOK FOR?

This is a practical textbook on reading, writing and critical thinking in the digital age, designed for undergraduate, college and pre-university students in the UK, USA and other English-speaking countries worldwide. It will be very useful for those who are going on to major in English Studies, Communication Studies, Media Studies, Journalism, Cultural Studies and Education. However, the first edition was originally designed for and tested on students who may not specialise in those areas, but who are taking a university/college foundation course in critical reading and writing.

0.2 WHAT IS CRITICAL READING AND WRITING?

Critical Reading and Writing in the Digital Age is an ambiguous title. *Critical* is, for a start, used to mean many things in an educational context. To some *critical thinking* simply means the ability to see logical flaws in arguments or to weigh up the evidence for explicit claims. In this coursebook we take a wider view. *Critical* partly means resisting the assumptions on which "rational" arguments are based, by explaining and questioning how common-sense "logic" establishes its categories in the first place. And this leads us to an even wider meaning for *critical*: "explaining how the world and our relationships within it and to it are constructed through reading and writing". By what *criteria* do we judge discourse and its claims, assumptions and values?

Another meaning for *critical* sees it as derived, not from the noun *criteria*, but from *crisis*. The world and its inhabitants face a number of crises. For many, life is still critical from day to day, with either unemployment or persistent food shortages threatening one billion. Others, especially perhaps women, find the relationships within the family and the demands of conflicting social roles increasingly intolerable. Meanwhile, whole populations in modern urban society have been subjected to scientifically based technological experiments. Some of these – like using plastic with its mimic oestrogens, putting CFCs in aerosols, putting fructose syrup in food and drink or allowing the car to be used as the primary means of transport – have turned out to have disastrous consequences, and have led to a crisis in confidence for science and technology. Linked to this is an ecological crisis, which calls into question the systems of economic and technological development of the last 250 years, and the culture of consumer capitalism which has established itself in the last 75. Moreover, the concentration of power in the traditional news media has brought about a crisis of democracy, as can be seen from the context and results of the UK general election in 2015. And the financial crisis of 2008 seems to have worsened the crisis of inequality already established by neo-conservative economic theory. How the ideology, the way of thinking that causes these crises, can be detected in and behind text and discourse is one of the themes running through this book.

Another theme is the way in which power and authority can be resisted and contested. This emerges particularly clearly in Part C. We show the need to look beneath the surface of the operations and publicity of large corporations. We suggest ways in which the internet can be used to challenge the power of the media by democratising and providing alternative news. We explore the potential of humour to be subversive, and of poetry to make us rethink our attitude to the environment.

0.3 HOW CAN I USE THIS BOOK?

Used intelligently, this textbook can provide a comprehensive introduction to the language and choices which writers consciously or unconsciously make in composing and revising texts. And it should also raise critical awareness of how these choices structure our thought processes and affect our social and environmental behaviour. With this in mind it is not supposed to be read in one go or even necessarily from cover to cover, but is designed as a practical and interactive textbook. Its **accompanying companion website at www.routledge.com/cw/ goatly** incorporates the following features **highlighted by this logo**.

- Many activities in analysis, writing and re-writing, which help to clarify the concepts introduced, and give practice in applying them to the production of texts. These might form the basis for class or seminar discussion on taught courses, or as exercises for self-study.

- Comments on these activities, which may be referred to by teachers and students, but which can often be the basis for debate. They will be especially useful for students studying on their own.
- Further reading references, which give guidance on how to explore the topics in greater depth.
- An index/glossary which defines the technical linguistic and discourse analysis terminology used and introduced in the text.
- Suggestions for extended writing projects, which will be targeted at a real readership, and which give scope for "writing back" against power through alternative discourses.
- Extra material which appeared in the first edition but which was replaced in the second.

The book aims to develop an understanding of how we are socially positioned by the discourse in which we participate, of how discourse enacts the power relations and conflicts within society. Since we only discover ourselves and our ideologies in relation to others, the writing projects suggested in this book should have a real readership. So they are designed to give experience of analysing and producing the kinds of texts which will be important in everyday life and professional life, or, which, for future teachers, are likely to be relevant to pupils.

0.4 E-PORTFOLIOS

Students may be encouraged to use an electronic portfolio to provide evidence of learning. An e-portfolio provides a means of collecting, documenting, reflecting on, and sharing various experiences and texts (written, visual, multimedia, etc.). It would, at a minimum, be a record of the coursebook activities and projects attempted, responses to any differences between their "answers" to activities and the comments provided, and feedback and reflection on the projects carried out. But it could include any other examples of texts which students came across which they can relate, through commentary, to the theories in the textbook and which may be shared with other students. It might also contain general reflection on their responses to the coursebook and what they find most useful and interesting, or contentious. Through an e-portfolio students will create their own personal learning space for the course.

While most institutions provide a platform, students can also create their own e-portfolio by using Google sites or any other freely available platform such as Foliospaces (www.foliospaces.org).

0.5 DESCRIBING TEXT, INTERPRETING DISCOURSE AND EXPLAINING IDEOLOGY

There are three levels at which we understand and analyse what we read and write (Fairclough 2001: 18–23; see Table 0.1). First of all we decode the surface forms and meanings of a text, and these meanings can be described. By **text** we mean "the physical form which the writing (speaking) takes on the page (in the air) and the meanings which this physical form encodes". This decoding depends upon **semantics** and answers the question 'What does the text mean?'

At a second level, we have to interpret what we have decoded, as part of discourse, working out, for example, who it refers to and guessing what inferences we are expected to make. By **discourse** we mean "the act of communication in which the writer intends to affect a reader, and the reader attempts to work out the writer's intentions". This interpretation of intention depends upon **pragmatics**, and answers the question 'What does the writer mean by this text?'

The third level, which we often ignore, is **explanation**, the end of critical discourse analysis (CDA), showing why the discourse and text are the way they are. It asks the question 'What social and ideological forces underlie or determine text and discourse meanings?' By **ideology** we mean "the ways of thinking which (re)produce and reflect the power structures of society", or, more briefly, "meaning in the service of power" (Thomson 1984).

An example will make this clearer. Let's look at the news report below ' "Superman" may never walk again' (from *The International Express*, 1–7 June 1995).

'Superman' may never walk again

(1) SUPERMAN star Christopher Reeve is in hospital with a suspected broken back.

(2) His family ordered hospital officials not to give out any information – but sources say he is partially paralysed.

(3) The actor's publicist, Lisa Kastelere, was plainly upset as she revealed that horse-mad Reeve was hurt show-jumping in Virginia.

(4) Witnesses saw him hit the ground hard as his horse shied.

(5) As doctors evaluated his condition in the acute care ward at the University of Virginia's Medical Centre in Charlottesville, it was not known whether he will walk again.

Table 0.1 *Three levels of discourse analysis*

Level 1	Coding and describing	Part A
Level 2	Interpreting and inferencing	Part B
Level 3	Explaining the ideology behind 1 and 2	Part C (A & B)

(6)   Reeve, 43 and 6 ft 4 in, was flown to the hospital by air-
       ambulance after doctors at the competition decided he needed
       special care.
(7)   Reeve, who starred in 4 Superman movies, lived with his British
       lover Gael Exton for 11 years.
(8)   They had two children.
(9)   Reeve then began a relationship with singer Dana Morosini.

At the first level, description, we could, for example, note that the first
two lines of the report and the headline are in larger font, and that
almost every sentence takes up a whole paragraph. These are features that
help us to place the text in the genre of news report. Or we might note a
shift in formality between sentence 4 and sentence 5, with 92 per cent
single-syllable words in sentence 4 and only 60 per cent in sentence 5.
We could also analyse the phrases used to refer to and describe the
named characters in this text, noting incidentally that these characters are
generally given first position in the sentence/paragraph:

Christopher Reeve	Superman star, partially paralysed, horse-mad, 43 and 6 ft 4 in
Lisa Kastelere	the actor's publicist, upset
Gael Exton	British lover
Dana Morosini	singer

Moving to the second level, discourse interpretation, it's quite clear
that we have to make several inferences in order to understand this
passage. We would infer, for example, that the events described in the
last two paragraphs took place before those in the first six. Or that
Reeve's hitting the ground hard (sentence 4) was the cause of his suspected broken back (sentence 1), since this is not actually stated. These
two inferences are quite uncontroversial, but inferencing is a risky business and a more controversial inference may be suggested by the
information in sentences 8 and 9. These may imply that Reeve somehow
deserved this "punishment" for abandoning his British lover and their
two children and striking up a relationship with Dana Morosini.

The description and interpretation levels of understanding and analysis
lead to ideological explanation. For example, the description phase shows
that Lisa Kastelere is depicted as 'upset'. This fits neatly into the stereotype of women as prone to emotions or unable to hide them (Fowler
1991: 101). In addition, the only nationality adjective used in the passage is 'British', used to describe Gael Exton. We can explain this if we
know the ideological position of the newspaper. Express Newspapers are
British with a capital 'B', unashamedly nationalistic and supporters of the
anti-immigrant party UKIP, featuring the Union Jack flag and a medieval

crusader as a masthead adjacent to their title. Reeve's former partner – who was a 'lover', by the way, not just someone like Dana Morosini with whom he had a 'relationship' – was British. This might make Britain somehow more important, or at least enable the British reader to relate more closely to the story. Such a nationalistic background also provides an ideological explanation for the doubtful interpretation – that the accident was deserved as a punishment for infidelity.

0.6 THE ORGANISATION OF THE COURSEBOOK

The way this book is organised roughly reflects these three levels of analysis (see Table 0.1). In Part A, at level 1, we analyse the forms and meanings that the text explicitly gives us. At this level we will be looking at text from three perspectives of meaning:

1   **Textual meaning**, to do with the ways in which texts can be organised, in sentences, paragraphs, visually and according to structures of a genre (Chapter 1). Examples are the headline and paragraphing of the superman report.
2   Conceptual or **ideational meaning**, in which the language and visuals of the text represent, sort and classify the outside world and the mental world (Chapter 2). This is exemplified by the descriptions which are used of Reeve, Exton and Morosini.
3   **Interpersonal meaning**, in which the text sets up relationships between readers and writers (Chapter 3). For instance, we noted the shifts in formality between sentences 4 and 5.

These three perspectives on the meanings encoded in texts derive from the functional grammar associated with Michael Halliday (Halliday 1994, Halliday and Matthiessen 2004). This sees grammar as designed to perform three functions within a social context – textual, ideational and interpersonal – and so Hallidayan grammar is particularly suitable for describing naturally occurring socially situated texts. It is also distinctive in the attention it gives to interpersonal meanings; most traditional treatments of semantics concentrate almost entirely on logical or ideational meaning.

Halliday's functions can also be applied to visual communication (Kress and Van Leeuwen 1996) and we will briefly analyse visuals in Part A. In Chapter 1 we explore the organisation of visually informative texts. In Chapter 2 we concentrate on what Kress and Van Leeuwen call 'represented participants' and in Chapter 3 'interactive participants'.

In Part B, Chapters 4, 5 and 6, we move to the discourse perspective, the production and interpretation of text as a social act. If Part A was about what the text means, then Part B is about what the writer means by and does with the discourse, or what meanings and effects are felt and created by the reader. Texts are by-products of this social interaction. As cues and traces of discourse acts, texts have to be produced and interpreted by reader and writer (Chapter 4). Irony and metaphors are prime examples where inferencing and interpretation are essential in getting at the writer's intended meaning. In discourse we do things to each other with texts, we position each other socially (Chapter 5). For instance, the 'Superman' report positions the reader as someone interested in the private life of a show-business personality. But texts do not work in isolation from each other. We make texts out of other texts, we use information from previously encountered texts to interpret the current one, in a web of intertextuality (Chapter 6): we notice that the news report is made up of texts first produced by, among others, the 'sources' (sentence 2) and the 'witnesses' (sentence 4).

Parts A and B show how the structures and the stated and implied meanings of texts can be analysed and then related to ideologies. But Part C starts at the other end by considering ideologies and how they are expressed in texts. We look at three sets of case studies from different ideological perspectives and in terms of three main crises: advertising texts as an expression of consumerism, the power of global capital and the crisis of inequality (Chapter 7); news reports as an expression of the dominance of powerful political, ethnic and economic elites and the crisis of democracy (Chapter 8); and environmental discourse and poetry in their contrasting representations of the human–nature relationship as a response to our ecological crises (Chapter 9). All three sets of case studies open opportunities for writing against power. But, Chapter 10, focusing on humour, parody and fan fiction, puts a major emphasis on their potential to resist and subvert the authority of powerful people, institutions and texts.

0.7 PATHWAYS THROUGH THE BOOK

Though the careful organisation of the book suggests that the most straightforward way of reading is in the order given, for students whose interests are less in the English language and more on these various ideological perspectives, there is the possibility of beginning with Part C, with its ideological background and analysis of media and poetic texts. If this option is taken, then there would have to be selective reference back to Parts A and B or to the website glossary in order to understand the relevant technical terms in the analyses. These pathways are illustrated in Figure 0.1, but the introduction to Part C also suggests how to read that section.

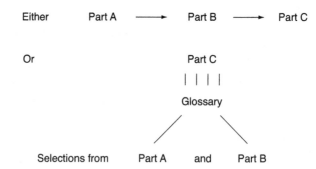

Figure 0.1
Pathways through
the book

See also the introduction to Part C for suggestions on how to read that section.

0.8 AN OUTLINE OF THE BOOK

PART A: CRITICAL LINGUISTICS: READING MEANINGS OFF THE TEXT

Chapter 1: Genre and the organisation of text
shows how texts are organised at the level of the sentence, paragraph and genre, and explores the use of visual information and graphics.

Chapter 2: Text and conceptual meaning
explains how the language and visuals in texts sort, classify and represent the phenomena in the outer world and the inner world of the mind, and explores the use of stereotyping.

Chapter 3: Texts and interpersonal meaning
surveys the main ways in which the text sets up relationships between readers and writers, reflecting and creating social distance, and expressing emotion.

PART B: CRITICAL DISCOURSE: READING MEANINGS INTO THE TEXT

Chapter 4: Interpreting discourse
shows how the meanings of texts are never complete without inferences on the part of the reader, and that in some cases like irony and metaphor, we cannot take the meaning of the text at face value.

Chapter 5: Reading and writing positions
views the production of texts as an action performed by the writer on the reader and as a means of setting up roles and positions for the reader and writer.

Chapter 6: Intertextuality
exemplifies how texts interpenetrate and influence each other: how a prior text provides information which influences the interpretation or production of later texts; and how through experience of varieties of texts we develop a sense of genres.

PART C: THE AUTHORITY AND POWER BEHIND DISCOURSE AND RESISTING IT

Chapter 7: Ads, consumer capitalism and the crisis of inequality
explores the ideology behind advertising and consumer capitalism, and analyses magazine advertisements and a webpage to see how this ideology is reflected in their language and visuals, contrasting this to the reality of the circumstances of production of the consumer products.

Chapter 8: News, institutional power and the crisis of democracy
argues that the notion of "unbiased news" is a myth, given the ownership of the press, the institutionalised racism in the selection of news and the access to the media by the rich and powerful; these arguments are supported by surveying the content and analysing the language of newspapers; it also explores the possibilities of social media and citizen journalism as alternative sources of news.

Chapter 9: Environmental discourse, poetry and the ecological crisis
makes the case for an ecological critical discourse analysis, suggests how linguistic resources can be most helpfully exploited to more faithfully reflect modern ecological theory, and shows how the poems of Wordsworth, Edward Thomas and Alice Oswald do so better than some environmental discourse.

Chapter 10: The power of fiction and comedy
considers the role of humour in challenging authority through its potential psychological, social and linguistic liberation, and the role of parody or fan fiction in writing back against the power, including the power of dominant fictional texts.

GLOSSARY
REFERENCES
INDEX

0.9 A GUIDE TO THE WEBSITE

This edition of the book comes along with a companion website at www. routledge.com/cw/goatly in order to help you better consolidate concepts introduced throughout the book. In keeping with the demands of the new age learner and learning styles, our companion website will act as a valuable resource to readers. It includes the following resources to make your learning experience useful and relevant to our times. Where this logo appears, these materials are available on the companion website.

Activities and comments
Every new concept introduced in a unit is followed-up with an activity – a sort of "check your understanding" task. You will also find comments on these activities, which can be referred to by teachers and students alike for better understanding and to provoke discussion.

Quizzes
You can check your understanding for the various concepts in each chapter with the multiple choice quizzes.

Further readings
The end of each unit will take you to a further reading list, which will help you to explore topics of interest in more detail. The details of these readings can be looked up on academic search engines instantaneously.

Glossary
A comprehensive glossary of key linguistic and technical terms used in the book.

References
A list of complete references, used for the materials in the book as well as in the website's further reading. This will make web links and/or PDF links mentioned in the references easily accessible.

Additional content
The website includes content regarding the role of computer-mediated participation for purposes of contesting discourses of power and authority: the use of social media platforms, blogs/wikis and different forms of popular culture used in the digital age. The section will emphasise how these forms of public contestation go hand in hand with the construction of identity within global cultural contexts.

Supplementary material
Finally, supplementary material includes further examples and sample analysis from the first edition for further discussion and analysis, and extra data for which there was not enough space in the hard copy book.

PART A

CRITICAL LINGUISTICS

Reading meanings off the text

GENRE AND THE ORGANISATION OF TEXT

1

The aim of this chapter
is to show how we can organise information in texts, through language, visuals and the structure of different genres.

Contents

1.0 Introduction: the need for organisation
underlines the fact that texts will be judged not only on their content but also on their organisation and textual impact.

1.1 Information in the clause and sentence
analyses the language resources for distributing old and new information in sentences, and patterns of organisation over sequences of sentences.

1.2 The structure of the paragraph
introduces four basic kinds of paragraph structure, and explores the differences between point-first and point-last structures.

1.3 Generic structure
explains the notion of generic structure, concentrating on narratives and news reports and showing how the latter's structure gives scope for bias.

1.4 Visual information in texts
surveys the devices at our disposal for making texts more visually interesting, and discusses their effects on reading.

1.5 Summary and postscript on genre, culture and ideology

Activities
As well as many small-scale activities, there are two major activities on

- making a text more visually attractive
- rewriting a narrative as a news report.

1.0 INTRODUCTION: THE NEED FOR ORGANISATION

Supposing you bumped into your new professor in the canteen and wanted to arrange to meet her in her office, and she gave you the following directions:

> It's the third office on the left on the corridor. You need the Arts building, that's three blocks down from here. It's on the second floor.

Though there is enough information here to get you to the office, it's so badly organised that it will be difficult to remember or to use. In fact it breaks two principles of the organisation of information. The first is that a speaker/writer should start from what the hearer/reader already knows. The second is that when a sequence is described its elements should be given in the order in which they take place. So it would be better to start with going to the Arts building, which you are informed is three blocks down from the canteen, and then to tell which floor you need, and finally where on the corridor it is:

> Three blocks down from here is the Arts building. Go to the second floor. It's the third office on the left.

Spoken text is entirely linear, and written text tends to be so. In other words, we have to listen in the order in which the words are spoken, and we often read the text in the order in which it is presented, though, as we shall see, this varies with the kind of text, and how visual it is. Because language text is largely linear, the order in which we present information is crucial in organising our material effectively.

In fact, reading a text is very much like making a journey from one point to another. If a longish text is well organised it will be possible for the writer to give a map and visual cues to the reader – indicate in advance and by graphic devices how the text is sectionalised, what point in the text we have reached and where we are going next. These are a great help to the reader and make the organisation clear. But a map is impossible without an underlying organisation. So let's examine the various ways in which information can be organised and presented in text.

1.1 INFORMATION IN THE CLAUSE AND SENTENCE

First of all we can consider how information is ordered in the sentence or clause. To analyse clauses for their information structure we can divide them into two parts called **theme** and **rheme**. Assuming the basic elements of the clause can be labelled **Subject**, **Object**, **Verb** and **Adverbial**, the theme will be the first of these elements to occur in the clause. Let's look at some examples.

1

Subject	Verb	Object	Adverbial
A strong earthquake	struck western	China	on Monday morning
Theme...	⏐ **Rheme...**		

2

Object	Subject	Verb	Adverbial
Western China	a strong earthquake	struck	on Monday morning
Theme...	⏐ **Rheme...**		

3

Adverbial	Subject	Verb	Object
On Monday morning	a strong earthquake	struck	western China
Theme...	⏐ **Rheme...**		

There are various additional grammatical tricks we can use to redistribute information. First, we can use the **passive**:

4

Subject	Verb	Adverbial
Western China	was struck	by a strong earthquake
Theme...	⏐ **Rheme...**	

Or we can introduce a second clause:

5   It was western China that was struck by a strong earthquake on Monday morning

6   It was on Monday morning that western China was struck by a strong earthquake

7   It was an earthquake that struck western China on Monday morning

Theme–rheme and given–new

In general, the most straightforward way of organising information in a text is to put old or given information, information the reader and writer already have, in the theme position, and information which is new to the reader towards the end of the rheme. We can see this if we imagine the sentences above are replies to questions.

 ACTIVITY 1 ━━━━━━━━━━━━━━━━━━━━━━━━━━━

Please refer to the companion website for the activity material.

> The guiding principle is, then, that the most important new information goes at the end of the rheme, and given or old information goes in the theme. If in your writing you bend this rule then you should have very good reasons for doing so.

ACTIVITY 2

Please refer to the companion website for the activity material.

1.2 THE STRUCTURE OF THE PARAGRAPH

Thematic strings or thematic development

Besides looking at the themes of individual clauses, we can consider the pattern of themes over a whole paragraph or passage. A clear pattern of **thematic development** will often be a sign of good organisation. Consider this short news item about Nelson Mandela's death, where the three themes, underlined, all refer to the dead man:

NELSON MANDELA DEATH

Anti-apartheid activist Nelson Mandela died on December 5th 2013. Mandela, also affectionately known as Madiba, spent 27 years in prison, many of them on Robben Island, before his release in 1990. He went on to become the first president of South Africa in the fully democratic post-apartheid era, serving from 1995 to 1999.

Or look back at the text about the late Christopher Reeve's horse-riding accident in the introduction (p. 4), where the themes are as follows:

Superman star Christopher Reeve
His family
Sources
The actor's publicist Lisa Kastelere
She
Horse-mad Reeve
Witnesses
Doctors
Reeve, 43 and 6 ft 4 in
Doctors
Reeve
They
Reeve

There is an obvious pattern here. The themes always refer to people, as normal in human-interest stories. Almost half of the themes refer to Reeve. The other people referred to are those who have reacted verbally to the accident or its aftermath.

ACTIVITY 3

Please refer to the companion website for the activity material.

> We have seen that the words in the theme of sentences and clauses have a very important role in making a text hang together, technically, giving it **cohesion.** Or to put it another way, repeated references to the same people or semantic areas throughout a text may well help the text cohere; but if the expressions which refer to them are in the theme position this cohesion will be more obvious and more organised.

We noted patterns of referring to one person in the Mandela text, various persons in the Superman text, and to seasons in passage 2 in Activity 3.

Paragraph structure

Thematic development is one area to consider when organising our text, but equally important is paragraph structure. Walter Nash (1980) suggested four quite typical ways of organising paragraphs in continuous prose, which he calls the Step, the Stack, the Chain and the Balance. These are not rigid patterns, and may be combined or modified, but they often give a basic shape to paragraphs and sections of writing.

The step

> Heat fat in frying pan. When hot add peas. Turn and stir-fry slowly over a medium heat. Add chicken broth and continue to stir-fry for one more minute. Sprinkle with salt, sugar and sherry and stir-fry gently for one further minute and serve.

This is part of a recipe, one example of a **procedure** – a text type that tells you how to carry out a process step by step in the right order. The **step** is probably the basic design which underlines procedures, as well as narratives, both of which depend upon an ordering of events in time. Notice that, in this recipe, there is very little attempt to make the text

It is clear there is a stack here because it is possible to enumerate the arguments, as indicated in brackets. These would be an example of signposts given to the reader to make the organisation of the text clear. However, quite apart from these, the paragraph displays cohesion through using vocabulary with related and contrasting meanings. 'Illogical' in sentence 1 is echoed by 'ill-considered' in sentence two and 'irrational' in the last sentence and contrasts with 'sensible' in the penultimate sentence. The word *government* recurs three times, and the related words *election* and *political* occur in the first and the final sentence. The word *self-contradictory* is expanded in sentences 3 and 4, which claim that the increase in the number of cars works against two government campaigns.

The chain

The two paragraph patterns we have looked at so far show very tight organisation. But the **chain** has a more exploratory feel about it. It is a design in which the sentences appearing in succession are linked most obviously only to the sentence before.

> Mosquitoes are the greediest creatures I have ever met, my children included. They combine the vice of greed with the virtue of persistence, and buzz around for hours in the darkness seeking out those few patches of bare white flesh I carelessly leave uncovered. Under that flesh, as they well know, flow pints of that red juicy food known as blood. Blood is to mosquitoes, what Foster's lager is to Australians. However, it is only the females which suck blood, the males feeding on nectar. If they both fed on blood there would be no hope. But, as it is, providing we can live far enough away from flowers there is some hope that, to find a mate, the blood-sucking sex will have to keep away from us.

The chain-like structure links one sentence to the next. This cohesion is achieved by repeating vocabulary, or using pronouns to refer "back" to something which has come in the previous sentence; for example:

Sentences 1–2	*mosquitoes*	*they*
	greediest	*greed*
Sentences 2–3	*bare flesh*	*that flesh*
Sentences 3–4	*blood*	*blood*
Sentences 4–5	*mosquitoes*	*males, females*
	blood	*blood*
Sentences 5–6	*males, females*	*they both*
	blood	*blood*
	feeding	*fed*
Sentences 6–7	*blood*	*bloodsucking*
	no hope	*some hope*

The balance

The last basic design for paragraphs or texts is the **balance**. The metaphor suggests a weighing up of descriptive facts, or arguments for and against a proposition, giving equal weight to each side, without coming down firmly in favour of one or the other.

> The Institute of Education certainly has a more human scale than the National University, both in the size of student population and in its architecture. On the other hand, the University, being more modern in its buildings and larger in size, can afford better resources than the Institute. Its library is one of the best in the region, and the computing facilities are second to none. However it is sprawled over Kent Ridge, with narrow bending walkways which never allow you to see anyone else from a distance, and this, coupled with its long, bare, windowless corridors gives it a rather impersonal and sinister atmosphere. The Institute, by contrast, may have decaying, termite-infested buildings, cave-like offices, and uneven floors, but it has a more homely, if messy, human feel to it. And while a larger proportion of students at the University are just after a degree to improve their chances of material success, the undergraduate at the Institute of Education is more likely committed to a worthwhile career, and may be a kinder kind of soul.

There are several balances in this paragraph. Very often one sentence is weighed against another by using words or phrases specifically to point to contrasts: 'on the other hand', 'by contrast', 'however'. At other times the point of balance occurs in mid-sentence through use of a **conjunction** like *while*. More generally the frequent use of comparatives – 'better', 'kinder, 'more' – gives an overall sense of weighing up two things placed opposite each other.

Sometimes the balance is unequal. We may have made up our mind already which side we come down on, and simply concede one or two contrary arguments to make us appear reasonable. For example:

> Although pet cats and dogs are invaluable companions for old people, and are creatures 'for children to learn benevolence upon', these advantages cannot outweigh the negative impacts they have on the environment. They consume huge amounts of protein in a world where a quarter of the population is hungry. They spread diseases and parasites to human populations, particularly when negligent owners do nothing to control their messing in public parks and on sidewalks. There are numerous instances of young children being attacked and disfigured by "guard" dogs. And the industry of dog- and cat-breeding simply reinforces and displaces snobbishness about human ancestry with snobbishness about canine and feline pedigree.

Here the first clause, 'Although ... upon', makes a couple of concessions to those in favour of pets. This makes the writer appear fair-minded, before the crushing weight of arguments against is "stacked" up against them.

This example, in fact, illustrates how the paragraph design of balance and stack can be combined in practice. There is a very small stack of two items on one side of the balance, but a much bigger and weightier one on the other side. There's no doubt which way the scales are supposed to tip:

ACTIVITY 4

Please refer to the companion website for the activity material.

The point of paragraph or text

Another crucial aspect of paragraph and text structure is the position of the point, or topic sentence. The main idea, the most essential new information, can appear in at least two positions. It may come in the first sentence as it does in the example of a stack. In other paragraph or discourse types it may come last, towards the end of the paragraph or text.

Point-first structures are called **deductive**, and point-last structures **inductive**. Deductive structures are generally easier to absorb than inductive ones. They allow skimming, or allow the reader to abandon reading half-way through the text, while still understanding the general idea, and so are less time-consuming. Inductive structures, on the other hand, are more enigmatic, suspenseful, demand more time, and place an emphasis on the process of reading rather than simply the information as a product. Good writers will always be careful to adopt the most appropriate structure, inductive or deductive, to match their purposes and the likely reading style.

ACTIVITY 5

Please refer to the companion website for the activity material.

1.3 GENERIC STRUCTURE

In the previous section we noted some general patterns of paragraph structure organisation that are employed in continuous prose. But it would be wrong to assume that when we are organising the complete texts we write we somehow start with a blank slate. The example given under the step paragraph above is itself the instruction part of a recipe with its larger standardised structure. So when we consider specific discourse types or genres we will recognise a more or less conventionalised **generic structure**, a kind of template into which we can fit our words and sentences. For example, a recipe will have the following compulsory elements of structure: TITLE ^ INGREDIENTS ^ INSTRUCTIONS and optionally PREPARATION/COOKING TIME, UTENSILS, NUTRITIONAL INFORMATION, NAME OF CHEF. (The carat, ^, means "followed by".) Or look at these adjacent entries from a dictionary.

cas-ta-nets /ˌkæstə ˈnets/ **noun** [plural] a Spanish musical instrument consisting of a pair of small round pieces of wood or plastic held in one hand and brought together quickly to make a CLICKING sound, used especially by dancers

cast-a-way /ˈkɑːstə ˌweɪ/ **noun** [C] someone whose ship has sunk and who is left on an island or beach where there are no other people

caste /kɑːst/ **noun 1** [C/U] one of the social classes that people are born into in Hindu society, or the system of having these classes **2**

[C] a group of people who have the same professional or social status

The generic structure for each entry is quite clear:

HEADWORD (syllables) ^ PRONUNCIATION ^ WORD CLASS ^
MEANING[S]

And the larger generic structure simply involves listing each entry alphabetically by HEADWORD.

Interestingly, different genres or different parts of the same genre might have distinctive features of graphology, phrase, clause and sentence structure. These are often known as **register** features. For instance, we note the omission of articles and objects of verbs in the instruction part of recipes:

Heat ~~the~~ fat in ~~a~~ frying pan. When hot add ~~the~~ peas. Turn and stir-fry ~~the peas~~ slowly over a medium heat.

Or one might note the use of abbreviations for different types of **noun** in the dictionary, e.g. 'C' for countable, and, graphologically, the bolding of the headword.

To illustrate generic structure we will concentrate on two genres – narratives and news reports – because these are both representations of events but have quite contrasting structures.

The generic structure of narrative

Investigating oral narratives, William Labov discovered the following elements of their generic structure (Labov 1972). (Readers unfamiliar with the story of Goldilocks and the Three Bears should read it on the internet before proceeding, for instance at www.dltk-teach.com/rhymes/goldilocks_story.htm)

Abstract

The **abstract** is a short summary of the story that narrators generally provide before the narrative begins. It encapsulates the "point" of the story, or what the story exemplifies. It is not compulsory, but it provides a signal that a narrative is about to commence, and that the speaker wishes to hold the floor uninterrupted until it is over. And it is also a bridge to make the narrative relevant to the preceding conversation. For example, the conversation might be about how frightening childhood experiences can give you phobias. To make the transition to narrative you could say 'There's this kid I knew when I was young who had a dreadful experience with bears, and it has still affected her behaviour for years afterwards.'

Orientation

The **orientation** gives information about the time, place, persons and situation/activity type they are engaged in. Typically this section will include adverbials of time and place and **relational** verbs like *to be* which describe states/relations rather than actions (see Chapter 2, pp. 54–55), for instance describing the place, time, weather or characters. When reference is to an action which is going on at the time the narrative commences, then the **progressive** *-ing* forms of the verb will be used. An example would be:

relational   relational
verb   verb
Her name <u>was</u> Goldilocks and she <u>was</u> very adventurous.

time adverbial progressive   place adverbials
<u>One June day</u> she was <u>walking</u> <u>to school along the edge of the</u>
<u>wood behind her house.</u>

Strictly speaking this orientation element is not compulsory either, but is normal in written narratives.

Complicating action

The **complicating action** and the resolution are the essential elements in a narrative. In fact, all a narrative needs is two or more clauses describing a pair of linked events or actions, ordered chronologically, such as 'Goldilocks went into the bear's house. The bears frightened her away.' These clauses will be in simple **present** or simple **past tense**, in contrast with the progressive forms in the orientation, e.g. 'went' not 'was going'. If the order of clauses is reversed the interpretation of the sequence of the events changes, and we have a different narrative. For instance: 'The bears frightened her away. Goldilocks went into the bears' house.' 'She went to Yale and got a degree' is a different story from 'She got a degree and went to Yale.'

Resolution

The **resolution** is provided by the last of the narrative clauses which began with the complicating action, bringing the sequence of actions and events to an end, for example: 'Goldilocks ran away from the house of the three bears and back home.'

Coda

The **coda** is the means by which the narrative is completed and the listener is brought out of the past back into the present time. Just as the abstract was a bridge from the surrounding conversation to the narrative, this is a bridge out of the narrative and signals that the speaker no longer has the right to the floor. Often it is changes of tenses and time adverbs that bring us back to the present, as in 'So, she <u>still</u> <u>doesn't</u> eat porridge, play with teddy bears or rock on chairs, and she <u>prefers</u> to sleep on the floor.'

Evaluation

Although these previous elements should occur in a particular order, evaluation may occur at any point in the narrative, scattered through-out the text between the abstract and coda. Labov defined **evaluation** as those clauses which don't belong to the narrative action, but which, on the contrary, delay its forward movement. These comprise:

Evaluative device		Example
Comments by narrator		'At that moment Goldilocks looked like a little Russian doll'
Evaluative comment of character		' "Eating my porridge was a horrible thing to do" '
Evaluative comments attributed to a third party		' "Mama said it was naughty not to lock the door" '
Emotive devices	Exclamations	'What a soft bed it was**!**'
	Interjections/swearing	' "**Oh shit**, look at my chair!" '
	Emotional vocab	' "The **horrible greedy slut!**" '
Comparators	If clauses	'**If** Goldilocks had cried
	Comparisons	**more like** a typical girl
	Modals (can, shall, might, etc.)	Baby Bear **might** have pitied her
	Negatives	But she did**n't**
	Futures	**Will** she ever go
	Questions	walking in the woods again**?**'

We can sum up Labov's model in the following formula, with optional elements in parentheses.

(ABSTRACT^) (ORIENTATION^) COMPLICATING ACTION^RESOLUTION (^CODA) + (EVALUATION).

This formula means that a minimum narrative consists of two linked clauses, the first belonging to the complicating action and the second constituting the resolution.

Why does the narrative genre have this particular structure? A **narrative** is a story (possibly fictional) which is an attempt to make sense of events and happenings in the world, rather than simply recounting events from experience (non-fictional) in the order in which they occurred. The Genesis creation myth, as an example of narrative, not only tries to make sense of the origins of life on earth, but more particularly explains why there are seven days in the week, why snakes have no legs, why women suffer in childbirth, why we wear clothes and why work is necessary (www. biblegateway.com/passage/?search=Genesis%204&version=GNT). This requirement that narratives make sense of the world provides some explanation for the elements of their structure. The abstract suggests that the story has a point, some topic or idea which it illustrates; or to put it the other way around, the abstract makes sense of the story. The same role may be fulfilled by the coda, for instance the moral at the end of a fable. The resolution also contributes to "making sense" – it gives a feeling of "closure", a conclusion to the episodes, a neat tying up of the narrative strands, or a solution to a problem. Real life, of course, seldom has such neat or final solutions – the marriage that ends a Shakespearean comedy would, in real life, be as much a beginning as an ending. In a similar way, whereas the clauses of a recounted incident could describe unrelated events or actions, the clauses of the complicating action of narrative are defined as linked in some way, for example by cause or effect, or condition and response (Montgomery *et al.* 1992: 177–178).

 ACTIVITY 6 ━━━━━━━━━━━━━━━━━━━━━━━━━━━━━━━━━

Please refer to the companion website for the activity material.

We notice that in narrative we have a basically inductive structure. In one sense, of course, an abstract, if there is one, might give a hint of the point of the story, which would make it point first, deductive. But the inductive movement towards the resolution is essential to the specific instance that proves the point. Unlike really deductive structures, the narrative cannot be abandoned part way through and still convey the main idea of the story. As we shall see this is one of the main differences between the generic structure of narrative and that of news reports.

The generic structure of news reports

The structure of news reports in "serious" newspapers is quite different from narrative, though popular newspapers tend to be more narrative-like. In this section we will be following the pattern of generic structure worked out by Van Dijk (1986), somewhat simplified and modified according to the structure of online news, and diagrammed in Figure 1.1.

The **summary**, to be distinguished from **the news story**, comprises the **headline**, sometimes with a sub-headline and the **lead**, generally the first paragraph (or two). The headline(s), and sometimes the lead too,

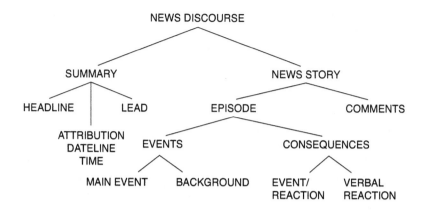

Figure 1.1
The discourse structure of news reports

will be graphologically prominent, in bigger, bolder or different colour type. The summary announces the main topic, and also includes a concise version of the main point, the main event. This makes the news report skimmable. A basic guideline for reporters is that the lead should contain information about who did what, when, where and how. However, it stops short of answering the question *why?* For example:

Big Sur wildfire destroys 15 homes and 500 acres of national forest

[HEADLINE]

Home of California town's fire chief among properties destroyed by blaze in Los Padres national forest [SUB-HEADLINE]

A wildfire in the Big Sur area of California destroyed at least 15 homes and forced about 100 people to evacuate as it burned through dry vegetation on its way towards the ocean on Monday. [LEAD]

The news story comprises the **episode** and **comments**. The episode is made up of **events** and **consequences**.

Dealing with the events first, these divide into the **main event** and the **background**. The main event(s) by Van Dijk's definition, based on a daily newspaper, must have taken place within the last two days.

If the event is one of a series in a previously reported ongoing story, then the last important event constitutes the main event. In short reports, the main event and the lead may be the same paragraph or sentence.

A wildfire in the Big Sur area of California destroyed at least 15 homes and forced about 100 people to evacuate as it burned

through dry vegetation on its way towards the ocean on Monday.
No injuries have been reported. [MAIN EVENT/LEAD]

Notice that more details of the main event may be given at later places in
the report, not necessarily continuous and following the lead. Also notice
that some of these details may be derived from and embedded in verbal
reactions, as in

The fire burned about 500 acres (200 hectares) in the Pfeiffer
Ridge area of Los Padres national forest near state highway 1,
forest spokesman Andrew Madsen said. [VERBAL REACTION [MAIN
EVENT]]

The **background**, most fully developed in broadsheet/serious papers,
helps us to activate or update the knowledge held in memory, thereby
making the news intelligible. Here we find references to previous events
sometimes stretching back even into history, and details of the physical
circumstances in which the event took place. This section has much the
same function as Labov's orientation. For example:

Big Sur is a popular tourist destination along the central California
coast with high-end resorts and beautiful views of the Pacific
Ocean. [BACKGROUND]

A lightning-sparked wildfire in 2008 forced the evacuation of Big
Sur and blackened 650 sq. km (250 sq. miles) before it was con-
tained. That blaze burned more than a dozen homes. [BACKGROUND]

Turning from events to **consequences**, these latter may be almost as
important as the main event, but they tend to come later in the report.
The consequences are anything which was caused by the main event,
namely another **event**, a **verbal reaction** or a human physical **reaction**.
For example:

Madsen said the fire had destroyed the home of Big Sur fire chief,
Martha Karstens.

"She left thinking that she was going to go protect other people's
homes," Madsen said, "and it turns out that her own home has
been consumed."

"This is a completely wind-driven fire," Madsen said. "We're cau-
tiously optimistic that we're going to pin this thing down within the
next couple of days." [VERBAL REACTION]

The Red Cross has set up an overnight shelter for people who have been displaced by the fire, Madsen said [VERBAL REACTION [REACTION]]

As we shall see in Chapter 8, the verbal reactions are usually those of powerful authority figures, stars, politicians, government spokespersons, police, lawyers, or scientists and other professionals.

The **comment** part of the episode comprises evaluations of the other elements and speculations about what might happen next. When doing analysis it is important to remember that these comments are those of the reporter or the editorial team producing the newspaper, and are different from the verbal reactions of eyewitnesses, politicians, etc. Generally news reports try to maintain the illusion of impartiality. It is only in the comments that the hidden ideology comes more or less to the surface. For example:

A wildfire so late in the year is unusual but not surprising given that California is enduring the driest calendar year on record. [COMMENT: evaluation]

Van Dijk's model is strictly applicable only to news reports, not to other articles in the newspaper such as editorials and features. In fact, newspaper feature articles can be viewed as an expansion of the background and consequences of newspaper reports, and editorials as an expansion of comments.

The elements or moves of news report generic structure have a certain amount of ordering built into them. Providing the lead and the main event are not combined, as is often the case with shorter reports, the summary must precede the main event, which may be followed by the background, consequences and comments. These last three categories do not, however, have to appear in any particular order. This could be diagrammed as follows:

SUMMARY ^ MAIN EVENT ^ (BACKGROUND) (CONSEQUENCES) (COMMENTS)
Less strictly ordered

We need to add a few optional elements to Van Dijk's model: the **dateline**, which gives the place from which the story was filed, the **attribution** which identifies the news agency from which some reports are compiled, and in online newspapers the **time** of publication. These tend to be placed between headline and lead, though in hard copy newspapers the attribution may come at the very end. In this example they are:

Associated Press [ATTRIBUTION] **in Big Sur** [DATELINE]

Tuesday 17 December 2013 08.51 GMT [TIME]

Sample analysis

To make the application of this analytical model clearer, here is a sample analysis of a news story about increased defence expenditure by Japan. The labels follow the discourse element. Double brackets indicate one discourse element inside another.

Japan increases defence budget amid tensions with China [HEADLINE]

Tokyo announces plans to buy drones, jet fighters and destroyers, and set up amphibious unit similar to US marines
[SUBHEADLINE]

Associated Press [ATTRIBUTION] *in Tokyo* [DATELINE]
theguardian.com, Tuesday 17 December 2013 09.53 GMT [TIME]

Jump to comments (43)

Japan has approved a plan to increase defence spending by 5% over the next five years to purchase its first surveillance drones, more jet fighters and naval destroyers [LEAD] in the face of China's military expansion. [BACKGROUND]

The revised five-year defence plan was adopted by the cabinet along with a new national security strategy that reflects Prime Minister Shinzo Abe's drive to raise the profile of Japan's military and expand the country's role in international diplomacy and security. [MAIN EVENT]

Experts say the plans are in line with a power shift that has been ongoing for several years, but Japan's neighbours and some Japanese citizens worry that they constitute a move away from the pacifist constitution the country adopted after the Second World War. [VERBAL REACTION]

'Many people worry inside Japan and outside that maybe Abe hasn't really learned the lesson from the wartime history of Japan and that there's a danger that a greater role played by Japan actually means the rise of militarism in the long-term', said Koichi Nakano, an international politics professor at Sophia University in Tokyo. [VERBAL REACTION]

The previous five-year plan for 2011 to 2016, which was adopted by the opposition Democratic party of Japan when it was in government, cut the defence budget by ¥750bn (£4.5bn), or 3%. It also cut troop numbers by 1,000. [BACKGROUND]

Abe's new plan maintains current troop levels. The strategy also reflects a shift in Japan's defence priorities from its northern reaches to the East China Sea, where Tokyo and Beijing dispute the sovereignty of a chain of uninhabited islands. [MAIN EVENT]

The new defence plan calls for setting up an amphibious unit similar to the US marines to respond quickly in case of a foreign invasion of the disputed islands. It will also deploy an early warning system, submarines and an anti-missile defence system in the area. [MAIN EVENT]

Broader defence programme guidelines also adopted on Tuesday stated that Tokyo was "gravely concerned" about China's growing maritime and military presence in the East China Sea, its lack of transparency and 'high-handed' approach. [VERBAL REACTION TO PREVIOUS EVENT]

Late last month, China said all aircraft entering a vast zone over the East China Sea must identify themselves and follow Chinese instructions. The US, Japan and South Korea have ignored Beijing's demand. [BACKGROUND: PREVIOUS EVENT]

Abe said the national security strategy set out Japan's diplomatic and security policy "with clarity and transparency". [VERBAL REACTION]

During the 2014 to 2019 period, Japan plans to buy three drones, most likely Global Hawks, 28 F-35A jet fighters, 17 Osprey aircraft and five destroyers, including two with Aegis anti-ballistic missile systems. The purchases would cost ¥24.7tn yen, up 5% from the previous plan. [MAIN EVENT]

The new plan says Japan would demonstrate its commitment to upgrade equipment, increase troop activity, step up defence capability and raise deterrence levels amid an increasingly tense regional security environment. [MAIN EVENT]

Narushige Michishita, a national security expert at the National Graduate Institute for Policy Studies, said Abe's plans set the stage for Japan to come out of its post-war isolationism. [VERBAL REACTION]

"Isolationism was very convenient and comfortable, but now China is rising rapidly and the US commitment to Asia is not growing, so maybe we should be a little more proactive," said Michishita, who helped develop the previous defence guidelines in 2010. [VERBAL REACTION]

(Retrieved 17 December 2013 from www.theguardian.
com/world/2013/dec/17/japan-increases-defence-
budget-tensions-china)

This particular text illustrates two more recent and radical modifications of the discourse structure of news reports in the digital age. First, the use of underlined hyperlinks which can be clicked to give more background information to the reader, about, in this case, Japan, China, Abe's drive to raise the profile of Japan's military, and so on. Hypertext complicates enormously the generic structure by introducing optional generic elements at multiple levels of discourse.

Second, you will notice, after the dateline and time, the hyperlink which gives the reader the option to read feedback from other readers and make comments themselves. This apparent democratisation of newspapers in giving readers a voice is a development we will explore in Chapter 8. Digital newspapers, and internet texts in general, are unlike traditional writing in allowing immediate feedback, making them much more like spoken genres such as conversation.

ACTIVITY 7 _____

Please refer to the companion website for the activity material.

Values and ideology in the ordering and selection of news

News is a manufactured and processed product. This is quite clear if you listen to the radio news late at night and then early the following morning. Very often it will be the same, since the people who manufacture news have been sleeping. In the BBC's early years the announcer would sometimes declare 'there is no news tonight' (Bell 1991: 2), meaning there was not sufficient manpower available, or no raw material had been found worthy of selection and processing into a story.

Let's look at the processing first. Because the generic structure of news reports is deductive and relatively visual compared with narrative, it allows for re-ordering, prioritising and highlighting of the events reported. This processing gives scope for bias. With its point-first structure the reader can abandon the reading and still get the main idea of the report. At the most extreme he might just glance at the headline or look at the lead, before moving on to something else. So the copy editor's selection of what goes into the headline and/or the lead can set up distortions by giving prominence to one aspect of the story rather than another (Davis and Walton 1983, Bell 1991: 80).

For example, take the headline lead and verbal reactions at the beginning of the following article.

UK unemployment rate at lowest since 2009

18 December 2013 Last updated at 13:44
www.bbc.co.uk/news/business-25428119

The UK unemployment rate has fallen to its lowest level since 2009, official figures show.

At 7.4%, this is the lowest rate since the February-to-April period in 2009, the Office for National Statistics (ONS) said.

The number of people out of work fell by 99,000 to 2.39 million in the three months to October, the ONS said.

Prime Minister David Cameron told MPs the figures showed that "the plan is working".

Mr Cameron said: "There should not be one ounce of complacency because we have still got work to do to get our country back to work and everyone back in work means greater stability for them, greater ability to plan for their future, greater help for their families."

At the end of the article we learn that

Average weekly earnings growth, including bonuses, picked up by 0.9% in the three months to October compared with a year earlier, the ONS said, a slight improvement on the three months to September.

Excluding bonuses, pay grew by 0.8%.

But this is still well below the level of inflation – currently running at 2.1% – meaning that people's earnings are still falling in real terms.

Even this section gives a pro-government selection of what comes first. It is only in the last paragraph that we realise that the growth in employment is based on reducing workers' wages.

It would be perfectly possible, therefore, to repackage, reselect and re-order information in this report to give us a headline and lead such as:

More employees taking home lower pay

People's earnings are falling in real terms, with inflation at 2.1% and earnings growth at a paltry 0.8%.

The headline and lead foregrounds one sort of information rather than another, and gives an inevitably biased representation of the facts (cf. Bell 1991: 224). The reader who only skims the headline and lead in this deductive text will come away with a very one-sided version of the employment and earnings situation in the UK.

The selection of the raw material out of which news is processed has nothing particularly objective about it either. Galtung and Ruge (1973) identified a number of factors or biases that determine what events get into the news and which get left out or "spiked". These **news values** include

a   reference to elite persons
b   reference to elite nations

c   cultural proximity
d   intensity
e   unexpectedness
f   negativity.

If a news story refers to powerful or famous people it is more likely to get in the news (a). If we broke our back in a horse-riding accident, we wouldn't get six column inches on the front page of the international edition of a British newspaper. But Christopher Reeve did. If Prince Philip, the Duke of Edinburgh and husband of the British Queen, is in hospital it will be reported for several days prominently in the news. If your grandmother is in hospital, I doubt it would even make the local paper. The newspaper texts quoted in the book so far figure the late famous show-business personality Christopher Reeve, alias Superman, and the (former) prime ministers Nelson Mandela, Shinzo Abe and David Cameron.

The appearance of Reeve in the news also illustrates the factor of cultural proximity (c). Hollywood culture has spread worldwide. So the wide dissemination of this culture makes the stories more understandable, relevant to existing knowledge in readers' heads. By contrast, a Malaysian takraw star wouldn't mean much to readers of the *International Express* or to many readers of this book.

It is quite obvious that citizens of Europe, Japan, Australasia and North America are more prominent in the news than citizens of countries with lower average GDP, such as those in Africa, China or the Indian subcontinent (b). Seventy-four Western and Japanese tourists killed in a "terrorist" attack in Luxor, Egypt, got 12 column inches on the front page of the Singapore *Straits Times* on 17 November 1997, while the same edition gave only two column inches, tucked away on page 23, to the 87 coal miners killed in Anhui, China, despite the latter's cultural, ethnic and geographical proximity. The British newspaper *The Independent* on Friday 20 December 2013 gave around 300 words of coverage to a UN report of 500 killed in South Sudan, 230 words to a story about an Australian woman who walked off a pier and fell into the sea while checking Facebook on her phone, and 250 words to a report about a new York postal worker who caught two babies thrown from a burning building. Such bias in the degree of coverage, which is endemic in newspapers worldwide, might be considered as an institutionalisation of racism (cf. Van Dijk 1988a, 1988b).

In other words, for citizens of non-elite nations the event has to have more intensity (d), as measured by numbers, to be considered newsworthy. And perhaps accidents in Chinese coal mines and civil wars in Africa are so common that one more is hardly unexpected – another news value (e).

In most newspapers in Western countries negativity is an important value (f); disasters, accidents and any threats to the public are more common than good news. However, in countries where the media is under state control, the home news, especially, is likely to be more positive.

1.4 VISUAL INFORMATION IN TEXTS

So far, we have been assuming the organisation of a text lies primarily in the words and clauses, its language. But, in fact, when we considered paragraphing and headlines, we were already paying some attention to the use of white space to indent the text and larger font for emphasis. When we look at a text, we are drawn to the special fonts, italics, bulleted points, indentations, graphs, diagrams and images. Alongside linguistic resources, these and other visual resources are available for making a text what Bernhardt (1985) calls **visually informative**. Bernhardt (1985) suggests a scale of visual informativeness ranging from, for example, the homogeneous text of the average novel, whose only visual features are paragraph indentation and chapter headings, to instructions for self-assembly furniture, which, unfortunately, are often almost entirely visual in their information.

Assured and non-assured readers

When deciding on how much visuality is appropriate for a text we have to take into account another factor – how motivated or assured our readers are. A reader looking through a telephone directory for a number, or reading the latest novel by their favourite author, does not need to be encouraged to continue reading, and can be described as an **assured reader**. But someone flicking through a magazine, nonchalantly looking at the adverts as he turns the pages, or glancing at brochures in a travel agency, needs to have his attention grabbed and sustained, and can be called a **non-assured reader**. The non-assured reader will need to be attracted by the visuals, so one would expect texts designed for him to be more visually informative. By contrast, the texts for an already motivated reader can afford to dispense with the range of graphic devices we have been considering.

ACTIVITY 8

Please refer to the companion website for the activity material.

With the emergence of the world-wide-web visual information or visual communication in written texts has gained more importance than ever before. So in this section we will be considering some of the resources for visual information, and the consequences which they may have for text organisation, ways of reading and meaning.

Resources for visual informativeness

In the past linguists have often insisted that the spoken language, with features like stress and intonation, speed variation, rhythm, loudness and voice quality, is much richer than written language. This is only partially true. There are a range of graphic resources which, for instance, a desktop publisher will have to decide on when it comes to creating printed text, and which give an extra layer of textual meaning.

1   At the global level she will decide if she is going to import graphics – pictures, graphs, pie-charts, etc.

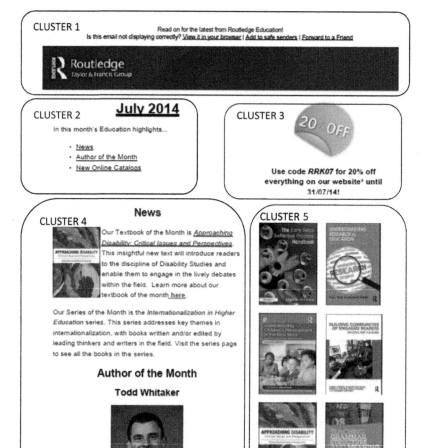

Image 1.1a
Clusters in a Routledge book promotion

reminding them that what they do matters. Todd's latest book is the third edition of *Dealing with Difficult Teachers*, published in July 2014. Learn more about our July Author of the Month **here**.

CLUSTER 6
Browse our newly updated catalogs:

CLUSTER 7

For more titles, please visit:

www.routledge.com/education

Connect with us!

*Offer valid only with web orders at routledge.com

CLUSTER 8

Image 1.1b
Clusters in a Routledge book promotion (continued)

2   She will consider how these can be integrated with global layout features – page size, number of columns, use of white space or colour.

3   At a slightly more detailed level she has the opportunity to use graphics for making textual organisation clear, for example by bullets, asterisks, dashes, enumeration (such as numbering or lettering).

4   More locally she has the choice of text features or highlighting: font type, font size, capitalisation, bolding, italicisation, underlining, outlining, shadowing.

ACTIVITY 9 ━━━━━━━━━━━━━━━━━━━━━━━━━━━━━

Please refer to the companion website for the activity material.

The visual resources under (1) to (4), in combination with the vocabulary and grammar of the written language, create the overall meaning of the text, making it **multimodal**. To understand this we can analyse the visual and spatial resources of a text and how they interact with the verbal resources to structure the text and to create meanings, while allowing different ways of reading.

Structure of a visually informative text

We have seen how a text is structured linguistically at the paragraph level, the sentence level and the clause level. In the same manner, a visually informative text is structured into several analytical units, the most basic of which is a **cluster** (Baldry and Thibault, 2006). This is a local grouping of items on a printed page or webpage. The items in the cluster are next to each other and may be visual, verbal and so on. Each cluster will be separated from the other clusters by the use of some of the resources (1) to (4) above, such as white space, outlining, columns, and different fonts or font size. For instance, the front page of a newspaper or a home page of a website, or a promotional email in your inbox can be divided into several clusters. Very often the different generic elements will form different clusters identified by visual resources. For instance, look at this online recipe (www.bbc.co.uk/food/recipes/how_to_make_trout_en_49680).

Let's look at an example of clusters in Image 1.1 which is an example of a promotional email from the publisher Routledge, featuring highlights related to their books in the Education series for the month of July 2014.

As we notice, the structure and layout of the email is very different from a conventional email as it makes effective use of extra visual resources. The email text can be transcribed into eight primary multimodal clusters which we have indicated by adding outlining. These clusters are identified and separated from each other using various visual resources. White space is generally important. But bolding, sometimes with larger fonts, helps divide cluster 2 from 1, 4 from 2, and 6 and 7 from 5. Internally the clusters are similar in graphic style or visuals: the same size font and bolding, which, for example, differentiates cluster 3, from 1, 2 and 4; or the repetition of the book covers in clusters 5 and 6.

The first cluster, with the title and the company banner, and the last cluster, with standing details of the company and its logos, form a vital part of the promotional text. The first cluster announces the text's basic topic and the last identifies the Taylor and Francis group, which is promoting its Education series. The other clusters use a combination of linguistic and visual resources and convey all the relevant details about the publications. These include the month's highlights in bulleted points (cluster 2), discounts offered with a coupon code for items that can be bought through their website (cluster 3), detailed information on a book in focus and its author (cluster 4), various books available in the series (cluster 5), catalogues of other series (cluster 6) and a call for action by connecting through social media (cluster 7). A further analysis reveals how each cluster contributes to a specific meaning by making use of various visual, typographical and linguistic resources. For instance, in cluster 1 the combination of linguistic information 'Read on for the latest from Routledge Education!' and the visual information with the Routledge banner and logo sets the tone of the text and marks its promotional theme.

Similarly, a look at other clusters will show how the combination of linguistic and visual or typographical resources plays variations on the promotional topic of the text. Cluster 3, for instance, borrowing from a different genre, creatively deploys a visual resource of a discount coupon sticker that can be peeled off. This deliberately folded sticker acts as an invitation to the reader to take advantage of the 20 per cent discount. The visual invitation combines perfectly with the language about the offer to fit the overall promotional purpose.

We also notice that alongside the promotional theme is an underlying expectation of action by the reader. In cluster 3 this might be a delayed action, since it requires the reader to physically do something after reading the email. On the other hand, the resultant actions expected from clusters 4 and 7 are instantaneous. In cluster 4 we are invited to click on the hyperlinks provided, the blue highlighted words, 'here', 'series' and the titles of the book and the series. In cluster 7, to click on the links to the website www.routledge.com/education (using verbal resources) and social media links (using the visual resources – logos of Twitter and Facebook). So the promotional theme of the email is extended with visual and verbal resources that invite the readers to take up the offers and engage with the Routledge series on Education. At the same time, when combined with other clusters as a whole, these clusters fulfil the specific purpose of the text, that of promoting the Education series offered by the publisher.

We can see how various resources are co-deployed and contextualised in the making of a text-specific meaning, as the different kinds of resources are combined through the **resource integration principle** (Baldry and Thibault, 2006). The tight integration of the verbal, the visual and the spatial emphasises details which would not have been so easy to grasp otherwise. For instance, the images of book covers with author names in cluster 5, and text along with catalogue covers showing respective titles in cluster 6 present detailed information without having the need to draw up a linear list of book or series titles. The visual presentation of the information effectively integrates relevant details required to be known by the reader. So what is it that makes visually informative texts so effective? The answer lies in the reading processes involved in these texts.

Reading paths in visually informative texts: cluster hopping and modularity

Degrees of visual informativeness and multimodality are likely to match reading styles and reading paths. Texts that are not visually informative tend to be linear and **progressive**. They only reveal their structure through reading in their entirety, which enables the text to form one large unit, with, perhaps, a point-last, inductive structure. Novels and poems are normally progressive; when you begin a novel written in English, you will typically read from the left to the right and move from the top to the bottom. In other words, you will follow a reading pattern prescribed to you by the author of the text. You are not supposed to turn to the last page of a murder mystery to find out who was the murderer. The homogeneous print of literary texts encourages such linear reading.

Visually informative genres, on the other hand, often follow a more complex reading path. In particular, if graphic devices of types (2) and (3) are employed to sectionalise the text into clusters, then the text can be described as **localised**. These sections can be read selectively, and in any order one chooses, a **modular** rather than progressive reading style (Kress, 2014). For example, in 'What's all the buzz about' (see Chapter 1 Activity 9 on the companion website) the reader can home in on the True or False cluster and choose to look at just one of the questions and answers without reading the other. Or in the Routledge email, depending on individual choices, interests or preferences, readers may first read cluster 3 or cluster 5 before they move on to cluster 4. So the reading process of a multimodal text usually involves a discontinuous path of reading where readers "hop" backwards and forwards to understand the text. This process is known as **cluster hopping** (Baldry and Thibault 2006).

The reading process as a result also follows the principle of **periodicity**, where structures repeat themselves in a patterned way, and allow variation within the textual framework. This framework is provided by the different clusters which combine linguistic, visual and typographical information in varied ways. Thus, certain contents in the clusters act as "entry points" that anticipate the development of the topic of the text. For instance, you will see in the Routledge email that clusters 1, 3, 4 and 7 act as entry points for its main topic of promoting its educational books. Thus, recurrent patterns of the underlying theme of promotion and an expectation of a resultant action to be taken by the reader become evident throughout all the clusters in the email.

This type of non-linear modular reading also extends to the manner in which readers may read online newspapers or websites. Instead of demanding a strongly sequential reading order, multimodal texts provide readers with navigational resources to choose their own reading path, as we saw with the use of hyperlinks in the generic structure of online newspapers (Lemke, 2002). Thus, the reading process of a visually informative text involves vertical, horizontal, circular or zigzag reading paths, as clusters escape from a linear sequence and take up constantly changing positions relative to each other. As a result, even if you choose to read cluster 3 first, and then hop to cluster 7 and leave cluster 4 to be read later, you will still get a sense that this is a promotional email. In other words, the periodic patterns of the individual clusters contribute to the overall meaning of the email.

ACTIVITY 10 ━━━━━━━━━━━━━━━━━━━━━━━

Please refer to the companion website for the activity material.

ACTIVITY 11 ━━━━━━━━━━━━━━━━━━━━━━━

Please refer to the companion website for the activity material.

1.5 SUMMARY AND POSTSCRIPT ON GENRE, CULTURE AND IDEOLOGY

In this chapter we have been exploring the ways in which text is organised or knitted together, its cohesion (Figure 1.2). We looked at how:

- to organise information within the clause or sentence, to preserve a given – new order in theme and rheme, and how to relate themes throughout paragraphs;
- to organise information and ideas in four basic kinds of paragraphs – step, stack, chain and balance – patterns which in practice we can blend;
- to position the point first or last in the discourse to give a deductive or an inductive structure;
- specific genres have their own organisational conventions, which may or may not be required or taught in schools;

- the generic structure of narrative contrasts with news reports, which provides opportunities for distortion of news;
- to use visual information to help with the organisation of text, in order to produce modular rather than progressive reading, and to make texts more attractive, so that they appeal to non-assured readers.

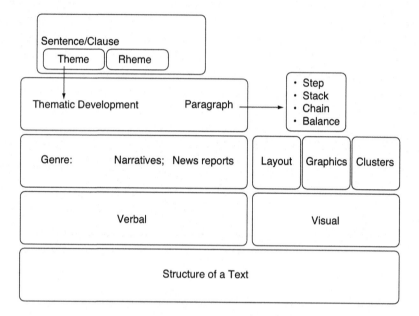

Figure 1.2
Summary of the chapter

Genres are discourse types which have achieved importance within a particular culture, society and institution. Another way of looking at it is to say that the culture values these particular forms of discourse, so that to be part of the culture and to participate fully within it one needs to master their linguistic and generic conventions. An imaginary person who was restricted in competence to the genres of sales encounters, jokes, conversation and chatting up members of the opposite sex would have less power, and be less valued and lower paid than a person who could, in addition, give public talks or lectures, write letters to the editor of a quality newspaper, conduct employment interviews, chair committee meetings and so on.

In an educational context it becomes important for students to be taught to operate successfully within the highly valued genres of a society, by being acquainted with their generic structures. This is part of what "empowering" students means, and it necessitates abandoning the overemphasis on narrative writing: 'stories are for those who, because of their social status and education, are denied the power of exposition' (Van Leeuwen 1987: 199). It is hoped that, if you missed out on explicit teaching of genre in school, this book will help at least to raise your awareness of the features of different genres.

Genres are, however, seldom absolutely distinct – one text will often include elements of different genres (Fairclough 1995: 88–90), and genres and generic combinations are evolving and emerging all the time. For example, 'What's all the buzz about' exemplifies a relatively new genre combining elements of the more traditional popular science feature article and interview/conversation. So school, college and university students should not simply learn to reproduce generically "pure" texts but also to experiment with combining and modifying genres. This will give an opportunity to question their structural and linguistic conventions, in order to explore their communicative justifications, if any, or their ideological underpinnings.

FURTHER READING

Please refer to the companion website for the list of further reading.

2 TEXT AND CONCEPTUAL MEANING

The aim of this chapter is
- to show how vocabulary, grammar, and visual images represent the state of the world, and, through stereotyping and obscuring responsibility reflect underlying ideologies;
- to demonstrate how to analyse the vocabulary and grammar of a longer text and the possibility of relating the findings to ideological concerns.

Contents

2.0 Introduction: language as a tool for thinking
argues that the way we think about and perceive the world around and inside us is more or less determined by the language we speak, and the choices we make within that language.

2.1 Ideology and vocabulary
shows how vocabulary is used to classify the objects and phenomena of our world, and that such classification leads to stereotyping, exploring in particular the representation of women.

2.2 Ideology, grammar and transitivity
gives a detailed explanation of how clauses represent states, actions, speech and mental processes; the section includes a substantial analysis of an online feature article linking the analysis of vocabulary and grammar to ideology.

2.3 Complications to transitivity
explains how grammatical structures like the passive, and the changing of verbs into nouns can be used to hide agency and responsibility.

2.4 Visual texts and conceptual meaning
explores how visuals can be used to classify and attribute qualities, confer extra meaning and represent actions and reactions.

2.0 INTRODUCTION: LANGUAGE AS A TOOL FOR THINKING

If Chapter 1 was about packaging, the emphasis of this chapter is content – the ideas we convey through language. One assumption of critical linguistics is that the language in the text affects the way we think. In a superficial sense this is obvious – the main reason for communication is to influence the thoughts of others. Practitioners of critical discourse analysis (CDA), however, consider the effect of language on thought in deeper senses:

1   The vocabulary and grammar of a particular language predispose the speakers/writers of that language to think in certain ways about themselves, other members of society and the world around them.
2   The grammatical and vocabulary choices which a speaker/writer makes within the resources of that particular language *construct* a representation of the world, rather than simply *reflecting* a pre-existing reality.

(1) is known as the theory of **linguistic relativity** (Whorf 1956: 57–65). The strong version claims that our language completely determines the way we think about the world and ourselves. But the weak version, which we accept, simply says that speaking one language makes it difficult to think like the speakers of another language.

ACTIVITY 12

Please refer to the companion website for the activity material.

The assumption (2) suggests that the "same" event may be represented differently. Look at this extract from a news report about riots in the English city of Bristol (*Straits Times*, 20 July 1992):

> The trouble erupted on Thursday night after two men were killed when the stolen police motorcycle they were riding was involved in a crash with an unmarked police car.

a   Two men were killed when the stolen police motorcycle they were riding was involved in a crash with an unmarked police car.
b   Police murdered two 17-year-olds on a motorcycle by ramming them with their unmarked police car.
c   Two youths killed themselves by driving their motorcycle into an unmarked police car.

The choice of (a), (b) and (c) represents or constructs the event in quite different ways.

ACTIVITY 13

Please refer to the companion website for the activity material.

Further evidence of the effect of texts in constructing our perception of reality comes from captions (As in Image 2.1). In caption competitions contestants provide a humorous representation of the photograph, one which is unlikely but still possible.

Another insight of CDA is that the influence of language upon thought and perception is most powerful when we are unaware of it, when it expresses hidden or **latent ideology**. We may be aware

Image 2.1
Captions as constructing reality: *Pensioner saves shop from collapse after Kent earthquake*

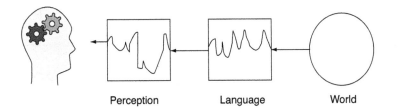

Figure 2.1
Distortions of reality through language and perception

Perception   Language   World

of alternative ways of conceptualising reality (1) because we speak a second language or (2) are sufficiently alert to notice the choices made within the language we speak. But, if not, the texts we encounter may seem the only natural way of representing experience. This mind-set is known as **naturalisation**. We often hear talk of "objective", "unbiased" description, as though our language and texts can simply and faithfully reflect a pre-existing reality. In fact we have no direct access to the world or reality out there. Even in the act of perception we interpret rather than simply register sensations of the world. For example, our brains invert the upside-down image on our retina, and we often interpret the size of that image as a cue to distance rather than an indication of the dimensions of the object. But language is even more important than perception as a distorting medium, coming between the reality "out there" and our perceptions/thoughts of it (Figure 2.1).

A particular problem might arise for less dominant groups of society, who cannot give expression to their experience because the vocabulary of the language includes only the terms of the dominant group. The feminist Betty Friedan (1964) spoke of 'the problem without a name', the alienated and oppressed experience which women felt as members of a patriarchal society. The lack of a term for this condition made it impossible for women to discuss it, and so to recognise it as a shared problem (Mills 1995: 122).

The conceptual or representational dimension of language shows itself in two ways: first, in the vocabulary we use to categorise and refer to phenomena, and, second, in the structures of clause grammar which relate the objects we refer to. We'll start with vocabulary and then move on to discuss the grammar of the clause.

2.1 IDEOLOGY AND VOCABULARY

First, the reality we experience has no inherent categories or classes and can therefore be categorised in any number of different ways. What goes on in an act of classification is shown by the following simple exercise. Look at the six boxes in Figure 2.2, and separate them into two classes containing three boxes each.

Figure 2.2
Alternative
classifications

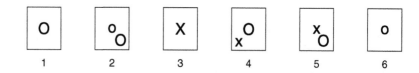

There are several valid ways of grouping these boxes in categories.
You could divide them into 1, 3, 6 and 2, 4, 5 on the criterion of containing one letter or two. Or into 1, 2, 6 and 3, 4, 5, because 1, 2, 6
contain only Os and no Xs. Or into 1, 3, 4, with upper case letters in the
centre, and 2, 5, 6 with lower case. Or any number of other alternatives.
Adopting any one criterion for classification means excluding other possible criteria.

The question is – why categorise in one way rather than another? The
answer is that the features we select for classification reflect our value
system. In Thai the primary criterion for categorising siblings is by seniority, rather than by sex as in English. So there are no words equivalent to
brother or *sister*, but "older sibling" *phîi* or "younger sibling" *nóoŋ*. This
is because seniority in Thai culture carries rights and responsibilities more
important than in the West. Traditionally Thais' elder siblings may take the
role of substitute parent and can give orders and make demands of younger
siblings. Along with this goes the responsibility for their welfare, for example helping to pay for their education.

Furthermore, "sibling" seniority transfers beyond the family. Thais use
the words *phîi* or *nóoŋ* as terms of address, rather like second-person pronouns, not only with blood siblings, but also with friends. So when you
start a conversation with a stranger and want to be friendly, and if you can't
tell if they are older than you, you have to ask them about relative age.

This example shows how common-sense categories are actually
language-specific and affect verbal and non-verbal behaviour. They also
influence perception, since Thai culture forces new acquaintances to look
for features of relative age when initiating friendly discourse. This is evidence for at least a weak form of linguistic relativity, and you may have
found similar evidence in your discussion of Activity 13.

Another way vocabulary reflects ideological values is the invention of
categories through new words. The new word or phrase, especially if a
noun, assumes that this is a useful, valid or "real" category for referring
to things, so this is a very clear example of language constructing rather
than simply reflecting reality.

The categories invented will sometimes reassure us or sometimes
alarm us. Doctors invented the term *colitis*. Perhaps if your doctor diagnoses your bowel problem as *colitis* this reassures you, at least more
than if she admits not knowing what the disease is. However, the label
colitis really only means "inflammation of the colon" and describes the
symptoms, rather than diagnoses the cause. If you ask what causes the

inflammation you may well be told it is 'idiopathic', meaning, more or less, "the cause is unknown". So how much faith should we have in the doctor for simply finding these labels?

By contrast the press and social media invent categories of people who are perceived as some kind of threat to themselves, their family or society: *couch potatoes, winos, chain-smokers, shopaholics, feminazis, sodcasters* (people who play music loudly on mobile phones in public), etc. Maybe the obsolete seventeenth century *sillytonian* ("a silly or gullible person") deserves a comeback.

ACTIVITY 14

Please refer to the companion website for the activity material.

Categorising the categories

Ideology is also powerful when the categories established by vocabulary are themselves categorised into more general groups. In contrast with the first level of classification these more general categorisations are less "natural" and more variable or debatable. So, sometimes we group dogs in a more general class with mammals like cows and whales, but on another occasion classify them as pets, along with goldfish and budgerigars. Very often such super-categories will be established or negotiated in particular texts or discourses.

The following extracts are taken from the report of a seminar on the physical abuse of women. Participants in this seminar obviously disagreed over the members of the more general category:

1   Road bullies and wife-beaters are the same type of criminals and should be treated with equal severity, pronounced Dr Alfred Choi.
2   'If counselling doesn't work, then drastic measures are called for. But let's not go overboard and equate the wife-beater to the road-bully, child-abuser and rapist' – Mrs Ruby Lim-Yang.
3   There is a big difference between the road bully and the wife-beater, Professor Anne Wee said. 'When you are punishing the road-bully you don't have to think in terms of the long-term relationship between the bully and victim … tougher measures could worsen the situation … in most cases wife-battering is not premeditated.'

(From 'Beating the wife-beater', *The Straits Times*,
14 August 1992)

This debate shows that the decisions we make about general categories are not simply academic, but have practical consequences. We tend to treat the people we group together in the same way, a point made very clear by comments (1) and (3). This is most obvious in legal cases where classification will have crucial consequences for sentencing or the allocation of damages and entitlements, e.g.

> A retired policeman won a unique court ruling to have his stress-related depression classed as an "injury" in the line of duty. The case means Bob Pickering, 52, of Brighton will be entitled to increased pension payments and may open the way to more claims against police authorities.
>
> (*International Express*, June 1–7 1995, p. 6)

Originally the Greek word *kategorein* ("categorise") meant "to accuse".

ACTIVITY 15

Please refer to the companion website for the activity material.

Often lists can imply membership of a super-category. Jonathan Swift put this to good satirical use in *Gulliver's Travels*:

> Here were no ... pickpockets, highwaymen, housebreakers, attorneys, bawds, buffoons, gamesters, politicians, ... tedious talkers, ... ravishers, murders, robbers, virtuosos.

The inclusion of attorneys, politicians, tedious talkers and virtuosos in a list mainly made up of criminals suggests that they, too, belong to that category.

Word-class, value and action

When classification leads to action the choice of a noun rather than a verb or **adjective** is important. Nouns represent categories of things, adjectives relatively permanent qualities and verbs quite temporary qualities. Consider the following possible ways of criticising your lecturer:

(1) The lecturer **bored** me	verb (past tense)
(2) The lecturer **bores** me	verb (present tense: habitual)
(3) The lecturer is **boring**	adjective
(4) The lecturer is **a bore**	noun

In (1) this may simply be a one-off failure to be interesting; perhaps the lecturer was tired, or hadn't had enough time for preparation. (2) is more damning, as he is in the habit of being less than interesting. (3) damns him still more, since the capacity to bore is one of a relatively permanent quality. Worse still is to label him a bore (4), equating his very existence with boredom. The solutions to this problem will be less or more drastic. In the case of (1) nothing may need to be done as next week he may not bore you. (2) and (3) are more problematic, but student feedback may encourage improvement. Since in (4) boring people is part of his nature, the only solution may be to remove him.

Stereotyping

One by-product of the categorising systems of vocabulary is **stereotyping**. This occurs when, on the basis of some members of a class having a characteristic or belonging to another class, other members are assumed to have that characteristic or belong to that other class. For example, because many Chinese students are short-sighted we assume that most Chinese students are short-sighted. Or because most nurses belong to the female class, we assume that all nurses are female.

Stereotyping is responsible for the puzzling humour of this joke:

> A father and son were travelling home late at night and were involved in a high-speed car crash. The father was killed outright, and the son was rushed to hospital to undergo surgery to save his life. But the surgeon said to the hospital administrators – 'Ethically I am unable to operate on this patient: he is my son.'

The stereotyping of surgeons as male is so strong that it might take the reader a while to work out that the surgeon was the boy's mother.

Stereotyping is a particular problem when we lack first-hand knowledge of the class members or their assumed characteristics. If we have never met a Nigerian in the flesh, then we will pick up our stereotypes second-hand.

Similarly, when judging someone's character or inner state of mind we make assumptions on the basis of their observable behaviour. For example, in some cultures people queue for buses and in others they do not. Does this indicate that the latter are competitive or lack a sense of justice?

ACTIVITY 16

Please refer to the companion website for the activity material.

Vocabulary, stereotyping and women

We can now look at a concrete example of how vocabulary, either by categorising through labelling or by stereotyping, serves ideology, in this case sexism.

ACTIVITY 17

Please refer to the companion website for the activity material.

There are perhaps three main areas where stereotyping women is most obvious in newspapers and magazines.

- First, in Activity 17 you may have found certain sub-categories or sub-classes to which women are typically assigned by nouns. Very often these sub-classes define them in relation to their family relationships rather than in terms of their jobs. 'Jane Martin, 28, mother of two', is probably more likely to occur in a newspaper report than 'John Martin, 30, father of two'. When women are defined by occupation, certain occupations are often stereotyped as female, and others as male. Therefore a longer form is used for what is regarded as exceptional, resulting in phrases like *lady doctor, male nurse, women MPs*. One other linguistic symptom of the stereotyping of women's roles is the use of suffixes to distinguish women from men, and convey different connotations, for instance *actress, authoress, hostess, stewardess, poetess, comedienne, usherette* (Mills 1995: 94–95).

- Stereotyping also emerges in the verbs and adjectives used of women, so that possible qualities come to be seen as expected, even inevitable, e.g. physically weak, emotional, irrational. Linked to the previous point, you may have noticed that the selection of vocabulary will emphasise the non-occupational qualities of women in society. So many words, and visuals, concentrate on describing women's looks, youth, sexuality and desirability for men. A particular semantic area which is **overworded** is in the vocabulary for hair colour, some of the terms having no equivalent for male hair: *brunette, blonde, auburn, redhead, peroxide blonde, ash blonde, natural blonde* (Mills 1995: 162). This suggests that women are still constructed in the media as objects for satisfying men's desires and, as a by-product, for producing children. For instance, female secretaries seldom refer to managers as 'the boys along the corridor', but managers might well refer to secretarial staff as 'the girls in the office'. Emphasising youth in relation to women is also reflected in the popular press's use of first names and short forms. Though male politicians and others in power are sometimes referred to by a shortened form, e.g. *Johnny Howard* (Australia), the tendency does seem stronger in the case of women, e.g. *Winnie* not *Winifred Mandela*, and *Maggie* for Margaret Thatcher, but not *Georgie* for George Osborne or *Kev* for Kevin Rudd (cf. Fowler 1991: 96, 100–101) 'The name is Bond. Jimmy Bond' sounds ridiculous. Of course, politicians pre-empt this if they already use the short form themselves, like Tony Blair, Tony Abbott or Bill Clinton.

ACTIVITY 18 ————————————————————————

Please refer to the companion website for the activity material.

- Finally, metaphors for women, especially in Japanese (Hiraga 1991: 55), often depict them as commodities, consumer goods or food. The ideological basis of these metaphors is obvious: commodities are inanimate objects; their sole purpose is to be used by consumers; they can be bought and become the property of their owners. All these assumptions suggest a society in which women are expected to be passive, powerless, valuable and desirable objects, and to be purchased, owned, used, consumed and enjoyed by men.

A development of stereotyping theory can be seen in the work of Helene Cixous, who shows that a binary opposition such as male/female can become a way of organising other oppositions.

> *Where is she?*
> Activity/passivity
> Sun/Moon
> Culture/Nature
> Day/Night
> Father/Mother
> Head/heart
> Intelligible/sensitive
> Logos/Pathos
>
> (Cixous 1981: 90)

These analogical oppositions reinforce each other, for example nature (not culture) is seen as both a woman (not a man) and passive (not active). Obviously enough, these oppositions cluster to produce strong stereotypical associations for women and men, as well as for nature.

The strength of the male–female opposition and obsessive insistence on its application leads to quite cruel medical practices. An article in the *New Internationalist* reports:

> According to the Intersex Society of North America one in every 2,000 infants is born with ambiguous genitalia from about two-dozen causes. There are more than 2,000 surgeries performed in the US each year aimed at surgically assigning a sex to these intersex patients.
>
> (Nataf 1998: 23)

The difficulty in assigning infants to the category of male or female prompts surgeons to change the infants' bodies to more neatly fit the framework of classification. There could hardly be a stronger example of the relationship between linguistic classification and (abuse of) power, unless it were Clinton's attempt to pin down the meaning of *sexual relations* as a synonym of *sexual intercourse*; he claimed after having oral sex with Monica Lewinsky in the Oval Office 'I did not have sexual relations with that woman.'

2.2 IDEOLOGY, GRAMMAR AND TRANSITIVITY

The conceptual aspects of ideology are not simply reflected in the vocabulary of a language, however. They are at work in the grammar and probably more dangerous there precisely because they are more latent. The part of the grammar of the clause which is relevant to conceptualisation, the representation of the world, is called **transitivity**. Let's see how it works.

We can divide lexical verbs and the processes they represent into five basic categories: Existential, Relational, Material, Verbal and Mental (Table 2.1). **Existential processes** represent the existence of some thing, the single participant, known as the **existent**, e.g. 'there was a flash of lightning'. **Relational processes** describe states of affairs, static situations. They relate two things, or a thing and a property, the **token** and the **value**, e.g. 'John (token) **is** a teacher (value)', 'John (token) **is** poor (value)'. They include verbs like *to be* and *to have*, e.g. 'I **have** two houses', 'that penknife **belongs to** Jim', 'the hairbrush **is** in the drawer'. Other Relational verbs are *remain, stay, equal, comprise, constitute, include, contain*, etc. And, as used in the

Table 2.1 *Process types in Hallidayan grammar*

Process	Meanings	Participants	Example
Existential	Existence	Existent	There are <u>six moons of Uranus</u> (Ext)
Relational	States, relationships	Token, value Carrier/attribute	<u>Peter</u> (T/C) remained <u>a teacher</u> (V/A)
		Identified/identifier	<u>Boris</u> (T/Id) is <u>the Prime Minister</u> (V/Ir)
		Possessor/possession	<u>Paula</u> (T/Possr) has <u>a cat</u> (T/Possn)
Material	Actions, events	Actor, affected, recipient	<u>Snow</u> (Act) blocked <u>the road</u> (Aff) <u>Jane</u> (Act) gave <u>me</u> (Rec) <u>a waffle</u> (Aff)
Mental	Perception, emotion, thought	Experiencer, experience	<u>The cat</u> (Excer) saw <u>the bird</u> (Exce) <u>Mat</u> (Excer) hated <u>dogs</u> (Exce) <u>He</u> (Excer) decided <u>to go home</u> (Exce)
Verbal	Speaking, writing, communicating	Sayer, receiver, verbiage	<u>Paul</u> (S) told <u>Mindy</u> (R) <u>he would go home</u> (V) <u>Deirdre</u> (S) whistled

following sentences, though not always, they include the verbs *stand, surround, occupy*. 'Big Ben **stands** next to the Houses of Parliament', 'a moat **surrounds** the castle', 'an oak tree **occupies** most of my back garden'.

Relational clauses may be divided into **attributive**, with a **carrier** and **attribute,** e.g. 'John (carrier) **is** sick (attribute)', 'Mark (carrier) **is** a nurse (attribute)'. And **identifying**, with an **identified** and **identifier,** e.g. 'Abe (identified) **is** the Prime Minister (identifier)', 'Mandy (identified) **is** the oldest in the class (identifier)', which, unlike attributive clauses, can be reversed, e.g. 'The Prime Minister **is** Abe', etc. And **possessive**, with a **possessor** and **possession** e.g. 'Ahmed (possessor) **has** a guitar (possession)'.

Material process verbs describe an action or event, and answer the question *what happened*? These are prototypical verbs, the "doing words" which we were taught at school, e.g. 'John **hit** the teacher', 'Harry **smoked** dope', 'Jemima **died**', 'Mary **ran** fast'. But material processes also include verbs without an animate agent, e.g. 'snow **fell** heavily and **blocked** the driveway', 'the car **slid** over the black ice'. Whether animate or not, the thing responsible for causing the action or event is called the **actor**: John, Harry, Jemima, Mary, the snow, and the car, respectively. All material process verbs will have an **actor**, the subject in active voice clauses. Some will take an object, the thing that the action or event affects, and we can call this the **affected**. In the previous examples the teacher, dope, the driveway, are the affected parties. There may sometimes be two affecteds, one of which can be called the **recipient**, for example, John in 'Mary gave John a potato.'

Mental process verbs are of three types, perception, cognition and emotion, e.g. 'John Kerry **saw** the Israeli Prime Minister'; 'Samantha **heard** the birds singing'; 'Bach **considered** resigning'; 'computers **think** fast'; 'Paris Hilton **loves** waffles'; 'the boss **annoyed** me'. The "person" who experiences these perceptions, thoughts, or emotions we can call the **experiencer**, in the previous examples John Kerry, Samantha, Bach, computers, Paris Hilton and me. Sometimes the **experience** (perception, thought or emotion) will be referred to by a **noun phrase**, 'waffles', 'the boss'. But often it is represented by a whole clause (underlined): 'Miliband **wondered** whether he should accept 1 million pounds for the Labour party. He **decided** not to accept the money, because he **thought** it might compromise his integrity.'

Verbal process verbs are verbs of saying or writing, e.g. 'He **demanded** an apology', 'he **nominated** a gorilla as chairman of the committee', 'the Indonesians **prayed** for rain', ' "Help me," he **cried**. "How, exactly?" she **asked**'. The person doing the saying or writing will be called the **sayer**. The person addressed is the **receiver**. Sometimes what is actually said, the **verbiage**, can be represented by a whole clause or sentence, as with mental processes: 'He said he would come on Monday'; ' "I ate the chocolate cakes", she confessed.'

Notice that in these analyses it is the lexical verb, the last verb in the verb phrase, which indicates the process. So that in 'Paul was **drinking** and John started **eating**' we ignore 'was' and 'started'.

ACTIVITY 19

Please refer to the companion website for the activity material.

A sample of transitivity and vocabulary analysis

Let's now demonstrate how to apply these vocabulary classifications and grammatical analyses to a longer text, to show the ways in which linguistic patterns can be used, deliberately or not, to construct a version of reality, and reflect ideology. The text is a comment column taken from the online BBC news magazine.

> www.bbc.co.uk/news/magazine-25334716
> **18 December 2013** Last updated at 00:51

What is the appeal of Candy Crush Saga?

Candy Crush Saga – the "match-three" mobile game – was the highest grossing app on both iPhone and iPad in 2013. How did millions of commuters become entranced by a grid of brightly coloured sweets, asks Chris Stokel-Walker.

Stand on a crowded commuter train in New York, Paris, London, Tokyo, or Berlin and you will see a multitude of people. Goldfish-mouthed, eyes glazed, deeply breathing, fixated on one thing only.

Getting rows of red jelly beans or orange lozenges to disappear.

The game is also immensely popular on Facebook, with the site hosting support groups for self-confessed addicts.

Worldwide, Candy Crush Saga is estimated to make £610,000 ($1,000,000) per day from its users, according to Appdata. It is one of a growing number that is free to download but generates extraordinary revenues by nudging addicted players into paying more to get gizmos that help them progress through difficulty levels.

They buy add-ons, extra lives and access to higher levels. These microtransactions have been criticised, but its British-based developer King is quick to point out that more than half of players who reach the last level in Candy Crush Saga have done so without any financial outlay.

The hefty revenues have led to speculation that King, which has its HQ at London's Kings Cross, is preparing for an initial public offering (IPO) of shares in the US.

King has taken advantage of a change in the way people play video games. There was a time when a particular demographic was overrepresented among gamers – young men at home, using consoles. The advent of smartphones and tablets has changed gaming – so much so that the typical Candy Crush Saga player is a woman aged 25–45.

Some people's devotion to the game leads to them changing their smartphone's internal clock so that they get more lives, an all-important (and scarce) commodity doled out at regular intervals.

One gamer, Laura Wilson, travelling on a Friday afternoon train from Kings Cross to Newcastle, played for only a few minutes before her lives ran out. With a small sigh she closed the app on her iPad and opened up an e-book. For her the e-book was scant consolation. "You get addicted," she explains matter-of-factly. She isn't alone.

An afternoon Tube journey across London saw a carriage full of players hunched over their phones. Two men, one in his 40s, one in his 20s, were sitting across from each other manipulating sweets into patterns, their lives measured out in cascading bon-bons and exploding chocolate buttons. Six in ten UK players while away their journey to work like this, though most are progressing through the hundreds of levels in the midevening, between 6 pm and 9 pm.

"It's a good stress relief," says Amy Bolton, a 21-year old student at Newcastle University.

Gamers like Bolton drop in and out during the course of the day, according to internal usage figures described by King. A quick session snatched here and there helps people progress through the hundreds of levels in the game. Some of the most eager gamers are keeping pace with King's coders, who have released more than 500 levels to date, snaking up a path that King readily admits owes a debt to the layout of popular board games.

They can start a game over breakfast on their laptop while scrolling through Facebook. They can then play it on their phone on the train to work, where they can switch on their iPad and continue their game where they left off. This smooth continuity of gameplay is something King believe is part of their success.

Candy Crush is not so much a new type of game as an incredibly well-researched and careful fine-tuning of existing concepts.

There have been plenty of games that follow the same basic format as King's creation. Candy Crush Saga owes a debt to the likes of Tetris and Puzzle Bobble/Bust-a-Move, both of which captivated audiences of yesteryear.

Candy Crush Saga displaced Bejeweled, a similar matching game originally developed 12 years ago, from the Facebook gaming charts earlier this year. Now other games aim to replicate Candy Crush's success with minor tweaks.

Sebastian Knutsson, chief creative officer and co-founder of King, says that none of his team foresaw Candy Crush Saga's success when developing the game, initially for the company's website.

Knutsson was and remains an avid gamer, and was especially enamoured of the early 1990s arcade games and their bright, brash colours. Working with artists and designers from a small office, he produced a game that stood out from the other "match-three" games that were on the market. Sweets were chosen, he reveals, to appeal to their core audience, which is far from the stereotypical gamer.

Not that Candy Crush Saga was perfect from the first iteration. "We had an early theme based around the French Art Deco style," Knutsson explains. That included an over-the-top French voice egging on players when they made good moves. "It didn't work out," Knutsson says. People hated the accent, finding it too jokey. It was replaced with a smooth, deep male voice whispering encouragement.

The function of the game, and the way it rations lives, has been carefully crafted by King to provide maximum enjoyment, and to keep people coming back for more. Players regularly check the countdown until their next life is released and they can play on. It's precision-engineered addiction, and it has resonated with the public.

"They give you unlimited lives, or the levels don't get more challenging in the same way," says Bolton, explaining why she prefers Candy Crush to its competitors.

Though Knutsson says that "we don't want to be a Candy Crush company", the game is far and away King's largest property. It makes up the lion's share of the company's 225 million unique monthly users. Appdata, an analyst of iOS and Facebook applications, estimates that Candy Crush Saga has 137 million active monthly users alone, topping charts.

There has been criticism of the revenue structure around the game – free to download but delicately engineered to get users spending money.

A recent Candy Crush expansion pack has had a 40-strong team of developers working on it, four times the number of programmers and artists who brought the original Facebook version of the game into existence.

Knutsson says that King will keep adding levels to the regular Candy Crush. The addiction will continue.

Nervously, Bolton admits that before she goes to sleep, she'll often fit in a game.

"And when I close my eyes to go to sleep, I can see all the shapes still, like a virtual Candy Crush in my head."

Vocabulary and the population or participants of the text

We noted earlier that vocabulary classifies and categorises. Let's look at the way this text categorises the people and other participants, technically called the **text population** (Talbot 1992).

'People' or 'the public' are sub-categorised as 'commuter(s)', and 'gamers' in general, who were traditionally mostly 'young men at home using consoles' but in the case of Candy Crush Saga (hereafter CCS) mainly 'women of 25–40'. Gamers using King products are the '225 million unique monthly users'. Of these CCS has '137 million monthly users' or 'players', including 'millions of commuters' some or all of which are 'addicts', a subgroup of which have formed 'support groups' to break their addiction. The specific users mentioned are the anonymous 'two men, one in his 40s, one in his 20s', and the women identified as 'Amy Bolton, a 21-year old student at Newcastle University' and 'Laura Wilson'.

A separate group of people are those associated with 'King' and the development of CCS: 'coders', 'a 40-strong team of developers', 'artists and designers', 'programmers and artists' and 'Sebastian Knutsson'.

But people are not the only or even main participants in the text. We have a list of different digital devices: 'consoles', 'laptop', 'ebook', 'smartphone', 'iPhone' and 'iPad'. Then there are the various 'apps' or 'games'/'mobile games' played on them. Some pre-date Candy Crush or are 'its competitors': 'video games', 'early 1990s arcade games', 'Tetris', 'Puzzle Bobble/Bust-a-Move' and 'Bejeweled'.

Unsurprisingly, 'Candy Crush Saga' figures prominently and repeatedly. So do its 'images' – more specifically 'bonbons', 'jelly beans', 'lozenges', 'chocolate buttons', all types of 'sweets' or 'candy', of course. As do its 'gizmos' – specifically 'add-ons', 'lives' and 'access to levels'.

Even a swift glance at the text reveals the importance of numbers. We already noted references to the number of users, 'usage figures' as measured by 'Appdata' and their ages, but we also have statistics like 'six in ten UK players'. These, with gender, clearly relate to the success of the app and its marketing, making it 'the highest grossing app'. Successfully penetrating the market also translates into 'money', 'revenues', '£610,000 ($1,000,000) per day' and the possibility of issuing 'shares' in an 'IPO'.

Other numbers associate with time. The history of gaming gives us the contrast between 'early 1990s', 'yesteryear', 'original' and 'present', '2013' 'to date', 'new'. More prominent are the time periods spent on the game: 'time', ranging from 'lives' to 'day' to 'intervals', 'minutes', the more specific 'Friday afternoon', 'midevening, between 6pm and 9pm' or the less definite 'breakfast', the time 'before she goes to sleep' and gamers' 'countdown until their next life'.

Places are featured, not so much those which passengers are travelling to or from – 'Newcastle', 'Kings Cross' – but those emphasising the global spread of CCS: 'New York', 'Tokyo', 'Paris', 'London', 'Berlin'.

From these patterns of vocabulary one might detect an ideology that celebrates the marketing and financial success of a new and developing gender-neutral digital product, which is very time-consuming and reaches beyond traditional gamer demographics. And an ideology which naturalises the ubiquity of digital devices with global reach.

However, this interpretation is based on analysing noun phrases. Adjectives and verbs provide a more or less obvious criticism of the CCS phenomenon. Admittedly, some of the effects on users are described positively or neutrally: 'devotion', 'stress relief', 'captivated', 'entranced'. But the words 'addicted'/'addicts'/'addiction' are repeated, and there is an unflattering description of players as 'goldfish-mouthed, eyes glazed, deeply breathing, fixated on one thing only'. Moreover, the very financial success of the company has been criticised, in so far as it relies on precision-engineering addiction to make gamers buy helpful gizmos.

Grammar and ideology: transitivity analysis

To fully investigate the use of verbs and adjectives we have to employ a transitivity analysis. In other words, having identified the major people and things in the text, we can explore how they function as participants in clauses. We examine, in turn, interesting patterns in the relational, material, mental and verbal process clauses. The large number of examples quoted and analysed here give you a model for any analysis you may wish to do yourselves, but you might wish to skim over some of them.

Relational processes

Relational clauses will be used to describe and explicitly categorise the participants in the text. The relevant kinds of question to ask will be 'what participants attract these relational descriptions?' and 'what kinds of qualities or categories are assigned to them?'

Relational clauses concentrate on three kinds of participants as tokens: the game itself (17 clauses); the players of the game (6 clauses); the company, King, and its personnel (7 clauses).

The Game

The game is positioned in relation to 'other "match-three" games (token) that **were** on the market (value)' and 'it (token) **is** one of a growing number that is free to download (value)', but not so original: 'Candy Crush (token) **is** not so much a new type of game as an incredibly well-researched and careful fine-tuning of existing concepts (value)'.

Its effect on users is also highlighted: ' "It (token)**'s** a good stress relief, (value)"'; it (token)**'s** precision-engineered addiction (value)'. This is not surprising since the stated aim of the article is to find out 'what (value) **is** the appeal of Candy Crush Saga (token)'. The qualities experienced by the player have something to do with it: 'this smooth continuity of gameplay (token) **is** something King believes is part of their success (value)', and one of the users, Amy Bolton, describes its uniqueness, since with other games 'the levels (token) don't **get** more challenging in the same way (value)'.

The changes to and improvement of the game are also emphasised: 'Not that Candy Crush Saga (token) **was** perfect from the first iteration (value)'; 'it [the first iteration] **included** an over-the-top French voice egging on players when they made good moves (value)'; it is the possessor/token of developers 'a recent Candy Crush expansion pack (token: possessor) has **had** a 40-strong team of developers working on it (value: possession)'.

Finally, its popularity and financial importance to the company, King, is stated: 'the game (token) **is** also immensely popular on Facebook (value)'; 'it (token) **makes up** the lion's share of the company's 225 million unique monthly users (value)'; 'Candy Crush Saga (token: possessor) **has** 137 million active monthly users alone (value: possession)'; 'the game (token) **is** far and away King's largest property (value)'. Note how the possessive clauses give CCS more power as a possessor than the attributive and identifying ones, which merely assign it to categories.

Players

Players as tokens are described in terms of their attachment to the game: 'How did millions of commuters (token) **become** entranced (value)'; ' "You (token) **get** addicted (value)" '; in which addiction 'She (token) **isn't** alone (value)'. Or in terms of the non-traditional demographic: 'their core audience, which (token) **is** far from the stereotypical gamer (value)'; 'the typical Candy Crush Saga player (token) **is** a woman aged 25–45 (value)'; 'there was a time when a particular demographic (token) **was** overrepresented among gamers (value) – young men at home, using consoles (token)'.

The Company

Another focus of attention as a token is the company, 'King, which (token) **has** its HQ at London's Kings Cross (value)', and its personnel including the founder Knutsson: 'Knutsson (token) **was** and **remains** an avid gamer (value), and **was** especially enamoured of the early 1990s arcade games and their bright, brash colours (value).' King/Knutsson's defence of the company, ambitions for it and description of early stages of the game all feature: 'but its British-based developer King (token) **is** quick (value) to point out that more than half of players who reach the last level in Candy Crush Saga have done so without any financial outlay'; 'we (token) don't want **to be** a Candy Crush company (value)'; 'we (token) **had** an early theme based around the French Art Deco style (value)'.

Material processes

The main reason for analysing material processes is to uncover who is represented as the most powerful participants in the text. It is important to note the main patterns of who/acts on whom/what. Material process verbs are of many kinds, and therefore vary in terms of the amount of power the actor is exerting on the affected. Crudely speaking, if the clause has an actor and an affected in a transitive clause, this actor is being represented as relatively powerful and responsible for the action. If there is only an actor and no affected in an intransitive clause, the actor comes over as less powerful. Affected participants are represented as passive and powerless. More delicately, there are material processes which just involve movement of oneself, such as 'John entered the room' or 'I climbed a mountain', where the room and mountain are hardly affected at all and the "affected" can be called a **range**. These attach relatively little power to the actor, not much more than intransitive clauses do. At the other extreme are the very powerful creative or destructive material processes which, being partly existential (or anti-existential) bring things into or take things out of existence.

As with relational clauses the main actors in our article are the players (40), the games themselves (21) and the personnel at King who developed CCS (15).

Players

The main actions performed by the players are playing the game, but these are during their travelling 'Laura Wilson (actor), **travelling** on a Friday afternoon train from Kings Cross to Newcastle' with other travellers – 'Two men (actor), one in his 40s, one in his 20s, were **sitting** across from each other' – and six out of ten of these '**while away** their journey to work (affected) like this'.

Amy Bolton's playing CCS is framed by sleeping ' "And when I (actor) **close** my eyes (affected) **to go to sleep**, I can see all the shapes still" '.

'Nervously, Bolton admits that before she **goes to sleep**, she (actor)'ll often **fit in** a game (affected).' So they also find time for playing: 'A quick session (affected) **snatched** here and there'.

Note that in these cases none of the players is actually affecting much, they are either intransitive or the actor is acting on themselves (closing their eyes). Fitting in a game, snatching a session and whiling away time are not prototypical actions affecting the game and time.

The other prerequisite for playing the game is being able to interact with digital devices. Previously players were '**using** consoles (affected)' but now they '**switch on** their iPad (affected)' or play while '**scrolling** through Facebook': 'With a small sigh she (actor) **closed** the app (affected) on her iPad and **opened up** an e-book (affected)'. The game also affects their interaction: 'Some people's devotion to the game leads to them (actor) **changing** their smartphone's internal clock (affected)'.

Generally these 'people (actor) **play** video games (affected)' in a new way and 'they (actor) **play** it [CCS] (affected) on the way to work' or in Laura Wilson's case '**played** for only a few minutes'. But what does playing involve? 'Two men, one in his 40s, one in his 20s (actor) ... **manipulating** sweets (affected) into patterns', '**getting** rows of red jelly beans or orange lozenges (affected) to disappear'. And once they have '**made** good moves (affected)' players can '**progress** through the hundreds of [difficulty] levels in the game', until they '**reach** (affected) the last level in Candy Crush Saga (affected)'.

Great emphasis is put upon the use of every spare moment to start, stop or continue with the game: 'They (actor) can **start** a game (affected) over breakfast on their laptop' and '**continue** their game (affected) where they (actor) **left off**' or '**play on**', in other words '**drop in and out** during the course of the day'. For the game is designed to 'keep people (actor) **coming back** for more'. Waiting to resume they regularly '**check** the countdown (affected) until their next life is released'. And even after reaching the highest level they continue to respond to new levels: 'some of the most eager gamers (actor) are **keeping pace with** King's coders (affected)'.

Another focus is on the possibility of gamers '**spending** money (affected)', '**paying** more (affected) to get gizmos that help them progress through difficulty levels', 'so that they (actor) **get** more lives (affected)'. 'They (actor) **buy** add-ons, extra lives and access to higher levels (affected).'

Notice that when players interact with computers or play the game there are far more instances of affecteds, suggesting this is the only way they can exercise their power, whether spending money or not. However, does playing the game really affect the game or it is rather like a range – climbing a mountain?

The Game

The game and similar games are quite powerful in their effect on users. 'The function of the game (actor) ... has been carefully crafted by King

... **to keep** people (affected) coming back for more', with 'their lives (affected) **measured out**' by it.

One of the attractions of the game is probably the imagery, the '**cascading** bon-bons (actor) and **exploding** chocolate buttons (actor)', and the '500 levels to date (actor), **snaking up** a path'.

Another addictive attraction is 'the way it (actor) **rations** lives (affected)', 'an all-important (and scarce) commodity (affected) **doled** out at regular intervals' with players waiting 'until their next life (affected) is **released** and they can play on'. Very often the game is able 'to **get** users (affected) spending money' for these lives, '**nudging** addicted players (affected) into paying more to get gizmos that (actor) **help** them (affected) progress through difficulty levels'.

The game is represented as more successful than competitors, 'a game that (actor) **stood out** from the other "match-three" games that were on the market' and which '**displaced** Bejeweled (affected) ... from the Facebook gaming charts earlier this year', though the competition is not over: 'Now other games (actor) aim to **replicate** Candy Crush's success (affected)'.

CCS, by persuading gamers to pay for extra lives '**generates** extraordinary revenues (affected)'. It is a huge commercial success: 'Worldwide, Candy Crush Saga is estimated to **make** £610,000 ($1,000,000) (affected) per day from its users.'

The Company

The final dominant group of actors are King and the team of developers. Knutsson '**working** with artists and designers from a small office, **produced** a game (affected) that stood out', '**developing** the game (affected)', '**crafted** by King (actor) to **provide** maximum enjoyment (affected)'. Recently it has had 'a 40-strong team of developers (actor) **working** on it, four times the number of programmers and artists who (actor) **brought** the original Facebook version of the game (affected) into existence'.

Features of the game and King's past and future development strategies are emphasised: 'King (actor) has **taken advantage of** a change in the way people play video games (affected)'; 'Sweets (affected) were **chosen** ... to appeal to their core audience'; 'an early theme (affected) **based** around the French Art Deco style ... was **replaced** with a smooth, deep male voice whispering encouragement'; '[coders] who (actor) have **released** more than 500 levels (affected) to date', and 'King (actor) will keep **adding** levels (affected)'. Because of the revenue from the addiction King may be '**preparing for** an initial public offering (IPO) of shares (affected) in the US'.

We can sum up the general pattern of power relations and of chains of cause and effect represented in this article. King and its game developers are the most powerful. This is because, though they are not actors as frequently as the players, the kind of creative material processes which bring into existence and develop this addictive game are very high up the scale of power. The players are, of course, often affected by the game which King produced. But even when they are playing the game they are relatively passive since, as a range it is not directly affected by them, any more than a mountain is much affected by people climbing it.

The control CCS and its developers exert over players is obvious from the vocabulary to do with addiction and from the relational clauses which describe its effect. But it is underlined when we look at the mental processes of affection with players as experiencers.

Mental processes

Mental processes indicate internal or perceptual processes, strictly speaking, only accessible to the experiencer. One question to ask is who the experiencers are – whether the writer claims to know the experiences of other experiencers, other characters, as is common with all-knowing narrators in some kinds of fiction. Another important question might be whether the mental processes are to do with thinking, feeling or perception.

Players

As experiencers players outnumber King/Knutsson 9 to 3. Most players' mental processes are affective or emotional, and in all cases the experiences are games, eight of the nine CCS or an aspect of it: 'it (experience) has **resonated with** the public (experiencer)', its sweets (experience) are able '**to appeal to** their core audience (experiencer)', who, like Amy Bolton (experiencer), '**prefers** Candy Crush (experience) to its competitors'. There is 'a multitude of people (experiencer) … [g]oldfish-mouthed, eyes glazed, deeply breathing, **fixated on** one thing only (experience)', a small sample of the 'millions of commuters (experiencer) [who have] become **entranced** by a grid of brightly coloured sweets (experience)', just as previous games, 'Tetris and Puzzle Bobble/Bust-a-Move (experience) **captivated** audiences of yesteryear (experiencer)'.

In only two cases are players experiencers of cognitive or perceptual processes, 'find' and 'see', respectively: '[People (experiencer) **hated** the accent (experience),] **finding** it (experience) too jokey', '"I (experiencer) can **see** all the shapes (experience) still, like a virtual Candy Crush in my head."'

The Company

There are a few mental processes associated with King/Knutsson but these are either cognitive – 'none of his team (experiencer) **foresaw** Candy Crush Saga's success (experience)', 'This smooth continuity of gameplay (experience…) is something King (experiencer) **believes** is part of their success (…experience)' – or negative – '"we (experiencer) don't **want** to be a Candy Crush company (experience)"'.

The general pattern is of players as experiencers of mental processes of affection with the game as the experience. Some of these seem to combine a mental process with a material one (what Halliday labels **behavioural** processes): 'a grid of highly coloured sweets (actor experience) has **entranced** millions of commuters (affected experiencer)', 'tetris (actor experience) **captivated** audiences of yesteryear (affected experiencer)', again attesting to the power of the games to influence emotions.

Although Knutsson's mental processes are not much represented directly, we get indirect access to his thoughts because he is quoted so often, as the next section shows.

Verbal processes

One reason for analysing verbal processes is to see who holds the floor, has their words (verbiage) reported. Another is to see what kinds of effect the sayers might have on those listening, whether they dominate, for example, or what speech acts they perform (see also Chapter 5). Analysis of the verbiage will also tell us the main concerns of the sayers.

Knutsson (The Company)

By far the most important of the sayers is Knutsson, whose views are therefore overrepresented. He talks of aspects of the game's past and future development '"We had an early theme based around the French Art Deco style (verbiage)," Knutsson (sayer) **explains**'; '"It didn't work out (verbiage)," Knutsson (sayer) **says**'; 'sweets were chosen (verbiage…), he (sayer) **reveals**, to appeal to their core audience (…verbiage)'. He (sayer) **says** 'that King will keep adding levels to the regular Candy Crush (verbiage)'; that 'none of his team foresaw Candy Crush Saga's success when developing the game (verbiage)'; and '"we don't want to be a Candy Crush company (verbiage)"'. King, the company he founded and represents, describes 'internal usage figures (verbiage)'. More important, against the accusation that the microtransactions exploit addiction 'King (sayer) is quick **to point out** that more than half of players who reach the last level in Candy Crush Saga have done so without any financial outlay (verbiage)'.

I think that particularly significant is the omission of the sayer in the following clause: 'These microtransactions (target) have been **criticised**'. The absent anonymous critic is negligible compared with the strongly present Knutsson/King, who defends the company and dominates the floor.

Players

Two players are quoted as sayers as well. Laura Wilson openly admits addiction: '"You get addicted," (verbiage) she (sayer) **explains** matter-of-factly.'

But Amy Bolton only implies her addiction: 'nervously, <u>Bolton</u> (sayer) **admits** that <u>before she goes to sleep, she'll often fit in a game</u> (verbiage)'. Otherwise all her verbiage is positive: '<u>"It's a good stress relief,"</u> (verbiage) **says** <u>Amy Bolton, a 21-year old student at Newcastle University</u> (sayer)'; '<u>"They give you unlimited lives, or the levels don't get more challenging in the same way,"</u> (verbiage) **says** <u>Bolton</u> (sayer), **explaining** <u>why she prefers Candy Crush to its competitors</u> (verbiage).'

So the weight of the verbiage provided by Amy Bolton and Knutsson as sayers is positive about CCS, which amounts to bias by selection.

Problems when identifying processes

Applying the Hallidayan transitivity scheme to texts is not always straightforward. Sometimes there are literal and metaphorical meanings for a verb, and it is important to choose the correct one. Reputedly, when the Earl of Sandwich said to the radical John Wilkes 'You will either die on the gallows or of the pox [syphilis]', the latter replied: 'That depends upon whether I embrace your principles or your mistress.' In this case 'embrace' is either a material process with 'your mistress' as the affected, or a mental process with 'your principles' as an experience.

Another complication arises when the metaphor is not just lexical but grammatical too as in '<u>An afternoon Tube journey across London</u> (experiencer) **saw** <u>a carriage full of players hunched over their phones</u> (experience)'. Here not only is a journey personified through the use of 'saw', but the **grammatical metaphor** redistributes participants and circumstances from the more literal: 'There was a carriage full of players hunched over their phones during an afternoon Tube journey across London.' It promotes a literal time/place circumstance 'during an afternoon Tube journey across London' into an experiencer, and a literal existent 'a carriage full of players hunched over their phones' into an experience.

A third complication is when a verb seems to involve more than one process in its meaning. We have already seen that creative material processes as in 'Knutsson **produced** a game' can be glossed as "cause to exist", so that it is partly existential. When players 'get more lives' this means "cause themselves to have" so the causal element is material and the having element is relational. The 'replaced' in 'an early theme was **replaced** with a smooth, deep male voice whispering encouragement' means "causes something to be there instead of something else" which also makes it material-relational, just as the 'topping' in 'Candy Crush Saga has 137 million active monthly users alone, **topping** charts' means "is at the top of".

Ideological factors in and behind the text

The purpose of performing such a detailed analysis of the lexis and clauses of a text is to reveal patterns which might be cues to the underlying ideology. This amounts to explanation, at level 3 in Table 0.1. It is, of course, rather more problematic than pure description of the text's meanings, so my explanation may be highly disputable.

The world represented here by the material processes is one where the public, commuters in particular, constantly interact with machines, where they are rather powerless to do anything else except act on themselves, especially travel. They spend most of their spare time playing CCS or similar games. This is because of the emotional power it has over them, shown by mental processes of affect. The developers of the game and the game itself are represented as more powerful than the players, who seem to lack the power to stop playing it. The text seems to celebrate CCS's ability to reach beyond the traditional demographic for gaming, especially its attraction to women, measuring its success by player numbers and geographical reach. This depends upon the qualities of the game that are spelt out in relational clauses. The text also celebrates CCS for the amount of revenue it generates. It is a capitalist success story depending upon establishing a market niche through clever strategic development and the manipulation of demand. The chain of cause and effect can be diagrammed as follows:

King Knutsson develops the game with cleverly attractive features
↓
Players play the game
↓
Its popularity spreads in terms of numbers and worldwide reach
↓
Players become fixated on it
↓
Some players spend money to help them progress through the game
↓
In this way the game generates huge revenues

Although there is some criticism voiced anonymously of the exploitation of players' addiction, the balance of the representation in the verbiage is given to King/Knutsson and gamers who enjoy it. King responds to criticism by pointing out that half of the most successful players spend no money.

Any disapproval by the writer is veiled or indirect and a matter of inference (see Section 4.4). The article may imply that literal lives and CCS lives are somehow crazily confused. In this quote are lives real or virtual or both? 'Two men, their lives **measured out** in cascading bon-bons and exploding chocolate buttons'. This echoes T.S. Eliot's satirical 'I have measured out my life with coffee spoons' ('The Love Song of J. Alfred Prufrock'), but the game measures out virtual lives too 'an all-important (and scarce) commodity **doled** out at regular intervals'. So is there an implication that using up virtual lives is equivalent to wasting your real life? 'Laura Wilson ... played for only a few minutes before her lives **ran out**.' And when Amy Bolton tries to get to sleep she ' "can see all the shapes still, like a virtual Candy Crush" ' in her head. So for her is Candy Crush real and her memory of it virtual, blurring or reversing the boundaries between real and virtual life?

ACTIVITY 20

Please refer to the companion website for the activity material.

Summary

We have now explored how the choice of vocabulary to categorise and the choice of processes and participants in the clause display underlying ideological positions. Some of these analyses might simply reinforce the obvious meanings which a reader gets from the text anyway. But in other cases the linguistic analysis will reveal latent patterns which escape an ordinary reading. Critical reading can benefit greatly from such analyses, precisely because it brings to light what is ordinarily latent or hidden. We could well, therefore, apply such critical reading to the drafts of our own writing, to reveal the categories we think in and the way we have represented participants.

2.3 COMPLICATIONS TO TRANSITIVITY

At this unconscious or latent level we often get manipulated by two major transformations or complications to the grammatical system: nominalisation and passivisation. We'll devote this next section to them since, unconsciously or not, they can be powerful ideological tools.

Passivisation

Passivisation allows you to leave out the actor in material processes, experiencer in mental processes, and sayer (speaker) in verbal process clauses:

> Material: Poachers killed the elephant → the elephant was killed
> Mental: Rangers noticed the vultures → the vultures were noticed
> Verbal: The marksmen told the poacher to freeze → the poacher was told to freeze

Notice that past participial clauses can achieve the same omission as passivisation: 'an all-important (and scarce) commodity (affected) **doled** out at regular intervals'.

Sometimes passivisation enables newspapers, among others, to protect sources by omitting the sayer, or to retail their own opinions as though they were someone else's, e.g. 'It is widely believed the BJP will not survive the confidence vote in the Indian Parliament.' In material processes, the omission of an actor will avoid apportioning blame or responsibility.

ACTIVITY 21 ━━━━━━━━━━━━━━━━━━━━━━━━━━━━━━━━

Please refer to the companion website for the activity material.

Nominalisation

Nominalisation turns a verb or an adjective into a noun (phrase). Most obviously it involves adding a suffix (e.g. *rough* → *roughness, imply* → *implication*), but less obviously using a noun which has the same form as a verb, e.g. *a catch*. Nominalisation allows even more omissions than passivisation. In

> Hutus killed one million Tutsis in the Rwandan civil war →
> There were one million killings in the Rwandan civil war

it omits both actors or perpetrators, and affecteds or victims.

In addition nominalisation suggests timelessness, since tense is no longer needed. Supposing we nominalise the clause (a) 'People are dissatisfied with the government policy on new golf courses' to make it part of the following sentence: (b) '*Dissatisfaction with the government policy on new golf courses* will cause a loss of popularity.' The hearer doesn't simply remain ignorant about who is dissatisfied, but about when they became dissatisfied, and whether they are still dissatisfied. The dissatisfaction sounds permanent.

Furthermore, noun phrases carry with them an **existential presupposition**. That is, since a noun phrase refers to things, when we encounter one we will assume something exists which is being referred to. So nominalisation is a means of smuggling in the presupposition, in this instance

> \>> There is dissatisfaction with the government's policy on new golf courses.

Nominalisation here is a sleight of hand which assumes propositions without stating them. If presupposed they cannot be easily argued against. For instance, if you say 'No' in reply to the statement in (b) then you are arguing against the claim of loss of popularity not about whether anyone is dissatisfied with the government policy. To argue against or disagree with a presupposition is much more difficult; you'd have to say something like: 'What do you mean by dissatisfaction with government policy on golf courses? Who's dissatisfied with it?'

ACTIVITY 22

Please refer to the companion website for the activity material.

A sample analysis

Nominalisation and passivisation are put to interesting use in the following news report. I have underlined the nominalisations and italicised the passives.

www.bbc.co.uk/news/world-middle-east-22261422
23 April 2013 Last updated at 17:27

Iraqi Sunni protest clashes in Hawija leave many dead (1)

More than 20 people have been killed in clashes between security forces and Sunni Arab protesters in northern Iraq, officials say (2).

Violence erupted when security forces raided an anti-government protest camp in Hawija, near Kirkuk (3).

Two Sunni ministers said they were resigning in protest over Tuesday's raid (4).

It was the worst violence between security forces and Sunni protesters in recent months (5).

Tens of thousands of Iraqis in Sunni-dominated areas have been protesting against Prime Minister Nouri al-Maliki, accusing his government of discriminating against them (6).

The government denies the accusations and says that *protesters have been infiltrated by militant groups* (7).

Hawija has been under siege since Friday when *an Iraqi officer was killed* in clashes with protesters (8). Residents refused a demand to hand the suspects over (9).

A final attempt at mediation broke down on Monday night and *troops were sent in* at dawn, the BBC Arabic's Rafid Jaboori reports from Baghdad (10). The government claimed its forces came under attack and had to respond (11).

The defence ministry said *20 "gunmen" and three officers were killed*, while other officials said that as many as 27 people had died (12).

After the raid, Sunnis briefly seized control of three checkpoints near Hawija before the army, reportedly using helicopter gunships, retook them (13). *A number of further deaths were reported* as *the checkpoints were attacked* (14).

In Hawija, the army cleared the square where the protest camp *had been set up*, burning tents, Reuters news agency reported (15).

Sometimes nominalisations are used to summarise a clause from elsewhere in the text, where the missing participants are provided. So that the 'protest' in the headline (1) is elaborated as a clause in

> Tens of thousands of Iraqis in Sunni-dominated areas have been protesting against Prime Minister Nouri al-Maliki (6).

Or 'the accusations' (7) refers back to the clause with explicit participants

> Tens of thousands of Iraqis in Sunni-dominated areas have been ... accusing his <u>government</u> of discriminating against them (6).

In other cases the missing participants are not made explicit at all. This may not matter when they can be inferred from the context, so that the '<u>demand</u> to hand the suspects over' (9) was presumably made by the government/security forces. But, in other, much more important cases, nominalisations leave us completely unclear about participants. We are told 'A final <u>attempt</u> at <u>mediation</u> broke down' but who attempted to mediate? And there were 'A number of further <u>deaths</u>', but who exactly died? (And how many of them for that matter?) 'The <u>government</u> claimed its forces came under <u>attack</u> and had to respond' (11) but who, if anyone, attacked the government forces? The nature of the participants in some cases may be debatable rather than unknown. What or who do the 'security forces' make secure? Who or what sections of the Iraqi population is the 'government' governing?

When we analyse the passives we see similar patterns. It is implied that protesters were the actors who killed the Iraqi officer in 'an Iraqi officer was killed in <u>clashes</u> with protesters' and who set up camp in 'the <u>protest camp</u> had been set up'. In 'the checkpoints were attacked', however, we do not know whether this is the original attack and takeover of the checkpoints by the Sunnis, or the retaking of the checkpoints by the government troops. In other instances we have no idea who was responsible for the killings: 'More than 20 people have been killed', '20 "gunmen" and three officers were killed'. And we can only guess who did the reporting in 'A number of further <u>deaths</u> were reported.'

We hope we have shown how nominalisation and passivisation to varying degrees distance us from the reality of what is going on, and from who is responsible. If, as is quite possible, a reader were just to read the headline of this article the heavy nominalisation and abstraction would leave huge gaps in representation and avoid assigning any responsibility for the killings:

Iraqi Sunni <u>protest clashes</u> in Hawija leave many dead (1).

ACTIVITY 23 ▬▬▬▬▬▬▬▬▬▬▬▬▬▬▬▬▬▬▬▬

Please refer to the companion website for the activity material.

Although nominalisation provides opportunities for manipulation, vagueness and failure to allot responsibility, it is extremely important in academic writing. Compare, for example, this paragraph written by a foreign student studying educational psychology, with its rewrite by an educated native speaker (nominalisations underlined):

Original
They (teachers) should know some of these students are misbehaving because they have problems coping with the life they lead at school. Because they can't solve it themselves they behave in ways that are totally foreign to them.

Rewrite
Student misbehaviour may be caused by problems with life at school. The student's inability to solve these problems may lead to kinds of behaviour that are totally foreign to them.

Importantly, nominalisation gives opportunities to vary the theme of the sentence. Whereas the original generally sticks to 'they' as the theme, the rewrite has 'student misbehaviour' and 'the student's inability to solve these problems' (Jones 1991: 181). Reinforcing this view, research has found a correlation between highly rated literature essays in schools and the use of nominalisations in the Theme (Tan 1993: 86).

As readers and writers we should be careful not to be enslaved by grammatical structures like nominalisation, but to use them consciously, remaining aware of how they leave out participants or mystify the processes they refer to. They are an important and powerful resource, but, if they muddle our thinking about causes and responsibilities can be dangerously abused. Warning: nominalisation and passivisation can seriously damage your mental health.

2.4 VISUAL TEXTS AND CONCEPTUAL MEANING

So far we have looked at the ideational or conceptual meaning conveyed through the vocabulary and grammar of the texts. Kress and Van Leeuwen (1996), in their 'grammar for visual design', assume that the visual mode draws upon the same semantic system as language.

The two major processes in visual grammar for representing conceptual relations and interactions are **conceptual** and **narrative** processes. **Conceptual processes** 'represent participants in terms of their generalised and more or less stable and timeless essence', that is, more or less permanent states, qualities and relationships. **Narrative processes** 'present unfolding actions and events, processes of change, or transitory spatial arrangements'. In a sense, conceptual processes are equivalent to Halliday's existential and relational processes and narrative processes are similar to material processes. Figure 2.3 diagrams the conceptual meanings involved in visual texts.

Conceptual processes

As mentioned above, conceptual processes represent a static concept rather than engaging their participants in some kind of action. Conceptual processes can be sub-divided into the classificational, analytical and symbolic types. Each of these three represent the world in different ways.

Classificational processes

Classificational processes assign to classes, rather like some kinds of carrier-attribute relational clauses, e.g. 'Paul is a teacher'. They may do this either in a *covert* or an *overt* way. So, for instance, in the Routledge email in Chapter 1 (see Image 2.2), the section showing their new book catalogues, the symmetrical spatial arrangement of the visual images of the catalogue covers helps to create the sense that these specific catalogues for Educational Psychology, Literacy and Language Education, etc. are all members of the class of book catalogues. This is an example of covert classification, which enhances the overt linguistic classification in the heading.

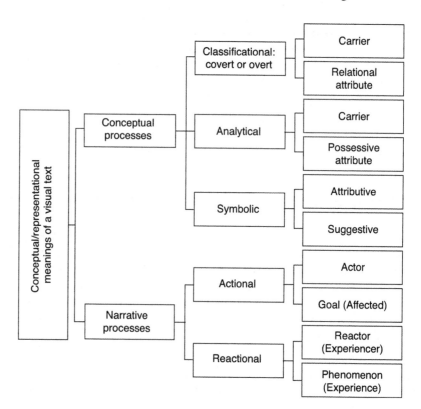

Figure 2.3
Visual representation of conceptual meaning

Image 2.2
Covert
classification in a
Routledge book
promotion

Analytical processes

Besides classifying entities in a hierarchical order, images can also display their possessive attributes, establishing between them a part–whole relationship. This is realised through **analytical processes**. Non-verbal texts create this part–whole relation through two kinds of participants: the carrier (whole) and its possessive attributes (parts), similar to possessive relational processes.

For example, Image 2.3 depicts a model (carrier), wearing business clothes (possessive attribute). By minimising background and other context, the visual takes the reader's attention to the business outfit, which is represented in its minimal defining features (striped shirt, tie and trousers). Another example is maps. In a map of a country, the carrier is the entire country, and the possessive attributes are the individual states or provinces, and both are labelled either inside the image or in a legend or caption.

Symbolic processes

The third type of conceptual processes, **symbolic processes**, do not try to find relationships between images, but to visually represent what a

Image 2.3
Analytical
attributive process
in ad for business
clothes

participant 'means or is'. Symbolic processes take two forms, symbolic attributive and symbolic suggestive.

When parts of visual images are made prominent by, for example, being placed in the foreground, exaggerated in size, well-lit or in strong colours, they become symbolic attributes. For instance, in Image 2.4 the two participants are depicted in black and white, and the apple is highlighted in a bright red colour (though reproduced in greyscale here). The carrier is the man, the devil in the Garden of Eden who is offering an apple to the other participant – the woman, Eve. In this context, the highlighted red apple in contrast with greyscale of the co-text is a symbolic attribute that defines the identity of the participants. Symbolic attributive processes are akin to relational clauses of the carrier-attribute type, e.g. 'the devil in the visual (carrier) is a symbol of temptation (attribute)' or even identifying process clauses 'the devil with the red apple (identified) is the most stereotypical icon of temptation (identifier)'.

In contrast to symbolic attributive processes, symbolic suggestive processes usually only have one participant, the carrier, whose meaning is established in some other manner, such as the atmosphere within the image. As you can see, the visual (Image 2.5) de-emphasises image detail – the partially lit face – to symbolically suggest a "frightening mood" or a "dark atmosphere".

Narrative processes

The second category of process for representing conceptual relations and interactions in visuals is the **narrative process**. Like material processes, they depict physical actions, events, movements or changes in state.

Image 2.4
Symbolic
attributive process
in Devil tempting
Eve

Narrative processes emphasise both actors and movement or direction. Actors can be made prominent by relative size, place in the composition, contrast against a background, colour saturation, sharpness of focus and by the "salience" or importance of the human face. And because narrative processes involve movements, the image will employ **vectors**, imaginary lines that can be projected from the actors and that indicate the direction of movement of the body or eyes/gaze.

Actional processes
Narrative processes can be either actional or reactional. **Actional processes** involve some kind of physical action. They can be 'transactional',

Image 2.5
Symbolic
suggestive
process in a
candlelit face

where there are two or more participants (equivalent to transitive material processes), or 'non-transactional' with only one participant (equivalent to intransitive). In transactional processes the vector extends towards the other participant(s), the affected. Image 2.6 illustrates a transactional narrative process, with one participant acting on another, and can be described and analysed as follows:

The woman	is kicking	the ball
Actor	**Actional process (transactional)**	**Affected**

In this photo the vector runs from the woman's right foot to the ball, linking the actor and the affected. Non-transactional processes have only one participant and therefore the vector is not directed towards anyone

Image 2.6
Transactional narrative process in woman kicking a ball

or anything; for example, an image of Barack Obama walking across an empty White House lawn.

Reactional processes

In **reactional processes** the reactor indicates that they are reacting to another process by the direction of their gaze. This makes them more like behavioural processes or mental processes of perception. These, too, can be transactional and non-transactional. Image 2.7 shows a reactional process of the football player looking at an unknown phenomenon or experience. It is non-transactional as the vector is formed solely by the gaze of the main participant and we cannot see the action or object towards which his gaze is directed.

Image 2.7
Reactional process in footballer observing

We have seen that Hallidayan transitivity systems can provide a way into visual analysis of conceptual meaning. And, though there is not space to explore it here, the linguistic and visual representations of the world around us clearly interact. However, in such interactions the clause is probably a more highly developed system for representing and constructing reality than images are, which is why, as for example in Image 2.1, the caption seems to construct what happened more precisely and unambiguously. By contrast, when we start with a verbalised idea and provide an image to elucidate it we tend to think in terms of illustration of a pre-existing idea rather than construction of reality.

 ACTIVITY 24

Please refer to the companion website for the activity material.

2.5 SUMMARY

In this unit we looked at the conceptual or representational dimension to ideology (Figure 2.4). We saw that:

- the language we use predisposes us to think and act according to certain value systems and ideologies, and to represent the world in certain selective ways;
- we encode value and ideology by vocabulary, which assigns to categories, categorises these categories, stereotypes and "invents" new categories, exploring how lexis represents women in newspapers;

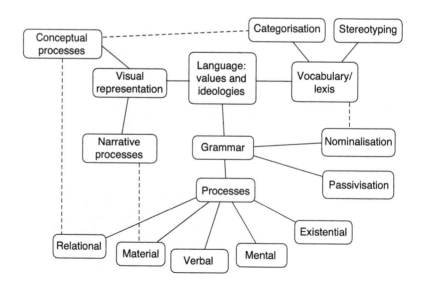

Figure 2.4
Summary of the chapter

- we can convey value and ideology less obviously by the choice of processes and participants in the clauses of texts, a choice which inevitably biases representation of the "facts";
- we can use nominalisation and passivisation for strategic purposes such as avoiding assignment of responsibility for statements or acts, or for preventing argument, and, textually, for allowing more choice of themes;
- we can understand visual texts and their representational meanings with a closer look at the classifying and narrative processes involved in the image.

FURTHER READING

Please refer to the companion website for the list of further reading.

3 TEXT AND INTERPERSONAL MEANING

The aim of this chapter
- to show how the vocabulary, grammar and visual features of texts reflect and create social relationships between reader and writer;
- to give practice in the rewriting of texts with similar content but for different readerships.

Contents

3.0 Introduction: understanding social relationships
provides a framework for understanding how our social relationships vary in terms of power, contact and expression of emotion.

3.1 Regulating behaviour
shows how the grammar uses commands and expresses obligations as a way of influencing others' behaviour.

3.2 Assertiveness
shows how degrees of dogmatism in a text depend on the linguistic resources for expressing probability, frequency, universality and subjectivity.

3.3 Pronoun use
gives an overview of the choices of pronoun and how their use reflects different kinds and extents of personality.

3.4 Contact and the imitation of speech
demonstrates how certain features of spoken language, like minor sentences and rhythm, can be incorporated into written texts to make them less formal and more expressive.

3.5 Formality of vocabulary

explores the varying strands of vocabulary in English from the informal Old English, to the more formal French, to the most formal Greek and Latin, and relates them to style markers in dictionaries.

3.6 Emotional meaning in lexis, and contested terms

illustrates how vocabulary can be used to express emotion, or euphemism to hide it, and the need for sensitivity to politically contested/incorrect terms.

3.7 Interpersonal meanings in visual texts

describes the various resources used in visual texts to create social relations with the viewer, to indicate the objectivity or subjectivity of the representation and the extent of the viewer's inclusion or engagement.

Activities

Besides small-scale exercises, there is one major activity – a rewrite of a formal information letter as though addressed to a friend.

Project 1

The first suggested project involves taking a short extract from an academic text, then adapting/simplifying it for schoolchildren, and testing the resulting text on a real readership.

3.0 INTRODUCTION: UNDERSTANDING SOCIAL RELATIONSHIPS

In Chapter 1 we discussed how writers organise information in a text, and, in Chapter 2, how the texts we read and write create a value-laden representation of reality. We now shift to the third aspect of description, how texts convey and create interpersonal relationships. If Chapter 1 was about packaging, and Chapter 2 about "content", then chapter three is about exchange.

We have all had the experience of reading articles or books whose content would be interesting enough, but whose author's personal style is off-putting. We might describe it as *stuffy, distant, unenthusiastic, unengaged* or, if the author errs in the other direction, *over-familiar, juvenile, condescending, patronising*. The appropriate interpersonal stance is quite difficult to judge, but this chapter aims to explore the language choices we have available to construct relationships between ourselves as writers and our readership.

Before we begin we can consider the different dimensions of relationships. Cate Poynton (1989), in her book *Language and Gender: Making the Difference*, suggests that interpersonal relationships can be analysed along three dimensions: **power**, **contact** and **emotion**.

The power someone has over you might be a matter of physical strength or force, for example Usain Bolt, riot police or the army; or the authority given to a person by an institution, such as the president of a university; or status which depends on wealth, education, place of residence, for instance the person in the Jaguar who has an MA and lives in a smart suburb; or expertise, the possession of knowledge or skill, such as the expert cook rather than the novice, the authority on bee-keeping compared with the person just starting up a couple of hives.

As for contact, we will communicate with some people more often than others, and so they will be more familiar to us. Members of our family we might see every day and provide a lifelong relationship. Fellow students who we have just met we might also see every day at the moment, but perhaps our relationship won't last a lifetime. We might consult our dentist regularly but with long time intervals in between. We recognise the bus driver who we see several times a month, but hardly talk to. And at the extreme there will be total strangers who we have never met before, and do not expect to meet again.

On the face of it we might think that there is only need for one dimension here, that those who have higher status and power are not the sort of people we will have much contact with. A moment's thought, however, indicates that this is not the case. Parents and their children are very close, seeing each other frequently on the contact axis, but there is clear inequality in terms of power. The same may be true of the relations between teachers and pupils.

The third dimension is emotion or affect. In some relationships we are unlikely to express emotion at all. If we do express it, emotion can

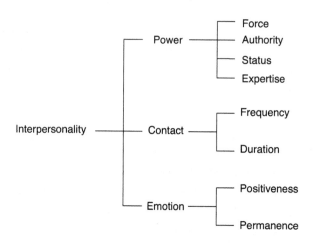

Figure 3.1
Dimensions of interpersonality

be positive or negative, and fleeting or permanent; for example, feeling annoyed with someone and then quickly forgiving them, or, by contrast, holding a grudge against them for years.

To sum up, we can think of interpersonal relationships as depending on contact or horizontal social distance, power or vertical social distance, and the kind and amount of emotion expressed. Emotion is partially dependent upon the contact and power dimensions; we tend not to express strong emotion to people of higher status or power, or those who are at medium distance on the horizontal axis. Conversely, the expression of emotion will often in itself be an attempt to change the horizontal distance between discourse participants.

ACTIVITY 25

Please refer to the companion website for the activity material.

Any writer should, then, be asking herself the following questions:

- Do I wish to come over as an authoritative expert or not?
- Do I wish to set myself up as of higher status than my reader?
- Do I wish to appear friendly/close to my reader or more distant and formal?
- Am I going to express feelings in my writing and will they be positive or negative?

One way of helping you judge the right interpersonal tone is to find the person in Activity 25 that best matches your ideal reader, and to visualise them as a reader while you are composing. This chapter surveys the linguistic means by which we express the appropriate interpersonal meanings in the text.

3.1 REGULATING BEHAVIOUR

The most obvious way in which we show our power is by regulating the behaviour of other people in line with our wishes or the wishes of the institution we represent. The most straightforward way to regulate their physical behaviour is to issue commands or insist on the reader's obligations. To regulate their verbal behaviour we will tend to use questions, demanding a reply. In either case there are more and less forceful ways of getting them to do what we want.

Commands and obligations

The strongest demand is conveyed by a command in **imperative** mood. For example: 'wash the dishes'; 'have a drink'; 'take a bath'; 'come on Tuesday morning'. However, there are other systematic resources in the grammar for telling or reminding people of what they are obliged to do. These are verbs and adjectives that are inserted before the verb referring to the action the speaker/writer wants done. They are known as **modal constructions**. Here are some examples, 1–8, in ascending order of strength of obligation. I have put some equivalent phrases to the right.

1	You **can** use a condom for casual sex	You are allowed/ permitted to
2	You **may** use a condom for casual sex	
3	You **might** use a condom for casual sex	It is suggested that you...
4	You **need to** use a condom for casual sex	It is necessary for you to...
5	You **will** use a condom for casual sex	You are required to...
6	You **should** use a condom for casual sex	
7	You **are to** use a condom for casual sex	You are obliged to...
8	You **must** use a condom for casual sex.	

Even 8, the strongest of these modal constructions, is less forceful or demanding than the imperative 'use a condom for casual sex'.

ACTIVITY 26

Please refer to the companion website for the activity material.

Imperatives and modals of high obligation generally indicate that the writer/speaker is in a position of greater power than the reader/listener. This power may be a question of authority or status, especially when the action to be performed is for the benefit of the writer or the institution that the writer represents and that gives her authority. In cases where the action is for the benefit of the reader, as, for example, procedural texts like manuals and recipes, the authority of the writer comes more from expertise. Either way, the power asymmetry is clear. As far as the horizontal axis is concerned, imperatives tend to be used either when we have a high degree of contact, or to people with whom we have very little contact, perhaps having met them once and never expecting to meet them again. We reserve the politer forms where there is a medium degree of contact, but where we anticipate that contact may increase – for example, people you quite like in your class, but who are not yet close friends (Wolfson 1989).

Questions

The most direct way of demanding verbal behaviour of a listener or reader is to use questions in the **interrogative** mood: 'Have you ever been to Sweden?' 'What time is it?' 'Can you swim?'

The effect of interrogatives on interpersonal relationships is not as clear as in the case of commands. On the one hand, on the power dimension, questioning assumes authority, the right of the writer to demand information from the reader, as, for example, in the composition and filling in of forms. On the other hand, a typical question assumes that the reader possesses knowledge which the writer does not have but wishes to have, so that the reader is something of an expert. (Though in the case of forms this is an expertise which only extends as far as personal details.) Horizontally, on the contact dimension, written questions can often be ice-breaking or a social lubricant. This is because they ask for a reply, which keeps the channels of communication open, and show interest in the state of the reader or what the reader is engaged in, as in a personal SMS or e-mail. However, in mass-produced texts interrogatives are rather odd, because there is no opportunity for the reader to reply to them. What kinds of question, then, might be used in such texts?

First, there are **expository questions**, like the one at the end of the previous paragraph. This is a question which the writer herself goes on to answer. It is a way of introducing or stimulating interest in an issue or discourse topic, of providing textual scaffolding for the discourse which follows.

Then there are **rhetorical questions**, which, unlike expository ones, do not demand an answer. This could be because the answer is supposed to be common knowledge in the first place. For example, if I say 'Was Tony Blair a real socialist?' I may expect that everyone believes he wasn't. Or sometimes the point of the question is really to make an indirect statement. For example, 'Doesn't the government realise that we no longer need the BBC?' is really a way of saying 'We no longer need the BBC.'

When discussing regulating behaviour above, we suggested that commands and questions are the main grammatical ways of getting other people to act or speak in accordance with our wishes. Consequently, written texts which use commands and questions assume, or pretend, the presence of the reader. This makes them more personal than texts which simply make statements. Often this personality is a fake, what Fairclough called **synthetic personalisation**, that is, treating a mass audience as though they are individuals being directly addressed (Fairclough 1995: 11; 2001: 52, 168ff.). For example, 'Have a nice day', the kind of notice used at the exit points of public buildings or by the roadside at the boundaries of towns, tries to give the impression that whoever reads it is being personally and individually addressed. In fact, it is quite general and indiscriminate, especially when you read it at 11 p.m.

3.2 ASSERTIVENESS

Most commonly writers make statements (rather than issue commands or ask questions), using what is technically known as **declarative** mood. When these are published, writers are claiming higher status or expertise than the reader, setting themselves up as an "authority". James Thurber said 'reason is six sevenths of treason' but he might also have said, '*author* is two-thirds of *authority*'. For example, if the writer makes informational statements or puts forward arguments, we expect from her a high degree of expert knowledge or rationality. If the writer is an entertainer then we assume that she has the special ability to amuse the readership. But this expertise and authority/status will be reflected in the degrees of dogmatism or assertiveness with which statements and arguments are made, as we discuss below.

The grammar of English provides plenty of resources for us to make our statements less assertive or less dogmatic. First, there are other modal structures, besides those used to regulate behaviour, which encode different degrees of certainty or probability. Then there are words which are used to claim different degrees of frequency or universality, how generally true the statement is. Finally, there are markers of subjectivity. Let's take a look at these resources in detail.

Modals of probability

1   This ten-year-old car doesn't have a smoky exhaust.
2   This ten-year-old car is unlikely to have a smoky   probably
exhaust.   doesn't have
3   This ten-year-old car may have a smoky exhaust.   possibly has
4   This ten-year-old car will have a smoky exhaust.   is likely to have
5   This ten-year-old car must have a smoky exhaust.   certainly has
6   This ten-year-old car has a smoky exhaust.

Items 1–6 are statements about a particular car rather than cars in general. At the two extremes, 1 and 6, we have the bare negative and positive statements. Sentences 2–5 express increasing degrees of probability/certainty. Sentences 1 and 6, the bare statements, can be seen as a kind of extreme pole for the scale of probability, as they allow no doubt about how possible it is for the car to have a smoky exhaust. You might think that sentence 5 with its *must* is more assertive or dogmatic than 6. However, think about a sentence like 'The stadiums for the football World Cup must be finished by now.' This actually expresses some uncertainty; it is as though the speaker is trying to reassure herself that they are finished.

Frequency

7   This ten-year-old car never has a smoky exhaust.
8   This ten-year-old car occasionally has a smoky exhaust.
9   This ten-year-old car sometimes has a smoky exhaust.
10 This ten-year-old car often has a smoky exhaust.
11 This ten-year-old car frequently has a smoky exhaust.
12 This ten-year-old car always has a smoky exhaust.

Sentences 7–12, like 1–6, are also about one particular car. They become progressively dogmatic because they make increasing claims about the frequency with which the car exhaust is smoky.

Universality

13 Ten-year-old cars don't have smoky exhausts.
14 No ten-year-old cars have smoky exhausts.
15 A few ten-year-old cars have smoky exhausts.
16 Some ten-year-old cars have smoky exhausts.
17 Many ten-year-old cars have smoky exhausts.
18 Most ten-year-old cars have smoky exhausts.
19 All ten-year-old cars have smoky exhausts.
20 Ten-year-old cars have smoky exhausts.

By contrast with 1–12, which were statements about an individual car, sentences 13–20 make statements about members of the class of ten-year-old cars. So they use quantifiers like *few*, *some* and *many* to indicate the rough proportion of the class. As with 1 and 6 in our first group, 12 and 20 are dogmatic statements, and even more dogmatic than 1 and 6 since they are universal generalisations.

ACTIVITY 27

Please refer to the companion website for the activity material.

Table 3.1 *Markers of subjectivity*

Certainty	Expression (personal)	Expression (impersonal)
High	I believe/I think/in my opinion/ to my mind	It's obvious that/obviously the plant is dead It's clear that/clearly she is tired It's evident that/evidently the food was bad
Medium	I presume I suspect I expect	It's apparent that/apparently she is tired It seems that the plant is dead It looks dead She sounds tired The plant feels dead The plant smelt bad

Markers of subjectivity

It has been suggested by Simpson (1993: 50–51) that verbs of thinking and perception reduce the assertiveness of statements, just like modals. In other words, instead of saying 'it may rain' we can say 'I think it's going to rain', or 'in my opinion it will rain' and 'it seems about to rain'.

Summary

This section has shown how we can tone down or reduce the strength of the claims which we make when we write statements. The devices for this are modals of probability, frequency adverbs, quantifiers – which indicate degrees of universality – and subjective markers. All these devices have consequences for the power dimension of interpersonal relations, because, generally speaking, the more universal or dogmatic the statement the higher the degree of authoritativeness or expertise the writer is assuming. Contrast, for example, 'I think this ten-year-old car may have a smoky exhaust', which is a very tentative statement about one particular car with the rather bold and assertive generalisation 'All ten-year-old cars have smoky exhausts.'

> It is important for you, as writers near the beginning of your academic career, to judge the degree of dogmatism or assertiveness to use in academic writing. Obviously if you are making use of a well-known and widely accepted formula or theorem in science or mathematics you can afford to be dogmatic. You would be unlikely to say 'The square on the hypotenuse may sometimes be equal to the sum of the square of the other two sides.' Similarly, you will be quite sure about the figures for results of an experiment. However, in the conclusion section of an experimental write-up you may want to make tentative explanations, or in a history or literary criticism essay you might consider being far less dogmatic: 'It seems to me that when Lady Macbeth says "I have given suck etc." this could be a confession to Macbeth of a previous marriage he knew nothing about.' In a sense being tentative about scientific conclusions does not diminish authority because scientists are self-assured enough to be cautious in their conclusions, and this is a feature of scientific writing.

ACTIVITY 28

Please refer to the companion website for the activity material.

3.3 PRONOUN USE

You can see that some of the modal devices listed above do not use the personal pronouns *you* and *I* – examples 1–20, and column 3 in

Table 3.1 – and some do – column 2. This section explores further how the degree and kind of personality relates to choice of pronoun.

In English we have several choices in the pronoun system which will affect the degree of contact expressed by the text. The pronouns available are listed in Table 3.2 and will differ between singular and plural, and between first, second and third person. But, if we want to be very formal and distant, we can avoid these choices by using impersonal constructions. In Table 3.1, column 3, we have already seen how *it* constructions can avoid mentioning the experiencer in mental processes. And in Chapter 2 we also introduced passives and nominalisation which may also reduce personality. By using the passive we avoid mentioning one of the participants in the clause, and by using nominalisation we can avoid mentioning either. For example:

ACTIVE   Our submarine sank your aircraft carrier
PASSIVE   Your aircraft carrier was sunk
NOMINALISATION   The sinking [took place on Wednesday]

So the first choice we have is between avoiding the expression of personality through nominalisation/passivisation or making our texts relatively personal. This choice between mentioning or avoiding mentioning participants is represented furthest left in Figure 3.2, as we read from left to right.

In certain genres, like scientific and academic writing, teachers often recommend an impersonal style through the use of the passive, and in this genre nominalisation, too, is widespread. The resulting impersonality presents science and academic work as entirely objective: as though a body of knowledge somehow exists independent of the scientist who makes the observations, and of the people who read the scientific report. However, there are strong arguments against the claim of scientific objectivity. For one, scientific discovery takes place in institutions and academic communities where struggles for funding, power, prestige and promotion make science political and personal. More seriously, quantum mechanics implies that the observed object and observer can no longer be separated, a point demonstrated by Heisenberg (Bohm 1980: 134).

Table 3.2 *The personal pronouns of English*

Person	Singular			Plural
1st	I			We
2nd	You			You
3rd	She	He	It	They
	One			

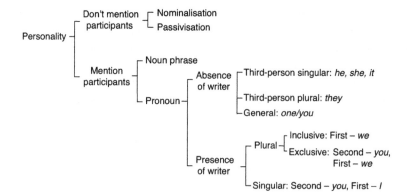

Figure 3.2
Personality and
personal pronoun
choice

Returning to Figure 3.2, if we opt to mention participants we can either use the explicit noun phrase or use pronouns. With pronouns our first major choice as writers is to decide whether we wish to represent ourselves and the reader in the text (absence or presence of writer in Figure 3.2). If not we should stick to third-person singular or plural pronouns, or general *you*. In fiction the distinction between first and third person depends on whether the narrator participates in the events of the fiction. If she does, she will be bound to use the first person singular pronoun *I*. A writer who only uses the third person automatically represents herself as less involved in the fictional world. In daily conversation we often hear complaints against the United Nations, the government, or Parliament or Congress which take the form of 'Why don't *they* do something about it?'. More surprising, but quite common, is for people to complain in the same terms about institutions of which they are members as though they don't belong – this amounts to a shift of responsibility onto and criticism of the leadership of the institution.

Incidentally, the choice of singular third person pronoun is problematic and ideological in gender terms. The use of *he* as a default pronoun, for example in university regulations, to refer to any student whether male or female should have been discontinued long ago. In such contexts it is quite acceptable nowadays to use *they* rather than the slightly clumsy *s/he*, e.g. 'If a student is ill on the day of the examination they should provide a medical certificate and lodge it with the registrar's office within one week.' The association of certain high-status jobs with males by using the masculine pronoun, is, however, still quite widespread. For example, in this extract from a secondary school textbook:

> A supervisor assigns a lighter workload to **his** friend than he does to another worker with whom **he** doesn't get along, although both workers share the same job description.
>
> (*New Clue 4 Normal Academic*: 163)

You may have noticed this book avoids the problem by consistently using *she* to refer to the writer (speaker) and *he* to refer to the reader (hearer).

A further ideological controversy may arise from attempts to human-ise and feminise nature by referring to the earth as *her* rather than *it*. You may be familiar with James Lovelock's *Gaia* theory, the idea that the earth's crust, the rocks and soil, the living things on them and the atmosphere are one large organism, *Gaia* the earth goddess. And that this goddess positively regulates the environment so that life can con-tinue (Lovelock 1988). Abolishing the distinction between "living" and "non-living" matter makes *he* or *she* sensible for referring to the earth, and the reconceiving of the earth as a goddess makes *she* the "natural" choice (providing this does not reinforce the stereotype of passivity).

Once the writer decides to signal her presence she has the choice of using *we, you* and *I*. But there are complications in the use of these pro-nouns. *You* immediately gives the impression of being in contact and of addressing her reader(s) and opens the way for more contact devices such as rhetorical questions and commands. But it is ambiguous between singular, plural and general, appearing at the end of three pathways in Figure 3.2. *You* can refer to

One individual addressee	e.g. *When did you first feel this pain?*
A group of addressees	e.g. *When did you as a family move to Washington?*
People in general	e.g. *When you run fast your heart rate increases.*

In the last of these *you* is the informal equivalent of *one*.

These ambiguities in the use of *you* become another resource for syn-thetic personalisation. We defined this, remember, as addressing a mass audience (the general or plural *you*) as though they were individuals, and it is particularly common in advertising. Consumer capitalism uses advertising to appeal to consumers as individuals; a consumer normally buys goods as an individual for themselves or other individuals, or some-times for their immediate family. It would be disastrous for consumer capitalist economies if whole streets or blocks of flats got together to buy and then share computers, power tools and washing machines. Not only advertisers, but any published writer must, in fact, be addressing more than one reader, and would often like to extend the readership widely, and yet, since silent reading is an individual activity, the reader will be positioned as though they are the only reader and will co-operate with this illusion. The ambiguity of *you* facilitates this, in ways which *one* never could because of its insistence on singularity.

An extremely important choice in terms of contact and solidarity is between *you* and *we*. *We* may include the writer and the reader together in the same group, whereas *you* unambiguously separates them. The teacher who begins a lesson: 'Today *you*'re going to find out more about the discovery of North America by the peoples of East Asia' constructs the finding out as an activity of the pupils. The teacher who begins 'Today *we*'re going to find out more about the discovery of North America by the peoples of East Asia' represents the learning as a joint enterprise. This is somewhat fake, of course, since she is likely to know roughly what she is going to find out before she starts! Contrast this with 'In the next unit we're going to discuss inferences' which equally artificially presumes the reader is as much involved in the discussion as the writer.

The main ambiguity in the use of *we* can be spelt out as follows, reflected in the options in Figure 3.2.

- **Inclusive** *we* to varying degrees includes the reader/hearer in the group referred to, as in the teaching/discussion examples above.
- **Exclusive** *we* refers to a group to which the reader does not belong. This is especially common when the writer represents an institution of which the reader is not a member, e.g. 'We at Toyota do our best for you.'

Finally, there is the option of using *I*. This is the most personal way for the writer to refer to herself, the only other option being the rather formal or distant noun phrase like *the present writer, this writer* or *the writer of this article*. *I* is informal, individual and "personal" too, though note that writers, especially entertainers, can use *I* as a persona or mask.

> I've always found myself challenged, not visually, mentally, physically or, as far as I know, sexually, but by the little mundane tasks of life. In the morning I have to remember to turn on the hot water switch outside the bathroom before entering to take my shower and to bring a towel into the bathroom with me. Next I must ensure that the socks I put on are a pair, neither of them inside out, and that I've done up my flies. I need to adjust the toaster accurately so that the bread comes out nicely browned, and if it's under-toasted adjust the control to a low level before re-toasting it. I try to avoid, not always successfully, having the porridge in the microwave boil over and ooze down the sides of the bowl so that it messes up the place mat on the table. It's a miracle if I ever leave the house without some trivial disaster or other. And did I shave? And have I got my umbrella?

The I, the persona of this passage, is a self-caricature of the real person of the writer, as synthetic as the synthetic personalisation of *you*.

The text you are reading is an academic textbook. The authors have, however, let themselves intrude in places, with anecdotes about student pranks, travelling to Cyprus, Christian evangelical upbringing and other examples of personal self-disclosure. Some of the reviewers of this manuscript welcomed these personal interludes while others thought them inappropriate to an academic style of writing. We kept them because we do not wish to disguise our identity and subject position as writers, nor the fact that our ideological position is only one of many and is determined partly by personal history. We hope this recognition of personality makes it easier for you to resist our position when it differs from yours.

ACTIVITY 29

Please refer to the companion website for the activity material.

3.4 CONTACT AND THE IMITATION OF SPEECH

The contact dimension depends on the frequency and duration of meeting and talking face to face. Although high contact can apply to the written medium in emails and text messages, we might wonder how it could apply to the print medium, which is, of course, rather impersonal compared with, say, radio, television or YouTube. But anything in a written text which gives the flavour of speech will be more personal and simulate some degree of contact. We have already seen how questions and commands are used for such purposes, and how pronouns like *you* and *we* are used for synthetic personalisation. Another linguistic device which is related to the imitation of dialogic speech is the use of incomplete sentences, technically, **minor sentences**.

Minor sentences are stretches of text punctuated as sentences but with the main verb or subject missed out (excluding imperatives, which don't normally have a subject in any case). In dialogue, obviously, such utterances or "sentences" occur quite naturally, for example in response to questions. Look at this extract from a policeman interviewing a witness. The minor sentences have been underlined.

P: Did you get a look at the one in the car?
W: I saw his face, yeah.
P: What sort of age was he?
W: About 45. He was wearing a . . .
P: And how tall?
W: Six foot one.
P: Six foot one. Hair?
W: Dark and curly. Is this going to take long? I've got to collect the
    kids from school.
P: Not much longer, no. What about his clothes?
W: He was a bit scruffy looking. Blue trousers, black.
P: Jeans?
W: Yeah

(Fairclough 2001:15)

So one way of imitating speech will be to write in minor sentences. This is a particularly common convention for ad copywriters.

The ARRIVAL
of the FITTEST

TACOMA
A whole NEW line of TRUCKS from TOYOTA.

STRONGER. FASTER. BETTER. That's the GOAL of every competitor.
To OUTPERFORM the field. To be the BEST there is.
Introducing TACOMA. The new BREED of Toyota Truck.
With three totally NEW engines that deliver MORE power up and down the line than ever before. A 4-cylinder 2.4 litre POWERPLANT that outperforms the leading competition's standard V6's, even carrying a half-ton payload.
And a 3.4 liter V6 that OUTMUSCLES their biggest V6's. RESPONSIVE handling. Braking power that stops shorter FASTER and more CONFIDENTLY. Even class-leading 4x4 ground CLEARANCE.
Plus the added safety of a driver-side airbag.
Altogether it's the heart and soul of a WINNER.
The new TACOMA has arrived. And it's every inch a CHAMPION.
Call 1800 GO-TOYOTA for a BROCHURE and the location of your NEAREST DEALER.

TOYOTA TACOMA
I love what you do for me

(*Popular Science*: 125, June 1995)

ACTIVITY 30 ▬▬▬▬▬▬▬▬▬▬▬▬▬▬▬▬▬▬

Please refer to the companion website for the activity material.

The minor sentences are very concentrated at the beginning of this advert, and suggest the writer (W) is voicing one half of a dialogue. Imagining a rather unsympathetic reader (R), we might fill in as follows:

W: The ARRIVAL of the FITTEST
R: What's arrived that's so fit?
W: **TACOMA**
R: It doesn't sound very fit to me. More like a nasty disease, a sarcoma, or something that gives you a coma. What on earth is it?
W: **A whole NEW line of TRUCKS from TOYOTA.**
R: How are they different from other trucks?
W: STRONGER. FASTER. BETTER. That's the GOAL of every competitor.

R: What is?

W: To OUTPERFORM the field.

R: What the hell does that mean?

W: To be the BEST there is. Introducing TACOMA.

R: Sorry I wasn't concentrating. What's that again?

W: The new BREED of Toyota Truck.

R: What does it come with?

W: With three totally NEW engines that deliver MORE power up and down the line than ever before.

R: So? What does it use to do that?

W: A 4-cylinder 2.4 litre POWERPLANT that outperforms the leading competition's standard V6's, even carrying a half-ton payload.

R: How extraordinarily interesting. So that's it, is it? Any other exciting features that make it more attractive than its wimpish opposition?

W: And a 3.4 liter V6 that OUTMUSCLES their biggest V6's.

When an utterance is incomplete, as in answers to questions or minor sentences, then the reader/hearer has to supply the missing information. This will either come from the previous question or from knowledge brought to the text by the reader. Incomplete sentences assume that writer and reader share a good deal of information which does not need to be made explicit. This is typical of diaries and postcards – 'On Monday went to the Eiffel Tower. Drizzled all day', where the subjects of the clause can be understood (Scott 2013). Or of commentary on sporting events where the actions, such as kicking the ball, are so obvious they need not be mentioned: 'Valencia to Giggs'. This presumption of shared information is why minor sentences suggest a high level of contact between writer and reader.

Of course, another related feature of connected speech is that words are often contracted, *can't* for *cannot*, *I've* for *I have*, *it's* for *it is* (contrast *its* meaning "of it" by the way). Abbreviations are common in internet chat, which as "chat" pretends it is spoken, although in essence it is written. They are a way of speeding up communication so that exchanges can be almost as fast as those in speech, but they also constitute a code which may exclude some users of English and thereby create a sense of intimate contact: *tuvm; 2d4; wtfigo*, etc. (thank you very much; to die for; what the fuck is going on).

ACTIVITY 31

Please refer to the companion website for the activity material.

How much shared knowledge to assume

In fact, one main problem in writing is judging how much knowledge your average reader possesses, and how much can be left out. Comparing texts A and B below, we notice that A is written for a more specialist readership than B.

A	B
An appreciation of the effects of calcium blockers can best be attained by an understanding of the activation of muscle groups. The proteins actin, myosin, troponin and tropomyosin make up the sarcomere, the fundamental unit of muscle contraction. The thick filament is composed of myosin, which is an ATPase, or energy producing protein.	The contraction of muscle depends on calcium. If we can understand how calcium activates muscle groups, we can appreciate how those groups are affected by calcium blockers. The fundamental unit of muscle contraction is the sarcomere. In the sarcomere are two filaments, one thick and one thin. They contain proteins that prevent contraction and proteins that cause contraction. The thick filament contains the protein myosin, which is an ATPase, or energy producing protein. (Colomb and Williams 1985)

A assumes knowledge of the following, but B makes it more explicit.

- The contraction of muscle depends on calcium.
- Calcium activates muscle groups.
- In the sarcomere are two filaments, one thick and one thin.
- They contain proteins that prevent contraction and proteins that cause contraction.
- Myosin is a protein.

Notice, incidentally, the differences between the first sentence of A and the second sentence of B. B is more personal and less formal because 'appreciation' and 'understanding' have been denominalised into 'we [can] understand', 'we can appreciate', which also gives the opportunity to use the first-person plural pronoun 'we'. And A's 'the activation of muscle groups' becomes B's 'how calcium activates muscle groups', removing the nominalisation to make clear the actor (calcium) and the affected (muscle groups).

Rhythm

In Chapter 1 we surveyed the graphic devices available for making texts visually informative, to give the kind of richness to the written medium which the spoken medium has by virtue of its loudness, tempo, voice quality, stress, intonation and rhythm. But writing can also borrow rhythm from the written medium, assuming that the text is read aloud or sub-vocalised. Prose writers, popular newspapers and, above all, advertising copywriters, often write rhythmically as though the written medium is to be translated into the spoken, with implications of higher contact. But what exactly do we mean by "rhythm"?

Rhythm is a regular pattern of stressed (louder) and unstressed (softer) syllables. In words of two syllables (or more) one syllable will be stressed and the other unstressed, e.g. NEver, reMAIN, alLOW, ALLergy. In addition, one-syllable nouns, verbs (not auxiliaries), adjectives and adverbs will tend to be stressed. So the following sentence, with the stressed syllables marked / and the unstressed *x*, has an observable rhythm, a recurring pattern of two unstressed syllables followed by a stressed syllable:

```
 x  x  / x  x  /  x    x  /   x  x  /   x    x / x   x
 I can never remember the months of the year when the eating of
 /   x   x  /
 oysters is safe.
```

You can find plenty of examples of the rhythms of speech by flicking through the adverts of magazines. These below come from *Popular Science*:

```
 /  /  x
 Just surfaced
  /  /  x
 Skyy vodka
  x x /
 the intell-
 x x    /
 igent drink
```

```
 / x   x  /  x  / x  /
 buying a more expensive paint
  /  /  x   x  / x  /
 won't buy you a better paint
```

In the last example the rhythm is not quite so clear, but notice that the rhythmical pattern of the first six syllables is repeated exactly in the last six syllables. And the two clauses each have four stressed syllables, like the lines in nursery rhymes.

```
 /   /   x / x  /
 Tom, Tom the piper's son
```

```
/  x /  x   x  /  x  /
Stole a pig and away did run
x  /  x  /  x  /  x  /
The pig was eat and Tom was beat
x  /   x  / x  /   x  /
And Tom went roaring down the street
```

Perhaps this rhythmical tendency in written adverts is a pale imitation of the rhythmical slogans and jingles of TV ads, which pretend a heightened emotion: the euphoria produced by the product becomes so powerful that one can only express it in song.

A general rule with rhythmical writing is that the higher the proportion of stressed syllables the slower we read and the more emphatic the effect. Conversely, the higher the proportion of unstressed syllables the faster the words flit by, and the more exciting or light-hearted it feels. You might like to compare the rhythmic effects of the second and third stanzas of the extract of the Larkin poem quoted on page 102.

3.5 FORMALITY OF VOCABULARY

The vocabulary of English is largely made up of three strata. There is a bedrock of basic **Old English** words, the most frequent, since they occur across the whole range of genres. These are generally quite short and either core or informal. Then there is a thick sediment of the many French words of medium formality, which flooded into English in the fourteenth century. And finally, as topsoil, we have the more cultivated, learned and technical Greek and Latin words which were borrowed into the language from the sixteenth to eighteenth centuries and are still being coined today.

Let's look at Table 3.3. The items in each row of the table convey the same logical concept, but differ stylistically, either in terms of positive/negative emotion, formality or geographical dialect. We can see how formal/technical vocabulary and informal vocabulary are distinguished from **core vocabulary** by looking at columns 1, 4 and 5. Good examples of the connection between borrowed words and formality are the quartet of informal *give a hand to* (all Old English words), core *help* (Old English), slightly formal *aid* (French) and the more formal French *assist*, originally from the Latin *adsistere*. Or consider the words *town* (Old English), *city* (French) and *metropolis* (Greek), though these are not listed as they do not have exactly equivalent logical meanings. Notice, too, that formality applies to all parts of speech – nouns, adjectives, verbs and even conjunctions like *therefore*, v. *thus*, v. *and so*.

Old English words are on the whole shorter than those from French or the classical languages. No doubt *supercalifragilisticexpialidocious* is not

Table 3.3 *Stylistic variations in vocabulary*

Core	Positive emotion	Negative emotion	Formal (technical)	Informal	Dialectal
House	Home	Hovel	Residence	Pad	Pad
Dog		Cur	Canine	Pooch, doggy, bow-wow	Pooch
	[Motion – negative]	Shit	Excrement, faeces	Poo	
Therefore			Thus	And so	
Thin	Slim, slender	Skinny	Emaciated		
Determination	Perseverance	Obstinacy stubbornness	Motivation	Will-power	
Ear, nose and throat			Otorhinolaryngology	ENT	
Bear			Tolerate	Stand, put up with	
Help		Interfere	Aid, assist	Give a hand to	
Prostitute	[Comfort woman – negative]	Whore Slag		Slag	Slag

Old English. Consider in Table 3.3 the perfectly understandable Old English *ear, nose and throat,* which any patient looking for the hospital department can understand. And contrast this with the formal, technical Greek *otorhinolaryngology,* incomprehensible for most outpatients, though this has not deterred some hospitals from snobbishly substituting it for the Old English terms. Notice *ENT* as well, which, as an acronym, is much shorter, and assumes a degree of familiarity or professional contact with medicine.

We can see that many informal equivalents use compounds and phrases rather than single words, *will-power* for *determination, put up with* for *tolerate, give a hand to* for *aid.* This is another way of reducing the length of words, and preserving the informal Old English flavour. Word length has, in fact, been used as one factor for computing the technicality and difficulty of a text. Readability measures are generally based on a combination of word length and sentence length. If you use Microsoft Word you can enter 'readability scores' in the Help menu to find out how to compute the readability of your document. This will give you two indices to tell you the grade level or reading level for which the text is appropriate (Grade 1 is 6 years old).

We notice from the rightmost column that many informal words are also dialectal. The reason for this is that dialect is an expression of contact: dialects can only be preserved if the speakers meet and use them. On the one hand dialectal usages affirm solidarity between speakers; on the other hand they deliberately exclude potential conversationalists who do not understand that dialect, or, for that matter, the latest slang.

It would be misleading to think that texts always keep up a consistent level of formality and informality throughout. Some writers even deliberately mix levels of style for poetic effect. Philip Larkin, for example, at the end of his poem *Toads*, recognises that the toad of work which oppresses him is matched by a psychological toad of conformity and timidity which ties him to his work. He expresses this in a mixture of styles – slang, archaism in a quote from Shakespeare's *Tempest* ('we are such stuff as dreams are made on'), the formal and the colloquial:

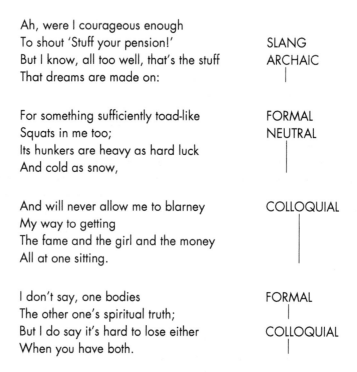

Ah, were I courageous enough	
To shout 'Stuff your pension!'	SLANG
But I know, all too well, that's the stuff	ARCHAIC
That dreams are made on:	
For something sufficiently toad-like	FORMAL
Squats in me too;	NEUTRAL
Its hunkers are heavy as hard luck	
And cold as snow,	
And will never allow me to blarney	COLLOQUIAL
My way to getting	
The fame and the girl and the money	
All at one sitting.	
I don't say, one bodies	FORMAL
The other one's spiritual truth;	
But I do say it's hard to lose either	COLLOQUIAL
When you have both.	

On the other hand, we would generally want to avoid the ludicrously inappropriate mixing of styles in sentences like 'After my considerable exertions throughout the day I couldn't be arsed to ascend to your 4th floor residence' or 'After working hard all day I had no inclination to climb up to your 4th-floor flat.'

However, one of the features of modern media discourse is the hybridisation of texts, especially the conversationalisation of public discourse in order to make it sound or read like private discourse. Fairclough (1995: 9–14) gives the example shown in Figure 3.3, from the British tabloid *The Sun*, which packages and retails a Parliamentary report for the British working-class reader.

Britain faces a war to stop pedlars, warn MPs

CALL UP FORCES
IN DRUG BATTLE!

By DAVID KEMP

The armed forces should be called up to fight off a massive invasion by drug pushers, MPs demanded yesterday.

Cocaine pedlars are the greatest threat ever faced by Britain in peacetime—and could destroy the country's way of life, they said.

The MPs want Ministers to consider ordering the Navy and the RAF to track suspected drug-running ships approaching our coast.

On shore there should be intensified law enforcement by Customs, police and security forces.

Figure 3.3
Extract from the
Sun, 24 May 1985
(source: Fairclough
1995: 69).

Notice how the headlines and lead have informal items like *pedlars/pushers, call up, forces* whereas the later paragraphs have more formal equivalents like *drug-running, ordering, security forces.* Or contrast the pair of sentences 'Britain faces a war to stop drug pedlars' and 'Call up forces in drug battle' with the later sentence 'On shore there should be intensified law enforcement by Customs police and security forces'. You might like to consider, as revision, what it is about the first two sentences that makes them less formal than the third.

3.6 EMOTIONAL MEANING IN LEXIS, EMOTICONS AND CONTESTED TERMS

There are three main ways of encoding emotion in our choice of lexis. First, there is what one might call **emotive "spin"**. In the first three columns of Table 3.3 we notice that words may share the same conceptual meaning but differ in emotive meaning. A famous example is:

POSITIVE	NEUTRAL	NEGATIVE
slim	*thin*	*skinny*

It is as though these words are three identical balls, three identical concepts, but *slim* spins positively, *skinny* negatively, and *thin* doesn't spin at all.

These words with emotive "spin" are different from a second class of words which are empty of conceptual meaning, what one might call **affective words**. Here we would include swear words. The fact that these are drained of any conceptual meaning is obvious when we consider that, as a swear word, *fuck* has no reference to sex, *bloody hell* no connection with blood, and *piss off* nothing to do with urination. They are simply strong expressions of negative emotion. Less strongly negative expressions include *terrible, horrible, awful, disgusting, pathetic*. At the positive end we have *nice, fine, cool, good, great, wonderful, smashing, awesome* and so on. Because these are evaluative terms expressing individual taste, likes and dislikes, they are subjective and cannot be verified or challenged. Perhaps this is one reason they are so often used in advertising copy, where they are difficult to contradict or disprove. Look back at the use of *winner, champion* and *best* in the Tacoma advert.

Many of these conceptually empty affective words can be used as adjectives/adverbs which add emotional intensity to the adjectives/adverbs they modify: *a **terrible** miss/**terribly** misguided, a **dreadful** experience/**dreadfully** hot, an **awful** mistake/**awfully** exciting*. These are called **intensifiers** and they also include *very, especially, complete/completely, absolute/absolutely, amazingly, madly, confoundedly*.

A further aspect of emotive meaning is illustrated in the second column of Table 3.3. Here, in brackets, are terms which are **euphemisms**, i.e. words used to avoid a direct reference to something considered impolite or unpleasant. Because the more common core word is taboo or has negative emotive spin, these terms are substituted – for example, *comfort woman* is substituted for *prostitute* or *sex slave*, and *motion* is substituted for *faeces/shit*. They are in brackets because, rather than being positively emotive, they avoid the negative emotion of the core, formal or informal equivalents. Sex, urination and excretion and death are the commonest topics for euphemism. It's quite usual to use the phrase *sleep together* as a euphemism for sex, though sleep is precisely what the sexual partners don't do! My favourite euphemism for a funeral wake is *cold meat party*. This uses the fact that cold meat is often served at wakes, because the mourners and relatives will be too busy attending the funeral service beforehand to cook a hot meal. However, it might fail by drawing attention to the cold flesh of the corpse!

Euphemism is often used by the powerful to disguise the horrors that they inflict during war:

> Israeli military commanders described the massacre of 2,100 Palestinians, most of whom were civilians (including 500 children), in Gaza this summer as "mowing the lawn". It's not original. Seeking to justify Barack Obama's drone war in Pakistan (which has so far killed 2,300 people, only 4% of whom have since been named as members of al-Qaida), Obama's counter-terrorism adviser Bruce Riedel explained that "you've got to mow the lawn all the time. The minute you stop mowing, the grass is going to grow back."
>
> (Monbiot 2014a)

A third way of conveying emotion is to conceptualise it. This is when you use words like *despair, depression, nervous, amazement* to describe, rather than express, one's own or other people's feelings as it were objectively and from the outside. These contrast with affective interjections (swear words) and adjectives (*nice*, etc.) because there is a degree of objectivity in their use – for example, there are ways of measuring degrees of clinical depression. Emotional attitude can also be conceptualised through the use of **modals of (dis)inclination**: e.g. *need, want to, am inclined to, am keen to, would like, would rather, unfortunately, hopefully*, etc.

ACTIVITY 32

Please refer to the companion website for the activity material.

Emoticons

Written language is relatively poor in the resources available for conveying emotion compared with face-to-face conversation. The latter has body language, and variations in volume, speed, voice quality, noises like sobbing or laughing, pitch and intonation. In internet chat or mobile phone messages, which are high on contact and therefore wish to imitate speech, there is a need to compensate for the lack of resources for emotional expression. The result is the large number of emoticons to represent emotion. We are now often provided with a menu to choose from, but keyboard symbols may also be used: :-) :-(;-) :~-(:-o ;-@ meaning happy, sad, winking, crying, shocked and screaming, respectively (Crystal 2001: 37).

Contested terms

In the climate of political awareness where we live today there is a heightened sense that certain words may unintentionally cause negative emotion or offence. We can call these **contested terms**. Their avoidance gives rise to groups such as the following:

> nigger v. black v. Afro-American v. person of colour
> crippled v. spastic v. handicapped v. disabled v. challenged
> poor v. underprivileged v. economically disadvantaged
> poor countries v. the Third World v. developing nations v. the
> South v. the majority world

Many of these groups display euphemism as we proceed to the right, as though calling something by a less transparent name disguises the negative emotion associated with the original term. But sometimes pressure groups, who wish to contest taken-for-granted practices and naturalised ways of speaking, do the opposite – deliberately replace quite neutral or positive terms with negatively emotive ones:

economic growth v. economic cancer
settlement (of Australia/North America) v. invasion
property is theft

Summary on style of vocabulary

Any good dictionary will give you an indication of styles: whether a word is formal, informal, has positive or negative emotion, is offensive or is dialectal. The *Collins Cobuild Dictionary*, for example, has the following style markers which tend to overlap. I have attempted to arrange them in some order in Figure 3.4.

What this diagram tries to indicate is that formal language tends to be written, technical language tends to be written, legal and medical language is technical; informal language tends to be spoken, as does emotive and offensive language, and dialect is most obvious in informal speech rather than in writing; literary and journalistic language tends to be less formal than the technical languages of medicine and law. More generally, of course, informality corresponds to closeness on both the power and contact dimensions, but especially contact. And informality, emotion and geographical dialect tend to converge.

ACTIVITY 33 ━━━━━━━━━━━━━━━━━━━━━━━━━━━━━━━━━━━━━

Please refer to the companion website for the activity material.

ACTIVITY 34 ━━━━━━━━━━━━━━━━━━━━━━━━━━━━━━━━━━━━━

Please refer to the companion website for the activity material.

3.7 INTERPERSONAL MEANINGS IN VISUAL TEXTS

So far we looked at how interpersonal meanings and social relations are created through the vocabulary and grammar of linguistic texts. Let's now consider the interpersonal or interactional meanings of visual texts, the relations between the producer of the visual text and the viewer. In discussing this, Kress and Van Leeuwen (1996) recognise three main dimensions: *contact, social distance* and *perspective*. Various resources are used to realise these three dimensions, as summarised in Figure 3.5.

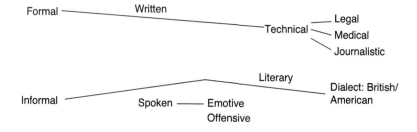

Figure 3.4
Style markers in the
Cobuild Dictionary

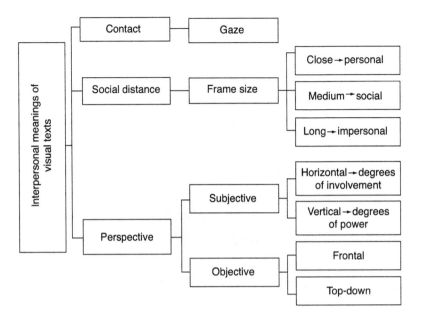

Figure 3.5
Visual resources for interpersonal meanings

Let's take a look at these resources for interpersonal meaning in detail. We begin by discussing visual contact and social distance, which belong under the contact dimension of Figure 3.5, and then proceed to perspective and the power dimension.

Visual contact

We can understand how **visual contact** is established between the image and the viewer by looking at how images directly or indirectly address their viewers. In other words, we can look at the kinds of "demands" or "offers" made by the visual texts. This dimension is realised through the resource of the **gaze**. The gaze is the vector formed by the glance of the participant(s) towards the viewer. It is the degree of "engagement" or "disengagement" of the gaze that determines the social relation with the viewer. For instance, when we look at the author-of-the-month section in the Routledge email in Chapter 1, we notice that in the posed photograph the author's gaze is directed at us (Image 3.1). This friendly gaze accompanied by a smile essentially makes a visual demand by requiring an acceptance of the promotional message that the email projects. So the directly engaging gaze of the participant demands acceptance and action by the reader.

On the other hand, the image in Image 3.2 is making a **visual offer**: the viewer is not required to enter a kind of interpersonal relation with the participants, but to look at the represented participants as items of information or objects of contemplation. The couple are continually looking at each other and smiling, without any demand for involvement beyond accepting or rejecting the offered information.

Author of the Month

Todd Whitaker

Todd Whitaker is a widely-recognised authority on staff motivation, teacher leadership, and teacher effectiveness. He has written more than 30 books and speaks all over the world, bringing his message to teachers and principals and reminding them that what they do matters. Todd's latest book is the third edition of *Dealing with Difficult Teachers*, published in July 2014. Learn more about our July Author of the Month **here**.

Image 3.1
Visual demand, social closeness and inclusion in author-of-the-month photo

Image 3.2
Visual offer in young couple smiling

Social distance

The second aspect of interactional meanings of visuals involves an understanding of the **social distance** between the viewers and the represented participants. This dimension is realised through the use of varying frame size, such as close shots, medium shots and long shots. A close shot implies personal engagement, where the object can almost be touched or used; a middle shot gives a sense of more distance and less engagement; and a long shot suggests that the object is there for the viewer's contemplation only, and that there is no possibility of engagement beyond this. In the author of the month section of the Routledge email, the frame size is a close shot with the head and shoulders of the participant. This indicates a friendly and personal social relation with the viewer, to establish an intimacy with the potential consumer.

Perspective

The third aspect of interactional meanings of visual texts is the "point of view" or **perspective** of the visual texts. The perspective can be either subjective (carrying a built-in point of view) or objective (with no built-in point of view). Visual texts with **subjective perspectives** require most of the viewer's attention as the selected point of view in the represented participants is imposed onto the viewer. This is done through two categories: **degrees of involvement** and **degrees of power**.

The degree of involvement is realised through the use of the visual horizontal angle between the frontal plane of the producer and the frontal plane of the participant(s). This can either be 180 degrees, a parallel alignment with a frontal point of view or an oblique point of view with a different angle. The frontal 180-degree angle projects a message of inclusion and involvement, suggesting that the represented participants are part of the viewer's world, as in the photograph of the author in Image 3.1. The oblique angle projects a message of exclusion, suggesting that the represented participant(s) or scene is not part of their shared world, and as a result there is a lack of involvement. The oblique point of view can be seen in Image 3.2.

The degree of power is realised through the use of the visual vertical angle between the viewer and the represented participants. (This relates to metaphors such as POWER IS HIGH – see Chapter 4.) So, if the viewer looks down on the participant in the picture, this indicates a more powerful position relative to the participant, and a less powerful position if the participant is viewed from a lower angle. Correspondingly, if the represented participant is at the same level as the interactive participant, then the relation is one of equality, or of neutral power. Image 3.3 is an example in which the viewer is in a less powerful position than the participant because of the low angle.

Image 3.3
Power perspective in rock climber photo

As mentioned earlier, **objective perspectives** in visual texts have no built-in point of view. No account is taken of the viewer, or where the viewer is. Scientific and technical graphics and drawings, maps and charts are examples of objective visual texts. The intention is to present all the information necessary, even sacrificing naturalistic depiction by, for instance, showing cross-sections combined with flow charts in biological drawings and straight lines in underground maps.

The encoding of the objective perspective is realised in two ways: (1) the use of a directly frontal angle, or (2) a perpendicular top-down angle. The sense of objectivity for the frontal angle is used for action-oriented visual texts used in schematic drawings or instruction manuals. In other words, the frontal angle is the angle of "this is how it works", "this is how you use it", "this is how you do it". The image in Image 3.4 is an example of a frontal angle scientific representation of one of the ways in which protein molecules are ingested into a cell.

On the other hand, the sense of objectivity for the top-down angle is used for factual or knowledge-based visual texts, usually seen in maps or diagrams of the structure of objects. Using the top-down perpendicular angle in which the object is viewed directly from above says "this is how it is" or "these are the facts". Image 3.5 is an example of a top-down angled diagram of the body of a generalised or typical insect.

So, just like the vocabulary and grammar of linguistic texts, visual texts employ various resources for establishing visual contact, social distance and perspective to express interpersonal meanings. Visual contact and social distance correspond to contact in Figure 3.1, and perspective corresponds to power, both more generally but also the power of the expert in conveying information according to an objective point of view.

Receptor-mediated endocytosis

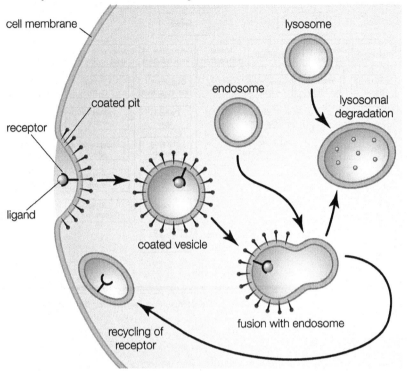

cell membrane

coated pit

receptor

ligand

coated vesicle

recycling of receptor

fusion with endosome

endosome

lysosome

lysosomal degradation

Image 3.4
Objective frontal angle in endocytosis diagram

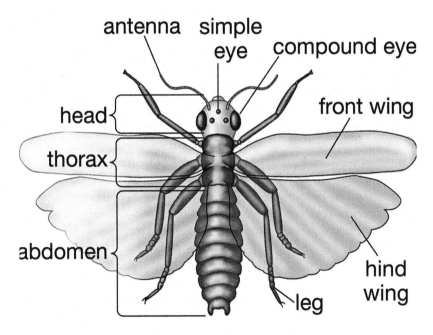

antenna

simple eye

compound eye

head

thorax

abdomen

front wing

hind wing

leg

Image 3.5
Objective perpendicular angle in insect diagram

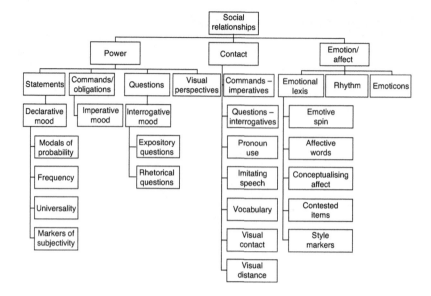

Figure 3.6
Resources for
interpersonal or
social relationships

ACTIVITY 35

Please refer to the companion website for the activity material.

3.8 SUMMARY

In this chapter we have looked at the various ways in which the text can encode interpersonal meanings, meanings associated with the social dimensions of power, contact and emotion (Figure 3.6). We saw that:

- we can demonstrate our power by regulating behaviour through the use of commands and questions, presuming, synthetically, the presence of the reader and making demands on him; and we can regulate less strongly by using modals of obligation;
- we can vary our level of authority, assertiveness and dogmatism in our texts by employing the scales of modal probability, frequency, universality or by using subjective markers;
- we can increase the personality of our text by the use of second-person pronouns or first person (exclusive and inclusive) or decrease it by using the third person, the passive or nominalisation;
- we can suggest closer contact and heightened emotion by imitating the rhythms and minor sentences of speech; though, with the latter, we must bear in mind the importance for the writer of correctly estimating the knowledge of the typical reader;

- we can create a closer contact by choosing from the different strands of English vocabulary – the more formal and longer Greek/Latin words, the French words of medium formality and the informal shorter everyday Old English words;
- we can use vocabulary and emoticons to convey positive and negative emotion, or cause offence with contested terms;
- visual texts also use resources of contact, social distance and perspective to create interpersonal meanings.

PROJECT 1

Please refer to the companion website for the activity material.

FURTHER READING

Please refer to the companion website for the list of further reading.

PART B

CRITICAL DISCOURSE
Reading meanings into
the text

In Part A of this coursebook we approached critical reading and writing through analysis of the surface grammar, vocabulary and visual aspects of texts. This is a semantic approach in which we describe what is encoded in the text and explain it ideologically, in terms of the ideas and power structures of a society. However, for critical analysis to be complete and valid we have to take a complementary discoursal approach, in which text is seen as a bridge between a writer and a reader. This is a more contextualised analysis which recognises the multiple meanings that a text can generate and the reader's work in constructing a meaning out of it. So in Part B the approach to text will not be decoding or semantic description, but making inferences and hypothesising. As a result this part corresponds to level 2 in Table 0.1, page 4.

We highlight three aspects of interpretation. Chapter 4 explains how the physical text which links writer and reader fails to fully convey the intended meaning, but is simply a trace of the writer's meaning and a cue for the reader's meaning. The second idea we explore, in Chapter 5, is that writing is a form of action involving a writer and an implied or ideal reader. Another way of putting it is to say that the reader is being constantly positioned by the writer, and may to varying degrees accept or resist this reading position. Chapter 6 develops the insights of both Chapters 4 and 5 by discussion of various types of intertextuality. The end of the chapter brings us full circle to the subject matter of Chapter 1 by considering genre as one kind of intertextual phenomenon.

INTERPRETING DISCOURSE

4

The aim of this chapter
- to show how implicit knowledge supplied from outside the text can interact with knowledge in the text to create inferences;
- to illustrate the ideological role of such implicit presupposition and inferencing;
- to give practice in analysing presupposition and inferencing.

Contents

4.0 Introduction: the need for interpreting texts
illustrates that meanings cannot simply be read off the text but that inferences and attitudes have to be recognised to make sense of it.

4.1 Presuppositions
surveys the main linguistic means for presupposing ideas rather than explicitly stating them, and gives examples of how presuppositions help create the sense of an ideal reader, or are used to smuggle in ideology.

4.2 Propositional attitude
points out how commands, orders and statements encode propositional attitude, and the problems when visual codes are used for conveying attitude.

4.3 Metaphor and irony
identifies metaphor and irony as prime examples of language uses where we need to recognise propositional attitude, and explores the uses to which they are put in writing.

4.4 Inferences and existing knowledge

shows how the background knowledge we supply for inferencing can be organised into stereotypical schemas; and illustrates how in interpreting jokes, racist and value-laden schemas are evoked and given currency, even though we do not accept them.

4.5 Adverts, association and inference

illustrates how sophisticated adverts can use visuals to create inferences about their products, so avoiding making explicit and indefensible claims.

Activity

A major activity is to find magazine ads and analyse them for the inferences they make.

4.0 INTRODUCTION: THE NEED FOR INTERPRETING TEXTS

The analysis of vocabulary, grammar and their meanings of the kind we did in Part A, Chapters 1–3 only takes us part of the way in understanding how texts are composed or interpreted and what effects they might have on the reader. Some early code models of communication proposed that communication works like this: a writer has meaning in her head, she encodes this completely in her text and the reader decodes it, resulting in a successful transfer of meaning from writer to reader. While, as we acknowledged in Part A, code is often important and necessary for communication, it is only one factor and is seldom sufficient. Reading is better modelled as 'a psycholinguistic guessing game', in which the text provides clues for the reader, and in which not only the meaning of the text but also the intentions of the writer have to be guessed (Sperber and Wilson 1995: 3–15; Mills 1995: 26–43).

Let's take a simple sentence like 'Shall I make a cup of tea?', uttered to your friend when she is visiting your flat or apartment. This won't be interpreted just by decoding. For a start you are not asking whether you should make a cup. Nor are you asking whether you are going to make tea (it grows on bushes), but rather whether to brew tea. Still, this doesn't take us far enough in our interpretation. You are not exactly asking about making enough tea to fill just one cup. If it's English tea you would have to leave some space for milk and sugar and, even if it's not, you wouldn't fill the cup completely to the top. Even more radically, you would probably want a cup of tea yourself, so you are asking about brewing tea in enough quantities to fill at least two cups. And, since brewing two or more cupfuls of tea takes some time, this question could be an indirect way of asking whether your visitor has enough time to stay and chat, or will soon be leaving (Boutonnet, personal communication).

This example illustrates that codes are not sufficient for communication. But, in fact, codes are not always necessary for communication. You might ask me how I feel today and instead of encoding an answer I could simply pick up a bottle of aspirin and shake it (Sperber and Wilson 1995: 25). There is no coded convention that suggests picking up a bottle of aspirin and shaking it means 'I am ill'; but probably I would have conveyed that meaning quite effectively.

What do we have to do to the decoded message in order to fully understand and interpret it? At least three things. We have to recognise propositions which are assumed rather than expressed. Then we must decide what attitude the writer has towards the propositions expressed or assumed. And, third, we have to guess what inferences the writer intended us to make on the basis of the proposition. Let's look at a small-scale example, borrowed from Sperber and Wilson, before we go on to explore these questions in more detail.

Imagine the following scenario. Mary is sitting in the living room reading the newspaper. John, who has been cooking dinner, comes in and puts two plates of food on the table and says: 'Your food will get cold'. First of all, the sentence makes a certain **presupposition**, an assumption which is not explicitly stated, namely that the food is warm or hot. Second, we have to decide on the speaker's attitude to this proposition and the presupposed proposition, technically **propositional attitude**. If the food happens to be a hot dinner, then John will probably have the attitude of belief towards the presupposition >> 'the food is warm or hot' and towards the proposition that it will get cold. (>> means "presupposes".) If it's ice-cream he would obviously not believe the presupposition or the proposition, and not expect Mary to think he believed them, and this would be a case of **irony**.

Third, in order to fully interpret this sentence as discourse, we would have to guess what John intended by uttering it, what he is **implying**, what **inferences** he wanted Mary to draw (Thomas 1995: 58ff.). By saying 'Your food will get cold', John might be communicating

'John wants Mary to eat the food at once.'

Inferences like this are created by using contextual information, or **schemas**. John has accessible a set of stored assumptions about "eating dinner at home" which contains the information

'John wants Mary to come and eat food at the time it is still hot.'

This assumption interacts with the full proposition/presupposition:

'The food on the table is warm/hot and will get cold'

to create the inference

'John wants Mary to eat the food at once.'

4.1 PRESUPPOSITIONS

In Chapter 2 we illustrated existential presupposition in discussing how vocabulary constructs or confers a reality: if a new word or phrase is invented, such as *feminazi*, then we assume that some people exist in the world who belong to this class. Also, when discussing complications to transitivity analysis, we mentioned nominalisation (turning verbs and adjectives into nouns) and the way this creates presuppositions. For example 'the ship sank' openly claims that the ship sank, whereas 'the sinking of the ship' simply presupposes it. We noted that arguing against a presupposition in noun phrase form is far more difficult than arguing against the equivalent explicit statement, because presuppositions cannot be negated.

In fact, a defining feature of presuppositions is that they remain unaffected when we negate the main clause in a sentence. For example, 'John's dog was killed' presupposes 'John has a dog'. If we negate this utterance to 'John's dog was not killed' it still presupposes 'John has a dog'.

Presupposition is a large and complex area in the study of meaning, and we cannot deal with the theories in detail. So in this section we will only discuss those linguistic devices which are commonly used for ideological or manipulative purposes, to smuggle in, as common-sense, assumptions which are debatable, controversial or simply inapplicable. We will illustrate not only possessive and existential presuppositions but also change of state, subordinate clause, *wh-* question, comparison, factive, implicative and *if* clause presuppositions.

Possessive presupposition

Close to existential presuppositions are **possessive presuppositions**. These occur when we use *'s* to indicate possession, or the pronominal "adjectives" *hers/his, their, my, our, your*. For instance, 'I looked under John's piano for your cat' presupposes >> 'John has a piano' and 'you have a cat'. To see how this works in practice, look at the following text. This is based on a horoscope taken from *Woman's World*, a magazine primarily targeted at 30–50-year-old American women. (We have had to rewrite it to avoid copyright infringement, though we have preserved the essentials of the presuppositions.):

Aries March 21 to April 19
With Mars in Libra's laid back domain, you should consider letting your mate take the initiative in romance. Any diet you begin now will be successful, making you look and feel beautiful.

Taurus April 20 to May 20
...be sure to take care of your pet's health in this period. On the 18th and 19th your mate will find you overwhelmingly attractive.

Gemini May 21 to June 21
...As your creativity blossoms, you'll become more self-assured and confident of your unique skills and talents.

Cancer June 22 to July 22
...You could be eager for career challenges as Mars' stimulating aspect increases your ambition.

Virgo August 23 to September 22
Your planetary rulers' positive aspects are giving you a sense of intense excitement. This energy spreads into your love life...

Libra September 23 to October 22
...Saturn's combative aspect perfects your diplomatic skills, preparing the way for career opportunities.

Scorpio October 23 to November 21
...let the tiger inside you emerge from her cage.

Sagittarius November 22 to December 21
Pluto's transforming power in your sign is stimulating you to rebuild your lifestyle to make it really comfortable for you.

Aquarius January 20 to February 18
You could feel a strong desire for novelty as Uranus in Aquarius reawakens your adventurous nature.

Pisces February 19 to March 20
...Fun becomes your top priority, as your inner child seeks your full attention.

(A rewriting of a horoscope from Woman's World
14 January 1997: 34)

The possessive presuppositions here make three sets of assumptions.

- First, that the readers have planetary rulers: 'your planetary rulers' >> 'you have planetary rulers', and that the effect of these rulers can be specified: 'Mars' stimulating aspect', 'Saturn's combative aspect', 'Pluto's transforming power' >> 'Mars has a stimulating aspect', etc.
- Second, that the readers have certain characteristics, presumably because they were born under a specific zodiac sign (e.g. 'Libra's laid back domain'): 'your unique skills and talents', 'your diplomatic skills', 'your ambition', 'your adventurous nature', 'your inner child' >> 'you have unique skills and talents', etc. Notice, too, in this respect, the existential and possessive presuppositions in 'let the tiger inside you emerge from her cage' >> 'there is a tiger inside you' and 'the tiger inside you has a cage'.
- Third, quite independent of specific zodiacal influence, one supposes, there are presuppositions about the general reader of these horoscopes: 'your partner', 'your love-life', 'your pet', 'your mate' >> 'you have a partner, love-life, pet and mate'.

Change of state presuppositions

In presupposing planetary influence, zodiacally determined characteristics and the possession of partners/pets/love-life, this horoscope positions the reader as someone who takes astrology seriously and has a certain lifestyle. But, in addition, there are frequent instances of another kind of presupposition – change of state presupposition – which construct the readers as unfulfilled in some way. We already illustrated **change of state presupposition** in the example 'Your food will get cold'. This presupposes that the food is not cold, i.e. it is hot or warm. Here are some examples from the horoscope which convey change of state presuppositions:

> It'll make you look and feel beautiful
> >> 'either you are not beautiful and/or you do not feel beautiful'

> You'll become more self-assured and confident of your unique skills and talents.
> >> 'you are not completely self-assured and confident of your unique skills and talents'

> Pluto's transforming power in your sign is stimulating you to rebuild your lifestyle to make it really comfortable for you.
> >> 'your lifestyle is not really comfortable for you'

> Uranus in Aquarius reawakens your adventurous nature
> >> 'your adventurous nature was once awake but has fallen asleep lately'

The horoscope seems to be reassuring women who are unfulfilled and dissatisfied with their lives that things are going to automatically improve under planetary influence.

To examine presupposition further, let's go from the sublime to the ridiculous, and look at the beginning of an editorial in Britain's *Daily Mail*, about the UK Meteorological Office's latest report on global warming, an editorial which attempts to support climate change sceptics.

DAILY MAIL COMMENT:
Global warming and an inconvenient truth

By DAILY MAIL COMMENT
PUBLISHED: 00:25, 10 January 2013 | UPDATED: 00:25,
10 January 2013

To put it mildly, it is a matter of enormous public interest that the Met Office has revised its predictions of global warming, whispering that new data suggest there will be none for the next five years. (1)

After all, the projection implies that by 2017, despite a colossal increase in carbon emissions, there will have been no rise in the planet's surface temperature for almost two decades. (2)

Why, then, did the Met Office choose to sneak out this intriguing information on Christmas Eve, knowing there would be no newspapers the next day? (3)

Isn't the inescapable suspicion that our national forecaster was anxious not to shake confidence in its Messianic belief that we are destroying our own planet? (4)

This paper keeps an open mind on climate change – and accepts that the Met Office's revised prediction doesn't prove the scientific establishment and its staunch disciples at the BBC wrong.

At the very least, however, it adds to the debate, lending support to those who argue that the threat to the environment has been greatly exaggerated. (5)

Meanwhile, ministers stake gargantuan sums of public money on their faith in the alarmists, scarring the landscape with wind farms, forcing up energy bills and threatening to shut down almost all our fossil fuel-dependent economy. (6)

The ideological manipulation brought about by presupposition is very clear in this passage, as it assumes the truth of a number of propositions which are highly questionable or extremely biased. We should be aware that the *Daily Mail* is right-wing, pro-corporate businesses, including those who make money out of burning fossil fuels. So its ideological agenda is obviously to cast doubt on the reality or danger of climate change.

There are some pretty obvious possessive and existential presuppositions here, some of which are controversial. In paragraph 5 we have the definite noun phrase nominalisation 'the debate'. For the vast majority (98 per cent) of scientists there is no debate any longer – man-made climate change and patterns of warming over the last 50 years are an undeniable reality. Then, in paragraph 6, we have 'their faith in the alarmists'. This not only assumes the existence of alarmists, who irresponsibly exaggerate the threat of climate change, but also that government ministers have a faith in them. 'Faith' suggests the possibility of a misplaced belief, of course. This belief is akin to the previous presupposition that the Met Office has a Messianic belief in destructive climate change: 'its Messianic belief that we are destroying our own planet'.

Subordinate clause, *wh-* question, comparisons, factive, implicative and *if* clause presuppositions

However, this editorial exemplifies several other kinds of presupposition. When we apply the negation test to diagnose presupposition, then it is only applied to the main clause of a sentence. This means to say that subordinate clauses or non-finite clauses regularly convey presuppositions. Look at this example:

> *Subordinate clause*   *Main clause*
> John, coming in, | noticed the dead dog.

Applying negation we get:

> *Subordinate clause*   *Main clause*
> John, coming in, | didn't notice the dead dog.

The negation test preserves the presupposition >> 'John came in'.

Let's apply this to the last sentence of the editorial: 'scarring the landscape with wind farms, forcing up energy bills and threatening to shut down almost all our fossil fuel-dependent economy' presupposes >> 'ministers are scarring the landscape with wind farms, forcing up energy bills and threatening to shut down almost all our fossil fuel-dependent economy'.

A further kind of trigger for presuppositions is *"wh-"* type questions, beginning *why, when, where* or *how*, that assume the truth of the embedded clause. For instance, 'When did John steal the mobile phone?' presupposes >> 'John stole the mobile phone.' So paragraph 3 'Why did ...' presupposes >> 'the Met Office chose to sneak out this intriguing information on Christmas Eve, knowing there would be no newspapers the next day'. Note, too, the negative spin of 'sneak out' instead of 'announce'.

There are some verbs and phrases which presuppose the truth or falsity of the statements they introduce. For example the verb *realise*. 'John realised that he had come to the wrong house' >> 'John had come to the wrong house.' In the first paragraph of the editorial we have the clause 'it's a matter of interest that' which presupposes >>'the Met Office has revised its predictions of global warming'.

Comparisons often automatically carry presuppositions. 'Paul, don't eat any more food' presupposes >> 'Paul has eaten some food'. In paragraph 5 of the editorial, 'at the very least' presupposes >> the report could do more than 'add to the debate, lending support to those who argue that the threat to the environment has been greatly exaggerated'. What exactly this more is we don't know, but can infer that it could support those who believe there is no threat to the environment at all.

There are also implicative verbs that trigger presuppositions. 'John managed/didn't manage to shut the window' presupposes >> 'John tried to shut the window'. The *keep* in 'This paper keeps an open mind on climate change' presupposes, possibly wrongly, that the paper has had an open mind on climate change. You can't keep something that you don't first have. In this case the implication is a kind of negative change of state presupposition.

If clauses and the main clauses they are paired with are particularly interesting in presupposing truth and falsity. To put it in a formula, 'If A had done X, Y wouldn't have happened' >> 'A did not do X'. Conversely, when the *if* clause is negative it presupposes that the positive equivalent did take place, 'If A hadn't done X, Y would have happened' >> 'A did do X'. In addition, the main clause in such pairs seems to presuppose its opposite: 'If A had done X, Y wouldn't have happened' >> 'Y happened'. And 'If A hadn't done X, Y would have happened' >> 'Y did not happen'. For example, although this does not occur in the passage, a sentence such as 'If Cameron hadn't talked about being the greenest government ever, then no one would have been surprised about Tory energy policies' presupposes that Cameron talked about being the greenest government ever, and that someone has been surprised about Tory energy policies.

ACTIVITY 36

Please refer to the companion website for the activity material.

4.2 PROPOSITIONAL ATTITUDE

Communication involves expressing propositions. But we have to recognise the writer's attitude to the propositions expressed. In Chapter 3 we discussed commands (imperatives), questions (interrogatives) and statements (declaratives). These are ways of encoding propositional attitude. In fact, linguists claim that three sentences like (1) 'John, wash the dishes!' (2) 'Does John wash the dishes?' and (3) 'John washes the dishes' express the same underlying proposition. What makes them different is propositional attitude. The command (1) indicates that the speaker thinks the proposition is desirable – it would be good for John to wash the dishes. The question (2) indicates that the speaker is uncertain about the truth of proposition – it is not known whether John washes the dishes or not. And the statement (3) indicates that the speaker believes this proposition is true – it is the case that John washes the dishes.

"Writing" is more and more visual on the internet, and the globalised world which demands language-neutral communication. So it's worth pointing out that one of the major differences between visual and verbal communication is that only the verbal has the resources to effectively convey propositional attitude. When one of the authors was a student at a college which was predominantly Welsh, a non-Welsh friend and he on St. David's Day, Wales' national day, attempted to fly a flag as a light-hearted protest against the celebration of Welshness. The flag depicted St. George, the patron saint of England, spearing a Welsh dragon, something like Image 4.1. But, if you think about it, the meaning was unclear, precisely because it did not signal propositional attitude. The proposition conveyed pictorially was simply 'St. George spears a Welsh dragon'. But whether it meant 'it's a scandal that St. George is spearing a Welsh dragon', or 'I wish St. George would spear the Welsh dragon' could not be conveyed graphically. Was it a statement or was it a command?

Of course, organisations like road traffic departments, airlines and multinational electronics companies, who communicate in ideograms to speakers of different languages, have managed to invent some crude markers of propositional attitude. They are, however, very crude. Although a diagonal bar usually means prohibition, as in Figure 4.1A, a sign like that shown in Figure 4.1B, found on the fold-down table of an

Image 4.1
Propositional attitude ambiguity in St. George and dragon cartoon

A

B

Figure 4.1
Graphic attempts
at propositional
attitude

Austrian Airlines plane going from Vienna to Cyprus, could hardly have conveyed the negative command 'do not bring pigs on board'. It was in fact a statement of fact: 'We do not serve pork.'

So we have seen that through commands (imperatives), questions (interrogatives) and statements (declaratives) language has resources to encode propositional attitude. And that visual attempts to indicate propositional attitude are often cruder or ambiguous.

However, propositional attitude is often not encoded or indicated at all in verbal, let alone non-verbal, communication. This makes it rather uncertain. A famous example occurs in Jane Austen's *Pride and Prejudice*, when Elizabeth Bennett is asked when she first fell in love with Mr Darcy. She replies 'I believe it must date from my first seeing his beautiful grounds at Pemberley.' (Pemberley is Darcy's magnificent mansion in Derbyshire.) We are uncertain whether she is being ironic – she really loves him quite apart from his wealth and property – or whether, to a greater or lesser extent, his wealth and property are a factor in her attraction. Does she believe the proposition she encodes and does she expect us to believe it? As another example, imagine that your parents went on holiday and in their absence you had a wild party involving, among other things, the consumption of 12 bottles of vodka. On their return the dialogue might go as follows:

DAD: I hope you behaved yourself while we were away.
YOU: Yes. <u>We put the twelve empty vodka bottles in the recycling bin for yesterday's collection.</u>

The underlined proposition is in fact true, and you believe it is true. But you expect your father to think you do not believe this proposition and are just kidding him.

This chapter concentrates discussion on two figures of speech in which propositional attitude is something less than belief in the proposition expressed. These are metaphor and irony.

ACTIVITY 37

Please refer to the companion website for the activity material.

4.3 METAPHOR AND IRONY

In one kind of **irony** the writer expresses a proposition which she does not believe to be true, and which she expects the reader to know is not true. For instance, a friend once wrote an ironic letter to the Forum Page of the Singapore *Straits Times* newspaper (24 May 1990), complaining indirectly about the nuisance of barking dogs.

Barking dogs of Chip Bee Gardens

I WRITE to express concern about the growing number of "burglaries" in the vicinity of my house in Chip Bee Gardens.

These burglaries occur at any time of the day or night. The burglars must work in large co-ordinated gangs because usually several houses are burgled at the same time.

I wish something could be done about it.

One night last week was pretty typical. There were burglaries at 9.30 p.m., 10.15 p.m., 11.40 p.m., 1.30 a.m., 4.20 a.m., 5.10 a.m. and 6.30 a.m. Most of the burglaries were over in 10 minutes, but some took as long as half an hour to be completed.

It is puzzling but the owners of the houses being burgled did not seem to be particularly bothered.

I never saw them checking if their possessions were being loaded into a waiting van during any of the burglaries.

They didn't call the police to the scene of the crime.

Ah, I know the answer ... the poor unfortunates are probably deaf, and they slept through the din of their guard dogs barking furiously as the burglars went happily about their work.

P. E. CLIFFORD
Singapore 1027

Paul Clifford obviously did not believe some of the propositions he expressed (or presuppositions he made), notably:

> These burglaries occur at any time of the day or night. The burglars must work in large co-ordinated gangs because usually several houses are burgled at the same time.
>
> . . .
>
> One night last week was pretty typical. There were burglaries at 9.30 p.m., 10.15 p.m., 11.40 p.m., 1.30 a.m., 4.20 a.m., 5.10 a.m. and 6.30 a.m. Most of the burglaries were over in 10 minutes, but some took as long as half an hour.
>
> . . .
>
> The poor unfortunates are probably deaf.

However, despite his signalling irony with scare quotes around the first occurrence of ' "burglaries" ', at least one reader did not detect his propositional attitude, which shows that irony can go unrecognised. This is the reply from the police (*Straits Times*, 7 June 1990):

Two burglaries in Chip Bee this year

I REFER to the letter 'Barking dogs of Chip Bee Gardens' by Dr P. E. Clifford (ST, May 24).

Our records show that there were only two cases of burglary at Chip Bee Gardens this year. Nothing was stolen in the first case and the second case resulted in the arrest of the culprit.

We would like to encourage Dr Clifford to help the police in apprehending the culprits by calling us if he witnesses any more burglaries in his neighbourhood.

ANG SIN PIN
for Director
Public Affairs Department
Republic of Singapore Police

Metaphor, too, runs the risk of not being detected. The following example is from the Bible, St. John's Gospel. Jesus' disciples had gone off to town to buy food. When they returned they offered him food:

> Meanwhile the disciples were urging him, 'Rabbi, have something to eat.' But he said, 'I have food to eat of which you know nothing.' At this the disciples said to one another, 'Can someone have brought him food?' But Jesus said, 'It is meat and drink for me to do the will of him who sent me until I have finished his work.'
>
> (John 4: 31–34)

It is hard to see how Jesus, in the context of the disciples returning with food, could have expected most of them to recognise the metaphor.

Given the risks of misunderstanding, what is the point of using irony and metaphor? Why do we complicate communication by saying things we don't believe – for example, saying our neighbours are deaf when they are not, distracting with irrelevancies, like burglaries, when we are really talking about barking dogs, and by being deliberately ambiguous and indirect?

Table 4.1 sketches some of the more obvious functions of metaphor, grouped according to ideational and interpersonal functions – explanation, ideological restructuring, cultivation of intimacy and the expression/hiding of emotion. The last two also seem to be the main functions of irony.

Table 4.1 *The functions of metaphor and irony*

	Function	Examples
Ideational	(1) Explanation/ modelling	*Electricity is like piped water. The pressure is the voltage, the rate of flow the amperage and the width of pipe the resistance.*
	(2) Ideological restructuring	*For mature economies growth amounts to economic cancer.* *Property is theft.*
Interpersonal	(3) Cultivating intimacy	*Thailand is becoming the Egypt of South-east Asia.* *What goes on four legs in the morning, two legs at mid-day and three legs in the evening? A man.*
	(4) Expressing/ hiding emotion	*Piss off.* *Europe's butter mountain.* *My mother passed away last year.*

(1) Metaphors are used in science and education both to build models and theories and to explain concepts to students. For example, physicists have two metaphors or theories for light, conceptualising it either as wave or particle. And it is common to explain electricity to secondary school students in terms of water flow through a plumbing system.

In fact, the dictionary is full of conventional metaphors which we use in order to understand abstract concepts (Lakoff and Johnson 1980). For instance, consider the metaphor theme POWER/CONTROL IS HIGH/ ABOVE (e.g. *high places* "circles of powerful people"; *high-handed* "exerting power tactlessly"; *top man/woman* "most powerful man/woman"; *at the top of the tree* "in the most powerful position"; *over, lord it over, oversight, overlord, superior, on top of,* all involving the meaning "in control of"). These metaphor themes can also be realised non-linguistically. We have already seen how visual perspective reflects this metaphor theme (Chapter 3 p. 109), when looking up at a participant in a picture indicates the viewer is less powerful. The demolition of the twin towers of the World Trade Center were an attempt to symbolically reduce the power of the USA.

(2) Ideology and its restructuring probably underlie most uses of metaphor, and examples of this function were discussed in Chapter 3 in terms of contested and offensive vocabulary. The metaphor themes represented in the dictionary often have an ideological dimension (Goatly 2007): metaphors of food for women – *cookie, honey, tart* – are particularly noteworthy, reducing women to objects for satisfying men's appetites. But if we call economic growth in mature economies *cancer*, and if we re-categorise property as *theft*, we are trying to get our readers to re-conceptualise and take a different ideological position. In this way metaphor can become a creative force, undoing our common-sense categories and transforming our perception of the world.

(3) Partly because some people will accept these restructuring metaphors as literal, while others will reject them, metaphor can make radical divisions in society. But metaphor is also divisive because it makes allusions which some of our audience will understand and others will not. Some readers can interpret the metaphor in Table 4.1 because they know the recent history of Egypt and Thailand: the military take-over and coup to prevent a demo-cratically elected Muslim Brotherhood taking power in Egypt in 2013 and the military coup in 2014 which removed from power the government of Yingluck Shinawatra; the lack of action by Western governments to pro-test against these coups; the adverse effect of the coups on the economies of both countries. Readers who have this background information feel included in the community of those who understand. Whereas those lack-ing enough political knowledge to make sense of it feel excluded. Similarly, riddles and jokes often depend on metaphors, and when our readers get the joke or riddle, or have it explained to them, this strengthens the social bond between them and the writer. The riddle of the sphinx in Table 4.1 – 'What goes on four legs in the morning, two legs at mid-day and three legs in the evening?' – depends upon the metaphorical analogy:

morning: mid-day: evening; infancy: adulthood: old-age

and the metaphorical equation between a walking stick and a third leg. Puns in adverts are a good example of jokes and humour which cultivate intimacy, and are probably used as synthetic personalisation to lower the defences of potential customers (see also Chapter 10, page 282).

(4) Lastly, metaphor has important relations to the expression of emo-tion. Some metaphors rely exclusively on emotional connotations, for example the swear words *piss off* and *shit*.

ACTIVITY 38

Please refer to the companion website for the activity material.

We will often use sensational or exaggerated metaphors if we wish to incite wonder or amazement in our hearers or readers. This is typical of popular newspapers:

ROGER Federer's career **resurrection** took another defining step last night when he outlasted Andy Murray.

The wine **lake** created by Europe's vineyards is now a mere **puddle**.

Roger Federer's career doesn't just become more successful again, it has a 'resurrection'; Europe didn't just have a few thousand overstocked cellars, but a wine 'lake'.

Conversely, when the event or object referred to has unfavourable emotive connotations we will often use metaphor for euphemism (see Chapter 3, page 104). In American English Louise Pound (1936) found the following metaphorical euphemisms for dying and funerals: *climbed the golden stair, called to the eternal sleep, crossed over the Great Divide, answered the last muster, planting* (quoted in Saville-Troike 1982: 201).

The metaphors we use, just like the other classifications, often have consequences for the actions we take. An interesting case in point comes from the actions of police on the street children in Rio, Brazil:

> 'Street children' ... are often described as 'dirty vermin' so that metaphors of 'street cleaning', 'trash removal', 'fly swatting', 'pest removal' and 'urban hygiene' have been invoked to garner broad-based support for police and death squad activities against them.
> (*New Internationalist* October 1997: 21)

When we turn to the functions of irony we see that they tend to be restricted to the interpersonal. One reason for using irony is similar to the euphemistic function of metaphor (4). It is to avoid responsibility for saying something that may cause offence or even bring legal punishment. Obviously Paul Clifford used irony partly to soften his criticism of his dog-owning neighbours, though because it misfired it ended up potentially causing offence to the police! This avoidance of taking responsibility for claims can also apply to metaphors. The headline of one Toshiba advert is **MAN'S BEST-EST FRIEND**, as though metaphorically the advertised TV is a faithful dog:

> The most **obedient** thing you'll ever own. Your Toshiba HDTV-compatible projection TV with the Power Focus HD 6-element lens system and new I.D.S.C. II Scan conversion technology. Oh yeah, and **it'll fetch anything you want to see** with the touch of a button.
> (Toshiba in *Maxim*, November 2000)

Although Toshiba might be sued if you find that the TV is not HDTV compatible, it is unlikely it could be sued for not fetching anything you want to see (like a dog fetches you a ball or a stick).

Irony often expresses disappointment that the actual state of affairs does not match up to the state of affairs described by the proposition in the text. If you say 'It's a lovely day for a barbecue' and then we go to the barbecue pit at the beach and there's a howling rainstorm, you might ironically echo the earlier remark: 'Yes, it's a lovely day for a barbecue.' Part of the function of this could be to express disappointment about the weather or to scorn the earlier stated proposition. The more or less veiled expression of emotion (4) is then often an important function. Certainly the Barking Dogs irony cited in the previous paragraph is an indirect expression of disapproval.

However, irony can sometimes exaggerate emotion rather than hide it, deliberately setting out to shock the reader. Jonathan Swift in 'A Modest Proposal for Preventing the Children of Ireland from being a Burden to their Parents' ironically suggests that the problems of poverty in Ireland could be solved by eating the babies of the poor:

> I have been assured by a very knowing American of my acquaintance in London, that a young healthy child well nursed is at a year old a most delicious, nourishing and wholesome food, whether stewed, roasted, baked or boiled, and I make no doubt that it will serve equally well in a fricassée, or a ragout.

Swift's proposal implies that such a policy is only an exaggeration of the kinds of cruelty and oppression already inflicted upon the poor children of eighteenth-century Ireland.

Irony, like metaphor, also cultivates intimacy (3) between the writer and reader who detects it, and even victimises those who fail to, like poor Ang Sin Pin. And irony seems to have humour as one of its main aims. According to Sigmund Freud (1963), jokes depend on initial confusion followed by a sudden flash of understanding. This is just what happens when we process an ironic statement, being puzzled by taking it at its face value, and then suddenly understanding that the writer believes the opposite of what she says.

Irony can often be used as a defence against accusations of racism or sexism. For instance, if you tell the joke 'Why do women have small feet? So they can get closer to the sink', you may claim that this is an ironic joke, a parody, and that you are targeting the people who tell such jokes. However, some of the hearers of the joke may take it at face value and revel in its sexism (Ross 1998: 57). Silvio Berlusconi, during a speech to the European Parliament, compared a German MEP to a Nazi concentration camp commandant. In response to the ensuing booing, instead of apologising, Berlusconi said he regretted his utterance had not been recognised as an ironic joke (Simpson and Mayr 2010: 80, quoting Billig 2005).

ACTIVITY 39

Please refer to the companion website for the activity material.

4.4 INFERENCES AND EXISTING KNOWLEDGE

When we use metaphor and irony, then, we do not believe the proposition we utter. But in addition we make the reader infer our intended meaning, and this will often necessitate supplying information from outside the text, as in the case of the Thailand–Egypt metaphor.

The background information or assumptions which we bring to texts in order to draw inferences are generally organised in our long-term memory in structures known as **schemas**. These are structures for storing stereotypical knowledge about objects and sequences of behaviour (Schank and Abelson 1979).

We can see how important schemas are in ordinary understanding of language by considering how we interpret a simple sentence such as 'I like apples.' Because our schema for apples includes the information that they are food, we will, by default, interpret this sentence to mean 'I like eating apples', rather than 'I have an emotional attachment to apples.' Do you know this joke?

> CHILD: Mummy, mummy, I don't like grandma.
> MOTHER: Well, leave her on the side of your plate and finish your potatoes.

Obviously it depends upon the fact that plates and potatoes belong to the schema for eating, and this forces us to abandon the default schema of family relationships cued by *grandma*. In one sense understanding a text means finding a schema which accounts for it.

A famous example of a schema for eating at a restaurant was provided by Schank and Abelson (1979):

RESTAURANT

props:	tables, chairs, cutlery, food, plates, menu, etc.
roles:	customer, owner, cook, waiter, (cashier)
entry conditions:	customer is hungry; customer has money
results:	customer has less money; customer is not hungry; owner has more money
Scene 1. <u>Entering</u>:	going in, deciding where to sit, sitting
Scene 2. <u>Ordering</u>:	(asking for menu, waiter bringing menu) choosing, signalling to waiter, giving order, waiter telling cook the order
Scene 3. <u>Eating</u>:	cook giving waiter food, waiter bringing customer food; customer eating food
Scene 4. <u>Exiting</u>:	customer asking for bill, waiter writing bill, taking bill to customer, (customer tipping waiter), customer going to cashier, paying cashier, leaving restaurant.

This is a pretty well-organised behavioural schema, traditionally stereotypical within Western culture. So that if you said 'I went to a restaurant yesterday evening' the hearer will probably infer that the standard schema was followed: this would be a default interpretation. It is only when there are non-standard occurrences that the speaker would think it worth her while elaborating on the restaurant visit. For example, there was a letter in a Singapore newspaper complaining about a visit to a Pizza Hut restaurant. The event schema developed against expectations. Scenes 1 and 2 proceeded as normal. However, Scene 3 was left out, despite the customers waiting an hour. Nevertheless, some of Scene 4 materialised, with the waiter writing and bringing the bill, and the customers leaving the restaurant, but without paying. Some scripts differ culturally and sub-culturally. Cheap Chinese restaurants often leave the bill at your table as soon as you order. And it's not clear in many English pubs that serve food whether you wait at your table to be served, or go to the bar to order.

Miscommunication will occur when the reader evokes a different schema from the one the writer intended. Activity 40 is a famous example of classroom discourse in which the student mistook what the teacher was trying to achieve, what schema she was following when she said 'what are you laughing at'?

ACTIVITY 40

Please refer to the companion website for the activity material.

> What is the relevance of schema theory to writing? Well, as we have seen, understanding texts is largely a matter of invoking the right schema. So it is vital, especially in deductive genres, for the writer to state clearly the topic or issue of the text adequately at an early opportunity so that the readers can supply the relevant schematic background information to make sense of it.

Newspapers face a particular problem with long-running stories, such as Julian Assange's taking refuge in the Ecuadorian Embassy. They cannot presume that every reader will have followed the story from its beginning, but they can probably guess that most have. There are two solutions to this problem. Introduce the earlier necessary background information in a shorthand way at the beginning and/or have a background section later in the article. We can see this in the very short news article about Mandela's death quoted in Chapter 1. After the headline and lead, important background information from Mandela's history is given, in case readers are unaware of the significance of his life/death. But even in the lead we are given the information that he was an anti-apartheid activist. I have italicised the background information.

NELSON MANDELA DEATH

Anti-apartheid activist Nelson Mandela died on December 5th 2013. [LEAD] Mandela, also affectionately known as Madiba, *spent 27 years in prison, many of them on Robben Island, before his release in 1990. He went on to become the first president of South Africa in the fully democratic post-apartheid era, serving from 1995 to 1999.*

For any writer the trickiest judgement to make is the state of the average reader's background knowledge, whether any particular schema exists for the topic of the piece of writing. She does not wish to tell the reader things the reader already knows, otherwise the writing will be laboured. On the other hand she does not wish to take the risk that the required inferences cannot be made because of inadequate background knowledge.

On which side did you err in preparing a simplified text for school children in Project 1 in Chapter 3? Note that hypertext providing links to extra background information makes digital media less problematic in this respect.

It's worth emphasising the stereotypical nature of many of the schemas we employ. The fact that we are constantly using such stereotypical information in our processing of text gives horribly wide opportunities for ideologies to operate latently and, as it were, naturally or common-sensically.

Let's illustrate this point by thinking about jokes which depend upon racial stereotyping.

> Q: What did the Japanese hostess say to the amorous stamp collector?
> A: Philately will get you nowhere.

Or

> There were an Irishman and a gorilla, and they were both preparing for a voyage to a space station. It was the end of their six-month course of physical and scientific training, and the evening before the mission was scheduled to commence. The head of the programme invited them into his office for a final briefing, at the end of which he wished them luck for the trip and handed them each a sealed envelope containing instructions for their duties during the three-week trip.
>
> When the gorilla got to his apartment on the base he opened his envelope and found five sheets of detailed instructions. They

told him that he should perform experiments on crystallography and heat conductivity, take various complicated astronomical readings, and monitor his and the Irishman's bodily functions including performing CAT scans at various intervals.

When the Irishman opened his letter, there was one small piece of paper which read: 'Feed the gorilla.'

To understand these jokes we have to supply various assumptions from our schemas for Japanese and Irish: that Japanese pronounce [r] as [l] and that Irishmen are stupid. (We also have to be aware of the proverb 'Flattery will get you nowhere'.) Of course, we need not *believe* these assumptions to get the joke, but simply by entertaining them we are, in a sense, giving them currency, acknowledging that other people believe or at least entertain them. In fact, there is plenty of evidence that Irishmen are highly intelligent. Anyone who knows about the literature of the British Isles will realise that a major contribution has been made by Irish authors – Swift, Goldsmith, Yeats, Oscar Wilde, Synge, and George Bernard Shaw – who are famous for their wit, intelligence and verbal dexterity. How this myth of Irish stupidity arose is itself instructive. Apparently, during the nineteenth century, if workers in the English mills went on strike, it was the management's policy to import Irish labour to keep the factories going. The workers who were locked out had a strong motive for spreading the idea that the Irish were stupid and incompetent in order to dissuade the employers from substituting their labour. This case illustrates clearly enough that the common assumptions of a culture, which we supply to make sense of discourse, very often have ideological dimensions, even though in the course of history their origins may have been lost.

The reason that inferencing has such a powerful ability to reinforce ideology is that somehow we don't feel forced to supply the premises which lead to the inference. If an ideological position is stated baldly we recognise it, and even if it is conveyed through presupposition we can detect the manipulation involved. But supplying information appears to be something we are doing rather than something being done to us. However, although we seem to be acting freely, we are actually being created as subjects, subjects who can or are willing to entertain the assumptions necessary to make sense of the joke or advert.

4.5 ADS, ASSOCIATION AND INFERENCE

Advertisements are particularly dependent for their effects and strategies on the inferencing process. In one kind of advertisement, the sophisticated ones which you find in glossy magazines, the product is more or less upstaged by the visuals, the setting, the characters and so on. These are notorious for using associations in a kind of behaviourist conditioning process in order to imply, most crudely, that by buying the product you buy other things as well. These things might be the "girl" who opens the door of the car being advertised, the kitchen in which the washing machine is located, the family and happy kids who are consuming the breakfast cereal. Another way of looking at this, less crudely, is to say that buying the product confers membership of the class of people for whom such a lifestyle is normal. By buying a Rolex watch you join a club of successful people including, according to the latest ad, Tiger Woods, Roger Federer, Marlon Brando, Robert DeNiro, Pablo Picasso and Martin Luther King Jr (www.hodinkee.com/blog/a-quick-look-at-the-new-rolex-ad-campaign-highlighting-innovators-and-rolex-wearers). The product becomes one prop in a schema for a stereotypically successful lifestyle.

Look at the advertisement for Dorma fabrics shown in Image 4.2. While most space in the picture does indeed display Dorma fabrics, our attention is immediately drawn to the heads and upper body of the couple, because these are placed centrally and brightly illuminated, which makes them into symbolic attributes of the whole picture (see Section 2.4). The caption above, 'One look creates perfect harmony', most obviously refers to the harmonious colours of co-ordinated fabric patterns, but the couple are gazing at each other – the vector of her gaze at his strong arm, the vector of his at her breasts. The advert promises, implicitly, then, through symbolic attribution, not only cloth, but a harmonious relationship. What is the nature of the promised relationship? The pun 'Don't just sleep on it' implies that there are other things to do on the Dorma-sheeted bed – presumably to make love, prompted by the idiom *sleep together/with*. The vectors of their gaze may indeed imply a future narrative process (see Section 2.4). (If this sexual meaning is the primary one, the implication might even be they are so good for making love on, that you could end up not literally sleeping on them.) 'Don't just sleep on it' implies more, too, certainly: that Dorma fabric can be admired as well as slept on, or, exploiting the idiom *to sleep on a problem/decision*, that the consumer shouldn't simply think carefully but go ahead and buy these fabrics. But the visual foregrounding of the couple through symbolic attribution guides us especially to the first implication – the promise of a harmonious sexual relationship.

Further aspects of the visuals imply more than this. The other light area of the picture shows a curtain billowing in the breeze, and a retro lion-claw-foot bath tub, still two-thirds full, with a towel carelessly left over its edge soaking up the bathwater. These become symbolic, we might infer, of a relationship in which the man and woman are too ecstatic to worry about closing windows or hanging up towels. And perhaps a slightly bohemian one – given that the bathtub is a bit spartan.

Image 4.2 Dorma fabrics ad

The pragmatic trick being played here is that the advertiser expects us to find a relevance through symbolic attribution for those foregrounded visuals which do not actually represent the products – the couple, the bathtub and towel. They can only achieve relevance if we accept some kinds of inferences, like those I have suggested. This implicit message is a strategic device, too. The Advertising Standards Authority would, presumably, not allow the advertiser to explicitly claim that if you buy Dorma sheets you also get a passionate, bohemian, heterosexual partner (cf. Tanaka 1994: 40–43).

We might also wish to think of the interpersonal implications created by visual codes in this ad (see Section 3.7). In terms of visual contact there is no demand made because the participants' gazes are directed at each other, not at the viewer. As the viewer seems irrelevant to the couple and is positioned behind the curtain, we almost feel that we viewers obtain the offered information by spying on them, like peeping toms. This sense of the hidden power of the spy is also conveyed by the slightly downward viewing angle. Secret observation is also consistent with the long shot of the couple, indicating a large social distance so that engagement with them is not possible, only contemplation. The oblique horizontal angle also suggests exclusion and non-involvement. However, the viewer has a closer shot of the fabrics of the curtain and the bed, and is at almost a 180 degree angle to them, which might imply the possibility of engagement and involvement by buying Dorma fabrics.

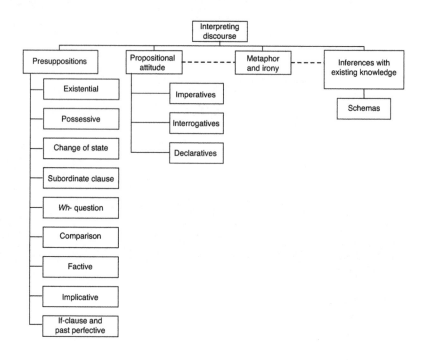

Figure 4.2
Summary of the chapter

ACTIVITY 41

Please refer to the companion website for the activity material.

4.6 SUMMARY

In this chapter we elaborated on the fact that as readers we need to interpret texts as well as decode them. In particular we noted that:

- writers can use presuppositions to dangerously and unconsciously structure our thinking;
- writers may have attitudes towards the messages (propositions) of their texts, attitudes which are not encoded in the text;
- writers can use irony and metaphor to cultivate intimacy and express emotion, to explain the unfamiliar or radically restructure thinking;
- writers expect readers to draw inferences by supplying background schematic knowledge;
- writers can exploit this schematic knowledge to reproduce ideologies and stereotypes and to make covert claims, for example in advertisements.

Earlier we introduced the notion of latent ideology, and suggested that when ideology is explicitly stated it is far less dangerous. When it becomes natural or common-sense, a background assumption, it is extremely insidious. The degrees of presence of meanings in a text might be represented on a scale (Fairclough 1995: 106):

Absent   Presupposed   Backgrounded   Foregrounded

Moving from right to left, foregrounded meanings are those which are explicitly stated. As for the backgrounding of information, in Chapter 1 we saw how this can be achieved through the generic structure of newspapers, or the sequencing of theme and rheme in the clause. This chapter has largely concentrated on the areas to the left of the scale – the presuppositions in the text and the absent meanings and information we have to supply from outside the text in order to make sense of it. It is in these areas that naturalised ideological assumptions are extremely powerful.

FURTHER READING

Please refer to the companion website for the list of further reading.

5 READING AND WRITING POSITIONS

The aim of this chapter
- to show the relationship between society's institutions and the subject positioning of the reader;
- to envisage written discourse as a writer acting upon a reader to construct a relationship;
- to raise awareness of politeness factors in positioning the reader;
- to encourage resistance against the reading positions imposed on us by texts.

5.0 Introduction: how texts position the reader
introduces the concept of subject positioning, and shows how the position of the reader and writer can shift in the course of a text.

5.1 Speech acts
shows how writing is an acting on the reader, illustrates different classes of speech acts and demonstrates how the kinds of speech act can reflect a relationship in a personal letter.

5.2 Indirect speech acts and politeness
outlines the factors influencing the politeness of requests and offers, and explores other aspects of politeness such as approval, modesty, sympathy and agreement.

5.3 Learning and resisting reading positions
shows how we might learn to adopt appropriate reading positions, identifies the various levels at which we can resist the reading position which the text invites us to adopt, and encourages this resistance when note-taking from written texts.

Activity
A major activity is to find a text which you wish to resist and explain/analyse your resistance to it.

5.0 INTRODUCTION: HOW TEXTS POSITION THE READER

In Chapter 3, when we considered the interpersonal elements of the grammar of English, dealing with matters such as power and contact, we were already providing one perspective on the relationships between the reader and the writer. In this chapter we are more specifically concerned with **subject positions**, the relative positions created for the reader and writer though texts; here, texts are seen as the means by which a writer performs an action on the reader. But before we consider in detail how subjects are created by texts, we ought to glance at a theory of the subject which relates it to the underlying ideological concerns of this book.

Louis Althusser (1984) argues that we become subjects through subjection to societal institutions such as the educational system, religious organisations, the family and the media. The texts produced by these institutions map out a role for the subject. Recognising your role confers identity on you as an individual, which to some extent empowers you, but also subjects you to the state and authority. For example, in the first few weeks of school children are taught and later internalise the rules of classroom interaction. Learning these enables them to act as subjects – for instance, knowing how to raise their hand to attract the teacher's attention and ask for information, but also subjects them to the authority of the teacher and the institution. The fact that pupils come to internalise these rules and regard them as obvious, unquestioned common-sense shows the link between subject positioning and latent, naturalised ideology (Mills 1995: 67–68). Another example would be the subject-positioning of women in Indian society. In a campaign to save girl children from being aborted in India, the prime minister remarked 'If daughters are not born, how will you get daughters-in-law?' This assumes a latent naturalised ideology of a society where women "will" get married and that they "will" take up the role of 'daughters-in-law'. Also, an obvious unquestioned common-sense assumption is that men will get married to women only. The statement thus confers and subjects the audience to gender roles which have been internalised. Let's explore more how language is involved in creating subject positions for readers.

In written media texts, one aspect of subject positioning is the general question of who the ideal or average reader is imagined to be, or invited to be. We saw an instance of this with the horoscope which we analysed for presuppositions in Chapter 4 (pp. 120–123), where the ideal or typical reader will be a rather unfulfilled 30–50-year-old conservative American woman with a partner and a pet, who believes in the power of the zodiac signs to determine certain aspects of character and in the influence of the planets.

However, there are more local aspects of subject positioning. Texts are seldom entirely homogeneous and writers will often adopt varying positions as the text progresses, and expect the reader to adopt matching shifts in position. For in the text in Chapter 2 about the Candy Crush Saga phenomenon, there is first the voice of the 'editor' introducing the main columnist Chris Stokel-Walker as a kind of researcher or pop sociologist. When the latter starts to speak in paragraph 1 he adopts the voice and position of a commuter observing other commuters' behaviour, and addresses the reader as a potential fellow commuter: 'Stand on a crowded commuter train…'. At other points his voice is that of an interviewer interviewing Laura Wilson and Amy Bolton, or criticising King, and we the readers are an audience for their replies. Besides his voice as a commentator on a social phenomenon or a historian of video games, he variously adopts the voice of a financial pundit, speculating on a likely IPO, or a statistician voicing data from Appdata, and in these cases the reader might be a potential investor.

More locally still in texts, we can identify the particular sentence or utterance of writer/speaker and give this a label as a speech act, for example *inform, command, question, reprimand, warn, protest, dare, confide*. Using sentences to act on other people in these differing ways positions both writer/speaker and reader/hearer: the informed and the informed, the commander and the commanded, the questioner and the questioned, the reprimander and the reprimanded, etc.

As writers we should be alert to the kinds of positions we are taking up and the matching positioning of our readers. This chapter will help to raise awareness of the factors affecting this subject positioning by discussing it from four angles: speech acts; indirect speech acts and politeness; the heterogeneity of positions in texts; and the contesting or resisting of positioning.

5.1 SPEECH ACTS

Speech act theory, beginning with Austin (1962) and elaborated by John Searle (1969, 1979), explores the notion that the sentences we utter and the texts we write are discourse acts which affect our addressees. From this perspective text is simply a trace of what we are attempting to do to other people.

In some kinds of speech act, **assertives**, the speaker/writer will be giving information, describing a state of affairs in the world, as in: 'There's a departmental meeting scheduled for tomorrow afternoon.' Examples are *state, inform, swear, remind*. In another type the writer/speaker attempts to make the reader/hearer do something, giving them a **directive**, as in 'Please type out the agenda.' Examples would be *ask, command, request, suggest, plead, beg*. In other speech-act types, **commissives**, the writer/speaker is giving a commitment to the reader/hearer that she will do something in the future, as with 'I promise to type the agenda by tomorrow evening.' Instances would be, *promise, threaten, vow, volunteer.* At other times the writer/speaker expresses an inner feeling in **expressives**, for example, gratitude when saying 'Thanks for typing this so quickly.' Here we find acts like *thank, congratulate, apologise* and *condole.* One of the most powerful of speech act types is the **declaration**, by which the speaker brings about a change in the institutional situation simply by her utterance. So 'Let's begin the meeting' declares the start of the meeting, providing the chairperson, who is institutionally ratified, makes the declaration. Other examples are *declaring war, christening, marrying* or *sentencing.*

ACTIVITY 42

Please refer to the companion website for the activity material.

5.2 INDIRECT SPEECH ACTS AND POLITENESS

The most straightforward way of using texts to perform speech acts matches assertives with declarative mood, directive commands with imperative, and directive questions with interrogative. However, it is also quite normal to use one kind of grammatical mood structure to indirectly perform a different kind of speech act. This is called an **indirect speech act**. You can use the declarative mood grammatical structure of a statement as an indirect directive or command, e.g. 'The dog needs to be fed' instead of the direct 'Feed the dog.' Or you can use the declarative mood to indirectly ask a question, e.g. 'You went to Starbucks' last night?' Or the opposite, use an interrogative mood associated with questions to make a statement. For example, 'Who left the door unlocked?' can be an indirect way of saying 'Someone left the door unlocked.'

This section concentrates on discussing directives, especially commands, requests and offers. We will consider when bald imperative commands should be avoided for the sake of politeness, and the various strategies of indirectness by which this can be achieved.

So what determines the politeness of directives? First, it is crucial to take account of the difference in relative costs and benefits to writer/speaker and reader/hearer of the action required. And this is recognised in the distinction we have between requests and offers. Requested acts benefit the writer and offers are costly to the writer. Second, the writer will need to take more pains to be polite if the reader has more power than her; she ought to be more polite in writing a memo to her boss than her subordinate. Third, as mentioned earlier, there is evidence to suggest that, at least in North America, a medium degree of contact necessitates politeness – in other words, the writer can afford to be less polite with intimates and complete strangers, but she is likely to be more polite with those acquaintances she anticipates might develop into friends.

To sum up, there is a need to use the politer forms of language when:

- the reader is of greater power than the writer;
- the reader has a medium degree of contact with the writer;
- the action demanded is of relative benefit to the writer and of cost to the reader.

What exactly are these polite forms? Leech (1983) identifies, as major factors in politeness, the features of **optionality** and indirectness. Optionality means giving the reader the option of refusing. Indirectness gives the reader the opportunity to deny recognising that a request is being made. This becomes clearer if we look at these examples:

direct/no option less polite

1. *Look after the kids.*
2. *I want you to look after the kids.*
3. *Will you look after the kids?*
4. *Can you look after the kids?*
5. *Would you mind looking after the kids?*
6. *Could you possibly look after the kids?*
7. *You couldn't possibly look after the kids, could you?*
8. *The kids have a holiday coming up.*

indirect/optional more polite

Item 1 is obviously the most direct of these requests. Items 2, 3 and 4 are less direct, not requesting the act itself. Of this trio, 3 and 4 are more tactful than 2 because they are in a question form and therefore allow for the possibility of a negative reply, the option to refuse. Items 5 and 6 are more tactful still: they recognise the reasons the hearer might have for taking the refusal option (he would mind it), and they are indirect because the *would* and *could* make them hypothetical, suggesting that the request has not actually been made (['If I asked you] would you mind looking after the kids?'). Item 7 is politer still – the question expecting the answer 'no', thereby making it even easier for the reader to take the option of refusal. Item 8 is the most indirect, simply being a hint, and cannot really be counted as an on-record request at all.

ACTIVITY 43

Please refer to the companion website for the activity material.

Leech has actually proposed a number of maxims that we more or less adhere to if we are being polite in our discourse (1983: 139). The first is **tact**, in directives, which means as we have seen, using indirectness and optionality when the action is costly to the hearer/reader. The second maxim is **approbation** or its converse, **modesty**, when you praise others and underrate yourself. One way of being modest is to pretend that as a writer you are deficient in your communicative skills. You can use all the modal devices of uncertainty (Chapter 3) to suggest that you could be misleading your readers: *possibly, I think, sometimes*, etc. You can pretend that what you say is redundant: *As you know, of course*, etc. Or that you have a tendency to ramble on: *This may be beside the point, but...* Or that you have put things more obscurely than need be: *In other words, or to put it more simply*, and *if you see what I mean....*

> Approbation is a telling strategy for effective communicators. We ought to take opportunities to praise or raise the self-esteem of the reader, especially when we have a potentially hostile or antagonistic readership.

Effective comments on blogs or letters to the editor, for example, which are inherently critical or express disagreement, might at least show some approbation or agreement. This is probably more important in cultures where a high value is placed on maintaining others' **"face"**. Look at the opening of the following letter, *Tough line must be taken to stop teenagers smoking* (*Straits Times*, 19 March 1997: 40).

> I REFER to the report "Community roped in to help smokers quit" (ST March 5).
> <u>I applaud Mr Alex Chan, chairman of the Committee on Smoking Control, for involving the community in a bid to discourage smoking among teenagers.</u>
> However, I disagree with his idea of dismissing the authoritarian approach when dealing with them.

The underlined sentence shows approbation before going on to criticise or show disagreement. In fact, this gives us a clue to another strategy for being polite – to agree wherever possible, Leech's **agreement maxim**. The next letter, *Sex scandals have a sordid tradition* (*Independent*, Monday 9 May 1995) shows a balance of agreement and disagreement in its opening paragraph:

From Mr David Turner
Sir: <u>Our attitudes towards sex and marriage may well have changed over time, as Professor Carol Smart suggests</u> ("Has adultery become a spurious issue?" 22 May), but the current stance taken by the popular media in its reporting of adultery is no recent development.

The last of Leech's maxims is the **sympathy** maxim. This suggests that one should at least take an interest in the readers' problems, and ideally claim the feelings they have about their misfortunes or fortunes are matched by yours. Typically, condolences and congratulations would figure here.

It should be clear from the last two maxims, concerning agreement and sympathy, that speech acts do not occur in isolation – you have to agree with a previous statement, or sympathise with good or bad news. Indeed, speech acts often form adjacent pairs, such as question/answer, greeting/greeting, inform/acknowledgement, statement/agreement, offer/acceptance, thanks/acknowledgement, command/compliance. The second act of the adjacency pair may be a **preferred second** or a **dispreferred second**, that is, more or less comfortable for the second speaker (Levinson 1983). The ones I have listed above are the preferred seconds. But offers and commands could, for example, meet with refusals and statements could meet with disagreements. These dispreferred seconds would be considered less polite, which is why they might be accompanied by an apology or a reason for why the preferred second cannot be performed. For example, in the following joke:

> An Irishman wanders into a library and says 'Fish and chips, please.'
> The librarian says, 'Sorry, this is a library.'
> The Irishman whispers, 'Sorry, fish and chips, please'.
> (Carr and Greeves 2007: 216)

The adjacency pairs in the dialogue of this joke could be diagrammed as follows:

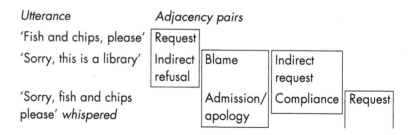

'Sorry, this is a library' is an indirect refusal, a dispreferred second, but the Irishman interprets it both as blame for speaking loudly in a library and an indirect request to speak more softly. So he goes on to make a dispreferred admission of/apology for the mistake for which he is blamed, and to comply with the indirect request by whispering a repeat of his own request.

Reflecting or constructing relationships

In our discussion of politeness we have assumed that the forms of language we choose simply reflect the existing dimensions of power and contact in our relationships. However, as we saw with ideational meanings in Chapter 2, language confers rather than reflects reality, and this is just as true of our social positions. It is through being talked and written to and by talking and writing in return that our social positions are established. For example, by using the imperative, advertisers constitute themselves as offering goods which are beneficial to the consumer, rather than requesting the reader to do them a favour. For there is, remember, no need to use less direct forms if the reader benefits. Or if a boss writes a note: 'I expect all members of the Division without exception to forward their comments to me on this matter by the end of next week' then this doesn't simply reflect a social positioning – it constitutes the relationship between boss and subordinates as an authoritarian one. In short, words create a social world rather than simply describing one.

5.3 LEARNING AND RESISTING READING POSITIONS

Up to this point we have been discussing subject positions as if they were simply a matter of individuals interacting with other individuals. In fact, however, we learn or are taught both how to be good subjects, and how to read texts in a certain way – what we might call a **reading position**. This process introduces us into a community with shared reading habits. In particular, in literature classes we spend a great deal of time learning to imitate the valid/fashionable ways of reading and to avoid the less valid/unfashionable. And very often in ordinary English instruction, for example, in reading a comprehension passage in an English textbook, we were expected to be quite naïve readers, to accept the text as given and to answer "factual" comprehension questions on it. The very point of this present book is to help students to move away from this naïve position and to think about why the text is the way it is, how it could have been otherwise and whose interests or purposes it serves.

The fact that different kinds of readers are expected of different kinds of texts is obvious enough from the following example (cf. Fish 1980). If you were given this text and were told it is a poem, you would read it in a particular way according to certain reading strategies.

> Black
> Fish
> Culler
> Leech
> White

You would, of course, initially apply the normal procedures for making grammatical and semantic sense of a sentence, which are not specifically literary ways of reading. Lines 2 and 4 of the poem are either nouns, in which case they represent two kinds of animal, or they are verbs meaning "to catch fish" and "to drain of blood". This last possibility makes sense for 'leech', since *to leech white* means "to drain of blood until it is white". 'Fish', on the other hand, looks like a noun since it has an adjective 'black' before it, and presumably both premodify 'culler', someone black who culls, not, in this case, seals, but fish. Since 'culler' is singular, 'leech' would then be an imperative command, and the first three lines would be a vocative address. The poem could then be rewritten: 'Black fish culler, leech white!'

Moreover, having been taught to read poems you would do much more than simply work out the grammar and meaning of the text. You might point out the symmetry of the poem, beginning with 'black' and ending with 'white', noticing that these words begin with sounds made with both lips, take special note of the pun on *colour*/'culler', and remark that this is the only two-syllable word and lies at the centre of the poem. You could also give some symbolic value to 'black' and 'white', perhaps good and evil, depending on how politically sensitive you are. You might then arrive at an interpretation of some literary significance: the poem is an ironic exhortation to an evil (black) exploiter of nature (fish culler) to drain nature of its lifeblood (leech white); with the consequence either of giving natural victims a sacrificial sanctity (white), or, more cynically, of the culler (exploiter), by economic gain, whitewashing his own evil.

However, when you are told that this refers to a reading list for a class in the language of literature, comprising just the surnames of the authors, you will read the text in a quite different way, not even trying to parse it as a sentence, let alone give it a literary interpretation:

> Black, Max, 'More about metaphor'
> Fish, Stanley, 'Is there a text in this class?'
> Culler, Jonathan, *The Pursuit of Signs*
> Leech, Geoffrey, *A Linguistic Guide to English Poetry*
> White, Hayden, *Metahistory*

Resisting reading positions

On the whole texts ask us to accept the position they set up for us. But there are various ways in which we can resist this position, and these are more or less radical. Most obviously and superficially we can resist the overt content of a text, the openly expressed ideational meanings. A few years ago there was an incident in the street where one of the authors was living in which a neighbour's dog was run over and left unconscious by a taxi who failed to stop. The neighbour chased the taxi and confronted the driver. The police arrived and charged the neighbour with grievous bodily harm. The dog was taken to the vet's and recovered fully after a few days. The case came to court two years later and the neighbour was acquitted. However, the two local newspapers both had factual errors in their reports of the court case. In one the dog died, in the other the dog was still recovering in veterinary hospital two years after the accident. Obviously, when the author read those texts he resisted the overt misinformation which the newspapers gave. This first kind of resistance is pretty obvious and widespread, deservedly so (Bell 1991: 218).

Second, as Chapter 2 suggested, you can resist the text's ideological categorisations and the construction of reality; for example, patterns of the depiction of women in tabloid newspapers. Turning to Chapter 3, one might resist the authority, dogmatism or level of formality of a text. More subtly, as Chapter 4 showed, one might resist its presuppositions, inferences or implications, and propositional attitudes. Finally, one might wish to resist the way of reading texts which seems to be natural, but which is in fact acquired through education and by example from other members of one's culture, sub-culture or community.

You might, for example, from an ideological perspective, resist the author's presuppositions and propositional attitudes in this extract about a Singaporean socialite.

> When you step into the home of X you enter a world of charmed gracious living.
>
> The black and white marble-tiled foyer of the Cluny Park bungalow leads to a drawing room. Here floor-to-ceiling French windows overlook a pool outside.
>
> Broad white sofas line one side of the airy room, showing off a costly Persian carpet on the maple parquet floor. At one corner is a gleaming baby grand piano, at another a French-Vietnamese cabinet displays figurines of geisha girls, samurai, and Chinese deities – all carved from ivory.
>
> Everything about the home, from the teak-framed modern Chinese paintings to a huge Filipino jade-bordered mirror in the toilet, reputed to belong to Mrs Imelda Marcos, is opulent but not ostentatious.

The home, you realise, is the sum of a determined woman, who took four years to tear it down and build it up again, until she could get it just so.

The ideal reader of this piece is supposed to admire the contents of this bungalow. More than this, he is supposed to accept that the character or identity of the woman depends on her valuable and tasteful possessions. And to accept the presupposition that she, despite the effect on her finger-nails, personally tore down the old bungalow and rebuilt it. However, one might refuse to accept this ideal reading position, especially if you have no admiration for furniture or *objets d'art* made of teak and ivory, because for you they symbolise reckless exploitation of the trees and animals in our environment. You may also be disgusted to read that a mirror has achieved a certain snobbish fame from having once belonged to Imelda Marcos, not the most ethical politician. Even more strongly you may resist the explicit claim that a person's value, identity and character is measured by their material possessions: 'The home is the sum of a determined woman'. And one can more easily believe that the original bungalow was torn down and rebuilt by poorly paid construction workers than by the lady whose 'gracious' lifestyle we are expected to admire.

Annotation and subject positioning

When you read texts, especially academic ones, you are probably in the habit of annotating them. Too often this annotation simply involves marking up the most important parts of the text by highlighting or underlining crucial points in order to clarify or summarise the author's meaning. But annotation should involve more than that. It should involve your evaluative response to the text, your awareness of subject positioning and your rejection, acceptance or qualification of that positioning. Charles Bazerman (1992) has listed a number of questions you can ask yourself to stimulate evaluative annotation, which have been modified below:

Questions	Comments
Do I approve or disapprove?	*????, NO!, not bad, not exactly, yuk, nonsense, right*
Do I agree or disagree?	*I don't agree because ... No, the actual facts are*
Are there exceptions/ counterexamples?	*Not true in the case of X... Case Y is just the opposite*
Are there examples which support the argument?	*Exactly what happens in the case of Z*
Can this argument be extended?	*This might also apply to ... This explains why...*

Questions	Comments
Do I accept the way the world/society is represented and categorised in this text?	It's good to see X coming over as powerful. I don't like the use of the term Y as it suggests...
What relationship is the writer striking up with me?	This text is too dogmatic/apologetic/ patronising The writer is on my wavelength/treats me with respect
Can I accept the presuppositions/implications of this text?	The presupposition X is unfounded I don't like the implications of this. The inference depends on racist/ sexist/ageist, etc. stereotyping
Can I accept the way of reading the text that I'm supposed to employ?	What's so great about this Shakespeare/Keats/Melville? Why must I read this Z (ad) like a W (poem) when it's just a Z (cheap publicity)

ACTIVITY 44

Please refer to the companion website for the activity material.

A good example of resisting the ways of reading expected by one's social group and subculture might be found in alternative readings of religious texts. One of the authors of this book was brought up as a fundamentalist Christian, and taught that the Bible was true from cover to cover, that it was the inspired word of God, and was not written in a normal human way, but by divine dictation. He was encouraged to believe that it could give him spiritual guidance for his life and daily behaviour, and to use it as a devotional text. However, as a teenager he noticed that the Bible had overt contradictions. Did Judas hang himself or simply fall over and break his neck? Did St. Paul's companions, during his experience of God on the road to Damascus, see the light and not hear the voice, or did they hear the voice and not see the light? Did one of the thieves crucified with Jesus repent or not? These overt contradictions led him to see the Bible in a quite different way. He could now no longer believe its texts were the result of God's Holy Spirit possessing the writers to produce an infallible text. He realised it was a flawed human product, like all other texts, and that it was written and edited/rewritten in a historical context, and had to be read in those terms, so that its injunctions could not simply be followed blindly in today's society. He came to the conclusion that it was only unique because it described a period of history in which God was particularly active. This meant, of course, that he would read it differently and more critically. And, socially, it meant, though remaining a Christian, he could no longer feel at home in the fundamentalist church community where he was brought up.

Another example closer to your experience might be in the reading of magazines for women. There has been a great deal of work on the construction of femininity by teenage magazines. When you read the Beauty sections of teenage magazines do you, if you are female, resist the way femininity is constructed there? Many such magazines reinforce and exploit the use of make-up as a ritual differentiating female adolescents from girls on the one hand, and adolescent men on the other. They suggest that a woman's status and identity depends upon her physical appearance. They tend to make girls dissatisfied with the natural changes to their appearance which accompany puberty, and introduce a sense of insecurity which can only be dispelled by buying a commodity. They also suggest a certain pleasure to be had from beauty rituals, once the commodity has been bought (MacRobbie 1991: 175–177). Or as a woman (Indian woman) you may resist the assumptions by the prime minister quoted above, that the role of women is to marry men and become daughters-in-law.

Resisting reading/subject positions entails challenging the beliefs, assumptions and authority figures of one's community. If one refuses to wear make-up as resistance to the kind of femininity constructed by magazines, this might alienate your peers. Or if you idealistically resist, for example, the worship of economic growth and consumer capitalism then this might spoil friendships with those whose major leisure activity is shopping, and put one out of step with the rest of the community. Only by subsequently joining a sub-culture which to some extent shares one's ideological position could one maintain enough sense of belonging to remain mentally healthy.

ACTIVITY 45

Please refer to the companion website for the activity material.

5.4 SUMMARY

In this chapter we explored the notion that texts create subject positions for readers and writers. We discovered that:

- the position created for readers will depend upon the kinds of speech acts we, as writers, perform on them;
- how polite we are affects the subject positioning of our readers. For directives which are costly to the unfamiliar reader, we will have to use indirect speech acts in order to be polite. In speech act sequences we will avoid dispreferred seconds;
- reading positions can be learnt or resisted. Learning them confers community membership, and resisting them excludes us.

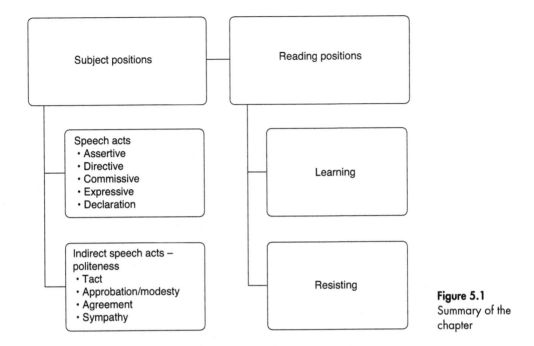

Figure 5.1
Summary of the chapter

FURTHER READING

Please refer to the companion website for the list of further reading.

6 INTERTEXTUALITY

The aim of this chapter
- to survey the various ways of representing another's text in one's own;
- to show how the deriving of one text from another gives scope for "bias" in news reporting;
- to illustrate how the meanings and purposes of texts depend on the previous texts they are reacting to, for example in parody.

Contents

6.0 Introduction: textual interaction
points out the importance of intertextuality for genre and in the inferencing process.

6.1 Meaning and social interaction
introduces the idea that the vocabulary and grammar of a language are a product of and reflect past social interaction.

6.2 Multiple voices in texts and genre-mixing
indicates how texts are not homogeneous but are often compounds of different text types, involving multiple voices.

6.3 The discourse of the other and reporting speech
details the different modes of representing another's speech, and linguistic criteria for recognising them, showing how bias can be introduced in this representation.

6.4 The news-making process as an example of intertextual chains
shows how news production depends on transmitting texts through a long series of readers and writers, with scope for distortion and changes to the original text.

6.5 Replies and reactions

illustrates how meanings depend upon which texts are being reacted to, or which previous texts supply the background knowledge against which the present text is interpreted.

6.6 Parody

explores the relationship between intertextuality and parody, and uses parody to underline the importance of attitude and purpose for making sense of texts.

Project 2

The second suggested project is a letter to a newspaper editor in which you explore your resistance and reaction to a text from that paper.

6.0 INTRODUCTION: TEXTUAL INTERACTION

This final unit of Part B is a discussion of **intertextuality**. Intertextuality simply means the way in which one text impinges on other later texts, or, to put it another way, how texts feed off and relate to each other.

But Charles Bazerman (2003) has made useful distinctions among the different levels and techniques of intertextuality. (1) One can quote or report a text as an authority, as a source of meanings to be taken at face value, when, for example repeating a law or a proverb. (2) You may report in order to dramatise an argument, by explicitly invoking conflicting views on an issue, for example opposing views on abortion. (3) You may explicitly use other statements as background, support or contrast, as when you explain a concept by referring to an encyclopaedia entry. More implicitly, texts may (4) simply rely on common beliefs, ideas or generally circulated statements or opinions. Sometimes these will just be common knowledge – e.g. that the Earth goes round the sun, or that adolescence can be a difficult transition period in life. At other times they may be controversial but still assumed or presupposed – that competition is necessary to enhance efficiency in industry. (5) You may use specific styles or genres and the subject positions or voices associated with those genres. (6) By using any words or grammatical structures of a language you are relying on language you have acquired through the experience of hearing or reading previous texts in that language (Bazerman 2003: 86–88).

We can see how these six categories might relate to the content of the first five chapters of this book. First, intertextuality type (4) is an aspect of the inferencing we discussed in Chapter 4. The "background" or "factual" knowledge, the assumptions and schemas which we bring to texts in order to infer meanings, are largely derived from other texts. Second, intertextuality type (5) relates to genre (Chapter 1) because it is through encountering examples of different texts in different social situations that we perceive typical text patterns and build up a mental model of the discourse structure of different genres. Within these genres or discourse types there will also be typical subject positions for readers and writers (Chapter 5). Third, intertextuality type (6) relates to the language system (Chapters 1, 2 and 3), the vocabulary and grammar used for expressing textual, ideational and interpersonal meanings. So we have already, though under other headings and labels, discussed aspects of intertextuality types (4), (5) and (6). This chapter will therefore emphasise the more explicit types of intertextuality (1), (2) and (3). But before doing so it is worth making a few more points about intertextuality (6) and (5).

6.1 MEANING AND SOCIAL INTERACTION

Type (6) claims there is a relationship between intertextuality and the vocabulary and grammar of a language. One important insight of the Russian linguist Bakhtin is that the meaning of words and grammar cannot be discussed in the abstract, since it is only achieved in the cut and thrust of dialogue, as part of social interaction:

> Meaning does not reside in the word or in the soul of the speaker or in the soul of the listener. Meaning is the effect of interaction between listener and speaker.... It is like an electric spark that occurs only when two different terminals are hooked together.... Only the current of verbal intercourse endows a word with the light of meaning.
>
> (Volosinov/Bakhtin 1973: 102–103)

Because words and their meanings emerge out of interaction they will always carry the traces of their past uses and evaluations by previous speakers. Language is therefore never "in one's own words", but other people's words: 'the trouble with words is that you don't know whose mouth they've been in'. The reason this is a "trouble" is that they will also carry with them the ideological imprint of their previous uses, which is why words and meanings are sometimes contested (Chapter 3, p. 103). They will also bear a cultural imprint, as the linguistic relativity theory of Whorf stresses.

6.2 MULTIPLE VOICES IN TEXTS AND GENRE-MIXING

We have already seen (Section 5.0) that it is rare for a text or genre to demand only one single subject position or voice for the reader or writer. Mary Talbot, in 'The construction of gender in a teenage magazine' took an article on lipstick and identified a multiplicity of voices: friend, interviewer, historian, advertiser, market researcher and facilitator (Talbot 1992). In the Sumo advertisement (Activity 45) you probably noted that the small print at the end of the form read more like a legal text, in contrast with the conversational features of the recommendation section.

Bakhtin saw the multiplicity of voices and positions in texts as valuable. He claimed that in the best novels, for example Dostoyevsky's, when the character/author makes an utterance or has an idea he is always replying or holding a dialogue, either with an imagined person he disagrees with, or with his other self, as well, of course, as when there is real dialogue between characters. Such diglossic (two-voiced) or **heteroglossic** (many-voiced) texts are preferable to the **monoglossic** (single-voiced). Monoglossic texts, which attempt to suppress dialogue, are often authoritarian and employed by totalitarian governments.

The multiplicity of voices and positions in texts is often a symptom of how one text type, discourse type or genre has colonised others. Fairclough has shown that conversational styles have colonised advertisements as an aspect of synthetic personalisation, as we saw in the Tacoma advert (pp. 96–97) with its imitation of the omissions and minor sentences of conversation. And, in turn, bureaucratic texts, like forms, have taken over some of the features of advertisements in order to become more reader-friendly (Fairclough 2001: 163ff.). Sometimes, indeed, the ambiguity of genre and voice may be taken even further; an advertiser may attempt to fool us by presenting an ad in the generic style of a news article or scientific report.

ACTIVITY 46

Please refer to the companion website for the activity material.

6.3 THE DISCOURSE OF THE OTHER AND REPORTING SPEECH

The most obvious way in which more than one voice can be overtly introduced into a text is through the reporting of speech. The reporting text and the reported text belong to different voices. Briefly speaking, the choices we have for representing speech are as in Table 6.1 (cf. Leech and Short 1973).

Table 6.1 *Ways of reporting speech*

Mode of representation	Example	Defining features
Free direct speech	'I will come tomorrow.'	Words actually spoken. No reporting clause.
Direct speech	John said, 'I will come tomorrow.'	Words actually spoken. Reporting clause.
Free indirect speech	*He would* come/go tomorrow/*the next day.*	Most of the words actually spoken, but some or all time, place and person shifters change. No reporting clause.
Indirect speech	John said *he would go the next day.*	Most of the words actually spoken but all time, place and person shifters change. Reporting clause.
Narrative report of speech act	*Mr J. Phillips indicated his intention of arriving on 21st November.*	Does not include most of the words actually spoken.

Note
Italic type indicates changes to words spoken.

The technical term *shifter*, used in the third column, needs some explanation. Some words will change their meaning according to who uttered them, when and where. For example, *I*, *here* and *now* mean something different if Barack Obama utters them in Detroit on 12 November 2015 at 4p.m., from what they would mean if Tony Abbot uttered them in Jakarta on 15 June 2013 at midnight. When indirect forms of speech representation are used these shifters change; for example, the *I* of direct speech becomes *he/she* in indirect, *you* becomes *he/she/they*, *we* becomes *they*, *here* becomes *there*, *now* becomes *then* and present tenses shift to past tenses.

As we move down column 2 we can see that the words are changed more and more from the original actual utterance. We can see this change in terms of the reporter's voice becoming more dominant than the original speaker's voice. Narrative report of speech act (NRSA) entirely obliterates the voice of the speaker.

We can relate these speech representation choices to questions of ideology and power in the press. Research into the language of news has shown that the more elite or powerful the speaker, the more likely that their speech will be represented verbatim (Glasgow University Media Group 1980: 163). Less powerful sayers are likely to have their actual words interfered with to a greater extent by being reported indirectly or paraphrased in NRSA form.

In addition, there is also less interference by the reporting voice in the case of free modes, where there is no reporting clause. A reporting clause allows the reporting voice to interpret, to give a speech act label to the speaker's utterance, e.g. *she complained, they confessed, he promised.*

ACTIVITY 47

Please refer to the companion website for the activity material.

The author's "interference" may not matter much in fiction, since, after all, it is made up by the writer. But when such interfering reporting clauses are used in newspapers and magazines to label and describe speech, this is capable of slanting the reader's interpretation, and is an aspect of the conferring of reality that we explored in Chapter 2. Several researchers have found that in stories about strikes or arguments between the US and Russian governments, verbs like *claim* were used for reporting the sayings of unions or the Russian government, in contrast with the neutral *say* for management and the US government. Unions and Russia were thereby represented as less credible than their antagonists (Glasgow University Media Group 1980: 184; Geis 1987; Short 1988).

Consider the following report of various Indian politicians' reaction to a doctors' strike:

> Meanwhile, political parties tried to make most of the opportunity. RLD leader Munna Singh Chauhan urged the UP government to shun its adamant attitude in public interest and resolve the crisis at the earliest. Congress leader Rita Bahuguna Joshi demanded that the inquiry in the case should be conducted by a retired high court judge. She also condemned the highhandedness of police in this case. Samajwadi Party leader Naresh Agarwal on the other hand saw a political conspiracy behind the doctors' strike. Accusing the opposition for extracting political benefits out of the crisis situation, he appealed the doctors to call off strike. "I think that there is some political conspiracy behind the strike because of the election season as opposition parties is making full utilisation of the situation," said Agarwal.

Only the words of the last speaker reported, Naresh Agarwal, are in direct speech. This means less interference and interpretation by the reporter compared with the narrative report of the speech acts of the other politicians. It also seems to give more presence, importance and legitimacy to Agarwal's voice and opinions, which are critical of the doctors.

Just as bad as interference and distorting the views of the second voice is plagiarism. This arises when you pretend to speak in your own voice but are really borrowing the voice of another, without acknowledging it. In one sense, of course, we can never speak entirely in our own words (Kress 1985: 49) since words, in order to be intelligible, have to be shared by a language community, but stealing text from another is an extreme appropriation. Most universities give advice and help to students on the different conventions for citations and references as a way of educating them to avoid plagiarism (e.g. http://library.dmu.ac.uk/Support/Heat/index.php?page=475).

6.4 INTERTEXTUAL CHAINS, THE INTERNET AND NEWS REPORTING

The texts we end up with often reflect a multiplicity of voices simply because they are the products of **intertextual chains**. Intertextual chains are probably more frequent than they used to be because modern technology has enhanced our ability to cut and paste and to access sources easily on the internet. E.M. Forster, whose prophetic short story *The Machine Stops* already at the beginning of the twentieth century imagines a world entirely dependent on the internet, also anticipates the way knowledge increasingly comes to us intertextually at second-hand:

> "Beware of first-hand ideas!" exclaimed one of the most advanced of [the lecturers]. "First-hand ideas do not really exist. They are but the physical impressions produced by love and fear, and on this gross foundation who could erect a philosophy? Let your ideas be second-hand, and if possible tenth-hand, for then they will be far removed from that disturbing element – direct observation. Do not learn anything about this subject of mine – the French Revolution. Learn instead what I think that Enicharmon thought Urizen thought Gutch thought Ho-Yung thought Chi-Bo-Sing thought LafcadioHearn thought Carlyle thought Mirabeau said about the French Revolution. Through the medium of these ten great minds, the blood that was shed at Paris and the windows that were broken at Versailles will be clarified to an idea which you may employ most profitably in your daily lives.
> (retrieved 26 July 2015 from http://archive.ncsa.illinois.edu/prajlich/forster.html)

Wikipedia is obviously a product of intertextuality. It is very difficult to know who the authors of such a text might be, as the texts can be subject to multiple edits, revisions, rejections and rewritings. It also demands citations as authority for statements in the articles, an insistence on intertextuality.

However, even traditional newspapers exemplify intertextual chains. The news article 'Big Sur wildfire destroys 15 homes and 500 acres of national forest' from Chapter 1 (p. 27) illustrates this point clearly enough. If we look at the last sentence and consider 'The Red Cross has set up an over-night shelter for people who have been displaced by the fire' we can trace the intertextual path by which this idea reaches the reader. Presumably a member of the Red Cross conveyed this fact to Madsen, who in turn communicated it to reporters from Associated Press, and similarly the news agency made it available to the *Guardian*, whose editorial team were responsible for the shape of the report as it appeared in the newspaper.

Red Cross → Madsen, forest spokesman → Associated Press [X → Y → Z...] → *Guardian* editorial team [A → B → C...] → reader

Even a direct quotation like this might well be transformed in the process of transfer. There is enormous scope for distortion by selection, omission and rewriting within such an intertextual chain, especially since, with tight time deadlines, the last person in the chain has little chance of checking for reliability with the initiator of the chain. Intertextuality and tight deadlines are two of the factors contributing to the kinds of factual misrepresentation illustrated by the story of the neighbour's dog and the taxi driver recounted earlier (Chapter 5, p. 151).

In fact, the chain we traced out considerably underestimates the number of links in the transmission process. The news team will include at least the journalist, the chief reporter, the news editor and various sub-editors. All these can make changes to the original report. Where international news is concerned, news agencies are also likely to pass the reports through quite complex internal chains of communications – their regional bureau, their central bureau, the bureau in the receiving country – even before they are received by the paper (Bell 1991: 44–50).

Sometimes in news reports it is not quite clear whose voice is being reported. It seems relatively common for an editor to save space by deleting the reporting clause, as in this example from Bell (1991: 71), date-lined Tel Aviv:

| An Israeli military force has crossed the border, an Army spokesman announced here, Agence France Presse reported. | → An Israeli military force has crossed the border. |

The minimal interference of the free form and the failure to identify the speaker blur the distinction between the newspaper's voice and the Army's voice. Another trick is for newspapers to use a sort of direct speech form without quotation marks and with the reporting clause at the end. Consider the last sentence of the Big Sur fire article again: 'The Red Cross has set up an overnight shelter for people who have been displaced by the fire, Madsen said'. The longer the verbiage the more ambiguous the kind of speech representation:

> ELECTRONIC road-pricing is starting a month early on the Central Expressway, not to generate extra income for the government, but to ensure a smooth extension of the system in September, Parliamentary Secretary (Communications) Yaacob Ibrahim said yesterday.
>
> (*Straits Times*, 20 July 1998: 1)

This, at least initially, as though it were a free form, blurs the distinction between the voice of the paper and the voice of the government, not surprising in Singapore, where the *Straits Times* is a government mouthpiece in any case.

Whose voices, then, get reported in the newspapers?

 ## ACTIVITY 48 ━━━━━━━━━━━━━━━━━━━━━━━━━━━

Please refer to the companion website for the activity material.

6.5 REPLIES AND REACTIONS

The general public's voices are not very prominent in news discourse. Of course, we may be free to react or reply to the voices of the media and the voices of the powerful, rich and famous reported in the media, though we seldom have the same degree of access to media as they do. Even if we did, through an online comment/blog or a letter to the newspaper, it is the originating voice which sets the agenda and makes various presuppositions which may be difficult to challenge.

We have already had an example of this specific kind of intertextuality, a reply or reaction to a previous text, in the letter about burglaries in Chip Bee Gardens, and the police reply (p. 128). That pair of texts showed that the meaning of a text often depends upon whether it is reacting to an intertextual context, and, if it is, what this context might be. More precisely, a preceding text will evoke schemas which we use to interpret or draw inferences from the second text.

 ## ACTIVITY 49 ━━━━━━━━━━━━━━━━━━━━━━━━━━━

Please refer to the companion website for the activity material.

Creative literature can also react against previous specific texts. As a secondary school student you may well have read Golding's *Lord of the Flies*. This book can be read as a reaction to the "normal" Christian imperialist ideology inherent in *Robinson Crusoe*, *Swiss Family Robinson* and, especially, *A Coral Island*, where white boys or men subdue evil black natives. In *Lord of the Flies*, by contrast, the Christian white boys rapidly degenerate into savages, the most religious of them, the choirboys, degenerating the quickest.

One further insight of Bakhtin's is that, even when we are not obviously reacting to a previous text, any utterance we make is in fact a reaction or a reply: we are writing as though an imaginary dialogue is taking place, and the imaginary reader is looking over our shoulder.

6.6 PARODY

Parody is a particularly interesting kind of intertextuality. The simplest form of parody is achieved by imitating the expression or style of a well-known text, author or genre and substituting an inappropriate style or content. You might, for example, take the content of a hairdresser's questions to a customer, and rewrite this in the style of a judge talking to a defendant: 'I put it to you that when you should have been washing your hair in anti-dandruff shampoo last night, you were in fact sitting in front of your computer all evening, is that not so? Do you plead guilty or not guilty of having dandruff?' What distinguishes parody from the text being parodied is obviously propositional attitude – the writer of a parody does not seriously believe what she is writing, and the propositional attitude might range from light-hearted fun to scorn or disgust.

Back in the 1960s and 1970s there was a TV advertisement jingle that went:

```
x  /x x  /  x      /x  /
A million housewives every day
```

```
/   x x  /  x  /   x   /
Pick up a can of beans and say:
```

```
    /   /     /
Beanz Meanz Heinz
```
               (see www.youtube.com/watch?v=RGhWcPRHMAI)

The following parody of this imitates the expression and style of the original very closely. The rhythm is identical. And the only substitutions are 'students' for 'housewives', 'put down' for 'pick up', 'spraypaint' for 'of beans', and 'D' for 'B', 'F' for 'H' in the last line.

```
x  /x x  /  x   /x  /
A million students every day
```

```
/  x    x  /  x    /  x  /
Put down a spraypaint can and say:
```

```
    /   /   /
Deanz Meanz Finez
```

The exact nature of the substituted content in parody is quite interesting. In the jingle above, a whole different schema is evoked: students being dissuaded from spray-painting graffiti by the threat of fines from the disciplinary figure of the Dean, rather than housewives deciding to buy tins of Heinz baked beans. But we should also note that the content is at one point reversed where *pick up* is replaced by its opposite, *put down*.

Sometimes it may be difficult to decide whether a piece of writing is serious or is intended as a parody. The letter to the editor below 'Reading between the railway lines' (*Independent*, 29 May 1995: 14) writes about the Thomas the Tank Engine books (substituted content) as though they are a moral and religious text.

Parodies are likely to misfire, of course, if the text or style being parodied is not recognised by the reader. Without explanation I don't suppose many readers understood the parody of the Heinz advertisement. This reinforces two points we made earlier: (1) a writer needs to correctly estimate the knowledge that readers can bring to the text being written; (2) the originating text in any kind of intertextuality – quotation, reaction or parody – must represent a powerful voice, one which is important enough to be worth quoting or famous enough to be recognised by the readership. Parody, although apparently a humorous putting down of the powerful and their texts, in fact pays them homage.

Reading between the Railway Lines

From Mr Barney Jeffries

(1) Sir: I feel I must reply to your attack on my hero Thomas the Tank Engine. As one who has read and re-read the stories many times, I hope I will be able to put you straight on a few points.

This opening sentence refers to the text to which the letter is replying. Often such reference is more explicit – see letter openings on p. 148. Note the presupposition carried by the nominalisation *attack*. The writer also announces what he is about to do, useful in a long letter.

(2) You suggest that the morality which Thomas and friends offer is nothing more than Old Testament retribution. In fact, the message is that if you say you are sorry, you will be given "another chance" (and probably end up pulling the special train). This surely represents a New Testament ethic of a loving Fat Controller who forgives all them who truly repent. And there are plenty of rewards for being good: a new coat of paint, a chance to pull the express or, the accolade, a branch line all to yourself.

The second paragraph has a kind of unequal balance structure, hinging around the *in fact* where the original text's position is stated first and then demolished. The low certainty verb *suggest* is outweighed by the modal devices of high certainty *in fact* and *surely*. Notice the lexical contrasts 'Old' v. 'New Testament', and 'retribution' v. 'reward'.

(3) The Fat Controller is not some distant, unapproachable ruler. He listens to the petitions of the engines (see Thomas and Gordon's alliance in *Gordon the Big Engine* and Percy's deputation in *The Twin Engines*).

(4) The books also make us re-examine our prejudices; the likes of Daisy and Boo show that diesels are not all bad, and "sinners" can often prove to be heroes.

(5) I can't agree with Thomas Sutcliffe's assertion that "there's no altruism here". Throughout the books, Thomas and friends continually work for the greater good of mankind (or, alternatively, enginekind). Often, the Fat Controller knows nothing of these deeds as the engines, being blessed with free-will make their own decisions. A good example of this is Douglas's heroic rescue of Oliver in *Enterprising Engines*.

(6) The value system nurtured in my impressionable mind (as a child born the year before Mrs Thatcher came to power) was obviously different from Mr Suttcliffe's son's. My favourite engine was always Toby the Tram Engine, perfectly content with his one faithful coach, Henrietta, rather than proud possessors of many coaches like Gordon and Henry. Blessed are the meek for they shall inherit their own stretch of branch line.

(7) Personally, I would like to wish Thomas and his friends a very happy 50th birthday, and best wishes for the next half century.

Yours faithfully,
BARNEY JEFFRIES
West Grinstead
Wiltshire

A new paragraph (3) for the second point, which concerns the Fat Controller. This paragraph gives specific evidence for the point stated in its first sentence.

Paragraphs 3–5 are deductive in structure, moving from the general to the specific.

(5): The writer restates his position on Sutcliffe's views.
A bit of humour lightens the interpersonal tone.

The themes of (5) are carefully chosen to underline the move from the general to the specific 'throughout the books', 'often' and 'a good example'

In (6) there is a telling presupposition that (story books) nurture value systems in impressionable minds; without such a belief this letter and the article which provokes it would be pointless or lack seriousness. There is a humorous inference that anyone born before Thatcher came to power is less likely to have a proud and competitive value system.

Paragraphs (6) and (7) are the most personal: (2)–(5) hardly mention the writer, but (7) climaxes in a personal birthday greeting.

The existence of parody is very clear evidence, too, that meanings cannot simply be decoded from a text, and that very often texts have to be interpreted according to the purpose and attitude of the writer, before we can go on to any ideological explanation. Parody is evidence for the importance of factoring in purpose and attitude, because on the decodable surface it is almost identical to the source text or genre. However, having humour as its main aim, it is by definition quite different in purpose and propositional attitude from the genre it imitates. In other words, parody highlights the difference between Critical Linguistics and Critical Discourse Analysis, Parts A and B of this book.

 ACTIVITY 50 ▬▬▬▬▬▬▬▬▬▬▬▬▬▬▬▬▬▬▬▬▬▬

Please refer to the companion website for the activity material.

6.7 SUMMARY

In this unit we considered how:
- writers can make texts heterogeneous in terms of genre and subject positions;
- writers can introduce another voice into texts by the representation of speech, and to varying degrees merge it with their own, though always preserving and acknowledging the distinct voices in academic writing;
- journalists and other writers might distort their representation of the world due to the long intertextual chains both in the process of news reporting and in using texts from the internet;
- writers can exploit intertextuality for humorous purposes in parody;
- language and discourse is fundamentally intertextual.

 PROJECT 2 ▬▬▬▬▬▬▬▬▬▬▬▬▬▬▬▬▬▬▬▬▬▬▬

Please refer to the companion website for the activity material.

6.8 SUMMARY OF PART B

This unit brings us to the end of Part B of the text, which has been concerned with the level of interpretation in Table 0.1. It is worth recapping and drawing together the main gists of this part and showing how they relate to earlier sections.

We'd like to stress once again the importance of taking into account the ideal reader when one is writing. We can sum this up in a number of questions:

- How much knowledge can we presuppose – what schematic resources does the reader have?
- How much acquaintance has the reader with figures like metaphor and irony, and will these misfire?
- What kinds of opinions do we suspect in the ideal reader? What might cause offence? What might be for him contested terms? What kinds of presuppositional smuggling can we get away with?
- What kind of subject position is going to be most effective in communicating with him, based on our degrees of contact, power and emotion?

And, of course, if we are planning to be teachers and expect our students to write in various genres, we might well ask ourselves the question:

- How much knowledge do students have of the discourse structure of the genres we require?

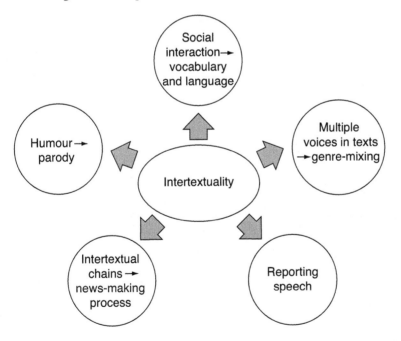

Figure 6.1
Summary of the chapter

FURTHER READING

Please refer to the companion website for the list of further reading.

PART C

THE AUTHORITY AND POWER BEHIND DISCOURSE AND RESISTING IT

The first two parts of this textbook started with language, text and interpretation and moved towards ideological explanation. This part moves in an opposite direction, outlining and critiquing various ideological positions and their related crises and showing how they underlie discourse. The underlying ideological positions and their crises relate to:

- the power of global capital and the crisis of inequality (Chapter 7)
- the dominance of powerful political, ethnic and economic elites and the crisis of democracy (Chapter 8)
- the authority of the scientific expert and the crisis of the environment (Chapter 9).

Some of the texts we analyse reproduce or reinforce these ideologies; for example in Chapter 7 we consider consumer advertising of global corporations, and in Chapter 8 media news reports. However, other texts have a more complex relation to power structures and current crises. Unlike media and advertising texts, which reinforce the ideology and help create the crisis, the texts of the environmental expert draw attention to the crisis, and may critique the economic system which has created it. We therefore explore how texts can counter political and economic power structures. So, in Chapter 8 we consider news blogs, where readers are invited to respond to and possibly resist news stories or comment/editorial columns in online newspapers, and the alternative communication networks of social media. In Chapter 9 we not only analyse the text of the environmental expert, but also the ways "nature" poetry can use grammar to resist the exploitation of the environment.

Chapter 10, concentrating on fiction and comedy, puts the most emphasis on resistance and writing back against power. How do the humorous texts of popular culture contest the discourses of authority? And how does reactive fiction – fan fiction – through parody and other kinds of intertextuality, subvert the power and ideology of the original text?

These four chapters link with the companion website with its suggestions for projects – publicity material for an organisation to which you
belong (7), and a news report for a student newspaper or a blog reacting
to the news (8), and a subversive fictional or comic text (10).

Using this part

There are various ways teachers and students can use Part C. You can
simply read straight through the analysis and commentary in these chapters. However, it would be better to read with the projects in mind and
to use the analysis, which revises Parts A and B, to inform the decisions when composing the text for the projects. More useful still would
be to examine and respond to some of the texts analysed before reading our detailed analysis, encourage more interaction and engagement.
For example, in Chapter 7 you might read Sections 7.1 to 7.7, and then
analyse some or all of the four texts in Sections 7.8–7.11 for yourselves
before reading (and hopefully resisting) our sometimes polemical and
ideologically positioned analysis.

Alternatively, Part C could be read more selectively, according to student interest. Or one could home in on parts of a chapter's analysis, for
example, visuals and implicature in some of the ads in Chapter 7, transitivity analysis in Chapter 9 and narrative analysis in Chapter 10. This
would give practice in applying the important concepts and analytical
procedures introduced in Parts A and B, without necessarily following all
aspects of analysis.

ADS, CONSUMER CAPITALISM AND THE CRISIS OF INEQUALITY

7

This ideological analysis is followed by four case studies:

7.8 The car, the individual and the road to success
An Opel Vectra ad.

7.9 A match for the jet set and the good Chinese wife
An ad for Emirates Airlines.

7.10 Unnecessary words and welcoming in style?
An ad for Sheraton hotels.

7.11 Global products, problems and production
The "Bablet" (iPad) webpage.

Project 3
Writing promotional or publicity material commissioned by a club, society, institution or company with which you are associated.

7.0 INTRODUCTION: CONSUMER CAPITALISM AND ITS PRESENT CRISIS

Roughly speaking, the last 250 years in Europe are a radical break with all the preceding historic and prehistoric ages. This is because technological advances of the Industrial Revolution allowed the mass production of manufactured goods and their quick and widespread distribution through transport systems like the railways. Later, from the 1920s onwards, capitalist manufacturing industry became organised around highly mechanised production lines such as the car-assembly plants of Henry Ford. Because this "Fordist" system involved a great deal of capital investment, its products had to be consumed *en masse*. The last 70 years represent another important and distinctive "post-Fordist" period. The development of electronic mass media, of radio, TV, etc. facilitated widespread advertising, so that most of the population could be targeted as potential consumers. These were the technological circumstances which enabled the development of modern consumer capitalism.

Current consumer capitalist economic models of growth operate as follows. To increase wealth, economies and their industries must produce more. And to sell more goods and services more people need persuading to buy them. In this, advertising plays such a crucial role. Since the advent of transnational corporations, market researchers have recognised or created new modes of consumption; the market has been fragmented into numerous specialised niches according to income level, age, household type and locality.

Simultaneous with this fragmentation of the market has been the break-up of mass culture. Instead of the two TV channels of the 1960s in the UK, and papers like the *Saturday Evening Post* in the USA, providing a common media experience, we have the diversity of cable and satellite TV, videos, the internet and many specialised magazines and websites (which record visits and recommend similar sites, reinforcing fragmentation). The rather conservative British foods of the 1950s have been replaced with a diversity of cuisines – Chinese, Italian, Indian, Greek, Turkish, Thai, Mexican, West Indian and vegetarian. Leisure and religion, too, have diversified, with exotic and eccentric options like tai chi, kung fu, judo, karate, taekwondo, Buddhism, Zen, Islam, Sufism, Hinduism, Scientology, Rastafarianism, Satanism, witchcraft and more (Faigley 1992: 12). In this fragmented culture the modern person has a bewildering choice of lifestyle and identity, a position, as we shall see, advertisers exploit (Sections 7.5, 7.6). Truth and being true to oneself has become a commodity, a consumer choice. How significant is the metaphor *I don't buy that* to mean 'I don't believe that'!

"Choice", in fact, lies at the heart of consumerism, especially when we shop for leisure, not necessity. For it is in leisure that the modern urban population, especially the young, find freedom of choice. Work, and to some extent family, represent authority and discipline and various kinds of coercion and responsibility. But as consumers in our leisure time we seem relatively free (MacRobbie 1991: 86, 88).

While society and the media have become locally fragmented, globalisation has intensified. Capitalism has embraced globalisation, seeking out locations for production where the costs are lower because of low wages and weak labour and environmental regulations, to maximise returns for investors and shareholders.

There are many downsides to this obsession with economic growth and consumer capitalist overproduction. Chapter 9 takes an ecological perspective on this system of increasing production and consumption, and critiques the outdated Newtonian worldview behind the Industrial Revolution. But, even superficially, it is obvious that manufacturing industry uses up non-renewable resources, and that broken or outmoded consumer goods create problems of waste-disposal in a finite environment. Very often obsolescence is deliberately built into these products: the technology is available to make them last much longer, but technological advance is ignored in favour of profits. The clothing industry unashamedly creates the concept of fashion, making last year's clothes psychologically obsolete, even though they may not be worn out.

Further downsides more relevant to this chapter are increases in inequality and in private debt (Figure 7.1; Table 7.1). These put into crisis the consumer capitalist system which created them: it seems on the verge of self-destruction. At the top of the pyramid (Figure 7.1) the

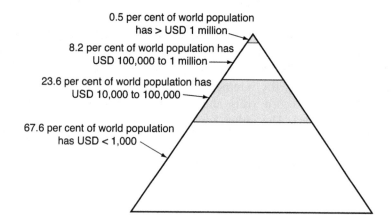

Figure 7.1
The global wealth pyramid (data from Credit Suisse Global Wealth Databook 2011)

0.5 per cent of world population has > USD 1 million

8.2 per cent of world population has USD 100,000 to 1 million

23.6 per cent of world population has USD 10,000 to 100,000

67.6 per cent of world population has USD < 1,000

Table 7.1 Trends in real household income by income group, mid-1980s to late 2000s (average annual change in percentages)

	Total population	Bottom 10 per cent	Top 10 per cent
Australia	3.6	3.0	4.5
Austria	1.3	0.6	1.1
Belgium	1.1	1.7	1.2
Canada	1.1	0.9	1.6
Chile	1.7	2.4	1.2
Czech Republic	2.7	1.8	3.0
Denmark	1.0	0.7	1.5
Finland	1.7	1.2	2.5
France	1.2	1.6	1.3
Germany	0.9	0.1	1.6
Greece	2.1	3.4	1.8
Hungary	0.6	0.4	0.6
Ireland	3.6	3.9	2.5
Italy	0.8	0.2	1.1
Japan	0.3	−0.5	0.3
Luxembourg	2.2	1.5	2.9
Mexico	1.4	0.8	1.7
Netherlands	1.4	0.5	1.6
New Zealand	1.5	1.1	2.5
Norway	2.3	1.4	2.7
Portugal	2.0	3.6	1.1
Spain	3.1	3.9	2.5
Sweden	1.8	0.4	2.4
Turkey	0.5	0.8	0.1
United Kingdom	2.1	0.9	2.5
United States	0.9	0.1	1.5
OECD27	1.7	1.3	1.9

Note
Income refers to disposable household income, corrected for household size and deflated by the consumer price index (CPI). Average annual changes are generally calculated over the period from 1985 to 2008.

wealthiest 29.7 million people, 0.5 per cent of the world's population, own 38.5 per cent of the world's wealth. At the bottom, by contrast, the poorest 3,054 million, 67.6 per cent of the world's population, own 3.3 per cent of the world's wealth!

Is the distribution of wealth becoming more equal or not? Table 7.1 shows the 25-year trends in real household income in 26 countries of the OECD (Organisation for Economic Co-operation and Development). It compares the total growth in income with the growth for the 10 per cent lowest income group and the 10 per cent highest income group. In only 8 of the 26 countries, in bold, has the income of the bottom 10 per cent grown faster than the income of the top 10 per cent.

As the mass of the population enjoy a relatively small share of increases in disposable income, they cannot afford the consumer goods which are brought to the market by producers. In order to assure consumption of this overproduction of goods the system has increasingly relied on credit.

Figure 7.2 shows alarmingly increasing levels of debt in the UK, Spain, South Korea and France over the 20 years from 1990 to 2008, levels which helped precipitate the financial crisis.

US personal debt rose sharply between 2000 and 2008 The percentage of debt to PDI (personal disposable income) was 90 per cent in 2000 and rose to 130 per cent in 2008. It began to fall equally sharply after the 2008 crisis but was still at unsustainable levels of around 105 per cent in 2013.

Total UK debt rose by a staggering 250 per cent from 1987 to 2011. It has levelled off since 2009, but the reduction in household debt has been accompanied by recession. This suggests that increased debt is essential for economic growth in the USA and UK.

The 2008 financial crisis was a symptom of the crisis brought about by inequality and debt. Credit had been extended recklessly to consumers,

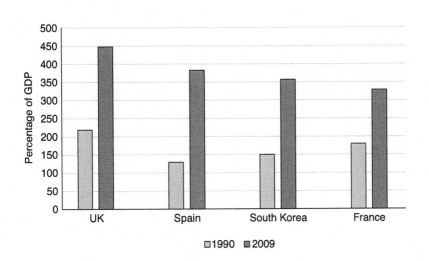

Figure 7.2
Increasing debt in mature economies 1990–2009 as a percentage of GDP (data sourced from Debt and Deleveraging at McKinsey)

especially property buyers in the USA, ignoring their credit risk, which resulted in the sub-prime mortgage crisis. Furthermore, even post-2008, the globalisation of capitalism has brought about increases in inequality, as capital becomes concentrated in the hands of fewer and fewer, the 1 per cent, and the wages of the middle classes and working classes fall behind inflation. Moreover, the average taxpayer has footed the bill for the bank bailouts. The result, which is a contradiction from the standpoint of consumer capitalism, is that growth and consumption is reduced, as potential consumers have less and less to spend. Advertising, can, then, be seen as a desperate attempt to revive a critically ill economic system.

7.1 DESIRE AND POWER

In this chapter we concentrate specifically on the kinds of ideological effects that consumer advertising has on society and the psychology of identity. First of all, in order to increase consumption, advertisers encourage human greed, envy and desire for power, even though most of the world's traditional religions and ethical systems regard these as antisocial, even evil. Consumers must be made to feel dissatisfied unless they buy a product or more of a particular product, whether they need it or not. If they needed it, the advertiser would not have to grab their attention, since the readership, as on eBay or Freecycle, would be assured. However, when luxury goods, like cars, become widespread society may arrange transport around their ownership, so that what once was a luxury becomes a necessity. In some places, like LA, life is very difficult without a car.

While buying a product directly satisfies (temporarily) the consumer's desires, the link between buying the product and attaining power or competitive advantage is less obvious. This is perhaps why, especially in a magazine like *Popular Science*, with a mainly male readership, ads appeal to the desire for power, usually to make money or to win the competitive race.

> Introducing the fraction of an inch that will put you miles ahead
> It's CompuServeCD. And it'll put you in the forefront of online technology, because of what it does and what it will let you do ...
> they'll start you down the road to where you've always wanted to be. Ahead.
> Compuserve
> The information service you won't outgrow.
>
> (p. 33)

> 7 surefire ways to be your own boss. If you want the final say ... if you want your name on the door ... if you want the profits that come from running your own business ... turn to the at-home training program that works: NRI

You Need the Edge. We deliver.
Every Edge product is covered by our famous lifetime guarantee.

(p. 45)

Slick 50 fuel system – more power to you.

(p. 35)

Notice how the last two examples transfer power from the product to the consumer, and how the Edge ad promises that the lifetime of the tools will match the lifetime of the consumer.

By buying powerful products we acquire power secondhand. We have already seen in Chapter 2, in our clause analysis of the X perm advertisement (Activity 20), that products are often represented as powerful actors. For instance, an Olympus camera which '**creates** impressive reproductions … **holding** as much as 80 images [sic] in its flash memory' (*Straits Times*, 20 August 1997: 27). When there might be doubts about the product's efficacy, as with skin cream, then its power as an actor over affecteds (your skin) tends to be stressed:

It [Bella] successfully **revives** your tired looking skin and **restores** it to its natural glow. At the same time it **minimizes** the look of lines and wrinkles on your complexion, **leaving** it totally refreshed and strikingly radiant.

(*Straits Times*, 20 August 1997: 29)

As in this case, what is claimed for the product is the power to solve a particular "problem", such as ageing skin.

7.2 BUYING AS PROBLEM SOLVING

Second, therefore, consumerism encourages the idea that buying a product solves problems. This idea can undermine the possibility of social organisation and political action. Imagine the following scenario. A jobless single mother, bringing up two small children in a public housing flat, suffers from headaches caused by stress. She might see advertisements for Panadol and treat her symptoms by buying and consuming it. Alternatively, she could attempt to remove the causes of the problem – contact other care-givers in the same position and organise a day-care centre, to give her and other parents a few hours respite from childcare. Consumerism favours the first alternative. Look at the average Beauty section in a teenage magazine to see to what extent readers are similarly encouraged to consume their way out of "problems" and "difficulties" with their appearance. And notice how many company slogans use the word "solutions".

One consequence of seeing products as solutions to problems is depersonalising or disempowering the consumer. Products, by being presented as achieving things that we cannot achieve, replace us. As Williamson illustrates:

> There is an ad for frozen vegetables which says 'Birds Eye peas will do anything to attract your husband's attention'. Presumably *you* would do anything to attract your husband's attention. A woman and a Birds Eye pea are made interchangeable. The peas represent what the woman can't do, they have the same aim: to make her husband notice something at dinner.
>
> (Williamson 1978: 38)

The problem–solution structure could be a basic template for many generic structures (Hoey 1973). Certainly it figures widely and obviously in many advertisements. This structure may be cued by the word *problem*:

> If you have a hair problem, visit Glower, a leading trichological centre.
>
> (*Straits Times*, 20 August 1993: 3)

or the word *solution*:

> Tailor made solutions available. (Give us your measurements) . . .
> So we take the responsibility of providing the most up to date communications solutions for voice, data and image, while you get on with what you do best.
>
> (*Asiaweek*, 14 February 1997: 11)

In other ads a negative state or state of mind is likely to be interpreted as problematic, even if the words *problem* or *solution* are not used.

> If you've been trying for a family and you haven't yet succeeded, don't worry, you're not alone. Every year at least 25,000 women try to get pregnant and fail. It doesn't mean there's anything wrong with them. It's usually just a case of bad timing. And that's when Discretest can be such a help.
>
> (*Good Housekeeping*, 8 May 1987: 10)

Maybe we invent problems. And perhaps, as Doris Lessing once suggested, some real problems have no solutions.

7.3 ACQUIRING QUALITIES

The third psychological effect of consumer advertising is to conflate the product with the consumer. Just as the power of the product gives power to the buyer, so, more generally, any positive attribute of the product is supposed to transfer itself to the possessor or their relationships.

Sometimes these qualities will be feelings or mental qualities, as if products have emotions: the shampoo Rejoice, or the slogan 'Happiness is a cigar called Hamlet' (Williamson 1978: 37). A particular favourite with advertisers is the word *intelligent*, as in 'Skyy vodka, the intelligent drink'. These slogans can only sensibly be interpreted as meaning "a cigar which gives you happiness" and "a drink for an intelligent drinker", even though spirits reduce the powers of reason.

Rolex and Breitling ads play an interesting variation on transfers of quality between product and consumer. Here, the stars – opera singers, sports celebrities, explorers – share qualities of reliability and excellence with the watch, if not imparting these qualities to the product they buy. The direction of transfer is perhaps beside the point – either way the quality of the star matches the quality of the watch:

> David Beckham. A global icon who insists on perfection. Precision and style. A legend forged by accomplishments. On his wrist is the Breitling Tranocean Chronograph Unitime, the ultimate traveler's watch.
>
> (www.coloribus.com/adsarchive/prints/breitling-watches-
> anthony-mandlers-breitling-watches-photo-shoot-with-
> david-beckham-16235005)

As far as the ordinary person in the street is concerned, the promised transfer will be from product to consumer. If a Rolex is a reliable watch then it might make you a reliable person. It is a small step from this to suggest that one's identity, character and worth depend less on what one is and more on what one has. Even in cities like London or Hong Kong, where having a car is not absolutely necessary for most people, many desire one, simply for status. Increasingly we are told we are only important if we are seen as the possessors of valuable property, and the more we own the more important we are.

The quality of a product can also be transferred to a relationship. A classic example is the series of De Beers ads with its slogan 'A diamond is forever' (www.debeers.com). If diamonds are indestructible and for-ever, then presumably the relationship with the person for whom one buys them will come close to being eternal too. Wedding rings prepare the ground for this slogan, as they are made of the most enduring metal, gold, and being a ring, have no end.

However, real human relations can often suffer from the advertisement-inspired drive to earn and consume more. Both partners go into full-time work in order, ironically enough, to buy labour-saving devices, in addition to houses, cars, home theatres, smart TVs, tablets, holidays. This earn-and-spend system may leave little time for interaction with children – except for our modern "quality time" – and creates the kinds of tensions between the roles of work, housework and care-giving which strain relationships and contribute to family break-up.

7.4 CHOOSING AN IDENTITY

Given the pace of change, the fragmentation of mass culture and the exploding numbers of possible lifestyles, modern individuals face an identity crisis. If advertisers can promise not only a product but an accompanying identity, then they have a very powerful strategy. As Lester Faigley puts it:

> The desire to consume is predicated on the lack of a stable identity. Purchasing and using a consumer object is a temporary and unstable attempt to occupy an imagined identity provoked by an image.
>
> (Faigley 1992: 13)

Some classes of advertisements – again Rolex/Breitling ads are good examples – exploit the fact that we achieve identity by identification, so the celebrity in the ad becomes a person to identify with. We'd all (?) like to be able to play football like David Beckham, enjoy his lifestyle, join his social set. Identity through shared product consumption can create a spurious social solidarity in the form of "consumer clubs" – the group of people who bought what you did (Williamson 1978: 45–47). The webpage http://minicooper.meetup.com will take you to a list of US Mini Cooper Meetup groups for 'local aficionados and lovers of the Mini Cooper automobile'. And the possession of a Samsung tablet rather than an iPad, or an Apple Mac rather than a PC, in some contexts, divides people along social lines. (When Apple announced to its loyalists its deal with Microsoft, the news was received as something like treachery: www.youtube.com/watch?v=WxOp5mBY9IY.) These clubs are a rather desperate antidote to the increasing anonymity of modern society.

Products therefore become a badge of membership. For example, the question 'Is your mum a Superfine mum?' asks whether the child's mother belongs to the group who use Superfine margarine. This ad simultaneously casts doubt on whether a mother can do her job really well, can be superfine, unless she has joined that club. A similar technique is used in the following, more extended ad:

IF THERE'S STILL A JAMAICAN BOBSLED TEAM, YOU'LL HAVE 350 CHANNELS TO FIND THEM

If you're a true sports buff, then get ready for a big change in your life. Or at least your weekends. Because with full-view satellite TV you get up to 350 glorious channels (including 100 radio). Which means you can watch virtually any football, basketball, hockey, or baseball game. And darn-near any other televised sporting event in the nation—even if it's the Mexican ping-pong team. With hundreds of program packages, intense laser disc quality picture and CD quality sound. Call 1-800-778-4900 now for the nearest authorised Full View TV dealer, a free brochure and free basic installation at participating dealers. Hey, if having 350 channels is a guy thing, it's the ultimate guy thing.

FULL VIEW TV

THE SATELLITE SYSTEM WITH THE BEST VIEW

(*Popular Science*, June 1995: 19)

Notice in particular the opening and closing lines 'if you're a true sports buff' and 'Hey, if having 350 channels is a guy thing, it's the ultimate guy thing', with their unashamed appeal to the product as a membership badge.

Both through the individual qualities they promise to impart to us, and through the social groups they associate us with, advertised products create illusory identities in our consumerist capitalist culture. The New Right in the USA and the UK see society simply as a collection of individuals, or at the most family units, responsible only to themselves rather than to society as a whole. These individuals compete against each other, and the most motivated and capable earn and spend more. In this antisocial society, identification and self-definition are achieved through levels and kinds of consumption (Faigley 1992: 49).

7.5 DISTINGUISHING YOURSELF: EXCLUSIVITY, UNIQUENESS, NEWNESS AND TRADITION

So we cannot allow ourselves to identify with all the other members of society as though we were uniform. To define ourselves as successful we must distinguish ourselves through the goods we consume. We need to feel special and superior since, after all, the goods we buy, often in fact very similar, are branded as *unique, unparalleled, special*, etc. This mind-set explains the exploitation of the consumer's snobbishness, as in the following, with its appeal to the exclusiveness of royalty:

EXCLUSIVELY FROM HARTMAN   Royal Club
The Ultimate
OUTDOOR LIFESTYLE
                           (*Good Housekeeping*, May 1987, p. 220)

A more euphemistic word for snobbery is *discrimination*: as in 'for discriminating chocolate lovers'. This concept suggests that, like the Rolex or Breitling superstars, we can match ourselves with the product, rather than simply deriving qualities from it – for instance: 'If you take pride in your handiwork, we think you'll appreciate the effort we put into ours.'

There is, of course, a startling paradox in pretending that products are exclusive, since they are mass-produced and ads are designed to increase the number of buyers, thereby making them less exclusive! So sometimes the appeal to exclusivity, taste and discrimination is social rather than individualistic, as in this Wedgwood ad, where the buyer is encouraged to start a little consumer club to reinforce existing friendships:

For richer for pourer. Wedgwood. If you can appreciate the finer things in life, you'll want your friends to do the same. Make some-one's wedding day with a Windrush fine bone china dinner service.

Another resolution to the exclusivity/mass-production paradox is appealing to the individual's exceptionally good taste while locating it within a tradition of previous consumers:

Jack Daniel's head distiller, Jimmy Bedford has lots of folk looking over his shoulder. Since 1866, we've had only six head distillers. (Every one a Tennessee boy, starting with Mr. Jack Daniel himself.) Like those before him, Jimmy's mindful of our traditions, such as the oldtime way we smooth our whiskey through 10 feet of hard maple charcoal. He **knows Jack Daniel's drinkers will judge him with every sip**. So he's not about to change a thing. The five gentlemen on his wall surely must be pleased about that.

In this, as in other whisky ads, the appeal to an exclusive tradition is probably a reaction against the fetishism of the new: 'The Famous Grouse. Finest Scotch Whisky. Quality in an age of change.'

But which categories of products have their value enhanced by being old or 'retro', and which have to be presented as new? The appeal of tradition is a strong one in a fragmented, insecure society where things are changing so fast. But ads for fashion items, electronic goods and digital devices always stress their newness, since this ensures the 'old' will be discarded for a more 'advanced' or 'hot' product.

The following Sainsbury's wine ad plays on snobbery and inverted snobbery simultaneously. While it overtly rejects the idea of pride based on wealth and product price, it nevertheless slips in the word 'pedigree' to suggest aristocratic tradition:

> It's a sparkling wine with a long and distinguished pedigree. It costs too little. At under £4 a bottle Sainsbury's Cava is something of a bargain compared to other sparkling wines. Perhaps at your next celebration you should pocket your pride and the difference.
>
> *(Good Housekeeping*, May 1987: 8)

Chevrolet seems to go further, implying that there is no exclusivity:

> At Chevrolet we believe that everyone, no matter how much they have to spend, deserves a safe car.
>
> *(Popular Science*, June 1995: 38)

Incidentally, this notion that the consumer "deserves" everything the manufacturer supplies connects to one argument in favour of advertising: ads make the poor aware of a quality of life to which they have a right, the simple essentials of life, like soap, decent sanitation, bedding, housing, clothing, etc. It's doubtful that this argument for advertising can be sustained in modern advanced economies.

7.6 BUYING A LIFESTYLE

Back in the 1950s and early 1960s advertisers often used conditioning strategies, like Pavlov on his dogs, by pairing the product with a desirable object (often an attractive woman (www.gettyimages.co.uk/detail/news-photo/models-helen-jones-and-sue-shaw-lying-on-a-car-without-news-photo/2633278)). The technique attempts to transfer the desirable connotations of the accompanying image of object or person to the product. More crudely, the strategy suggests that buying the product will bring you the desirable object too. For example, the right toothpaste or perfume will bring you the attractive woman or sexy man. This naïve technique is now less common, but there is a similar technique which suggests that the product gives access to a certain "lifestyle" or "way of life". Recall, for example, the Dorma fabrics ad (Chapter 4), which seemed to promise a passionate heterosexual relationship, not just cloth.

Judith Williamson, in her book *Decoding Advertisements*, explains how such appeals to a way of life achieve their signification:

> A product may be connected with a way of life through being an accessory to it, but come to signify it, as in the car ad which starts 'Your way of life demands a lot of a car' and ends by making the car signify the life-style: 'Maxi: more a way of life'. So the product and the 'real' or human world become linked in the ad, apparently naturally, and the product may or does take over the reality on which it was, at first, dependent for its meaning.
>
> (Williamson 1978: 35)

The promise of a new way of life is not always an empty one. With the penetration of computing technology into more and more areas of our lives, the communication devices which we own radically affect the way we live. Behaviour has been transformed since the first edition of this book in 2000 by the internet, mobile phones, tablets and the apps accompanying them, such as satellite navigation devices. In particular, we have global reach with our new digital communications, and may think of ourselves as belonging to a global rather than local community.

An explicit and doubtful promise of a lifestyle appears in the ad for AGA cookers (*Good Housekeeping*, May 87: 212–213; Image 7.1). Not only do we have AGA. IT'S A WAY OF LIFE, but the contact details at the bottom read: 'if you'd like to find out more about life with ... Aga ... send off this coupon', almost suggesting your cooker is equivalent to your partner. Such a personification of the stove may also be suggested by the visual echo of the shape of the woman's head and body in the shining pan and the left hand panel of the cooker.

Image 7.1
Aga stove ad
(a clearer similar
PDF image is
available at
www.agaliving.
com/media/
1139264/1985.
pdf)

The ad is explicit about selling a lifestyle, but not about the kind of lifestyle. The advertiser cannot openly promise that by buying the product you are also buying something else. This has to be inferred from the accompanying visuals. The AGA ad implies a simple and natural lifestyle. The substances in the kitchen are natural – the wicker basket, wooden chest, chest of drawers and spoons, stoneware vases, fruit, flowers, leather sandals, cotton nightdress and the flagstone floor suggesting a country cottage. The simplicity is symbolically attributed by the bare, homogeneous surfaces such as the whitewashed wall, with only a plain wood-framed mirror, the plain white nightdress, the woman's lack of jewellery or make up.

Since lifestyle is not just a matter of our surroundings but also our behaviour, we can infer a little narrative as well. The weak sun slanting into the kitchen is low in the sky, suggesting early morning or late evening. As the woman is dressed for bed, it implies she has just got up in the morning. The flowers on the chest of drawers are the daisies of an English summer. The flowers lying beside her imply that after rising early she went out into the garden to pick them, despite the chill of early morning, and returned, took off her sandals, and is blissfully warming her feet and dozing by the stove. There is a vector between her feet and the stove, but perhaps its direction is not significant. Is the actor of this narrative process the stove or the woman or both?

In visual symbolic process terms the AGA and the woman are foregrounded by illumination, but the AGA is central and therefore dominates. This makes it symbolic of the implied natural way of life. The full frontal horizontal 180 degree angle suggests engagement with the cooker and a demand for involvement and inclusion, which matches the idea that the viewer, too, can live a life with AGA as a partner. The AGA is in closer shot than the woman, also suggesting potential "closeness". The slightly blurred or fuzzy images in the ad imply, by a symbolic suggestive process, a "dream" relationship.

7.7 SUMMARY

We have seen, in the first part of this chapter, how, besides encouraging consumption, which is in some cases quite unnecessary, ads appeal to and reproduce value systems and mindsets. Besides generating envy, greed and wastefulness, ads also suggest that by buying a product or service we are:

- solving our problems
- acquiring quality or qualities
- choosing our identities

- distinguishing ourselves
- buying a lifestyle.

We now look in detail at four advertisements, to illustrate how these psychological appeals are manifested in the linguistic texture of the copy, and also to apply many of the discoursal aspects which have been touched upon in Parts A and B. The fourth ad, based on the Apple webpage, demonstrates how ads may ignore the realities of the globalised production process, even when they appeal to the global consumer.

7.8 CASE STUDY 1: THE CAR, THE INDIVIDUAL AND THE ROAD TO SUCCESS

This ad for Opel (Image 7.2) is a prime example of the blending of the personality of the consumer and the "personality" of the product. This is clear from the striking visual image – part woman, part car. The ad copy is, however, not quite sure about whether the qualities of the car – individuality and the power to make independent decisions – transfer from product to consumer through the act of purchasing, or whether the buyer already has them. The opening of the copy suggests the first: 'Remember all those moments when you wanted to say something, do something, but didn't? Times when you held back, because you were happier to let others take the lead.' But later it suggests that the car simply matches these pre-existing qualities of the consumer: 'And yet you know deep down that you wouldn't be who you are today, if it weren't for the decisions you'd made. Decisions that let you discover the power of individuality and the reward of independence.' In either case the appeal is the match between mental characteristics and mode of travel: 'So why should your mode of travel be so different from your mode of thought?'

We notice, too, the appeal to three other consumer values identified earlier: power, identity and distinction. For the copy promises the following characteristics:

- decision-making power: taking control of a situation and directing it;
- individual independence: the power to go where you want when you want;
- personal "advancement": leading the pack, being head of the class, moving while others are stationary.

Possible tensions between individuality and social membership are resolved by the notion of leading the pack; you are a member, but

WHEN YOU'VE MASTERED THE ART OF CONTROL
PEOPLE WILL KNOW

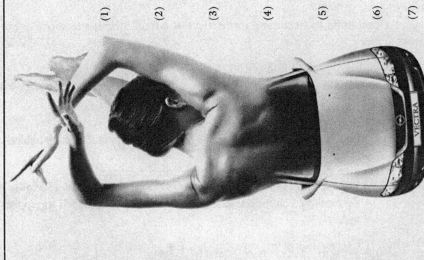

(1) Remember all those moments when you wanted to say something, do something, but didn't?

(2) Times when you held back, because you were happier to let others take the lead.

(3) And yet you know deep down that you wouldn't be who you are today, if it weren't for the decisions you'd made.

(4) Decisions that let you discover the power of individuality and the reward of independence.

(5) So why should your mode of travel be so different from your mode of thought?

(6) Why, indeed should you follow the pack when you could be leading it?

(7) When we designed the Opel Vectra, we set out to create a car that would sit

(8) at the very head of its class. A car that gives you the power to go where you want, when you want. And be capable of

(9) taking you the distance in comfort, safety and, yes, we dare say it, style.

(10) You know what it is to be an individual, to move while others are stationary, to take control of a situation and direct it in the way you want.

(11) When you drive the new Vectra you'll be reminded of all those moments when you pushed on with what you truly believed in. And when you move others

(12) will follow, as they come to realise you have mastered the art of control.

OPEL ⊙

JAPAN TEL 0120-55-5367 • TAIWAN TEL 886-02-5075311 FAX 886-02-5075505 • THAILAND TEL 662-5601609 FAX 662- 5611565 • INDONESIA TEL 62-21-4610138 • SINGAPORE TEL 65-4780766 FAX 65-472273 • MALAYSIA TEL 03-2419450 FAX 03-2419382 • HONG KONG TEL 852-28918400 FAX 852-28828560 • CHINA TEL 86-10-5012617 FAX 86-10-512-1618 • VIETNAM TEL 84-8-2948826 FAX 84-8-2948828 • SRI LANKA TEL 94-1-432858 FAX 94-1-446129

Image 7.2 Opel car ad

distinguished at the same time. Nevertheless, the main thrust is an appeal to identity and individualism. In the USA the car is almost synonymous with rights and social identity. As Baudrillard puts it: 'Disenfranchising. You lose your rights one by one, first your job, then your car. And when your driver's licence goes, so does your identity' (Baudrillard 1989: 112). The car is, moreover, the epitome of the individualism of laissez-faire consumer capitalism. It is individualistic, because it is for the private use of the individual or the nuclear family, rather than a shared resource like public transport. It is laissez-faire, allowing you to go where you like without making messy or inconvenient social compromises. However, it is not the most rational means of transport, given the problems of climate change. It is no accident that the most thoroughly consumer capitalist society, the USA, is the most addicted to cars. And partly as a result, in 2012 it produced 5.19 billion tonnes of CO_2 out of the world total of 34.5 billion tonnes. That is 15 per cent of total carbon emissions produced by roughly 4.5 per cent of theworld'spopulation.(http://edgar.jrc.ec.europa.eu/news_docs/pbl-2013-trends-in-global-co2-emissions-2013-report-1148.pdf).

The wording of the copy in this ad exploits a particular metaphorical theme or conceptual metaphor in the vocabulary of English: DEVELOPMENT/SUCCESS IS MOVEMENT FORWARDS (Goatly 2007; 2011). This equation gives rise to the following metaphors in the English vocabulary (in bold).

Success is moving forwards:

> John has made great **advances** with his mathematics

Developing or becoming more successful than others is to move ahead in a race:

> One element in the rat **race** is the desire **to get ahead**.

So failures cannot keep up with the front-runners:

> Paul is a **backward** child so it's difficult for him not to **get left behind**.

Difficulty in succeeding is difficulty in going forward:

> Persuading Londoners to switch from cars to buses is an **uphill** task.

What prevents success is an obstacle:

> Environmentalists are **obstructing** the government's attempts to manage Canadian forests effectively.

So solving a problem or avoiding failure is passing through, round or over an obstacle:

> He **scraped through** his exam.
> Can't you **find a way around** that problem?

This metaphorical equation is obviously suited to the advertising of cars. It enables the car to symbolise independence, leadership and success, as we can see when we use it to interpret extracts from the copy:

> Times when you held back, because you were happier to let others take the lead =
>> Times when you were inactive and were happier for the others to do something first.

> Why, indeed should you follow the pack when you could be leading it? =
>> Why should you imitate other people's behaviour instead of initiating or modelling an activity (or obey other people instead of giving orders)?

> A car that gives you the power to go where you want, when you want. And be capable of taking you the distance =
>> A car that gives you the power to do what you want when you want, and is capable of making you succeed.

> To move while others are stationary, to take control of a situation and direct it in the way you want =
>> To achieve things while others are doing nothing, to take control of a situation and make what you want happen.

> When you pushed on with what you really believed in =
>> When you did the difficult things you really believed in.

> And when you move others will follow =
>> When you do things other will imitate and obey.

Besides illustrating these three kinds of psychological appeal, this ad exemplifies a range of interpersonal linguistic features. High contact is simulated by pronouns, interrogative mood "questions" and fake dialogue, and minor sentences or other shortenings.

First the use of pronouns. Paragraph 1, sentences 1–6, uses just *you*. Obviously this has to be interpreted as an individual reader, given the emphasis on independence and individuality. The next paragraph, sentences 7–9, shifts to exclusive *we*, which includes only the members of the Opel company and introduces the car, briefly. Sentences 10 to the end shift back to *you*, the potential customer, emphasising now not just her individual psychology, but also how she can make a social impact on 'others'.

Turning to mood, note the prevalence of the interrogative in the first section (sentences 1, 5 and 6) which button-holes and engages the reader. In fact, there is only one other complete sentence (3) which is a statement in declarative mood; (2) and (4) are minor sentences. All interrogatives in this section fail the tests for normal questions. The first is really an indirect statement or reminder. The second and third are one kind of rhetorical question, 'Why...?', which demands an answer in the negative, and is a formula for dissuasion, in this case not to 'follow the pack' or 'allow your mode of travel to be so different from your mode of thought'. Later the flavour of dialogue is given by 'and yes, we dare say it, style', with its mock reply and its choice of the word *say* rather than *write*.

If interrogatives give the flavour of speech, so does the use of compound sentences, where clauses are joined by co-ordinating conjunctions like *and* and *but*. Beginning a sentence with these conjunctions makes the copy even more chatty, as in (3), (5), (9) and (12).

In addition, a number of shortenings and minor sentences give the impression of conversational contact. Contractions are everywhere: 'didn't', 'wouldn't', 'weren't', 'you'd', etc. Shortening of sentences is common: (1), really an interrogative, looks like an imperative because the words *do you* are omitted. (2) and (4) have been shortened into minor sentences – the major equivalents would begin: 'Do you remember the times when...'; 'You'd made decisions that let you ...'.

This use of shortenings and omissions in the first section contributes to a chain-like rhetorical structure, because it demands a compensating repetition in adjacent sentences: moments (1) → times (2); decisions (3) → decisions (4). Chains give the impression of unplanned afterthoughts, and so contribute to informality. These two chains are suspended on different ends of a balance, of course, the pivot of which is 'and yet' (3). Elsewhere in the copy stack structures emerge: (7), (8) and (9) stack up positive claims about the car.

In its affect there seems to be a growing confidence and heightening emotion towards the end of the copy. This is achieved by the repetition of grammatical structures, as in sentence (10), which suggest a rhythmical pattern – four beats per line, all starting with the infinitive form of the verb, with the *x/* pattern figuring prominently:

You know what it is
    x / x / x/x /
    to be an individual,
    x /   x / x x / x /x
    to move while others are stationary,
    x /   x / x x /x/x
    to take control of a situation
    x   x/ x / x /   x /
    and direct it in the way you want.

This detailed analysis helps us see the overall shape of the ad and how the linguistic details fit the copywriter's strategy. The structure is that of problem–solution. The writer takes on the subject position of psychological counsellor, perhaps in assertiveness or confidence building, beginning by establishing the patient's past. This accounts for the very personal beginning of the ad and the interrogatives. Having diagnosed the problem, though with a balance structure which prevents the ad from being too insulting, and having given some interrogative advice, she provides the solution in the form of the Opel Vectra. This will afford the female buyer decision-making power, independence and noticeable success, underlined by the triumphant affective rhythms. And the metaphors of movement forward for success, along with the visual which blends car and person, vouch for the fact that cars confer identity and guarantee success.

Just like the linguistic analysis, visual analysis reveals how ideational and interpersonal meanings contribute to the overall effect of the ad. First, let's consider ideational or representational meanings. As mentioned earlier, the striking visual image, part-woman, part-car, aligns the product with the character of the consumer. The image of the woman in an elegant posture, perhaps from ballet, with hands arched above the head and pointed toes, works to indicate elegance, style and control. In this way, the product (the car) becomes synonymous with features of the represented participant (the woman posing in an elegant and stylish dance posture). To use Kress and Van Leeuwen's terms, we have a conceptual process of a symbolic suggestive type, as the meaning of the participant is established by de-emphasising detail, and emphasising mood or atmosphere. As you can see, with her well-toned open back (and not her face) facing the viewer, the image of the woman as a person is de-emphasised and the posture and style of her body are emphasised (reflecting the metaphor of a car "body"). It is her pose that creates the mood suggestive of a certain class and identity: stylish, sophisticated and at the same time individualistic by being in control.

Regarding the interpersonal meanings of the visual, the image makes a visual offer, where the viewer is required to look at the posing woman, as an item of information or contemplation; we may either accept or reject this offer to see the car as a symbol of style and elegance. Since the back of the woman is facing the viewer, there is no gaze, and hence no demand for involvement. However, the medium-close shot creates a social or "one of us" relation with the viewer, a sense of social engagement.

Moreover, the 'point of view' is clearly a subjective perspective imposed on the viewer. This can be seen in both degrees of involvement as well as degrees of power. Involvement is realised by the horizontal 180-degree frontal angle of the image. This signifies inclusion, where the posing woman as well as the car form part of the viewer's world, a world projecting consumer values such as control or power, and style or distinction. At the same time, the degree of power is realised in the vertical high angle, with the viewer looking down on the car from 'above'. This confirms the decision-making power and individual independence of the consumer.

So we can see how both the representational and interactive meanings of the visuals reflect consumer qualities of sophistication, individualism and power, reinforcing the messages conveyed by the linguistic resources.

7.9 CASE STUDY 2: A MATCH FOR THE JET SET AND THE GOOD CHINESE WIFE

The selling point of this advertisement (Image 7.3) is the matching of a famous personality with the service advertised. This match is implied by the first two lines of the copy, with its parallel syntactic structure of two apposed noun phrases:

> (NP1) Mary Cheung, (NP2) award-winning photographer,
> On (NP1) Emirates (NP2) (award-winning airline)

The parallelism of the second NP2 with the first NP2 is slightly obscured by using parentheses rather than commas. Presumably this is a gesture of politeness through modesty, unusual self-effacement by a company advertising. Once this link between product and famous personality is achieved, buying the goods or service secures us identification with the famous and successful. The various real selling points of Emirates business class – the seatback video, the classy wine, the fax facility – are all mediated and validated through the eyes (camera) of Mary Cheung; as if they are not real until the famous photographer perceives and shoots them.

But, besides this, there is the appeal to distinction in the service provided. The wine Chateau Malescasse (or is it Malecasse?) '88, connotes

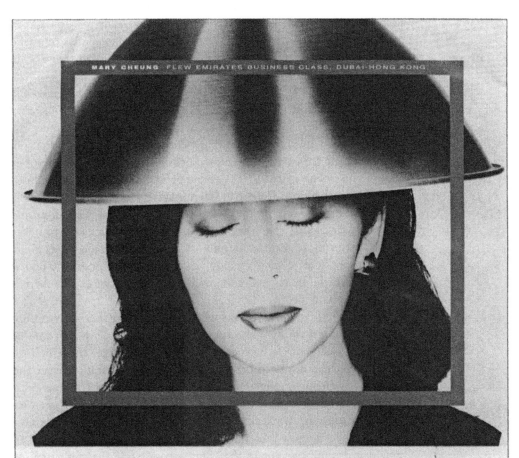

MARY CHEUNG FLEW EMIRATES BUSINESS CLASS, DUBAI-HONG KONG

Mary Cheung, award-winning photographer, on Emirates (award-winning airline).

9D enjoyed the Malescasse '11

A few verbal snapshots from 34,000 ft

9D is relishing the Chateau Malescasse. 7E likes the seatback video but unfortunately is willing to talk to anyone who'll listen about industrial polymers! As for 10B, I miss my family — so I'll send them a "love-you" fax!

Mary Cheung

Emirates

THE FINEST IN THE SKY

OVER 100 INTERNATIONAL AWARDS, 42 INTERNATIONAL DESTINATIONS. FOR DETAILS CALL EMIRATES OR YOUR LOCAL TRAVEL AGENT.
ON THE WEB AT: http://www.ekgroup.com/

Image 7.3 Emirates airline ad (*Asiaweek*, 14 February 1997: 19)

French sophistication and exclusivity (wine of a certain chateau and vintage comes in limited quantities, after all). This detail alludes to a whole way of life. We pick up on this detail, of course, because of the very visually prominent, red, thumbnail sketch of 9D.

The previous Opel Vectra ad celebrated the individualism of car transport. What, then, is the ideological significance of air-travel? Mary Cheung, though rich enough to enjoy the exclusivity of business class, cannot achieve the privacy and independence of private air transport. What does she feel about this enforced contact with the two other members of the public in seats 9D (a man) and 7E (probably an industrial chemist and therefore stereotypically a man)? 9D she just watches, but 7E's conversation on industrial polymers she regards as unfortunate. Apparently industrial chemistry is not the kind of topic likely to interest women, even those technically minded enough to invade the traditionally male preserve of photography. In any case, she does not find the company sufficiently engaging to dispel her homesickness, and therefore sends a 'love-you' fax back home.

This ad simultaneously breaks with gender stereotypes and reinforces them. It breaks them by presenting a woman successful in a traditionally male career who travels business-class. But it reinforces them by insisting on her close ties with her family, as though separation from them denies her fundamental instincts. Moreover, traditional Chinese culture might frown on a woman travelling alone in the presence of men with the opportunity to drink alcohol. Though she endures 7E's talk about polymers, she doesn't take much interest in the male passengers, who remain just numbers, nor in the wine, whose name she can't spell, but keeps herself to her sober self and for her family. She is a good Chinese wife and mother at heart. (Does the contraption in the photograph suggest a traditional Chinese peasant hat, in shape if not in sheen, or an inverted wok?)

In pragmatic terms the ad relies on two parallel schemas: photography and air travel. These make possible a kind of punning in the underlined handwritten 'A few verbal snapshots from 34,000ft'. The snapshot pun is obvious, but the 'from 34,000ft' demands a bit more processing. It's impossible to take a snapshot *from* 34,000ft, so we have to reprocess this to mean "*at* 34,000ft". Alternatively, we interpret the fax as a kind of snapshot which is sent to her family *from* 34,000ft.

The photography schema also contributes to visual impact. The black-and-white photograph of Mary Cheung – black hair and shoulders, white face – marked for cropping by the purple frame, is echoed in the text immediately below in its no-nonsense bold black-and-white font, something like Chicago.

In representational terms, we can see a conceptual classification process being realised overtly as Mary Cheung's photograph has the caption 'award-winning photographer'. The ad clearly takes advantage of her celebrity status as a marketing strategy. When consumers fly Emirates, they are not just flying any airline, they are flying an airline with a symbolic value attached to it through this classification process.

The rather impersonal font below contrasts markedly with the handwriting which follows. Since handwritten letters are always sent to individuals it obviously symbolises a high level of informal contact and synthetic personalisation. The significance of fonts is difficult to describe. But a comparison between the *Emirates* under the picture and the *Emirates* below the logo alerts us to it. The second suggests style and sophistication, where the first connotes bare efficiency. The three graphic choices, at the centre of the ad's body, are in marked contrast with each other.

Let's return now to the interpersonal features of the text. In the handwritten section they include pronouns, markers of inclination/ emotion, and punctuation. What is remarkable is the sudden intrusion of the first-person pronoun in the last sentence of the handwritten message. The impersonality of number '10B', suddenly gives way to the presence of the author 'I', 'my', 'I', '"you"', and the signature with first and second name. Markers of emotion/inclination are present throughout. At first they are applied to the other passengers: 'relishing', 'enjoyed', 'likes', 'is willing'. Note that they become less strong, though this contradicts the inference that 7E is absurdly keen to talk about industrial polymers. 'Unfortunately' probably expresses the disinclination of Mary Cheung, as does possibly the first 'll'. In the last sentence the positive emotions of Cheung are forcefully expressed when they are paired with the first person pronoun – 'miss', 'love'. The steady degree of informality and a crude marking of propositional attitude are also achieved by the punctuation, perhaps the dash, but certainly the exclamation marks.

Lastly, in the signature line, there is an expression of emotion in the symmetry of sound and syntax. Taking the two phrases together there is both repetition of rhythm |/x x x |/x x x |/|, and overall symmetry /x x x/x x x /.

    / x x   x /x x   x /
    Emirates the finest in the sky

If we take the second phrase as a unit, we have syntactic symmetry, emphasised by the repetition of [ai], underlined:

Noun phrase	Prep	Noun phrase
the finest	in	the sky

In relation to the visual interactive meanings of the ad, we notice that Mary Chueng's eyes are closed, so the picture is offered as an object of contemplation. In terms of visual distance, the very close shot of frame size (within a photographic frame) establishes an intimate personal relation with the viewer, implying maximum engagement. Moreover, the subjective perspective of the image invites the viewer to join the producers of the image – an 'us' with respect to the represented participant, Mary Cheung. This is confirmed by the frontal angle of the photograph, with a message of involvement and inclusion suggesting that the represented participant is part of the viewer's world. The possibility of engagement and inclusion is further underlined by situating Mary Cheung at the same level as the viewer (neither at a high angle nor at a low angle) indicating equality in terms of power.

To sum up the advertising strategies along with linguistic and visual features of the ad: the celebrity of the famous client rubs off on the product, and promises a similar distinction to customers buying the service. The features and awards of the offered service are downplayed and somehow become less important than the fact that a celebrity perceives and snaps them. Mary Cheung comes over very personally to the reader, both through the handwritten note, the pronouns and expressions of feeling, as well as through visual strategies conveying engagement, inclusion, equality and closeness. She is portrayed ambiguously as part professional business woman, but more basically as a "family woman", slightly out of place in this wine-drinking, job-obsessed male company. The copy and the visuals engage the reader through the schematically clashing puns, the three styles of print, one of which echoes the picture, and the use of parallel syntactic and rhythmical structures which convey both craft and an emotion of gentle admiration.

7.10 CASE STUDY 3: UNNECESSARY WORDS AND WELCOMING IN STYLE?

The paradox of this advertisement is that it keeps on reiterating it is telling you nothing new: 'exactly what you'd expect'; 'there are no surprises; but then you knew that'; 'as you know you'll find just what you are looking for'. What is the point? It may imply that these hotels need no special gimmicks to attract clients, simply the ordinary things a hotel offers but to a high degree of excellence. This possibility is, however, undermined by the phrase 'special programs'. A second possible intention might be to suggest that most readers and business travellers would be aware of the quality of ITT Sheraton hotels, and that, if the particular individual reader is not, then they are strangely ignorant.

Three nights with us is exactly
what you'd EXPECT.

A
TASTE of LUXURY
Stay three nights and enjoy
a sumptuous
daily breakfast for
one appealing rate.

There are no surprises when you stay at a Luxury Collection hotel.
Only sublime comfort and unparalleled service. But then, you knew that.
Allow us to welcome you at any of the 48 properties in 20 countries
that comprise The Luxury Collection.
Perhaps you'd like to sample our hospitality in Bangkok at the
Sheraton Grande Sukhumvit, or Bali at the Sheraton Laguna Nusa Dua
or even in Sydney at the Sheraton On the Park.
For AT&T cardmembers, a complimentary welcome gift
is yours when you check in. Simply show your
AT&T Calling Card. You'll be assured
of fast, clear connections when you call
home using AT&T Direct℠ Service.
Ask your travel professional about "Taste of Luxury" and all our
other special programs. Or in Malaysia call toll free
1-800.80-1510. Hong Kong 800.6812. Or in
Singapore 65.732-6000.
As you know, you'll find just what you're looking for.

THE LUXURY COLLECTION
ITT SHERATON

Europe Asia Australia The Americas Africa
For further information, please visit our Web site at www.ittsheraton.com

 AT&T

Image 7.4
Sheraton hotels ad
(*Asiaweek*, 27
June 1997: 7)

Evidence from the analysis of presuppositions supports this second interpretation. Perhaps in keeping with the pretence that the information in the copy is redundant, the existence of the properties making up the hotel group is also assumed rather than stated. The noun phrases carrying an existential presupposition are underlined.

> Allow us to welcome you at any of the 48 properties in 20 countries that comprise The Luxury Collection. Perhaps you'd like to sample our hospitality in Bangkok at the Sheraton Grande Sukhumvit, or Bali at the Sheraton Laguna Nusa Dua or even in Sydney at the Sheraton On the Park.

We don't dispute the existence of these hotels, or even their 'other special programs'. But more disputable is the nominalisation of 'we are hospitable' to 'our hospitality'. This smuggles in an existential and possessive presupposition, assuming rather than stating the claim.

For positioning the readers several other presuppositions are used. Readers are assumed to have travel professionals – 'your travel professional'. It is presupposed that AT&T cardmembers exist – 'For AT&T cardmembers' – and that they have Calling Cards – 'your AT&T Calling Card'. It is also assumed that they use them to call home – 'when you call home using AT&T Direct Service'. (Clauses introduced by *when* presuppose that the act has occurred or will occur.) These three presuppositions about AT&T cardmembers and their cards would have a different impact on different readers. Those who are not cardmembers might feel they were losing out, with the result that the ad seems to be indirectly advertising AT&T cardmembership, as well as hotels. This interpretation matches our earlier suggestion – the motive for insisting that the ad copy contains nothing new is to make readers for whom it is in fact new feel unusually ignorant and excluded. Notice that the *when* presupposition is also used about staying at one of the hotels, constructing it as something inevitable and normal:

> There are no surprises when you stay at a Luxury Collection hotel

The appeal of this ad is to a certain lifestyle, albeit one that can only be 'sampled' or 'tasted' for three days. And one strand of vocabulary underlines this selling point: 'luxury', 'sumptuous', 'sublime comfort', 'unparalleled service', 'welcome', 'hospitality'. Many of these adjectives are quite empty affective ones – certainly 'sublime' and 'unparalleled' as well as 'appealing' and 'special', and possibly 'sumptuous' too.

Another aspect of the vocabulary is **upgrading**, using a less core word when the core word would be just as good, and a tinge of euphemism. Instead of a *group* of hotels we have a 'collection of properties'

– *collection* connoting fashion houses or high-class art, as though the hotels were carefully assembled over time. Then we have the phrase 'travel professional', smarter than *travel agent* though probably referring to the same people. And 'calling card' conjures up the respectable society of previous centuries, like Jane Austen's England, when the idle rich spent their afternoons visiting and left behind a card if the people visited were out.

Some of this euphemistic upgrading indicates formality and deference, also detected in the tentativeness of the directives at the beginning. 'Allow us to welcome you at any of the 48 properties in 20 countries that comprise The Luxury Collection', despite the imperative, counts as asking permission, a low degree of obligation, thereby recognising the authority of the client. The next request/offer is phrased 'perhaps you'd like to sample our hospitality in Bangkok ... or Bali ... or even in Sydney...'. Remember that tactful directives build in optionality and indirectness. There is plenty of optionality in the 'perhaps' and the 'or's. Indirectness is achieved by guessing whether the reader wants the act to take place, this want being a condition for the speech act offer. Indirectness is taken even further by having 'would like' rather than *want*, suggesting that the offer is hypothetical rather than actual. (See Leech's (1983) hierarchy of tactful forms of request/offer on pp. 146–148.)

Synthetic personalisation surfaces periodically. There are the explicit promises of hospitality and welcome, as though a friend is staying for the weekend, rather than a paying guest. Though the extent of this hospitality is restricted since the welcome gifts are reserved for AT&T 'cardmembers' (used instead of *cardholders* to indicate a consumer club). More generally, the pronoun *you* is used throughout, often followed by the contracted *'ll*, and the less common *us*. Along with *you(r)* there is imperative mood, which recognises the existence of the reader, sometimes bordering on the tactless, in the technical sense of that word:

> Simply **show** your AT&T Calling Card...
> **Ask** your travel professional about "Taste of Luxury"
> Or in Malaysia **call** toll free
> For further information, please **visit** our Web site at
>   www.ittsheraton.com

It's worth thinking a bit about the particular structure of imperative clause + *and* + imperative clause, which is a stylistic peculiarity of ad copy. The example here is 'Stay three nights and enjoy a sumptuous breakfast at one appealing rate.' Is this equivalent to 'if you stay three nights you enjoy a sumptuous breakfast' etc.? Almost, but on top of this promise is a stronger imperative invitation. The problem with this structure is that unscrupulous copywriters use it to make false promises, as in 'Open an account with Standard Chartered Bank and win a Volvo.'

To sum up. The existence and quality of the hotel chain, and of the services to AT&T cardmembers, are taken for granted both through explicit claims that the reader knows this already, and through various presuppositions. This gives the impression that these facilities are already well-known to the vast majority of business travellers, so that if any readers haven't experienced them, they are somehow atypical. So this is a covert appeal to join the consumer club of guests at these hotels. Especially at the beginning of the copy there is some deference, which meshes well with the personal pronouns, contractions and the upgraded and euphemistic vocabulary to create a degree of interpersonal politeness, though without quite avoiding some empty affective adjectives. Imperatives are also present, however, with the co-ordinated imperative structure used to simultaneously persuade and promise.

7.11 CASE STUDY 4: GLOBAL PRODUCTS, PROBLEMS AND PRODUCTION: THE BANANA BABLET WEBPAGE

What will your poem be?

We all have something we can share. See how people use Bablet in their own special ways to add to the human story.

Discover →

What will your poem be?

Everyone has something to share. An opinion, a passion, a vision. The potential to add a verse to this earth's story. We were so excited by how people use Bablet every day, we tried to capture a few of these moments.

Watch "Your Poem" and explore

Exploring new depths

The ocean takes up 70 per cent of our planet's surface, but most remains a mystery. With the BaDive housing, marine biologist Martin Bloomer develops his research in protecting coral reefs by taking the Bablet deep under the sea.

Explore →

Mounting the expedition

World-famous mountaineers Amy Harrison and Andrew Bollinger have ascended some of the world's highest peaks, from Mount Everest to Mont Blanc. They use their Bablet to help them plan itineraries, climb safely and share their experiences with the world.

Explore →

Catching the vision in Bollywood

Farid Khan, Agra, India

Farid Khan, one of Bollywood's best choreographers, uses Bablet in many ways in production – from finding locations to mixing sounds to framing every shot and polishing every dance move. With Bablet, Khan quickly and easily shares his vision with the director, dancers, musicians and production team.

From composition to stage

Yo, Beijing, China

The rock band Yo writes and records music with Bablet. And in live shows, Bablet comes on stage with them. Two musicians play a Bablet on stage, using two percussion apps. With Bablet, they've found a new way to create and perform music with a new sound.

Far-reaching resources for education

School in a Box, Humla, Nepal

For tens of millions of kids in the poor world, having no electricity means little or no access to the best educational tools. But Study in a Box, a solar-powered educational tool-kit developed around Bablet, facilitates interactive learning anywhere.

A new game plan for head injuries

Chicago Clinic, Detroit, USA

Chicago Clinic in Detroit is using Bablet to pioneer the field of head injury assessment and treatment. In a pilot programme at St. Edmund's High School, sports coach Jimmy Hasslebank uses the Bablet and software from BaComet to measure athletes' baseline balance, cognition and memory. When sportspeople are injured, this innovative programme can help diagnose their injuries.

On-the-fly movie production

Josh Lecter, Iguazu Falls, Argentina

New Brunswick-based filmmaker Josh Lecter has developed a housing for Bablet that makes it into a lightweight, portable, film-making camera. With attached microphones, SLR lenses and further accessories, he brings Bablet on the go to film his documentaries.

The Bablet page is designed to emphasise the universality of the product, both through the examples and the images. Universality is first presented on the vertical dimension 'deep under the sea' and 'the world's highest peaks'. The headlines 'exploring new depths' and 'mounting the expedition' not only highlight this literal vertical dimension, but also hint at a metaphorical meaning (SERIOUSNESS IS DEPTH, and POWER/STATUS IS HIGH). The horizontal dimension, world-wide universality, is emphasised in the case studies from India, China, Nepal, the USA and Argentina. And various professions and industries are exemplified: film-production, medicine, education, dance-theatre and rock-music recording.

The universality is also underlined by quantifiers and general vocabulary: '**every**one', 'we **all**', '**every** day', '**many** ways in production', '**tens of millions** of kids', 'facilitates interactive learning **anywhere**', 'people', 'the world', 'the earth', 'far-reaching'.

Other noticeable aspects emerge from patterns of lexis. The text stresses the Bablet's adaptability to new and unique uses: 'new depths', 'a new way', 'a new sound', 'special', 'pioneer', 'innovative', 'on-the-fly'. Less strong is the emphasis on its collaborative communicative function in the repetition of the verb *share*.

Most of the presuppositions are existential or possessive: 'your poem' >> you have a poem; 'their own special ways' >> they [people] have special ways; 'the potential to add a verse to this earth's story' >> there is a potential to add a verse to this earth's story; 'this earth's story' >> this earth has a story; 'the human story' >> there is a human story. There are also subordinate clause presuppositions 'how people use Bablet in their own special ways to add to the human story' >> people use Bablet in their own special ways to add to the human story; 'how people use Bablet every day' >> people use Bablet every day. And there are change of state presuppositions 'they've found a new way to make and perform music with a new sound' >> they did not know/have a new way to make and perform music with a new sound. The presuppositions tend to be used strategically to make us accept the notions introduced by the lexis and quantifiers – the universality of the Bablet, and its everyday use for new purposes. From another angle, they assume that there is a human story (or poem) in which everyone has the potential to share by adding a verse, a potential which, it is inferred, can be realised by using the Bablet.

The Bablet is, then, primarily a 'tool', and it is people who use it in the various occupations, professions and artistic spheres exemplified. So an analysis of the grammar of clauses shows the Bablet is seldom the original actor or initiator of the process. Sometimes, indeed, it is simply the affected:

> People use Bablet every day
>
> Farid Khan … uses Bablet in many ways in his production –
>
> Two musicians play a Bablet on stage, using two percussion apps.

However, it is more generally represented as an instrument to achieve various people's purposeful actions. This is conveyed by adverbial phrases (clauses) of instrumentality/accompaniment, introduced by *with* (or *by*).

> With Bablet, Khan quickly and easily shares his vision with the director, dancers, musicians and production team.
>
> The rock band Yo writes and records music with Bablet.

The Bablet tool is represented as more powerful in clauses with the repeated 'use Bablet to':

> People use Bablet in their own special ways to add to the human story.
>
> Chicago Clinic in Detroit is using Bablet to pioneer the field of head injury assessment and treatment.
>
> Sports coach Jimmy Hasslebank uses the Bablet and software from BaComet to measure athletes' baseline balance, cognition and memory.
>
> They use their Bablet to help them plan itineraries, climb safely and share their experiences with the world.

In the last example the Bablet is certainly the actor of the process in the infinitive clause, who helps the mountaineers plan and so on. But in the previous examples it is the secondary or co-operating actor of the process referred to by the infinitive, jointly adding, pioneering, measuring, etc.

To sum up our findings from a transitivity analysis: the centre of attention and activity are the various professional people and artists who use the Bablet and demonstrate its adaptability and versatility as part of new technologies. The Bablet is an essential tool for these activities.

But who are these people? We saw earlier that celebrities are often used in ads to suggest transfer of status and admirable qualities to the buyer.

However, though the artists and professionals on this webpage are portrayed as successful and groundbreaking, they are not well-known celebrities. This is presumably because the main message is that quite ordinary people can participate in adding to the world's story by buying and using a Bablet. Creating too large a status gap between the artists and professionals portrayed and the reader/consumer might undermine this message.

The hidden people behind Apple: workers' conditions

So the iPad alias Bablet webpage stresses universality both in terms of worldwide global reach and in terms of the possibility of "ordinary" people owning it and contributing to communicative sharing as part of the earth's human story. However, it, of course, neglects important parts of the story of the people involved in the globalised production of the iPad and other Apple products.

In 2010 Apple relied on electronic components from its major supplier, Foxconn, a unit of Taiwan's Hon Hai Precision Industry, which employs around 900,000 workers in Chinese factories. But Foxconn came under scrutiny for the conditions of its workers, mainly due to a spate of suicides at its factory/dorm complex in Shenzhen, southern China.

The worker's rights group China Labor Watch (CLW) alleged that Foxconn enforced military-style working conditions. Workers toiled for up to 12 hours continuously, sometimes even through weekends, performing repetitive, assembly-line tasks. As the labour group Students and Scholars Against Corporate Misbehavior reported: 'Most of the workers agree that they feel stress in the production lines. They are not allowed to talk to each other when working. Even in the same production line, workers do not have chance to get to know their colleagues.' According to the newspaper *Southern Weekly*, Foxconn's workers rarely stopped working except to eat and sleep, and needed to work overtime to supplement their monthly wage of $130.

To prevent the incidence of suicide, Foxconn strung up netting between the high-rise dormitories to catch anybody who tried to jump.

This was in 2010. Partly in response to these criticisms, and partly because the minimum wage was increased in Shenzhen, by 2012 Foxconn had increased basic wages to $250 a month, possibly with a subsidy from Apple itself (http://appleinsider.com/articles/12/09/03/apple_believed_to_be_subsidizing_wage_increases_at_foxconn, retrieved 28 February 2014).

However, recently, in 2013, Apple began to move production to another company, Pegatron, with factories in Shanghai and nearby Suzhou. Between March and July 2013, from undercover investigations and 200 interviews with workers, CLW discovered 86 labour rights violations, including 36 legal violations and 50 ethical violations.

Workers have to work almost 11-hour shifts, at a rate of less than $1.50 an hour ($270 per month). This is far below a living wage for an expensive city like Shanghai, forcing workers to rely on long overtime hours. Though Apple claims that its suppliers are 99 per cent compliant with its maximum working week of 60 hours, the CLW found average weekly working hours in the three factories to range from 66 to 69 hours. Incidentally, the maximum legal working week in China is 49 hours!

None of the Pegatron factories provided sufficient safety training to workers or cared about their living conditions and well-being. Workers live in 12-person dorm rooms and take cold showers, when water is available (www.chinalaborwatch.org/pdf/apple_s_unkept_promises.pdf, retrieved 28 February 2014).

7.12 SUMMARY

One of the flaws of consumer capitalism is its tendency for the overproduction of goods. Advertising is, therefore, key in persuading people to buy goods which may in fact be surplus to their real needs, and does so by using a number of strategies – suggesting buying the product will satisfy your desire, particularly your desire for power, solve your problems, endow you with certain qualities and help you to establish a distinctive identity and lifestyle. The cult of the new is observable whether in relation to fashion or the potential of modern technology, and this encourages obsolescence and repeated consumption.

Another flaw in capitalism is the tendency of wealth to become concentrated in fewer and fewer hands. This means that the majority of the population may be getting poorer or having only modest increases in income. Under these circumstances, particularly when many Western economies have been stagnating or contracting, it is difficult to sustain the necessary levels of consumption for the system to continue. So this economic model has to rely on increasing levels of consumer debt. China has been lending money to Western consumers and governments so they can buy things, often made in China, which they do not need with money they do not have. Eventually this burden of debt becomes unsustainable, as it did in the 2008 crisis.

A third feature of capitalism is its tendency to buy cheap and sell high – in the case of Apple to seek out countries where environmental and labour laws are weak or weakly regulated so that they can buy cheap labour and the cost of production can be kept low. This is a somewhat desperate bid to keep prices down so that more can be consumed at less cost to the consumer, but it cannot solve the problems of capital accumulation or overproduction inherent in the system. Especially, as we shall see in Chapter 9, resources for production are becoming scarcer as our ecological footprint undermines sustainability.

PROJECT 3

Please refer to the companion website for the activity material.

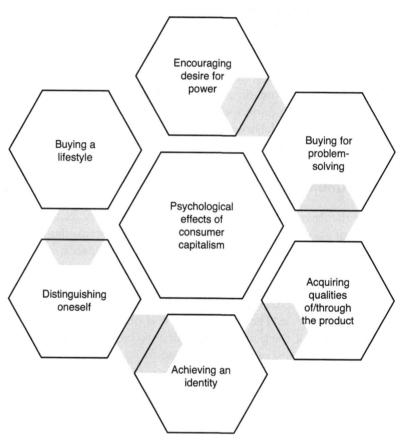

Figure 7.3
Summary of the
chapter

FURTHER READING

Please refer to the companion website for the list of further reading.

NEWS, INSTITUTIONAL POWER AND THE CRISIS OF DEMOCRACY

8

The aim of this chapter
- to argue that the idea of unbiased news is a myth, given the powerful economic and political interests behind the publishing and production of news;
- to argue that, given the unanimity with which corporate media promote market-driven economics and austerity, political choice has been minimised and democracy put in crisis;
- to analyse the tendencies of news to reinforce the power structures of global society, including sexism;
- to give practice in the composition of an online news blog, an opportunity to resist the normal ideological patterns of news discourse.

Contents

8.4 The sources of news
describes how news is predicted and gathered from the rich, famous and powerful and how this might influence its content and agenda.

8.5 Case study 1: representation and voices in the news
analyses and categorises the people named, and the proportion of men to women in each category, in online editions of *Japan Times*, *Times of India*, *USA Today*, Australia's *Herald Sun* and the UK's the *Mirror*, and reveals which of these named people have their words reported.

8.6 Case study 2: fighting power – representation of the US empire
introduces a study which shows how linguistic resources were used to challenge US imperialism.

8.7 Fighting power: information democratisation and voice on the internet
argues the case for citizen journalism as a force for democratisation and alternative news.

Project 4
Writing an alternative news blog showing awareness of factors influencing your selection of news and of quotes, and your sensitivity to linguistic strategies in the representation of characters.

8.0 INTRODUCTION: FREEDOM OF THE PRESS? THE CRISIS OF DEMOCRACY

No one doubts the power of the media, and no one doubts the media is useful to those in power. Newspapers, either in print or online, have vast circulations compared with any other published media, they are published or updated frequently and are accessible through wide distribution networks and online, often for free. For many people they constitute the most substantial consumption of written discourse. That the powerful in society should attempt to control and influence them is beyond question. The question of editorial independence is particularly sensitive, for example, in places like Hong Kong, where the mainland Chinese 'communist' party is often perceived as influencing the press (www.scmp.com/news/hong-kong/article/1426666/beijing-blamed-hong-kongs-press-freedom-declines).

However, there is also a conflicting myth of the freedom of the press, that journalists are free to give an objective account of anything they think newsworthy. And that, even if journalists on a particular newspaper may be constrained about what they can report, the reader has a choice because of the variety of newspapers on offer. Newspapers in this regard have been held up as the fourth estate, an essential ingredient of democracy. Because democracy relies on a public that takes responsibility for the choice and functioning of government, it is essential that the public have some knowledge of politics and society. The information and news that outlets give is supposed to be sufficiently important and trustworthy to allow voters to make judgements about the record of the political parties contesting elections, about the relative merits of their economic beliefs and vision for society, so they can make informed decisions about which party to vote for.

But suppose there is very little difference in parties' records, beliefs and vision? The fact is that most "democratic" governments since the late 1970s have embraced the economics of neo-liberalism. The main idea of neo-liberalism is that the best outcomes for the economy and society will be achieved if the supply and demand for goods and services is determined by the market, without any intervention from government. The result has been an attempt by governments to make themselves smaller and to "interfere" less. So governments have increasingly transferred the responsibility for services such as prisons and security, transport, welfare, health and education to the private sector. The majority of the mainstream media, owned as it is by large, private corporations, has supported this neo-liberal orthodoxy. And, at least in the UK and the USA, politicians, both Labour and Conservative, Democrat or Republican have followed the dominant media message. The result has been a more or less monologic discourse of the kind Bakhtin (Chapter 6) associated with authoritarian regimes.

However, this mantra of non-interference with the market was spectacularly abandoned during the 2007–2008 financial crisis, where huge sums of public money were devoted to saving the banking system from its market failure. Instead of regarding this as evidence of the flaws of an unregulated market system, politicians and the media started talking about the need for austerity to reduce the public debt incurred by bailing out the banks. This austerity was an excuse to cut government spending, to diminish the role of the public sector even further, and to transfer even more public assets to the private sector. The failure of neo-liberalism was used as an excuse to promote it!

Given the virtual unanimity of voices promoting neo-liberalism and austerity, even against the evidence, it is, therefore, not surprising that a crisis has emerged for democracy, reflected in the voter turnout for elections showing a downward trend (Table 8.1). Taking the first

Table 8.1 Voter turnout in parliamentary elections

France		Germany		Italy		Japan		New Zealand		South Africa		UK		US	
Year	%	Year	%	Year	%	Year	%	Year	%	Year	%	Year	%	Year	%
2012	55	2013	72	2013	75	2014	53	2014	77	2014	73	2015	66	2014	43
2007	59	2009	71	2008	81	2012	59	2011	74	2009	77	2010	66	2012	64
2002	60	2005	78	2006	84	2009	69	2008	79	2004	77	2005	61	2010	49
1997	68	2002	80	2001	81	2005	67	2005	80	1999	89	2001	59	2008	64
1993	68	1998	82	1996	83	2003	60	2002	77	1994	87	1997	71	2006	48
1988	66	1994	79	1994	86	2000	61	1999	85			1992	78	2004	69
1986	78	1990	78	1992	87	1996	60	1996	88			1987	75	2002	45
1981	71	1987	84	1987	89	1993	67	1993	85			1983	73	2000	64
1978	72	1983	89	1983	89	1990	73	1990	85			1979	76	1998	52
1973	81	1980	89	1979	90	1986	64	1987	89			1974	73	1996	66
1968	80	1976	91	1976	93	1983	68	1984	94			1970	72	1994	58
1967	81	1972	91	1972	93	1980	75	1981	91			1966	76	1992	78
1962	69	1969	87	1968	93	1979	68	1978	85			1964	77	1990	56
1958	77	1965	87	1963	93	1976	73	1975	83			1959	79	1988	73
1956	83	1961	88	1958	94	1972	72	1972	90			1955	77	1986	55
1951	80	1957	88	1953	94	1969	69	1969	90			1951	82	1984	75
1946	82	1953	86	1948	92	1967	74	1966	87			1950	84	1982	61
1945	80	1949	78			1963	71	1963	90			1945	73	1980	77
						1960	74	1960	93					1978	57
						1958	77	1957	95					1976	78
						1955	76	1954	96					1974	58
						1953	74	1951	96					1972	80
						1952	76	1949	97					1970	70
						1949	74	1946	98					1968	90
						1947	68								
						1946	72								

Note
Percentages have been rounded up to the nearest whole figure.

parliamentary elections after 1980 as our baseline and comparing figures for the most recent elections, we have a reduction in turnout from 71 per cent to 55 per cent in France, 89 per cent to 72 per cent in Germany, 89 per cent to 75 per cent in Italy, 75 per cent to 53 per cent in Japan, 91 per cent to 77 per cent in New Zealand, 87 per cent to 73 per cent in South Africa, 77 per cent to 63 per cent for the UK, and 77 per cent to 43 per cent for the USA.

Why this universally increasing reluctance vote? If the government is constantly making itself smaller, while promoting and, during the financial crisis, protecting the private sector at public expense, then the areas of life that can be affected by voting in one government rather than another will diminish too. Moreover, since we have a monologic discourse, in which the difference between parties might just be a matter of the scale and timetable of cuts to the public sector and welfare, voters might be inclined to think there is no point in voting as 'they are all the same'.

In the first part of this chapter we wish to challenge the view that the press is free, or that, for example, the citizens of the UK, or the USA, or Singapore, or South Africa have a diversity of points of view on offer in the news in their respective countries. We also want to challenge the view that it is even theoretically possible, let alone practically so, for the press to give an objective representation of the world.

Lord Northcliffe, the newspaper owner, once said 'News is what somebody somewhere wants to suppress; all the rest is advertising.' He obviously saw the role of the press as a watchdog for any inefficiency, irrationality, injustice, corruption or scandalous behaviour for which those in power may have been responsible. However, news media as we know it has been hi-jacked by those with political and economic power. First, they have done this through ownership. Second, they have done so by the dependence of newspapers on advertising. Third, they have exploited the ambiguities in what is newsworthy to their own ends. And lastly, they dominate the way the world is represented in the news since they are gatekeepers controlling the sources of the news and are being constantly quoted in it.

8.1 OWNERSHIP OF THE PRESS AND OTHER MEDIA

Ownership of the press tends to be concentrated in the hands of a few companies. An extreme case of this is Singapore, where all the newspapers – *Berita Harian, Berita Minggu, Business Times, Lianhe Wanbao, Lianhe Zaobao, My Paper, Shin Min Daily News, The New Paper, tabla!, Tamil Murasu, The Straits Times, The Sunday Times, Thumbs Up* and *zbCOMMA* – are owned by Singapore Press Holdings. Their most significant online presence is The AsiaOne Network, which their website describes as follows:

> **The AsiaOne Network** covers a whole suite of online platforms, including our flagship websites such as AsiaOne, STOMP, Razor TV, The Straits Times, The Business Times, Zaobao.com, and Omy. Collectively, our news, lifestyle and services portals command close to 160 million page views, and are read by an audience of over 11 million.
>
> Majority of our readers are professionals, managers, executives and businessmen – influential decision-makers who make these websites their daily read.
>
> Our advertisers include Fortune 500 corporations and leading brands, which use our websites and services as effective vehicles to reach affluent, brand-conscious and upwardly mobile individuals aged between 25 to 49 years. The sites are also well frequented by senior decision makers in governments, multinational corporations and institutions across Asia.
>
> (www.sph.com.sg/our-businesses/online/the-asiaone-network,
> retrieved 20 March 2014)

But in the UK the situation is not much better. The best-selling tabloid newspaper is the *Sun*, with a circulation of around 2.5 million. The most widely read broadsheet is the *Telegraph* (circulation around 570,000), but the most influential serious newspaper is probably *The Times* (circulation around 400,000). Both the *Sun* and *The Times* (and the *Sunday Times*) are owned and controlled by Rupert Murdoch, who in addition owns 39 per cent of the satellite broadcasting network BSkyB. Daily Mail and General Trust (DMGT), along with their subsidiary Northcliffe Media, own *The Daily Mail* and *The Mail on Sunday, Ireland on Sunday* and *Metro*, the free London daily newspaper. They also have a controlling interest in a large swathe of regional media, and a high proportion of shares in ITN and GCap Media. Richard Desmond owns *OK! magazine, Channel 5*, the *Daily Express, Sunday Express* and the *Daily Star*. The *Evening Standard* and the *Independent* are both owned by Russian businessman and ex-KGB agent Alexander Lebedev.

The news and entertainment empire of Rupert Murdoch, which, in 2013 split into 21st Century Fox and News Corp, extends into many countries. It owns a large group of newspapers in Australia, the *Wall Street Journal* and *New York Post*, Harper Collins the book publisher, the 20th Century Fox film studio and the Fox Broadcasting company, one of the USA's major television networks.

Along with the Murdoch empire, the following US companies and corporations dominate the media in the USA:

- Disney owns ABC, Buena Vista Motion Pictures Group, and ESPN; it is a partner in A&E Networks, which includes History, A&E, and Lifetime.
- CBS Corporation/Viacom owns CBS, CBS Radio (formerly Infinity Broadcasting), Simon & Schuster editing group, a 50 per cent ownership stake in The CW, MTV Networks and several cable television stations.
- Comcast owns NBC Universal, The Weather Channel, G4, Versus, style, E!, a share of A&E Networks, and Comcast SportsNet. As of 13 February 2014, Comcast also owns Time Warner Cable.
- Time Warner owns CNN, TBS,TNT, *Sports Illustrated*, *Time* and a 50 per cent stake in The CW.
- The Dolan family's companies and Cablevision own AMC, IFC, Sundance Channel, WE tv, News 12 Networks, MSG Network, Fuse TV, SportsTime Ohio.
- E.W. Scripps Company owns 14 newspapers, nine broadcast television stations, Travel Channel, HGTV, Food Network, DIY Network, Cooking Channel, GAC.

The advent of the internet has probably increased the diversity of views and voices in the news media. However, if one looks at the 15 most popular news websites in Table 8.2, we note some very familiar names, including CNN, Fox News and NBC, already mentioned in our analysis of the concentration of media ownership.

In South Africa there are similar concentrations of press ownership. Table 8.3. shows that the press is dominated by the Times Media Group and Media 24.

This means to say that, particularly in Singapore, as well as in the UK, South Africa and even in the USA, the owners of newspapers and other media have enormous scope, should they so wish, to exert pressure to suppress or highlight certain topics or events, or to mount campaigns, and to establish consensus, by denying alternative agendas or silencing opposing views. The scope for influence is facilitated by the process of manufacture of news. The source's or reporter's original text is filtered through a hierarchy which might include sub-editors, revision editor and editor in chief, making it possible for editorial policy to reject, interfere with, cut and distort the original text in line with editorial policy.

Pressure to interfere with the news may come from government, but just as important are influential commercial interests including those of the proprietor. Richard Desmond is the owner of *The Daily Express* and *Sunday Express* and, Michael Pilgrim, the editor of the latter, 'complained

Table 8.2 *Top 15 most popular news websites in March 2014*

Rank	News site	Estimated unique monthly visitors
1	Yahoo! News	150,000,000
2	Huffington Post	110,000,000
3	CNN	95,000,000
4	Google News	90,000,000
5	New York Times	70,000,000
6	Fox News	65,000,000
7	NBC News	63,000,000
8	The Guardian	60,000,000
9	Mail Online	53,000,000
10	USA Today	50,000,000
11	Washington Post	47,000,000
12	Wall Street Journal	40,000,000
13	BBC News	35,000,000
14	ABC News	33,000,000
15	Los Angeles Times	30,500,000

Note
The data for this table was extracted from *eBizMBA Rank*, a constantly updated average of each website's *Alexa* Global Traffic Rank, and US Traffic Rank from both *Compete* and *Quantcast*. www.ebizmba.com/articles/news-website, retrieved 20 March 2014.

that he had been obliged to spike stories about Desmond's commercial allies and publish critical pieces about rivals he did not like' (Greenslade 2009; 'Controlling Interest', Roy Greenslade, *Guardian* Monday 27 July 2009, www.theguardian.com/media/2009/jul/27/newspaper-owners-editorial-control, retrieved 26 March 2014). Similarly, Rupert Murdoch, according to Andrew Neill, former editor of the *Sunday Times*, claimed that he came under pressure to spike, i.e. reject, stories that might upset Mahathir Mohammed, Prime Minister of Malaysia (Greenslade 2009; www.theguardian.com/media/2009/jul/27/newspaper-owners-editorial-control, retrieved 26 March 2014).

Table 8.3 *Press ownership in South Africa*

Newspaper	Publisher	Language	Circulation (Q2 2013)
Sunday Times	Times Media Group	English	368,974
Daily Sun	Media24	English	287,222
Rapport	Media24	Afrikaans	192,293
Sunday Sun	Media24	English	170,843
Sunday World	Times Media Group	English	123,515
City Press	Media24	English	119,959
Isolezwe	INMSA	Zulu	110,753
Ilanga	Independent	Zulu	107,102
The Sowetan	Times Media Group	English	95,068
Die Son (daily)	Media24	Afrikaans	91,735

Note
The data for this table is compiled from http://en.wikipedia.org/wiki/Times_Media_Group and http://en.wikipedia.org/wiki/Media24

8.2 NEWSPAPERS' DEPENDENCE ON ADVERTISING

Newspapers are not simply a service to the public, but must make a profit for the corporations to which they belong or for their owners and shareholders. Where do newspapers get their revenue? The largest part is from advertising, not from the cover price charged to the readers in printed newspapers, and obviously not from free online newspapers. As Norman Fairclough puts it

> The press ... are eminently profit-making organisations, they make their profits by selling audiences to advertisers and they do this by achieving the highest possible readerships ... for the lowest possible financial outlay.
>
> (Fairclough 1995: 42)

There are two effects of this. For one, newspapers will not wish to run stories which might put off advertisers. This means that advertisers can threaten to withdraw their advertising if newspapers publish stories or implement policies which are critical of them or undermine their position. This may well restrict the range of political views, agendas or topics of investigative journalism to those acceptable to the particular companies advertising, or more generally to those which support the capitalist system of which advertising is a part. In February 2015 Peter Oborne, chief political analyst for the *Daily Telegraph*, resigned. He did so because he believed the fact that HSBC was a major advertiser with the paper had persuaded editors to downplay coverage of the scandal over HSBC's Swiss subsidiary's encouragement of tax evasion. It seems to us unfortunate that BBC World Service TV broadcasts ads, since traditionally the BBC's strength was its distance from commercial advertising and any influence it might exert.

But, second, and more important, the dependence of newspapers on advertising makes it very difficult for newspapers representing the views of the poor and the working class to be viable. Papers with a less affluent readership get much less advertising revenue per copy than papers with richer readers. This is because the advertisers can push more expensive products, not, for example, dog food, soap powder or toothpaste, but flat-screen televisions, mobile phones, computers, printers and cars.

The 2014 figures for advertising cost compared with circulation given in Table 8.4 prove the point. The *Financial Times* (*FT*) has less than 12 per cent of the circulation of the *Sun*, and yet is able to charge more for a full-page advertisement. This is quite out of proportion, even allowing for the fact that the *FT* is a broadsheet and the *Sun* a tabloid, with pages half the size. The explanation is that the readers of the *FT*

Table 8.4 *Advertising rates compared with circulation*

Paper	Circulation	Price of full-page display ad (£)	Cost per reader
Sun	2.5 million	51,000	2
Daily Mail	1.5 million	45,612	3
Daily Mirror	1.08 million	36,800	3.4
Times	400,000	27,195	6.8
Guardian	212,000	18,000	8.5
Telegraph	570,000	59,000	10.4
Independent	76,800	13,050	17
Financial Times	300,000	58,600	19.5

Note
The data for this table were extracted from www.themediabriefing.com/article/how-much-do-newspapers-think-their-audiences-are-worth (retrieved 5 March 2014).

have much more buying power per head than readers of the *Sun*. The cost, and presumably therefore the estimated value of an *FT* reader is nine times more than that of a *Sun* reader. The same goes if we compare the *Telegraph* with the *Daily Mail*, the former's readers costing three times that of the latter's. In the USA, *USA Today*, with a circulation of roughly 1.7 million, charges $125,000 for a full-page black-and-white ad, whereas the *Wall Street Journal* (global edition), with roughly the same circulation, charges $278,000. In Singapore *The New Paper*, a down-market tabloid with a circulation of 90,000, charges S$10 per column centimetre, while the elite readership *Business Times* with a circulation of 36,000 charges S$14.5 per column centimetre. An anomaly is the relatively upmarket Singapore *Straits Times* which, with a circulation of 325,000, charges S$44.5 per column centimetre, which is in line with the cost per reader of tabloid *The New Paper*.

Since the financial viability of newspapers depends upon their advertising revenue, this makes it very difficult to run a national newspaper which represents the views of the poor, or takes their political agenda seriously.

The history of radical working-class newspapers in the UK gives a clear picture of the problem. The *Daily Herald*, which was just such a paper, folded up in 1964. At that time it had 4.7 million readers, almost double the readership of *The Times*, the *Sunday Times* and the *Guardian* put together – that is 8.1 per cent of newspaper circulation. However, it had only a 3.5 per cent slice of the available advertising revenue. This did not stop Sir Denis Hamilton, editor in chief of Times Newspapers, saying at the time 'The Herald was beset by the problem which has dogged nearly every newspaper vowed to a political idea; not enough people wanted to read it'! (Similarly, *Life* magazine had more than five million subscribers when it folded in 1972, due to loss of advertising revenue.)

So, popular newspapers, in order to reach as wide a readership as possible, and to avoid tackling issues of inequality which may threaten the interests of advertisers and the capitalist system of which they are part, have to trivialise their news. In the UK there is at present no attempt to create a taste for anything much except sensationalism and prurient gossip about the private lives of celebrities. During the aftermath of Princess Diana's death, when the TV and radio were looking for someone to blame for the accident, the first tendency was to accuse the so-called "paparazzi", the photographers who were pursuing her on motorcycles, and the newspaper editors who were in the habit of buying their photographs. The focus of blame then shifted to the readers and purchasers of these newspapers. The problem is that the majority of the English population really have little choice if they wish to read a daily newspaper. What national newspaper is there in England which deals with serious issues with depth and intelligence and which a person of average education can understand? The tabloid newspapers make no attempt to cultivate a taste for clear thought or discussion of serious political issues.

Indeed, because their main aim is entertainment and not education, the papers turn political issues into matters of personality, as though political matters can be reduced to a soap-opera drama, sometimes with the kind of intertextuality labelled as *dramatisation of argument* in Chapter 6. The Gulf War was presented as a conflict between Bush and Saddam Hussein, the war in Afghanistan as a conflict between Obama and Osama bin Laden and finding and killing the latter was seen as some kind of victory for Obama. Needless to say, the deaths of Saddam and Osama have not solved the political and economic problems of Iraq and Afghanistan. But personalisation has become one aspect in the selection and presentation of news, or news values, the topic of our next section.

Now that we have online news, and a decreasing circulation of print news, a somewhat disturbing trend has emerged. Because ad revenue has declined along with circulation, both print newspapers, and even more online news outlets, have less to spend on investigative journalism and have become increasingly reliant on news agencies or wire services as their sources (Tewksbury and Rittenberg 2012). This may mean that the agenda and sources of news providers could become less varied, more monologic. However, because the online audience is more segmented and fragmented, the agenda may be less uniform.

Another feature of the relationship between online news and advertising mirrors the problems with traditional news. While there is a tendency for specialisation of readership in online news, as this allows advertisers to target a specific demographic more likely to be interested in their products, the information for specialised news is often rather costly to gather. The specialised audience, therefore, has to be sufficiently rich to compensate for the cost of obtaining specialised information.

8.3 THE SELECTION OF NEWS

What gets selected as news and why? We already looked at some of Galtung and Ruge's news values in Chapter 2, but here we have the space to consider all of them in more detail (Table 8.5). If we assume that newspapers have a role in informing and highlighting actions, events and processes which represent a threat to the general public, including political inefficiency or corruption, it will be obvious that most news will come over as bad news (1). No news is good news, as they say. The question is whether newspapers really do their job in this regard.

One problem is the question of frequency (2). In order to get into the news, events, actions or processes should take place over a time period which is shorter than the time between publications of the newspaper. This means to say that newspapers find it difficult to cope with major threats to the public from processes like climate change, which take place over years and decades. The only time these will be reported is when there is some discrete event, like a politician's speech, or the Paris Summit, which has a shorter time span. Our perceptual apparatus is not, of course, very good at taking in these more extended processes, so that we find short, isolable material or verbal processes much more meaningful (3).

Another factor which makes climate change difficult to get into the news is that it is a rather new cultural phenomenon: it's difficult for us to believe that the solid land on which we stand may in 50 years or so be under water, or that the familiar weather patterns which we have experienced all our lives may be disrupted. Of course, scientific investigations of the mechanisms of global warming, of meteorology and the chemical reactions of the upper atmosphere are very remote from most people,

Table 8.5 News values

#	Value	Explanation
1	Negativity	Generally bad
2	Frequency	The span of the event/action less than the length of time between publication
3	Meaningfulness	Familiar and comprehensible within the cultural mindset of the reader
4	Persons	Interest in people acting/talking/suffering
5	Consonance	The usual, predictable or expected
6	Unexpectedness	The unusual or abnormal
7	Continuity	The topic is in the news, continuing there
8	Composition	Variety in one particular edition of the newspaper
9	Threshold	Large scale events, numbers of people involved
10	Elite nations	Reference to the powerful nations – USA, Japan, Europe
11	Elite persons	Reference to powerful people – politicians, monarchs, the rich and famous

and perhaps difficult to understand. So they may not make it as news since they are distant from the human life-world as we understand it. Most newsworthy topics are those which involve human interest stories, are personal and can be dramatised (4).

This brings us to the next pairs of values, which represent a tension between the expected and the unexpected. Generally, news might be thought of as the reporting of exceptional or abnormal events (6). If everything goes according to the schema, it is hardly worth mentioning. The problem here is that certain normal and recurring events, and processes and states, which nevertheless represent a threat to many people, tend to be ignored in the news. Take for example the carnage on the roads caused by car transportation. In 2010 to 2011, road accidents were the world's ninth most common cause of death, with 1.24 million killed in 2010, and 92 people killed on the highways in the USA every day. These facts seem to be such an accepted, frequent and predictable threat to the public that newspapers and media hardly think traffic fatalities worth mentioning, unless there is some spectacular accident with a high death toll (9), or unless it involves an elite person such as Princess Diana (11). Similarly, the background noise of human misery caused by poverty, malnutrition, disease, pollution and ignorance is effectively filtered out from the mainstream media. By contrast, what really makes the news is the much less frequent phenomenon of terrorism and violent crime. From the period 1985 to 2013 the total number of deaths from homeland terrorism in the USA was just 3,487, and in Israel 2,061 (www.johnstonsarchive.net/terrorism/terror-rate.html, retrieved 26 March 2014).

There are, of course, powerful ideological reasons why terrorism should make the news, when car accidents and infant mortality do not. Terrorism is often of a political nature, and depending on allegiances one person's terrorist is another's freedom fighter. As such, terrorism represents a challenge to the political or economic status quo, and threatens those who have an interest in maintaining it because they at present have authority, fame or wield political or economic power. By contrast, the World Bank's loan and repayment system, which means a poor country like Mozambique had to spend 2.5 times as much on servicing debt as it did on health care (Hanlon 1999: 27), is very much part of the economic order. Consequently, to draw attention to the threat it poses to the well-being of poor nations is not a high priority among newspapers owned by transnational corporations. Highlighting the deaths of poor children in Mozambique might lead to political action to change the economic world order. But instead, deaths from 'terrorism' are highlighted because it threatens existing political orders.

By ignoring the real and pervasive threats to the well-being of humankind, newspapers are accomplices in one aspect of the crisis of modernity: the fact that the system is so rotten and out of step with human and ecological well-being that co-operating with and abiding by social norms is non-sustainable or brings tragedy or suffering. It was the playwright Arthur Miller who pointed out the difference between the heroes of traditional tragedy and the heroes of his own modern tragedies, like Willy Loman in his play *Death of a Salesman*. The traditional tragic hero experiences suffering and death because he rebels against society's valid norms – for example, Oedipus by marrying his mother, or Macbeth by killing King Duncan. But Willy Loman suffers because he wholeheartedly embraces the suspect values of the American Dream: the drive for status, money, possession of the latest consumer goods; the obsession with being liked, with indiscriminate sexual gratification and with fame and success for one's children (Miller 1958: 22–36). The interesting, or vital, question is, how long can the media go on ignoring the increasing background problems created by a flawed economic and political world order, simply because the human misery they cause is so widespread as to be no longer newsworthy?

On the other hand, we have the expected nature of the news (5), and we can relate this to what we have said about stereotyping in Chapter 2. We expect certain nationalities to behave in predictable ways, and events or actions which conform to our stereotype are likely to be more newsworthy than those that do not.

Look at the following lyrics of a song, and then watch it on YouTube at www.youtube.com/watch?v=5EjEH9YnD-U

> Since you love me and I love you
> The rest matters not.
> I will cut grass in the fields
> And you will sell it for beasts.
>
> Since you love me and I love you
> The rest matters not.
> I will grow maize in the fields
> And you will sell it for people.

Now, guess where the lyrics, here translated into English, originated from. Such is the stereotyping we have undergone, that I doubt any of us would associate these words with Afghanistan, for which we have many negative stereotypes concerning violence, arranged marriages and female oppression, rather than romantic love.

Continuity (7), the bandwagon effect, is very noticeable in news, and obviously contributes to stereotyping. In 2013 there was a near hysteria generated by stories of male celebrities having indulged in sex with underage girls, with Jimmy Saville the prime example. Many other celebrities were subsequently accused of sexual molestation or rape, and some of the accusations were not upheld by the courts. Sometimes newspapers wage campaigns, either of their own ideological making, or taking the cue from government. One current *Daily Mail* campaign is against families who are welfare-dependent and have been for generations (e.g. 'Families where generations have never worked because they don't want to cut the benefits "umbilical cord"', www.dailymail.co.uk/news/article-2526878/Families-generations-never-worked-dont-want-cut-benefits-umbilical-cord.html#ixzz31UnSiEfO, retrieved 12 May 2014). But

> The Joseph Rowntree Foundation published a study in December testing whether there were three generations of the same family that had never worked. Despite dogged searching, researchers were unable to find such families. If they exist, they account for a minuscule fraction of workless people. Under 1% of workless households might have two generations who have never worked – about 15,000 households in the UK. Families with three such generations will therefore be even fewer.
> (www.theguardian.com/politics/2013/apr/06/welfare-britain-facts-myths, retrieved 12 May 2014)

News value (9) is threshold, the idea that the larger the event or action in terms of casualties, numbers killed, cost of damage and so on, the more likely it is to make the news. The fact seems to be that this value, an absolute one if we accept that each human life is as valuable as the next, is largely overridden by factors such as threat to the status quo (as already noted, deaths from terrorism have a lower threshold than deaths from car accidents or starvation), or by the notion of elite nations (10) and elite persons (11), the last two values. As we shall see, rich and powerful people are the ones who are more newsworthy.

8.4 THE SOURCES OF NEWS

The dominant members of society also exert considerable influence on the selection of news because they tend to be the gatekeepers and the sources of news. On the global scale the international news which appears in national newspapers and online is increasingly provided by one or more of the Western-based news agencies: Associated Press, Reuters, Agence France-Presse, mostly, by the way, operating in English with all the cultural biases that this entails. Traditionally, at a more local level news was routinely gathered by journalists from the established and powerful institutions of society. Reporters checked with the police and the courts to find out if there were any interesting crimes or legal cases, and with hospitals to see if there were newsworthy accidents. Reporters still attend the press conferences at which politicians, company chairmen and spokespersons for important organisations pronounce on political issues or company financial results, plans for expansion or streamlining, retrenchment and redundancy. Should a journalist's report have been critical of the police, the courts and these other powerful figures, she might well have found her sources of news drying up afterwards. So this dependence was likely to dampen her campaigning zeal.

Every editor will keep a press diary so that the paper can routinely cover scheduled events featuring the rich, the famous, the very important people: international conferences, press conferences, sittings of Parliament, political speeches, state visits by foreign politicians or monarchs, concerts and so on. While this kind of routine makes the news production manageable, and means that it can be planned for, it also reinforces the power structures of society. Only relatively rich organisations can afford to employ press officers and stage press conferences, for example. So it is these powerful institutions who become the originating sayers. Their views and values, their versions of economic and political reality, are passed around and become common-sense and natural, hiding their ideological nature and exerting "untold" influence.

However, as we shall explore later in this chapter, the monolithic control of the news has been to some extent challenged by the new digital media. With the internet there is at least the theoretical possibility that the public consumers of news can also be the producers of news. Citizen journalists using portals like Ushahidi, Demotix, You Witness News, All Voices or Wikinews promote alternative news networks. The project suggested at the end of this chapter invites the reader to realise this possibility.

Moreover, through social media, ordinary members of the public may even put pressure on the more established and traditional online news sites to cover stories that would otherwise be ignored. An instructive example is that of Jody McIntyre, a student who suffers from cerebral palsy and who took part in the London demonstration against the increase in university fees on 10 December 2010. He was being pushed by his brother towards the police cordon when a police officer grabbed him by his shoulders and dragged him out of his wheelchair onto the road. When his friends tried to help him they were beaten with batons by the police. The incident was recorded and posted on YouTube, and such was the uptake and volume of internet discussion that the BBC were finally forced to cover the story in its morning news bulletin on 14 December. However, the BBC interviewer's unsympathetic attitude towards Jody provoked more social media outrage, and the BBC received at least 500 complaints. Nevertheless, the deputy head of the BBC newsroom, Kevin Backhurst, rejected the public's criticism, which again provoked anger in the digital media. By the end of December there were over 100,000 results for the phrase 'Jody McIntyre and BBC' on the Google search engine, most of them comments by ordinary citizens (Batkiewicz, 2011). Nevertheless, the BBC's refusal to apologise indicates some of the entrenched forces preventing the alternative social media penetrating the traditional establishment media.

A similar, if rather more exaggerated, pattern of social media influence and eventual establishment resistance is observable in China. Weibo, the Chinese equivalent of Twitter, had been instrumental in exposing corruption among Communist Party officials and campaigning against the building of hazardous industrial plants near centres of population. For example, Luo Changping, a business and economics reporter, in his microblog back in December, accused Liu Tienan, the Deputy Chairman of the cabinet's National Development and Reform Commission of falsifying his CV, using his power as a top official to enrich his family and issuing death threats to his mistress. Though the Chinese authorities initially denied these allegations, five months later, after a tide of negative comments on social media, they launched an investigation and sacked him. Official reports at the time praised the role of social media in aiding Xi Jinping's campaign against corruption (China: social media tools embolden anti-corruption activists, www.france24.com/en/20130515-china-social-media-tools-embolden-anti-corruption-activists%20, retrieved 12 May 2014).

However, according to *Fortune Magazine/CNN Money*, more recently, the Chinese government have perceived the social media and online blogs as a threat and launched a comprehensive crackdown against them. Three big-Vs (online commentators with verified large followings, in these cases of over ten million) were arrested in 2013. Between 21 and 23 August Beijing and Suzhou police detained Qin Huohuo, Yang Qiuyu and Zhou Lubao, charging them with rumour-mongering, defamation and blackmail. Zhou Lubao had previously become famous for spotting an expensive watch worn by a smiling official at a traffic accident years before (http://management.fortune.cnn.com/2013/09/12/china-social-media, retrieved 12 May 2014).

Even with the potential democratising influence of digital media on news content, the news is not objectively gathered, and is still often selected according to the values which suit and reflect the dominant elites of society, the interests of the newspaper owners, and through the powerful international agencies and local institutions who act as sources of news. Furthermore, once a particular item has been selected as newsworthy, it still has to be presented and shaped on the page of the newspaper and this provides further scope for "bias". The selection of lead and headline in a deductive, point-first genre like news reports can distort the facts, and mislead the reader who only skims the paper. We noted this in our discussion of the article 'UK unemployment rate at lowest since 2009' in Chapter 1.

Besides this, we explored in some detail in Chapter 2 how the language we use and the choices we make within it inevitably suppress some aspects of the world out there and highlight other features. For example, seniority was seen as being relatively important in the way Asian languages classify relatives. Language, then, is no transparent medium for representing reality but inevitably highlights and hides, is essentially "biased". We can only conclude that the notion of objective unbiased news published by a free press is a myth and a mirage.

Even were this not the case, we need to be aware of the patterns of representation in the news. Is it the rich and powerful who are mentioned, and is it their voices that are given the most prominence? This is the topic of the next two sections.

8.5 CASE STUDY 1: REPRESENTATION AND VOICES IN THE NEWS

To investigate representation and whose voices appear in the news we looked at the most prominent news stories appearing on 5 March 2014 in the online editions of the *Japan Times, Times of India, USA Today,* Australia's (Victoria and Melbourne) *Herald Sun,* and the UK's the *Mirror.*[1] We identified all the named people and categorised the major groups (see Table 8.6), and then noted whether they had their words reported. This analysis gives a fair indication of who gets to be mentioned in the news and whose voices are quoted.

Representation of named individuals in the news

The power structures of modern society are reflected in the data. The power of physical force is represented by the military, police and judiciary. The power of government by national governments and politicians, with Obama and Kerry, as leaders of the 'most powerful nation on earth' over-represented, along with leaders from Russia and China. The power of institutions is represented by officials. The power of knowledge by experts, doctors and academics. The power of economics by business people. And the increasing power of celebrity by entertainers. In the UK, at least, entertainers and celebrities seem to have more power than politicians – the campaign for nutritious school meals was spearheaded, not by the minister of health, but by Jamie Oliver, and the entertainer Russell Brand's views on politics are deemed more important than those of, say, the Green Party. Indeed the dividing line between entertainer and politician is a permeable one – think of Ronald Reagan, Arnold Schwarzenegger or Glenda Jackson – and in this data we have Kinky Friedman, a novelist and country music performer with political ambitions.

It is interesting to note the phenomenon of famous historical figures who have given their names to facilities or institutions – the Hubble and James Webb telescopes, the Menzies, Lowy, M.S. Ramaiah, and Sanjay Gandhi Institutes, the Moti Lal Nehru Medical College, and Sir Sundar Lal (SSL) Hospital. Maybe these names represent the power of history. None of them are the names of women, which may reflect the position of women historically, but which nevertheless reproduces a pattern of sexism.

Named individuals who represent ordinary or powerless people are found in the categories of patients, victims, criminals, relatives, friends and neighbours, and other members of the public. The fact that victims and patients are major categories simply underlines the general powerlessness of the public. When named people appear in court either as plaintiffs or accused, such as a girl who is suing her parents for college tuition fees, or when they are victims of crime, such as a policeman killed in a shootout, then very often friends, relatives and neighbours will be interviewed for their opinions of their character or behaviour or will themselves appear in court as witnesses. Or when gossip about celebrities is the news topic, less well-known friends of the celebrity might be questioned. A few members of the public might achieve a limited power by their skill or activism – a teenage boy whose poem can be read backwards and scored a hit on Twitter, or Bajrang Dal activist Ashok Mochi, a cobbler, or one Joy Botton who is organising a campaign against the ban on dogs on a beach in Australia.

Women in the news

From Table 8.6 it is immediately obvious that women, underlined in the table, are under-represented, except in the categories of patients, victims and relatives (where there are six mentions of wives and girlfriends). Indeed in these latter categories they are over-represented, underlining the fact that women are often seen as passive and achieve status through relationships, especially with husbands/partners. Murdered Muslim bride Farkhanda Younis exemplifies passive victimhood; Michelle Obama exemplifies importance by relationship to a famous male partner; and Reeva Steenkamp exemplifies both. Women as the victims of crime was still a hot topic in India after the rape and murder of Nirbhaya in Delhi, and the ongoing phenomenon of acid attacks. But it is also typical to represent women/girls as suffering victims in the West, for example in this quote from a *USA Today* article in the corpus: 'I can't even say the number of times my daughter has fallen and gotten a boo-boo, and he took her inside and washed her and bandaged her up.'

Women are also well-represented as entertainers, 10/23, especially in the 'acting' category, where they are often described in terms of their sexual relationship with men – one of the *Daily Mirror* articles is all

Table 8.6 *Categories of named and reported individuals in a selection of newspapers*

Category	Named individuals
National government	PRESIDENT BARACK OBAMA (× 5), RUSSIAN PRESIDENT VLADIMIR PUTIN (× 4), PREMIER LI KEQIANG (× 2), (PRIME MINISTER) ARSENIY YATSENYUK, US SECRETARY OF STATE JOHN KERRY (× 2), TRADE MINISTER TOSHIMITSU MOTEGI German Chancellor Angela Merkel (× 2), (fugitive) President Viktor Yanukovych (× 2), Prime Minister Shinzo Abe, French President Francois Hollande, British Prime Minister David Cameron, President Xi Jinping, Foreign Minister Fumio Kishida, Russian Foreign Minister Sergei Lavrov
Politicians and local government	CONGRESS LEADER RITA BAHUGUNA JOSHI?, CONGRESS VICE-PRESIDENT RAHUL GANDHI (× 2), AAP LEADER ARVIND KEJRIWAL, RLD LEADER MUNNA SINGH CHAUHAN?, SAMAJWADI PARTY LEADER NARESH AGARWAL, BJP'S PREEMINENT PARTY ELDER LK ADVANI, MADHYA PRADESH CHIEF MINISTER SHIVRAJ SINGH CHOUHAN, SENATOR ORRIN HATCH?, REP. DAVE CAMP CHAIRMAN OF CONGRESS' CHIEF TAX-WRITING COMMITTEE, REP. STEVE STOCKMAN, POLICE AND EMERGENCY SERVICES MINISTER KIM WELLS, BASS COAST MAYOR NEIL RANKINE Sheila Dikshit governor of Kerala (× 2), Democrat Wendy Davis, Sushma Swaraj, BJP's prime ministerial nominee Narendra Modi (× 4), Chief Minister Akhilesh Yadav, SP MLA Irfan Solanki, Rajnath Singh, Narendra Manish Sisodia, Sanjay Singh, Prithviraj Chavan, Texas Gov. Rick Perry, Rules Committee Chairman Pete Sessions, Texas Republican Sen. John Cornyn, GOP Rep. Ralph Hall the oldest member of Congress, conservative firebrand Ted Cruz, Dwayne Stovall a rival conservative challenger, Jim Hogan, *Kinky Friedman a novelist and country music performer, former El Paso Democratic Mayor John Cook, Florida governor Jeb Bush
Officials and diplomats	DEPUTY SECRETARY OF STATE HEATHER A. HIGGINBOTTOM, NASA CHIEF FINANCIAL OFFICER ELIZABETH ROBINSON, PARENTS VICTORIA CHIEF GAIL MCHARDY, CHIEF CABINET SECRETARY YOSHIHIDE SUGA (× 2), RUSSIA'S AMBASSADOR TO THE UN VITALY CHURKIN, DAVID HELVEY US DEPUTY ASSISTANT SECRETARY OF DEFENSE FOR EAST ASIA, CHIEF ELECTION COMMISSIONER V.S. SAMPATH, ELECTION COMMISSIONER H.S. BRAHMA, UNIVERSITY VICE-CHANCELLOR MANZOOR AHMED, VICTORIAN ASSOCIATION OF STATE SECONDARY PRINCIPALS PRESIDENT FRANK SAL, FIRE SERVICES COMMISSIONER CRAIG LAPSLEY, DAVID LO, A SPOKESMAN FOR TAIWAN'S DEFENCE MINISTRY, POLICE SPOKESMAN STEVE MARTOS, OPPOSITION EMERGENCY SERVICES SPOKESMAN WADE NOONAN, FU YING A SPOKESWOMAN FOR THE PARLIAMENTARY SESSION Treasury Secretary Jacob Lew, Republican State Attorney General Greg Abbott, Election Commissioner S.N.A. Zaidi, John Ratcliffe a former US attorney, Principal Colin Graeme Davis
Police and military	RETIRED PHOENIX POLICE OFFICER LISA WILSON CARNAHAN, REAR ADM. WILLIAM LESCHER DEPUTY ASSISTANT SECRETARY OF THE NAVY FOR BUDGET, CAPT. NIKOLAI SYOMKO AN AIR FORCE RADIO ELECTRICIAN, PAVEL SHISHURIN THE DEPUTY HEAD OF THE BORDER GUARDS, SEAN MATTSON PRESIDENT OF THE 500-MEMBER PHOENIX POLICE SERGEANTS AND LIEUTENANTS ASSOCIATION, SUNSHINE POLICE SERGEANT CALLUM MCCANN?, POLICE CHIEF COMMISSIONER KEN LAY, DETECTIVE SENIOR CONSTABLE JASON BENBOW? Phoenix police Detective John Hobbs, Rifat Gedik, former detective Paul Dale, Phoenix Police Chief Daniel V. Garcia
Judiciary	LAWYER TANYA N. HELFAND?, PRESIDING JUDGE CHIIWA KURASAWA, ADVOCATE LAWRENCE LIANG OF THE BANGALORE-BASED ALTERNATIVE LAW FORUM, JUDGE PETER BOGAARD OF MORRIS COUNTY SUPERIOR COURT'S FAMILY DIVISION?, TRIAL COURT ADMINISTRATOR RASHAD SHABAKA BURNS, FAMILY LAW ATTORNEY EDWARD O'DONNELL OF MORRISTOWN, CHIEF LAWYER BARRY ROUX?, ALISDAIR WILLIAMSON FOR THE DEFENCE, JOHN JONES QC Lawyer John Inglesino
Criminals /accused	ELIZABETH CANNING (SUEE)?, SEAN CANNING A RETIRED LINCOLN PARK POLICE CHIEF (SUEE) Carl Williams, Oscar Pistorius, "jealous" husband Jahangir Nazar 35 takeway delivery driver, Romanian teenager, a 19-year-old Japanese boy
Victims	QUTUBUDDIN ANSARI, ACID ATTACK VICTIM LAXMI Nirbhaya the courageous 23-year-old girl gang raped and murdered, Reeva Steenkamp Pritorius' girlfriend, "promiscuous" Muslim bride Farkhanda Younis

Category	Named individuals
Doctors	DR SEANA GALL A RESEARCH FELLOW IN CARDIOVASCULAR EPIDEMIOLOGY *DR ALEXANDER THOMAS CEO BANGALORE BAPTIST HOSPITAL, *DR NARESH SHETTY OF AHPI
Patients	Rekha Kumar (35) of Sitapur, Raisa Bano of Kunda in Pratapgarh, frail 70-year-old Shafiq
Business-people	GENERAL MOTORS CEO MARY BARRA, TOM O'SULLIVAN FOUNDER OF INDEPENDENT ENERGY CONSULTANCY MATHYOS JAPAN, SUREN RUHELA DIRECTOR AND PRODUCT MANAGER INDIA GOOGLE MAPS, MAYI GOWDA OF BLOSSOM BOOK HOUSE?, GM PRESIDENT DAN AMMANN, JEREMY ROBINSON-LEON COO AT GROUP GORDON NEW YORK CRISIS PUBLIC RELATIONS FIRM, GIRIDHAR K. GYANI DIRECTOR GENERAL AHPI NEW DELHI, FIRST NATIONAL SOUTHCOAST REAL ESTATE OWNER BLAIR HODGES Yahoo chief executive Marissa Mayer, Yahoo then CEO Carol Bartz, businessman David Watts, businessman David Alameel
Academics/experts	DAVID MADDEN MARKET ANALYST AT IG, RUSSIAN MILITARY ANALYST ALEXANDER GOLTS, RORY MEDCALF A REGIONAL SECURITY ANALYST AT THE INDEPENDENT LOWY INSTITUTE IN SYDNEY, HEMANT JOSHI WHO OVERSEES THE TELECOM PRACTICE AT CONSULTING FIRM DELOITTE, RANJITH CHERICKEL A TELECOM PROFESSIONAL WHO HAS WORKED AT NOKIA SIEMENS NETWORKS VERIZON WIRELESS AND SKYPE, RENSSELAER POLYTECHNIC INSTITUTE ASTRONOMER LAURIE LESHIN, HARVARD UNIVERSITY ASTRONOMER AVI LOEB, CITIGROUP'S ECONOMIST MINGGAO SHEN, CITIGROUP'S ECONOMIST DING SHUANG, CAL JILLSON A POLITICAL SCIENTIST AT SOUTHERN METHODIST UNIVERSITY IN DALLAS, MARK JONES CHAIRMAN OF THE POLITICAL SCIENCE DEPARTMENT AT RICE UNIVERSITY IN HOUSTON
Students	RACHEL CANNING HONOR STUDENT AT MORRIS CATHOLIC HIGH SCHOOL? *YASHAS SHEKAR A 23-YEAR-OLD college-mate Vijayakumar Umaluti, college-mate Sandesh Eshwarappa
Entertainers	AMY CHILDS THE REALITY STARLET (× 2), JOURNALIST WILL PAYNE, MICHAEL LE VELL, JOHN TRAVOLTA, JIMMI HARKISHIN?, SIMPSONS CREATOR MATT GROENING Wendy Doniger (author), Saheed Rumi who penned Ansari's biography, Tony Award winner Idina Menzel, Tom Kitt, Brian Yorkey (story writer) Michael Greif (director), Sir Steve Redgrave, Jordan, Kerry Katona, Lilia Kopylova, executive producer Stuart Blackburn, Craig Charles, Ellen, Bradley Cooper, Kevin Spacey, Julia Roberts, Pittsburgh Steeler Dave Meggett, Darren Gough (cricketer)
Historical figures/names	Mahatma Gandhi, Hitler, the late supreme leader Deng Xiaoping, Gov. Ann Richards, President George W. Bush, President George H.W. Bush Menzies Research Institute University of Tasmania, Lowy Institute in Sydney, M.S. Ramaiah Institute of Technology in Bangalore, Sanjay Gandhi Post-Graduate Institute of Medical Sciences, Moti Lal Nehru Medical College, Sir Sundar Lal (SSL) Hospital, James Webb Space Telescope, Hubble (space telescope)
Relatives, friends, neighbours	MOTHER LISA KITZMILLER, JOHNSON'S WIFE MICHELLE BURGER?, US FIRST LADY MICHELLE OBAMA, DEREK NICHOLS HIS OLDER BROTHER, NEIGHBOUR JAMES BRENN, ANOTHER NEIGHBOUR NICK ARCAN, CHARL JOHNSON A NEIGHBOUR OF OSCAR PISTORIUS? members of Steenkamp's family including her cousin Kim, long-term pal Emma Dodd, Le Vell's ex-girlfriend Chilean Blanca Fouche 31, (Terence Hodson and) his wife Christine, his wife Janette, Commons Speaker's wife Sally Bercow, Gough's former wife Anna George P. Bush 37 son of former Florida governor Jeb Bush and relative of George W. Bush and George H.W. Bush, her best friend Jaime Inglesino, his close friend detective Denis Linehan, boyfriend Lucas Kitzmiller
Other members of the public	WORLD'S OLDEST WOMAN MISAO OKAWA, JOY BOTTON (ORGANISER OF A RALLY AGAINST THE DOG BANS) BAJRANG DAL ACTIVIST, ASHOK MOCHI 39 A COBBLER, STEVEN DURETTE (FRIEND OF HOBBES), TEENAGE BOY JORDAN NICHOLS (WHO WROTE A REVERSIBLE POEM), INVERLOCH RESIDENT SHANE CLEMENTS police informer Terence Hodson, Jonathan Reed (would-be poet)

about Darren Gough the cricketer and Amy Childs 'the reality starlet'. The headline is followed by two photos of a semi-naked Childs.

Although we have a sprinkling of female doctors, high-flying business-women and politicians, women are totally absent from the experts category and only one appears in the police/military category. Moreover, we see that women's lack of power in politics in the USA is an angle in one of our stories: 'Democrat Wendy Davis became the first female gubernatorial nominee in the state since former Gov. Ann Richards almost a quarter century ago'. Female politicians in India seem to be better placed, especially Sheila Dikshit, governor of Kerala, a state which, through the socialist policies of its communist government, has championed the cause of women more than most.

Voices in the news

We used the same corpus of data from these online newspapers to investigate a related question – whose voices, whose representations of events, are reported in the news? In Table 8.6 all those who have their verbiage represented are capitalised. Where the reporting is indirect or a narrative report of speech act, then a question mark follows the capitalised named person.

Clear patterns seem to emerge in terms of the proportion of each category that have their speech reported: all the academics/experts and doctors; all the members of the judiciary, except one; more than three-quarters of officials/diplomats; three-quarters of the public; two-thirds of the police and military and of business people; around one-third of government figures and politicians, relatives/friends/neighbours, entertainers, criminals and victims. And no historical figures/names, or patients.

One factor here is accessibility. Many historical figures and some victims are dead. Government ministers and entertainers, especially those involved in a scandal or subject to gossip, may not wish to give interviews. Indeed, many gossip articles about entertainers quote anonymous PR agents or friends/sources. On the other hand, members of the public or their friends/relatives may well be flattered and eager to be interviewed. Similarly, experts see themselves as authorities and are therefore only too pleased to be quoted. Lawyers in court have no option but to go on the record. And officials, including spokespersons, are often paid to give their opinions to maintain good public relations.

This was a small-scale survey, but the findings are nevertheless quite telling. The number of women whose voices are represented is just a small proportion (at the head of the lists). Women often get to the news because of their relationships with more famous men. The most powerful countries militarily and economically have their governments and ministers mentioned the most. And power in general is the factor determining mention and voice, with the slight exception of voices of the public, over-represented, and entertainers/politicians, under-represented.

ACTIVITY 51 ━━━━━━━━━━━━━━━━━━━━━━━━━━━━━━━━━━

Please refer to the companion website for the activity material.

8.6 CASE STUDY 2: FIGHTING POWER – REPRESENTATION OF THE US EMPIRE

In the last two sections of this chapter we look at the ways in which news can be consciously used and manipulated to resist the power structures of society. First we consider how Singapore in the 1990s attempted to redress the balance against the domination of the West over the world-wide news machine. In 1994/1995 Shieh Yee Bing made a study of the way in which China and the USA were represented in the *Straits Times*. She analysed locally written editorials and features concerning China and the USA for the month of May 1994, and also the whole of the *Straits Times* newspaper for 27 December 1994. The stance taken represented a conscious attempt to counter the values of American society. The pro-Western media and their news agencies often depict Europe and the USA and its values as superior to those of the cultures and governments of the East. It was interesting to see that writers in a small nation state like Singapore can use the linguistic tricks employed by the Western media to counter and overturn their cultural imperialism, and to construct a representation which gives credit to Confucian and Asian values.

Transitivity

Shieh's first finding was that Americans tended to be represented as experiencers in mental process clauses a whole lot more than the Chinese – 10.04 per cent versus 3.02 per cent in the 27 December paper (pp. 65–66). This can be interpreted in various ways. Probably most obviously that China's behaviour prompts the USA to think and worry about it, to be emotionally or perceptually affected by the economic rise of China. China becomes something to be wondered at.

Reporting verbs

There is also widespread use of reporting clauses which make negative evaluative judgements about the USA:

> While many Americans <u>claim</u> that China's treatment of 'dissidents' are crimes, it may come as a surprise to many Americans that 'dissidents' in the Chinese vocabulary is not a synonym for reformers.
>
> (p. 47)

> The arguments about Americans <u>preaching</u> on 'universal individual freedom' is that human rights are also conditioned by local culture.
>
> (p. 47)

Nominalisation

More subtle is the use of nominalisation to make existential presuppositions. First, there are those which depict the USA as weak, decadent or inconsistent:

> It is difficult to see how capitalism can survive the decline of pax Americana.
>
> (p. 52)

> the inconsistencies evident in the US policy towards the Asia-pacific region are partly a consequence of the end of the Gulf War.
>
> (p. 52)

> the afflictions of American society, from unwed motherhood to street crime.
>
> (p. 58)

> America's eroding economic power.
>
> (p. 57)

By contrast, Asians are successful and self-confident in the superiority of their values:

> their success is due to the superiority of Asian values over those of the decadent West.
>
> (p. 52)

> the new burgeoning self-confidence of Asian countries.
>
> (p. 53)

The economic growth of China is presupposed, as is its authoritarianism, and the fact that it has opened, is opening or will be opening to outside influences:

> the resounding expansion of Chinese economic growth has raised the possibility that such economic growth could undermine powerfully the authoritarian system.
>
> (p. 69)

> China's economic boom.
>
> (p. 57)

> robust economic development in China.
>
> (p. 69)

> the opening of China.
>
> (p. 69)

Images of belligerence

The verbal and economic disagreements and unwelcome changes of trade policy are metaphorically represented as fighting, war or, at the least, a confrontational staring match. Very often the USA comes across as the initial aggressor, and China as the victorious party:

Bill Clinton could wield the MFN sledgehammer to advance US moral intervention in China.

(p. 54)

the US brandishing trade threats to force China to respect human rights.

(p. 54)

China and the other Asian nations are uneasy over US threats to unleash its prime trade weapon.

(p. 54)

China is waging war against the invasion of fancy foreign liquor
China triumphs over the US in diplomatic victory
China hailed its success in facing down Washington

(p. 70)

Premodification

The pattern of conscious bias is probably most clear in the contrasting adjectives which are used to premodify China and the USA, in the features and editorials, as in Table 8.7. All the adjectives are intended as positive towards China and Asia, but negative towards the USA and the West; though, personally, one might contest the negative affect of 'static' – no-growth economies are certainly more sustainable and inflict less harm on the environment.

Table 8.7 Premodifying adjectives for China and the USA

Attributive adjectives for China	Attributive adjectives for the US
booming China	weak dollar
rich East Asian countries	failed Western welfare states
prosperous East Asian societies	abysmal failure of US trade policies
spectacular economic growth in China	static economy
robust economic growth in China	feeble economic growth in America
collectivist Asia	individualistic Western societies
strong and different Asian cultures	hypocritical western liberals
China's 2500 years of highly moralist	decadent west
teachings	violent America
superior Asian values	

Source: from Shieh 1994/1995: Figure 4.3, p. 63.

One particularly interesting finding of Shieh's is the ambiguity of **premodification** and its relation to stereotyping. Adjectives before the noun can either be **restrictive** or **non-restrictive**. In their more usual restrictive meaning they define a subclass of the class picked out by the noun, e.g. in 'ginger cats are nervous', *ginger* defines one subclass of cats. In their non-restrictive meaning adjectives presume that all members of the class picked out by the noun share the quality referred to by the adjective. Take, for example, 'cacti are the only large plants to flourish in the barren desert'. 'The barren desert' refers to deserts in general, since they are all barren; it is not defining one particular kind of desert which is barren and distinguishing it from those deserts which are not. The interesting finding is that there is a potential ambiguity in many of the noun phrases which Shieh isolated (Table 8.8). For example, does 'fancy foreign liquor' mean "the subclass of foreign liquor that is fancy" or "foreign liquor, all of which is fancy"?

In summary, Shieh's analysis shows the *Straits Times* as using:

- mental process verbs to depict the USA as wondering at the economic success and social and moral superiority of the Chinese;
- reporting verbs to represent US statements and criticisms of China as unreliable;
- presuppositions portraying the USA's economic decline and social decadence;
- metaphors to paint a picture of a USA aggressive towards but defeated by China;
- ambiguous modifiers to stereotype US and Western people as individualistic, violent and failed hypocrites.

Table 8.8 *Restrictive and non-restrictive interpretations of adjectives*

Noun phrase	Meaning 1 restrictive	Meaning 2 non-restrictive
The angry American middle class	'That part of the American middle class that is angry'	'The American middle class, all of which is angry'
Failed Western welfare states	'The subclass of Western welfare states which have failed'	'Western welfare states, all of which have failed'
Individualistic Western societies	'The subclass of Western societies that are individualistic'	'Western societies, all of which are individualistic'
The decadent West	'The decadent parts of the West'	'The West, all of which is decadent'
Violent America	'The violent areas or parts of America'	'America, all of which is violent'
American individualism	'The special (prototypical) kind of individualism found in America'	'Individualism, all of which is American in origin'

The analysis suggests that the existing resources of grammar and vocabulary can be exploited for whatever ideological purposes – while much of the news is still post-imperialist there is the potential, given media access, to put forward an alternative ideology. However, our next chapter claims that there is something intrinsic to the grammar of English which makes certain ideology difficult to express, namely an ideology or worldview which matches that of modern ecological science.

8.7 FIGHTING POWER: INFORMATION DEMOCRATISATION AND VOICE ON THE INTERNET

In the internet age there is more scope for deliberately "biasing" the news to resist traditional control. Information democratisation might be defined as "the increasing involvement of private citizens in the creation, distribution, exhibition, and curation of civically relevant information". It not only has the potential to change control over information, but might even lead to political action:

> Information regimes ... have been interrupted by information revolutions, which involve changes in the structure or accessibility of information.... An information revolution disrupts a prior information regime by creating new opportunities for political communication and the organization of collective action.
>
> (Bimber 2003: 18)

Technology is key to changes in the structure and accessibility of information. Just as printing, in Europe, facilitated power struggles against the dominance of the Roman Catholic Church, and was instrumental in the Reformation, so, it is to be hoped, will the internet allow for challenges to the powerful, those people who controlled the media in the nineteenth and twentieth centuries, and who belonged to socio-economic elites. During the pre-printing era of the Middle Ages, ordinary people, often illiterate in any case, had very restricted access to the consumption of written information (even the Bible). Printing massively widened this access, and allowed people to interpret the Bible for themselves, without the intermediary of the Catholic priesthood. Now we have the prospect of ordinary citizens not only having access to huge, if not overwhelming, amounts of information, but also of using the internet to create information, distribute it, for example through social networks, and to guard it and keep it. Of course, this is a major threat to the existing power structures, as the cases of Bradley/Chelsey Manning, Edward Snowden and Julian Assange make clear.

The onset of the digital era has made news omnipresent. Instead of relying only on one single platform for the news, the digital era has made it possible to access news through multiple platforms on any given day. Studies have shown how the internet has surpassed newspapers and radio in popularity as a news platform after TV (Figure 8.1), and that sharing of news appears to be the most important development of the digital age. The rise of social media and its potential impact on news can be seen as social networking sites become critical players in the dissemination and consumption of news. Social networking sites like Facebook and Twitter dominate the intersection of social media and news (Figure 8.2).

Figure 8.1
Percentage of news sources from a 2012 survey (How Social Media is Taking Over the News Industry, infographic by Sam Laird, 18 April 2012 http://mashable.com/2012/04/18/social-media-and-the-news, retrieved 20 May 2014).

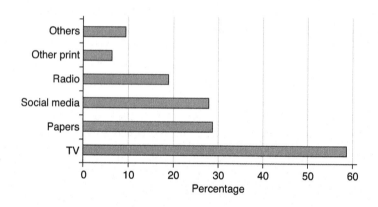

Figure 8.2
Social media as a news source (data from Pew Research Center, www.journalism.org/2013/11/14/news-use-across-social-media-platforms)

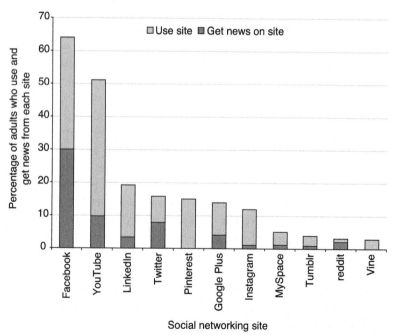

According to a study by the Pew Research Center, in the new multi-platform media environment, people's relationship to news is becoming portable, personalised and participatory. These new metrics stand out:

- *Portable*: 33 per cent of mobile phone owners now access news on their mobile phones.
- *Personalised:* 28 per cent of internet users have customised their homepage to include news from sources and on topics that particularly interest them.
- *Participatory:* 37 per cent of internet users have contributed to the creation of news, commented about it or disseminated it via postings on social media sites like Facebook or Twitter.

So, where the internet is available, news is, nowadays, becoming a two-way or multi-directional communication and a shared social experience. People swap links in emails, post news stories on their social networking site feeds, highlight news stories in their Tweets and haggle over the meaning of events in discussion threads. Bloggers can post their reactions to news stories or opinion pieces online, and journalists are sometimes expected to engage in dialogue with these public reactions. Readers thereby exert some control over what news is offered to them.

Even more radically, any member of the public who has internet access can, in theory, break a story or even create news. Famous examples of Twitter and Facebook users breaking news stories were American forces' raid on Osama bin Laden, Whitney Houston's death and the Hudson River plane landing. Figure 8.1 gives statistics from a survey of news sources in 2012. It is clear that social media is close to surpassing print newspapers as a primary source of news.

Newsblogs may be able to do away with traditional gatekeepers of news and set agendas that mainstream news ignores. Blog-based investigations led to the removal of journalist/news anchor Dan Rather from CBS because, during the 2004 presidential campaign he broadcast falsified Air National Guard documents critical of the performance of George W. Bush.

The project suggested on the website invites you to become a citizen journalist, and to contribute to the "revolution" brought about by social media and the democratisation of news. Unlike many citizen journalist blogs, which tend to be opinion pieces referring to existing news stories, you will be invited to create the news for yourself. In doing so you may be able to contribute to the revolution in news, by reversing the concentration of power over information in the traditional media, the top-down dissemination of news by those in power with their agenda-setting and filtering out of unwelcome or embarrassing news.

ACTIVITY 52 ▬▬▬▬▬▬▬▬▬▬▬▬▬▬▬▬▬▬▬▬▬▬▬▬▬▬

Please refer to the companion website for the activity material.

 PROJECT 4 ▬▬▬▬▬▬▬▬▬▬▬▬▬▬▬▬▬▬▬▬▬▬▬▬▬▬▬▬

Please refer to the companion website for the activity material.

8.8 SUMMARY OF CHAPTERS 7 AND 8

In Chapters 7 and 8, we've looked at the discourse of advertisements and the news. What overall pattern of cultural values and preoccupations does our analysis present? Not a very reassuring one. None of these discourses, if our samples are typical, both deal with serious political concerns and strive to encourage social engagement on the important issues facing the world in this century. Advertising unashamedly appeals to the individual consumer, and holds out the illusory promise of identity and social membership through the power of purchasing, or as personal dream fulfilment. Moreover, though serious newspapers deal with political issues, very few of them can be easily read by the powerless members of society, because of the economics of newspaper production. Also, issues persistently important to the powerless are not aired in the serious papers because of the values and controls which determine the content of the media, and reinforce the neoliberal consensus. News for the working and middle classes has become a matter of entertainment and amusement rather than political debate and engagement. However, one glimmer of hope is the way in which digital news and citizen journalists can bypass the traditional news channels and their gatekeepers, to create, spread and preserve information which the powerful may wish to suppress.

As Frith (1981) puts it, 'the problem [for capitalism] is to ensure that workers' leisure activities don't affect their discipline, skill or willingness to work'. Consumption advertising and being entertained by the news solve this problem quite neatly. The more important problems of survival of humans on earth and the degradation of the environment, vital to powerful and powerless alike, seldom stay in the centre of the news agenda for long. So our next chapter is concerned with the representation of the nature–human relationship.

 FURTHER READING ▬▬▬▬▬▬▬▬▬▬▬▬▬▬▬▬▬▬▬▬▬

Please refer to the companion website for the list of further reading.

NOTE

1 *Japan Times*: Japan's embrace of Russia under threat with Ukraine crisis; Romanian teen gets life sentence over Kichijoji robbery-murder; U.S. seeking to bolster naval presence in Japan, defense report says; Putin, Kerry engage in war of rhetoric over Ukraine; Longevity advice from world's oldest woman: 'Eat a good meal and relax'.

Times of India: Lok Sabha polls to start on April 7, vote count on May 16; LK Advani joins Rahul Gandhi in criticising BJP for being 'one-man show'; UP university suspends Kashmiri students for celebrating Pak's win against India; 12 years on, faces of Gujarat riots share a room and a dream of peace; Private hospitals to stop CGHS cashless scheme from March 7; China's Xi Jinping ramps up military spending by 12.2%, Japan expresses disquiet; Centre reduces Kerala eco-sensitive area by over 3,100sqkm hours before poll date announcement; Michelle Obama felicitates Indian acid attack victim Laxmi; Kejriwal arrives in Gujarat to verify Modi's development claims; 'Let us see,' says Kejriwal on contesting LS poll against Modi; Whether I become PM or not is immaterial – Rahul Gandhi; Passive smoking causes irreversible damage to kids' arteries; Google launches indoor maps in India; FreeKall–Bangalore students launch free voice calling service to those without internet; Nasa plots daring robotic mission to Jupiter's watery moon; After Penguin, another publisher recalls Wendy Doniger's book; Yahoo to disable Facebook; Google sign-in for its services; Obama, Germany's Merkel discuss resolution to Ukraine crisis; UP doctors on strike, 8 more die.

USA Today: China pledges to keep hold of 7.5% growth rate; In rare move, GM CEO says she's directing recall; Obama's budget eyes $1 trillion hike in tax revenue; Slain detective's final act of bravery; Cornyn, Davis survive Texas primary tests; High school senior denied 1st request for college tuition; NASA budget would ramp up asteroid mission; John Travolta apologizes to Idina Menzel for flub.

(Victoria and Melbourne) *Herald Sun*: Police hero among three officers sacked over racist stubby holders; Police fear arsonist may have struck again but Hazelwood mine battle almost over; Teacher ban for sex with student; Students' weekend bingeing stresses teachers; Ukraine crisis – US and Russia to hold key talks; Day three of Oscar Pistorius trial for murder of Reeva Steenkamp; Ban on dogs from Bass Coast beaches riles locals.

The *Mirror* (UK): 'Just good friends'– Amy Childs denies 'relationship' with Jump co-star Darren Gough; Michael Le Vell axed from Coronation Street and admits 'I need help' in cocaine use showdown with bosses; Teenage boy's incredible poem which can be read backwards re-Tweeted 120,000 times; The Simpsons recreate Ellen's Oscar selfie with Homer and Bart getting in on the action; Jealous husband killed 'promiscuous' Muslim bride after she had 'birthday sex' with another man.

9 ENVIRONMENTAL DISCOURSE, POETRY AND THE ECOLOGICAL CRISIS

The aims of this chapter
- to illustrate how the authority of climate scientists is challenged by powerful vested interests and the media;
- to introduce the idea of an ecological critical discourse analysis;
- to suggest how the conventional vocabulary and grammar of English might be changed to resist the technological ideology of the exploitation of nature;
- to illustrate how human-centred attitudes to the environment, reflected in the vocabulary and grammar of environmental discourse, represent nature as powerless or exploitable;
- to investigate how poetry, by contrast, can use language to represent nature as more powerful and more independent from humans.

Contents

9.3 Grammatical modification

argues that advances in scientific and ecological theory makes changes in the use of English grammar imperative.

Challenges to Newtonian dynamics

sketches major changes to scientific models in the past century, stressing the spontaneity and interdependence of natural systems.

Ordinary grammar and scientific theory

argues that ordinary English grammar is out of step with the new scientific models of the natural world.

What can we do about grammar?

suggests how we might exploit and modify grammar to better reflect science.

9.4 Case study 1: anthropocentrism and the grammar of environmental discourse in *SOTW*

analyses the typical ways in which nature is represented in the environmental discourse of the *State of the World 2012*, showing how nature is reduced to serving human needs and represented as powerless.

9.5 Case study 2: poetry and an alternative representation of nature

Explores and summarises the use of grammar and vocabulary to represent the power of nature in the poetry of William Wordsworth and Edward Thomas.

9.6 Case study 3: analysing individual poems by Edward Thomas and Alice Oswald

analyses grammar, metaphor and personification in representing nature in three poems.

9.0 INTRODUCTION: CHALLENGES TO THE AUTHORITY OF CLIMATE SCIENCE

In the previous two chapters we illustrated the power of multinational corporations as exerted through advertising, and the power of the media and the interests which control them. In both cases we advocated resistance, either through a critical approach to the linguistic, pragmatic and discourse strategies of advertising, or more actively through engagement in alternative news-making. However, this chapter is less straightforward in its attitude to resisting power and authority. We try to make the case that the powerful forces in business and the media, seen operating in Chapters 7 and 8, have encouraged a scepticism towards the authority of science. Big business often regards as threats the economic and lifestyle changes that climate scientists believe necessary to save the environment. They would prefer business as usual – that is, growth-led consumer capitalism controlled by neo-liberal market forces.

In any case, popular attitudes to science are often ambiguous and change over time. In the 1950s and 1960s science had more prestige – TV ads commonly showed white-coated "scientists" endorsing products. Such changes in attitude are apparent historically. Oswald Spengler in *The Decline of the West* (1922) claimed that science proceeds in cycles – romantic periods of investigation of nature are followed by periods of consolidation, with scientists becoming more arrogant and less tolerant of other belief systems, such as religious ones, so that society rebels against science and retreats into fundamentalism (pp. 23–24). We seem to be moving into this latter state at present. Ulrich Beck, in *Risk Society* (1992), explores the political consequences of scepticism of scientific and technological progress, a scepticism caused by technologically inspired disasters like Bhopal, Chernobyl, BSE, Fukushima and the devastation of bees by pesticides.

Politicians and the corporate media tap into this current scepticism to ignore scientific evidence in areas like drugs policy and, more relevant to the present unit, climate change. A clear example of how the fossil-fuel lobby influenced the Bush administration to interfere with the reporting of climate science comes from the United States House of Representatives Committee on Oversight and Government Reform, who in December 2007 issued a report *Political Interference with Climate Change Science*. The executive summary states:

> The evidence before the Committee leads to one inescapable conclusion: the Bush Administration has engaged in a systematic effort to manipulate climate change science and mislead policymakers and the public about the dangers of global warming. In 1998, the American Petroleum Institute developed an internal 'Communications Action Plan' that stated: 'Victory will be achieved when … average citizens "understand" uncertainties in climate science … [and] recognition of uncertainties becomes part of the "conventional wisdom".' The Bush Administration has acted as if the oil industry's communications plan were its mission statement. White House officials and political appointees in the agencies censored congressional testimony on the causes and impacts of global warming, controlled media access to government climate scientists, and edited federal scientific reports to inject unwarranted uncertainty into discussions of climate change and to minimize the threat to the environment and the economy.
>
> (www.astrid-online.it/rassegna/Rassegna-25/10-01-2008/
> US-HR_COMMITTEE_OVERSIGHT-Report-Climate-change.pdf,
> retrieved 19 July 2014)

We have already observed in Chapter 4 (p. 124) the way in which the media persist in emphasising uncertainty by using the phrase *the climate change debate*.

However, as we shall see, even "pro-environment" discourse can undermine its own position: the grammar it uses may just treat nature as a resource or commodity for humans to use, in line with a consumer capitalist agenda. Attention to the grammar and vocabulary of texts representing nature is therefore essential.

9.1 THE NEED FOR AN ECOLOGICAL CRITICAL DISCOURSE ANALYSIS

So far in Chapters 7 and 8 we have taken quite familiar ideological perspectives on discourse, explaining texts and their interpretations as sexist, capitalist and militarily and economically imperialist. Of course, ideology is not simple (Williams 1997), and though these ideologies are dominant they co-exist with strong ideologies of feminism, and weakened oppositional ideologies of socialism, anti-racism and internationalism.

However, though feminist and socialist critiques are academically fashionable, they are not fundamental. Our most urgent priority must be to address the ideology of the exploitation of nature which has developed over the last 200 years since the Industrial Revolution in Europe at the end of the eighteenth century. In 1992, David Orr cited the rather alarming results of our attitudes towards nature:

> If today is a typical day on planet earth, humans will add fifteen million tons of carbon to the atmosphere, destroy 115 square miles of tropical rain forest, create 72 square miles of desert, eliminate between forty to one hundred species, erode seventy one million tons of topsoil ... and increase their population by 263,000.
>
> (Orr 1992: 3)

The situation is still alarming. For example, since 1992 the situation seems to have deteriorated markedly in terms of CO_2 emissions, and hasn't improved much in terms of rainforest loss and population growth. The anthropogenic CO_2 emission rate for 2010 was 95 million tons a day, the population was going up by 213,000 per day in 2008 and 110 square miles of rainforest are lost each day.

Or listen to the recent report from the Intergovernmental Panel on Climate Change (IPCC):

> Human influence on the climate system is clear, and recent anthropogenic emissions of greenhouse gases are the highest in history.

> Recent climate changes have had widespread impacts on human and natural systems. Warming of the climate system is unequivocal, and since the 1950s, many of the observed changes are unprecedented over decades to millennia. The atmosphere and ocean have warmed, the amounts of snow and ice have diminished, and sea level has risen. Each of the last three decades has been successively warmer at the Earth's surface than any preceding decade since 1850. The period from 1983 to 2012 was likely the warmest 30-year period of the last 1400 years in the Northern Hemisphere, where such assessment is possible (medium confidence).
>
> (http://ipcc.ch/pdf/assessment-report/ar5/syr/AR5_SYR_FINAL_SPM.pdf, retrieved 28 July 2015)

According to the IPCC the consequences of global warming could be disastrous. We must expect more extreme weather, causing droughts, heatwaves and floods, with their attendant loss of life, and damage to infrastructure and agriculture. Should the permafrost melt, releasing methane (a far more dangerous greenhouse gas than CO_2), then these threats will be multiplied.

In the context of this ecological crisis a single-minded emphasis on sexist and capitalist-imperialist critical discourse analysis (CDA) is rather like considering the problem of who is going to fetch the deck-chairs on the *Titanic*, and who has the right to sit in them. So CDA has to address the basic problem of the ecological health of the planet – where we are steering the earth.

Even so, familiar ideological concerns can reinforce the ecological one. A broader socialist view might be linked with a plan for more sustainable ways of living: a simple lifestyle, in which consumer products are shared by neighbourhoods rather than owned by nuclear families, would reduce consumption and waste. High taxes with good publicly owned facilities make ecological sense. For, however hard we work, we are unlikely to be able to afford a garden with an Olympic-sized swimming pool, so we might just as well willingly pay taxes to fund civic swimming centres. Greens, like watermelons, are likely to be red inside. Equally, an anti-imperialist ideology could celebrate the harmonious relationships with nature of many native peoples; biological diversity and cultural/linguistic diversity most probably go hand in hand. Feminism too, by celebrating women as more caring, less aggressive people than the typical male, could help to resist hi-tech weaponry destruction of the environment. So though ecological critical discourse analysis might seem a new field, it actually relates to and supports more traditional forms of CDA.

Consequently, in this chapter we will consider the ways in which vocabulary and grammar represent ecology/the environment and the ways humans relate to it. We argue that grammatical representations are often out of step with the findings of modern science. We show how various strands of environmentalism continue to put humans at the centre of the biosphere, and adopt the natural capital agenda – as though the only point of nature is as a resource for human consumption. By contrast, poetry will be seen to use grammatical resources to represent nature in quite different ways.

9.2 METAPHORS, THE HUMAN–NATURE BOUNDARY AND CO-ORDINATION

An ecological discourse analysis has something to learn from feminist critiques of language. In the popular consciousness the "politically correct" language of feminism is a result of a campaign to change vocabulary and pronouns (Fowler 1991: 96–97). Similar campaigns might be launched ecologically.

Metaphor replacement and modification

For example, what do you make of the following text?

> **Consumption tax may 'slow down' Japan's cancer**
>
> . . .
>
> The lesson for Singapore was never to take things for granted, he said, since it only had 25 years of cancer compared to 200 years for the Swiss, and half the Swiss population.

In cases of mature economies such as Japan, Switzerland or Singapore, the metaphor of "cancer" can justifiably be substituted for "growth". It draws attention to the fact that growth in an already mature economy threatens the life-support systems of the planet, in much the same way as a cancerous growth eventually threatens the vital organs of the human body. Modifying or replacing one metaphor with another can both draw attention to the common-sense metaphor and help readers to challenge common-sense ways of thinking.

Another candidate for lexical and metaphorical modification is the substitution of *ecology* or *nature* for the word *environment*. *Environment*, meaning "surroundings", tends to be interpreted according to the metaphor IMPORTANT IS CENTRAL: **central** means "most important" (*investment was central to our economic success*), **centrepiece** "most important, interesting or attractive feature", **centre** "the place which exerts the most important influence" (*Boston became a centre for genetic modification*) and **core** "most basic and important". By contrast, the unimportant or less important elements are **peripheral**, **marginal**, or **fringe**.

If we use the word *environment,* presumably we suggest that humans are central and thus more important than nature. The candidates to replace the word *environment* are perhaps *ecology* and *nature. Ecology,* which includes in its original semantics the Greek word for home, is also human-centred, but, as most of us don't detect this metaphor perhaps that doesn't matter. Even so, *nature* seems a more "ecologically correct" word, however difficult it might be to distinguish what is natural from what is human-made.

Metaphors blurring the nature–human boundaries

Besides these specific cases of using *cancer* and *nature* it might be possible to change vocabulary use on a wider scale. For example, we could exploit the existing metaphorical equations LANDSCAPE IS HUMAN BODY and HUMAN BODY IS EARTH to blur the human–earth distinction, either through **personification** or **dispersonification**.

It is quite common to personify places, especially natural landscapes, using as metaphors parts of the human body. Proceeding from the top of the body downwards: **head** "upper part" (*the head of the valley*), **fringe** "edge of an area", **crown/brow** "summit" (*as we came over the brow of the hill we saw a dog*), **face** "front slope of a hill or mountain", **mouth** either "estuary" or "entrance to a cave", **tongue** "promontory" (*at the end of the tongue of land is a small town*), **neck** "isthmus" (*the neck of land links to a peninsula*), **shoulder** "more steeply inclined slope" (*we climbed round the hill's shoulder to the waterfalls*), **arm/finger** "promontory" (*the arm/finger of land extends out into the ocean*), **backbone/spine** "central row of hills or mountains" (*a backbone of limestone stretches from China to Siam*), and **foot** "lower part" (*the foot of the mountain is five miles from town*).

Furthermore, actions performed on the landscape are metaphorically actions on a human body, often violent, not **environmentally-friendly**: **gash** "deep trench" (*the bombs have left deep gashes on the landscape*), **scar** "scrape the vegetation off" (*the crashed plane had scarred the jungle clearing*), **rape** "environmental destruction").

Verbs and adjectives normally used for humans can be metaphors for the landscape: **lie, sit** and **stand** can all mean "be situated or positioned" (*the Sierra Nevada lies/stands to the east of California; Istanbul is sitting on extensive coal deposits*); **bald/bare** can mean "without vegetation" (*the hillside was bald/bare with only a little grass*); **hospitable** "with good living and growing conditions", and its opposite **hostile** (*hardly anything grows in the inhospitable soil*); **virgin** "unused, uncultivated" (*Costa Rica still boasts many virgin forests*); or **treacherous** "very dangerous" (*this swamp is very treacherous, keep to the path*).

Working in the opposite direction is the dispersonifying metaphor theme HUMAN BODY IS EARTH. Types of soil or rock can be applied to humans as nouns or adjectives. These are often evaluative: **grit** "bravery", **clod** "stupid person", **flinty** "severe and hostile" (*the headmaster gave me a flinty stare*), **craggy** "strong rough and attractive" (*Julia was attracted by his craggy jaws and chin*), **gravelly** "rough and low (of a voice)" (*he has a handsome face, blue eyes, black hair and a sexy, gravelly voice*).

The shape and area of land gives metaphors for the human body and its parts: **contour** "shape of the body" (*your bikini shows off your contours wonderfully*), **tract** "connected tubes in the body" (*he suffered from irritation of the digestive tract*), **furrow** "lines or wrinkles in the forehead" and, by implication, **stubble** "short growth of beard" which grows out of the skin as cereal crops from the ground.

The physiological processes or behaviour may be associated with earthquakes and volcanoes: **eruption** "pimple or spot, such as acne, that suddenly appear on the skin" (*the eruptions of adolescent acne are caused by blocked hair follicles*), **quake** "shake with fear", **tremor** "nervous shaking of the body" (*the disease causes tremors in the hands*).

Adjectival participles of transitive verbs literally used for actions on the land can indicating physique or character: **parched** "extremely thirsty", **rugged** "rough and strong" (*the sweat streamed down his rugged face*), **cultivated** "educated and cultured" (*my great aunt was a very cultivated lady who had been to university*).

Both these sets of metaphors blur the boundaries between humans and the landscape, though only the first personify the landscape as something human. One of the advantages of such personification is that it allows environmental destruction to be seen in terms of morality (for example, *rape of the countryside*) (Harvey 1996: 389).

Co-ordination and the human–nature boundary

In Chapter 2 we noted the effects that lists can have in suggesting membership of a common category, with an example from *Gulliver's Travels* (p. 50). So another way of blurring the distinction between humans and nature might be to include them in the same list or co-ordinate them with *and*. We will give more examples of this later in poetry, but for a taster consider these lines from Edward Thomas:

> And **I and star and wind and deer**/Are in the dark together.

Here, the human and natural are not only listed but are joint subjects of the predicate 'are in the dark together'.

9.3 GRAMMATICAL MODIFICATION

We have seen how metaphorical vocabulary and co-ordination can make us rethink assumptions about our place and practice in relation to nature. But these are fairly superficial kinds of linguistic strategy. We now turn to a deeper approach where it is the transitivity systems of the grammar, as outlined in Chapter 2, which are re-formed in directions favourable to ecology. As we shall see, the English language in its most simple material process grammar represents the world in ways that are in tune with the worldview which grew up out of Newtonian physics, but out of step with modern science and modern ecological theory. The next few sections suggest how a few less obvious grammatical choices can be exploited for pro-ecological ends.

One of the main features of Newtonian theory is its emphasis on movement. Newtonian dynamics concerned itself solely with the laws of motion:

> There is only one type of change surviving in [Newtonian] dynamics, one process, and that is motion. The qualitative diversity of changes in nature is reduced to the study of the relative displacement of material bodies.
>
> (Prigogine and Stengers 1985: 62)

In concentrating on changes which involve movement (rather than chemical changes or evolutionary changes), Newton represented objects as basically passive or inert until they were acted upon by some external force.

It was Newtonian physics, particularly dynamics, which made possible, 250 years ago, the Industrial Revolution in whose aftermath we are struggling, ecologically, to survive. This scenario of an external agent applying a force to an inert object to set it in motion has been transferred to our dealings with nature. We are the external actor, and we apply force to an apparently inert nature, which is seen as separate from us. The Newtonian world view and the technological world view must be abandoned if we are to stop desertification, species destruction, excess carbon emissions and the problems identified by Orr and the IPCC listed in Section 9.1. As we shall see, and as modern scientific theory realises, we have for too long forgotten that nature is far from inert, that we are part of it, so that we will suffer if we assume blindly that we can dominate it.

Challenges to Newtonian dynamics

If this chapter is partly about challenges to the authority of science, we also need to be aware that traditional science may itself be challenged by new scientific theories, so that there is an internal struggle for authority within science. There are three aspects of twentieth-century science which challenge the Newtonian view of matter – that the world can be divided into objects and processes, that nature is passive and controllable, and that humans are separate from nature.

First, relativity theory undermined the belief in the existence of permanent things that could be acted upon:

> Indeed it is not possible in relativity to obtain a consistent definition of an extended rigid body, because this would imply signals faster than light.... Rather ... [this has] to be expressed in terms of events and processes.
>
> (Bohm 1980: 123–124)

In the early 1980s superstring theory suggested matter is more like music. Just as vibrations of a violin string create different notes, so the vibrations of these superstrings might create all the forces and particles of the physical universe (Horgan 1998: 61). As Rifkin puts it: 'What we perceive as solid, material forms, may be a macro-expression of rhythms, vibrations, pulsations' (Rifkin 1987: 44).

Second, the second law of thermodynamics and the theory of entropy challenged the idea that natural objects can be completely controlled. This law states that it is impossible to make an engine which will continuously transform heat into an equivalent amount of mechanical work. The law states that the energy in the universe is necessarily and spontaneously being lost, or dissipated.

> Thus the "negative" property of dissipation shows that, unlike [Newtonian] dynamic objects, thermodynamic objects can only be partially controlled. Occasionally they "break loose" into spontaneous change.
>
> (Prigogine and Stengers 1985: 120)

According to this second law, the universe is gradually winding down to a disordered state, a structureless, homogeneous equilibrium. For example, if cold water and hot water are separated this is a relatively ordered state. But if they are put in the same container they will gradually become a homogeneous mass of lukewarm water, relatively disordered and structureless.

However, spontaneity also operates in another direction. Evolution shows increasing order among living beings, with more and more complex structures evolving, and less equilibrium.

A modern ecological theory, such as James Lovelock's *Gaia* hypothesis, reinforces these challenges to the Newtonian physics view of the natural universe. Lovelock believes the world, or the earth goddess *Gaia* – including the atmosphere, the oceans, living things, the rocks and minerals of the crust – functions as one large organism. It is rather like a giant redwood tree, more than nine-tenths of which is dead wood, with only the outer skin and leaves "alive". Such an organism is self-regulating. Active feedback by living things keeps the temperature, oxidation state, acidity and aspects of the rocks and waters constant at any one time. For instance, we would expect that the oxygen and methane in the atmosphere would react in the sunlight to produce carbon dioxide and water vapour, and that the atmosphere would return to a state of stable equilibrium. In fact, the amount of oxygen and methane in the atmosphere remains more or less constant. It can only remain constant because the living sub-systems of the *Gaia* system actively and continuously work to keep the environment suitable for life. And as these subsystems are interdependent, evolution and life concerns *Gaia*, not the organisms or the environment taken separately (Lovelock 1988: 19). If one wants to be optimistic about global warming, consider that the melting of the ice-caps and rising sea levels will put more pressure on the earth's crust, leading to more frequent volcanic eruptions, which will throw dust into the atmosphere and thereby reduce warming. An ingenious self-regulating device.

Gaia theory, which has recently been endorsed by geophysicists (Goatly 2007), implies the first challenge to Newton: *Gaia* is a set of interacting processes. But most obviously it reinforces the second challenge: the earth goddess *Gaia* is not passive, but is constantly organising and regulating herself. Moreover, it makes a third challenge: from a *Gaia* angle, human and other systems of the biosphere are interdependent, so exploiting nature as a resource becomes an obvious threat to the well-being of the human race as part of it. Mining the earth for minerals is about as sensible as eating one's liver for nutrients.

Ordinary grammar and scientific theory

We have sketched briefly how modern physics and ecology undermined several assumptions in the worldview of classical science. But what has this to do with the grammar of English? I would suggest that English grammar typically structures reality according to a Newtonian view of the world. Let's take an example of a fairly ordinary sentence.

> Fishermen traditionally caught 100,000 tons of fish per year in the North Sea.

This grammatical construction of reality encourages us to think in ways which are Newtonian in essence, but according to modern science, misguided. It is wrong in three ways:

1   The division into nouns, referring to permanent things, fish-
     ermen, fish, the North Sea, and verbs, referring to processes,
     catching. If all matter is, at a basic level, process, then this is a
     misleading representation. It would be more scientific to think of
     fish and fishermen and catching and the North Sea as four inter-
     acting processes.

2   The division into the actors who apply force or energy, the fish-
     ermen, and the inert or passive affected, the fish. This makes us
     think of the fish as inactive, ignoring any feedback within the *Gaia*
     mechanism, as though cause and effect only operate in one direc-
     tion. The fish and their commercial value in fact cause the fish-
     ermen to catch them. Take a clearer example: 'John drove the car.'
     In the longer term the actor, John, will be affected by the con-
     sequences of his actions: the car will produce sulphur dioxide and
     nitrogen dioxide which may contribute to John or his children suf-
     fering from asthma, and will definitely contribute to global
     warming which is already affecting him. He may appear to be doing
     things to the car, and the car to the atmosphere but the atmo-
     sphere will actually be doing things to him too.

3   This sentence marginalises the "environment" or **location circum-
     stance** ('in the North Sea') suggesting that the North Sea is either
     powerless, or is not affected. In fact the catching of so many tons of
     fish obviously changes the North Sea's ecosystem. This, too, denies
     the inter-relatedness stressed by *Gaia* theory.

What can we do about grammar?

We need a grammar which constructs a worldview which better reflects
modern scientific/ecological theory. Here is a selection of structures and
grammatical resources which could be used in this way.

Location circumstance as actor

Instead of marginalising the environment by referring to it in a location
circumstance, we have the option of turning it into a subject, or actor.

> *Ants are crawling all over the bed* →
> *The bed is crawling with ants*

The environment, the bed and the participants – the ants – become, in
the transformed version, mutual participants in the process, not separate
or in the background.

Ergativity

There are many verbs which belong to what is called the **ergative** paradigm (Halliday 1994: 163–172), for example, *sail, tear* and *cook* (see

Table 9.1). With ergative verbs, we use other terms to replace actor and affected, namely **instigator** and **medium**. And instead of using the terms transitive and intransitive, we replace them with **middle** and **effective**.

The difference between ergative verbs and non-ergative verbs is when two participants, actor/instigator and affected/medium, are involved; in other words, in the transitive or effective version, the clause is extended in a different direction (Table 9.2). With non-ergatives the clause is extended to the right, with ergatives to the left.

Ergative verbs without an object, i.e. intransitive or middle, represent changes to an object, the medium, as self-generated. For example, 'the door opened' suggests that the energy for this process originated in the door. When so-called inanimate natural objects are agents in such clauses they suggest they are active, not inert, better reflecting the second thermodynamic challenge to Newton. 'Occasionally they "break loose" into spontaneous change' (Prigogine and Stengers 1985: 120).

Muhlhäusler suggests that the use of middle ergative verbs is one of the features of Australian aboriginal languages which reinforces the identity between people and things (Muhlhäusler 1996: 123). The ergative verbs of these languages are usually middle, making human agency a special case.

Nominalisation

Nominalisation represents processes as nouns. By blurring the distinction between processes and things, nominalisation can suggest that things are in fact processes, in step with the first scientific challenge to Newton. Moreover, even more than middle ergative clauses, nominalisations may exclude any reference to an agent or external cause, with the same effect of suggesting a self-generated process. We can illustrate with an example

Table 9.1 *Ergative clause patterns*

Intransitive/middle		Transitive/effective		
Medium	Process	Instigator	Process	Medium
The boat	sailed	v. Mary	sailed	the boat
The cloth	tore	v. The nail	tore	the cloth
The rice	cooked	v. Pat	cooked	the rice

Table 9.2 *Participants and ergativity*

	Non-ergative	Ergative
Intransitive	John swallowed	The cloth tore
Transitive	John swallowed a grape	Paul tore the cloth
	→	←

from a geography textbook. Instead of *water condenses* we have the nominalised wording 'condensation' which, later in the text, reappears as a process: 'condensation occurs' (Wignell *et al.* 1993: 159). The water, the medium, disappears into the process, and when the discourse needs a clause rather than a noun the possibility of referring to the medium, water, is resisted.

However, in (ecological) discourse ergativity and nominalisation are double-edged. Though they reflect modern science more accurately, by obscuring human agency they may avoid telling us who is responsible for destroying the environment (Schleppegrell 1996).

Animation or personification

We saw earlier that we can use metaphorical vocabulary already in the dictionary of English to blur the distinction between humans and the landscape. In addition, grammar can be systematically used to represent nature as less than inert, as animate.

First, we can metaphorically reconstruct experiences in mental process clauses as though they were actors in material processes, e.g. *we noticed the river* → *the river arrested my gaze*, or *we love the forest* → *the forest touches my heart*. Let's call this **activation of experiences**.

Second, we can metaphorically reconstruct relational and existential processes into material ones, so that instead of nature being static it is seen as active. For example: *There are five trees in the valley/five trees are in the valley* → *Five trees stand in the valley, There is a boulder on top of the hill* → *a boulder tops the hill*. Let's call this **activation of tokens** or **existents**.

Besides these more specific patterns of activation, there are general patterns of animation and personification: natural, traditionally inanimate, things may become subjects of verbs normally used for living things (**animation**) or humans (**personification**), e.g. *the echoes died, the wind complained*.

We should sum up our discussion up to this point, so that we can bear it in mind as we proceed with our case studies. We discussed:

- the urgent need for an ecological CDA as being more fundamental to our survival than feminist, anti-imperialist or socialist CDA;
- examples of how metaphorical vocabulary could be changed or exploited to influence our attitudes to and impact on nature (Figure 9.1);
- how modern science and ecological theory has challenged some of the following incorrect assumptions of the Newtonian cosmology:

  - fundamental particles are things not processes
  - nature is passive and controllable
  - humans can be separated from their environment;

- how basic grammar is essentially Newtonian, which has led us to think in terms of the technological domination of nature;
- the possibility of grammatical modification using the following structures:

  - circumstances as actors
  - ergativity
  - nominalisation
  - animation/personification
  - activating experiences, tokens and existents (Figure 9.1).

9.4 CASE STUDY 1: ANTHROPOCENTRISM AND THE GRAMMAR OF ENVIRONMENTAL DISCOURSE IN *THE STATE OF THE WORLD 2012*

Our example of an environmental scientific text is the 2012 Worldwatch Institute report, *The State of the World 2012* (*SOTW*). This report gives plenty of statistical evidence for trends and possibilities in the areas of economics, urban development, transportation, technology for sustainability, political governance, population studies, building and architecture, food security, biodiversity and ecology.

In order to determine how nature is represented in this book we identified all nouns referring to natural phenomena that were participants in clauses, and also nouns in noun phrases involving nominalisation, whenever their participant roles in the equivalent denominalised clause could be determined, for example 'the **degradation** of our shared

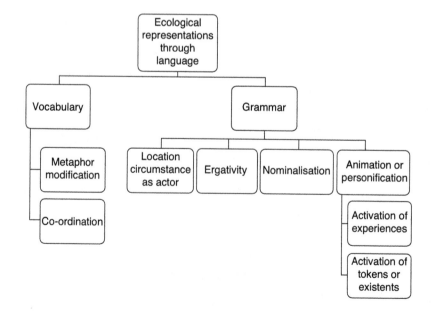

Figure 9.1
Linguistic strategies for a modern scientific representation of nature

environment' ('*x* degrades our shared environment'). These were then classified according to the Hallidayan scheme of transitivity introduced in Chapter 2, including the ergative option explained in this chapter. You will notice that the grammatical choices do little to challenge the dominant Newtonian paradigm of human relationships to nature, with nature as affected, usually by human actors.

Tables 9.3 and 9.4 indicate the main findings (for the full analysis see Supplementary Materials on the website). Natural element participants are predominantly affected, both in clauses (48 per cent) and even more in nominalisations (78.5 per cent). Natural elements as transitive actors and token-carriers have some significance in clauses, but natural elements in the other categories are negligible.

Most common nominalisations

The most common phrases involving nominalisation are *climate change* (59 times), *land use* (23 times) and *air pollution* (10 times). As in the

Table 9.3 *Natural participants in clauses*

Participant	Examples	Number	%
Affected	Programs that **improve** the environment; farmers **raise** enormous numbers of animals; China is **buying** more soy; metals are **recycled**; values that **protected** animals and habitats	127	48
Actor transitive	The forest now **provides** the village with food; the beluga sturgeon of the Caspian sea **produce** roe that can be worth up to $10,000 per kilogram; different species of coral **build** structures of various sizes	36	13.5
Token-carrier	Forests **are** a source of food, energy, medicine, housing, and income; water is **becoming** scarce; they [rabbits] **are** also responsible for serious erosion problems	32	12
Medium middle	Domestic animals **grow** quickly on feed; phytoplankton have **increased**; their [corals'] shell or skeleton may even start to **dissolve**	14	5.5
Experience	Why **worry about** a few thousand rare species that no one has ever **heard about?**; **enjoy** exciting and diverse nature; culture that **values** the environment; environment and equity are **considered** when making development decisions	13	5
Actor intransitive	A tree **falls** in the forest; a long-suffering waterway that **flows** through the nation's capital; 90% of chickens in India **arrive** from industrial facilities	12	4.5
Medium effective	Human activities **warm** the world; 40% of vegetables ... were **grown** in home and community gardens; composting ... **builds up** soil nutrients;	5	2
Other		28	10.5

Table 9.4 *Natural participants in nominalisations*

Participants	Examples	Number	%
Affected	The **degradation** of <u>our shared environment</u>; <u>land</u> **use**; <u>forest</u> **management**; **control** of <u>our atmosphere, land, forests, mountains and waterways</u>	167	78.5
Medium	<u>Climate</u> **stabilization**; <u>oil</u> **spill**; <u>soil</u> **erosion**; the **regrowth** of <u>forests and vegetation</u>	9	4
Actor intransitive	**Flows** of <u>minerals</u>; <u>saltwater</u> **intrusion**; <u>land</u> **subsidence**; the **collapse** of <u>the whole ecosystem</u>; the **effect** of <u>rabbits on the ecology of Australia</u>	8	4
Experience	**Keeping** <u>the global environment</u> **under review**; **attention to** <u>the environment</u>; integrative **concept** of <u>the environment</u>; **knowledge** and **information about** <u>weather</u>	7	3
Actor transitive	<u>Climate</u> **shocks**; <u>drought</u> **strikes**; **impacts** of <u>GM soy</u>; <u>ecosystem</u> **services**	5	2.5
Other		17	8

majority of nominalisations with natural elements as affecteds or mediums, the actor or instigator of the process is usually unstated. As far as *land use* and *air pollution* are concerned, it is obvious that it is humans using the land, and presumably some external actor or agent is responsible for polluting the air. However, *climate change* nominalises an ergative verb, which makes the medium more powerful, and might also excuse those changing the climate, the instigators, from some of the responsibility. If climate can change spontaneously, then who is to say that we are responsible for bringing about this change? Is this phrase then inherently problematic? Would the nominalisations *modification* or *destruction* or *heating*, where the underlying verbs are not ergative, more clearly emphasise human responsibility?

Most important processes by which nature is affected

We can now look at the verbs and their nominalisations which figure most prominently. Power over nature is very much assumed as the figures show. Although there is some recognition that humans cannot create nature, with talk of 'God's creation' and 'a freshwater environment created by nature', in places the book arrogantly assumes that humans produce natural objects, with the lemma *produc** and *raise** furnishing many examples:

> meat, egg and dairy production; chicken production; the production of timber; farmers who previously produced small quantities of

> low-quality honey; half the world's meat is now produced and consumed in developing countries; etc. etc.

> farmers raise enormous numbers of animals; cows raised for beef; raising livestock; the foxes and rabbits were raised.

Apparently bees, chickens and cows contribute little to this process of production!

Patterns of interaction with the environment also stress the power of humans over nature. First, the environment, especially land and water, is used by humans:

> land use (23 times); use less land; how land is used; using other land; use soils and water more sensitively; water usage (3 times); water use (3 times); using huge quantities of water; Lake Taihu is used for aquaculture farming.

> killed just to use their [animals'] skins; to use maritime and air space; the use of mangrove areas; use of palm oil; use of ecosystems; 12% of the world's corn was used for animal feed; cereals that were used for animal feed; 60 billion land animals are used in meat; wood was used for the walls; some products that used the fur of foxes.

Use is very often a matter of *consumption*:

> impacts of consumption on the environment; disruptions that human consumption patterns have caused; meat consumption (2 times); consumption of meat; fish consumption per person; half the world's meat is now ... consumed in developing regions; 40% of vegetables consumed by households; water consumption.

Consumption in these examples often refers to *eating* and *feeding*:

> corn and soyabean are fed to animals, animals are fed to us; grain eaten by people; ruminants are fed; cereals that were used for animal feed; 12% of the world's corn was used for animal feed; cattle raised; people in industrial regions still eat much more meat; eat meat every day; eat fewer vegetables; to eat more vegetables; grain eaten by people; eating more locally grown food; eating meat.

Another kind of domination of the environment by humans is the extraction of minerals:

> to extract the same quantity; to extract precious metals; extraction of key metals; the extraction of oil, gas and coal.

The kinds and extent of humans' use of the environment often leads to excessive exploitation:

> exploit the turtle population; commercial fish stocks are fully exploited; severe overexploitation of sturgeon; the over-pumping of groundwater; overgrazed and overharvested lands.

Though note that 'Ecuador said it would not exploit the 900 million barrels of oil in the ground under Yasuni National Park.'

The results of this human use, consumption and exploitation are negative effects on ecology. Degradation:

> land degradation (3 times); ecosystem degradation (2 times); degradation of environment; the degradation of our shared environment; physical degradation of freshwater; degradation of land and water; human induced soil degradation; degraded savannah.

Or pollution:

> air pollution (10 times); water pollution; the pollution of the Mezan river; the tons of consumer refuse polluting the Anacostia river; pollute the air, atmosphere, soil or water.

Or even more severely, destruction;

> habitat destruction (2 times); destruction of ecosystems; the destruction of planet earth; destruction of wetlands; companies that were destroying Indonesian rainforests; the current model of consumer societies is destroying the planet; rather than destroying ecosystems.

In keeping with *SOTW*'s representation of humans as dominant and nature as generally rather passive, it depicts the solutions to environmental problems as more human action on the environment. It needs to be managed:

> water management (3 times); river basin management; forest management; pest management; the management … of public and marginal lands; the ability to manage the forests.

Negative effects need to be prevented by preserving or saving it:

> preservation of natural resources; preserve forested areas; preserving the world's forests; preserving all life in all its forms; preserving an ecosystem and its services intact.

> save the planet; saving the panda; saving coral reefs.

Or reversed by restoration:

> restoring ecosystems like forests and wetlands; restore Earth's systems; the restoration of public and marginal lands; ecosystem restoration.

To sum up: humans act on a passive nature, by using and exploiting it and therefore degrading, polluting and even destroying it, and the solution to this problem is more human interventions and action on a relatively powerless nature.

The representation of active nature

However, from Table 9.3 we see that, though natural elements are mainly represented as powerless affecteds, in 13.5 per cent of clauses they are represented as powerful transitive actors. Analysing these clauses shows that the majority represent nature as serving the needs of humanity, by providing, producing and supplying goods and services to sustain and support human populations.

> *Provide*
> the ecological systems that provide us with fresh water, soil, clean air, a stable climate ... pollination and dozens of other ecosystem services; a finite world can sustainably provide enough for all; ecosystems provide services; ecosystems provide essential services; the services that ecosystems provide to humans; resources provided by nature; 50% more renewable resources than the Earth can sustainably provide; the forest now provides the village with food and tradable forest products; coral structures providing habitat and shelter for a large diversity of sea creatures.

> *Produce*
> 26,000 food gardens ... producing 25,000 tons of food annually; 40,000 cows producing milk; the beluga sturgeon of the Caspian sea produce roe that can be worth up to $10,000 per kilogram.

Sustain, support, supply
the ability of the planet's ecosystems to sustain future generations
can no longer be taken for granted; ecosystems support human
well-being; the 60 billion livestock animals that now supply the
world's meat, eggs and dairy products.

Natural elements may be positive in other ways too:

the forest ... absorbing 144,000 tons or carbon a year; a green-
belt of farms and forests that will form the backbone of a robust
local economy; individual gardens have played an essential role
in Cuba; trees filtering water to make it drinkable.

And, contrary to the general pattern, may even be acknowledged as a
creative force:

natural burial grounds that create new community parklands;
resources created by nature; a freshwater environment created by
nature.

However, when not serving human needs, natural elements might just as
often have negative effects:

areas hit by extreme weather and droughts; soot caused 3000
deaths, 200 hospital admissions ... and 6000 emergency department visits for asthma; feral animal populations which can damage
bird populations and even threaten people; bad weather ruined
their harvests; [rabbits] leaving the topsoil exposed and vulner-
able; the next surprise that nature throws at humanity.

Analysis of these grammatical patterns and the most commonly used
verbs in clauses and nominalisations shows clearly that the view of nature
in *SOTW* is predominantly centred on humans, i.e. anthropocentric.
Nature is used by humans, and if over- or mis-used the resulting environmental destruction is important simply because it threatens nature's
ability to provide humans with the necessary resources and services. As
the report itself states, 'Everything humans need for survival and well-
being depends ... on the natural environment.'

Anthropocentrism, vocabulary and the neo-liberal colonisation of the green movement

Such anthropocentrism is also evident in many of the vocabulary items
which refer to natural objects. Nature is often seen through the lens of
human needs, desires and evaluations: *energy, fuels, food, meat, natural*

resources, raw/materials. Or human evaluations are imposed on nature: *pests, animal wastes, feral animal populations.*

More significant, perhaps, is the way in which nature is viewed in terms of economic units such as assets, money or capital:

> Earth's natural capital (3 times); natural assets; common assets, and eco-system services; the world's common biological wealth; environmental bankruptcy.

Look, too, at the examples above under the heading of the verb *provide* and the repeated mention of ecology in terms of *services.* These phrases suggest that, in the modern economic regime of neo-liberalism, where all economic problems are supposed to be solved by the markets, the way to save the planet's ecology is to make it marketable as an asset valued in terms of money. The argument is that, unless this can be done, economists will continue to ignore nature and its goods and services and ecological destruction will continue apace. This is known as the Natural Capital Agenda: pricing, financialisation, valuing of nature in terms of money in an attempt to save it.

Several problems with this have been pointed out by George Monbiot (www.monbiot.com/2014/07/24/the-pricing-of-everything, retrieved 26 July 2014). First, how do you value natural assets? Often the figures put on the value of nature are quite nonsensical. The Natural Capital Committee set up by the UK government claims, for example, that protection of the freshwater ecosystems would give them an additional aesthetic value of £700 million. The National Ecosystem Assessment in 2011 said that looking after our parks and greens well would be worth £290 per household per year in 2060, because they provide solace, a sense of place and social value and supportive personal relationships creating strong and inclusive communities. Surely an underestimate?

The second problem is the irony of entrusting nature to the deregulated economic system based on debt and growthism that has been responsible for destroying the environment in the first place. According to Dieter Helm, the Chairman of the Natural Capital Committee, 'The environment is part of the economy and needs to be properly integrated into it so that growth opportunities will not be missed.'

The third problem is to do with power relations. For example, the Economics of Ecosystems and Biodiversity project, overseen by Pavan Sukhdev from Deutsche Bank, estimated the value of cutting down a mangrove forest for shrimp farming as $1,200 per hectare per year, compared with the value of leaving it standing which is $12,000 per hectare per year, because it protects local communities and provides a breeding ground for fish and crustaceans. However, such a valuation does not solve the problem. A businessman or local politician who wants to turn it into a shrimp farm is still likely to do so because he/she is far more powerful than the community of poor fishermen to whom the existing forest has far greater value.

Moreover, more fundamental problems in attempting a monetary valuation of nature have been noted by David Harvey. (1) Money is calculated as the equivalent of the market price of goods and services but many natural "assets" do not directly provide such services or goods; (2) the ecological organic whole of nature cannot be separated into parts that are valued separately; (3) the future benefits of natural goods are impossible to calculate since natural phenomena are often unpredictable; and (4) monetary valuation of the environment takes no account of the importance of nature in religious or cultural terms. Harvey concludes: 'it is hard, in the light of these problems, not to conclude that there is something about money valuations that makes them inherently *anti-ecological* confining the field of thinking and of action to instrumental environmental management' (Harvey 1996: 152–155).

However, despite its widespread use of the Natural Capital Agenda vocabulary, *SOTW 2012* does not monologically advocate this approach. While on the one hand it talks of making natural elements 'a tradable commodity like petroleum, minerals and grain', it also warns of the 'limitations that human perception-centred valuation creates'.

9.5 CASE STUDY 2: NATURE POETRY

We now undertake some case studies of poetry and the grammatical representation of natural elements within it. First, let's compare its representation in *SOTW* with that in *The Collected Poems of Edward Thomas* and Wordsworth's *The Prelude* using statistics compiled from previous research.

Sayers and actors in *State of the World* contrasted with Edward Thomas and Wordsworth

In the poems of Edward Thomas 31.5 per cent of natural element participants in clauses are actors/sayers; in *SOTW* the total is 23.5 per cent, including mediums in middle clauses. Of these there are no sayers and

Table 9.5 *Actors and sayers in Thomas' poems and* State of the World

	Experiences	Transitive actors	Intransitive actors	Sayers	Total actors + sayers
Thomas (%)	10.5	10.5	15	6	31.5
SOTW (%)	5.0	13.5	10	0	23.5

more than half, 13.5 per cent, are transitive actors, mainly like those noted above where natural elements supply or provide goods and services to humans.

Actors

In Thomas, natural elements are more frequently intransitive actors (15 per cent) than transitive (10.5 per cent), and the figures for animals and birds in Wordsworth are even more different (9.2 per cent intransitive to 0.7 per cent transitive – see Table 9.6, column 2). These figures give an opposite pattern to that in *SOTW* (10 per cent, if we include ergative middles, to 13.5 per cent). While natural elements in *SOTW 2012* have to make an impact and benefit humans to be actors, in *The Prelude* natural elements' actions are worth describing, quite apart from any effect they may achieve beyond themselves.

> The eagle **soars** high in the element
> That lowly bed whence I had heard the wind
> **Roar** and the rain **beat** hard

Landscape, as a proportion of participants, also figures quite frequently in *The Prelude* as an intransitive actor or medium (Table 9.6, column 4). The following passage describes the young Wordsworth ice-skating, and the highlighted clauses in the last ten lines illustrate a dynamic inter-action between humans and nature, as though the skater's movement makes him aware of an energy inherent in the banks and cliffs:

> So through the darkness and the cold we flew,
> And not a voice was idle; with the din
> Smitten, the precipices **rang** aloud;
> The leafless trees and every icy crag
> **Tinkled** like iron; while far distant hills
> Into the tumult sent an alien sound
> Of melancholy not unnoticed, while the stars
> Eastward were sparkling clear, and in the west
> The orange sky of evening died away.
> Not seldom from the uproar I retired
> Into a silent bay, or sportively
> Glanced sideway, leaving the tumultuous throng,
> To cut across the reflex of a star
> That fled, and flying still before me, gleamed
> Upon the glassy plain; and oftentimes,
> When we had given our bodies to the wind,
> And all the shadowy banks on either side
> **Came sweeping** through the darkness, **spinning** still

The rapid line of motion, then at once
Have I reclining back upon my heels,
Stopped short; yet still the solitary cliffs
Wheeled by me even as if the earth had rolled
With visible motion her diurnal round!
Behind me did they stretch in solemn train,
Feebler and feebler, and I stood and watched
Till all was tranquil as a dreamless sleep.

One of our grammatical modification devices is prominent here: the use of ergative verbs: *sweep, spin, wheel, ring* and *tinkle*. (They are ergative, remember, because when transitive, the extra participant will be subject rather than object.)

Landscape actors in intransitive clauses give us an example of a second kind of pro-ecological grammatical modification. The example below promotes what is literally a location circumstance into an actor:

and all the pastures **dance** with lambs

Compare this with the more common-sense 'Lambs dance in all the pastures'.

We have been looking at the way landscape features as an actor in intransitive clauses. However, in *The Prelude* landscape is an actor 50 per cent more in transitive clauses than intransitive (Table 9.6, column 4), and it is this active nature of the landscape in Wordsworth which sets it apart from landscape as we common-sensically conceive it. Typically mountains feature as these transitive actors:

I had seen . . .
The western mountain **touch** his setting orb
A huge peak, black and huge,

Table 9.6 Participant roles as a percentage of all noun phrases within natural categories in The Prelude

	Animals/birds	Water	Landscape	Weather	Plants
Actor trans	0.7	5.8	4.8	22.6	5.8
Actor intrans	9.2	6.2	3.2	24.8	9.7
Sayer	10.7	5.8	1.1	3.0	1.8
Experiencer	4.6	1.2	1.4	0.75	1.1
Experience	19.8	4.6	4.4	3.8	6.9
Affected	19.8	9.3	16	16.6	15.5

Note
The percentages do not add up to 100, because the 100 per cent includes participants in relational and existential clauses, and non-participants, e.g. NPs in post- or pre-modifying structures or adjuncts.

> As if with voluntary power instinct
> **Upreared** its head.
> And <u>mountains</u> over all, **embracing** all;

The last example suggests the unity, connectedness and indivisibility of nature as though Wordsworth were prefiguring Lovelock's *Gaia* theory, or Lovelock echoing him.

Weather is the most important transitive actor (Table 9.6, column 5), but, whereas landscape seems to act on other natural objects, weather affects humans and the poet in particular. The very opening of *The Prelude* demonstrates:

> Oh there is blessing in <u>this gentle breeze</u>,
> A visitant that while <u>it</u> **fans** my cheek
> Doth seem half-conscious of the joy <u>it</u> **brings**
> From the green fields, and from yon azure sky.

In another famous passage the boy Wordsworth feels the wind (and grass and rock) supporting him as he climbs steep crags:

> Oh! when I have hung
> Above the raven's nest, by knots of grass
> And half-inch fissures in the slippery rock
> But ill **sustained**, and almost (so it seemed)
> **Suspended** by <u>the blast</u> that blew amain,
> Shouldering the <u>naked</u> crag, oh, at that time
> While on the perilous ridge I hung alone,
> With what strange utterance did the loud dry wind
> Blow through my ear! The sky seemed not a sky
> Of earth—and with what motion moved the clouds!

In sum, what distinguishes the actors in *The Prelude* is the energy and potential given to natural elements usually regarded as lifeless – weather, water and even landscape.

Sayers

There is a total lack of sayers in *SOTW 2012*. In fact, instead of nature speaking for itself, the report expects the United Nations Environment Program 'to serve as the voice of the environment'.

By contrast Edward Thomas and Wordsworth see nature as a communicator. Almost two-thirds (47/72) of the instances of natural element sayers in Thomas are birds. For instance:

This was the best of May – the small brown birds
Wisely reiterating endlessly
What no man learnt yet, in or out of school.

('Sedge Warblers')

Sayers in *The Prelude* tend to be associated with, on the one hand, animals and birds (Table 9.6 column 2), where 10.7 per cent of the natural element noun phrase are sayers, and rivers and streams (column 3) where 5.8 per cent are. Let's look at some examples of animals and birds first:

By the still borders of the misty lake,
Repeating favourite verses with one voice,
Or conning more, as happy as the birds
That round us **chaunted**.

The heifer **lows**, uneasy at the voice
Of a new master; **bleat** the flocks aloud.

As for bodies of water as sayers, Wordsworth is, by his own admission

...a spoiled child ... in daily ***intercourse***
With those crystalline rivers, solemn heights,
And mountains, ranging like a fowl of the air

Indeed, in Wordsworth's ideal world, we should not interfere with rivers and treat them as affecteds since this will actually inhibit their powers of communication:

The famous brook, who, soon as he **was boxed**
Within our garden, found himself at once,
As if by trick insidious and unkind,
Stripped of his voice and left to dimple down
(Without an effort and without a will)
A channel paved by man's officious care.

Nature as experience rather than affected

Sayers need someone to listen to them, so predictably there is a much higher number of natural elements as experiences in Thomas compared with *SOTW 2012* (10.5 per cent compared to 5 per cent in Table 9.5). For example,

[A]ll things **forget** the forest
Excepting perhaps me, when now I **see**
The old man, the child, the goose feathers at the edge of the forest,
And **hear** all day long the thrush repeat his song

('The Green Roads')

And in Wordsworth we see a significant representation of nature as experiences in birds and animals (19.8 per cent in Table 9.6 column 2) and plants (6.9 per cent in column 6).

> I **spied**
> A glow-worm underneath a dusky plume
> Or canopy of yet unwithered fern
>
> At leisure, then, I **viewed**, from day to day,
> The spectacles within doors, birds and beasts
> Of every nature
>
> . . . **see** that pair, the lamb
> And the lamb's mother, and their tender ways

In Thomas the affective mental process responses to experiences of nature are crucial, in, for example, these lines from 'November':

> Few **care for** the mixture of earth and water,
> Twig, leaf, flint, thorn,
> Straw, feather, all that men **scorn**,
> Pounded up and sodden by flood,
> **Condemned** as mud
>
> . . .
>
> Another **loves** earth and November more dearly
> Because without them, he **sees** clearly,
> The sky would be nothing more to his eye
> Than he, in any case, is to the sky;
> He **loves** even the mud whose dyes
> Renounce all brightness to the skies.

In this and the previous section we have shown that in Thomas and Wordsworth nature, especially birds, animals and water, are much more serious communicators than their counterparts in *SOTW 2012*, and therefore figure more as experiences to which we pay attention. In *SOTW*, by contrast, they are never sayers, and the ratio of experiences to affecteds is much lower.

Thomas and Wordsworth convey the idea that nature can speak to us as a sayer or affect us as an experience. Being receptive to nature's messages as experiencers can, of course, give us a different direction for our scientific and technological advances, perhaps a more positive one than using technology to enhance our material power as actors over an affected nature. Scientific measuring instruments convey messages from nature which may lead to a more reciprocal relationship. We have responded to messages about the ozone layer which nature has been sending us. It remains to be seen whether we will respond in the same way to anthropogenic climate heating.

Activation of experiences, tokens

We noted earlier the grammatical resource of upgrading experiences and tokens to actors. This is a widespread and stylistically significant phenomenon in *The Prelude*. It applies most obviously to plants, landscape and weather. Many of these actors are only metaphorically material. In a more common-sense syntax they would be experiences, though paraphrasing into such syntax (attempted in brackets) becomes increasingly problematical in the following examples:

> Till <u>the whole cave</u>, so late a senseless mass,
> **Busies** the eye with images and forms
> Boldly assembled

(cf. I saw the whole cave…)

> Oh there is blessing in <u>this gentle breeze</u>,
> A visitant that while it fans my cheek
> Doth seem half-conscious of the joy <u>it</u> **brings**
> From the green fields, and from yon azure sky.

(cf. I enjoyed (the breeze fanning my cheek))

> …<u>my favourite grove</u>,
> Tossing in sunshine its dark boughs aloft,
> As if to make the strong wind visible,
> **Wakes** in me agitations like its own

(cf. I fear my favourite grove/my favourite grove worries me)

> …<u>Lofty elms</u>,
> Inviting shades of opportune recess,
> **Bestowed** composure on a neighbourhood
> Unpeaceful in itself.

(cf. I felt calm in the shade of the lofty elms)

> Yet, hail to you
> <u>Moors, mountains, headlands, and ye hollow vales</u>,
> <u>Ye long deep channels</u> for the Atlantic's voice,

> Powers of my native region! <u>Ye that</u> *****seize**
> The heart with firmer grasp!

(cf. ? I adore/love/worship/am obsessed with the moors mountains, headlands etc.)

> Oh! *****wrap** him in your shades, <u>ye giant woods</u>
> And you, <u>ye groves</u>, whose ministry it is
> To **interpose** the covert of your shades

(cf. Ye giant woods and groves, prevent me seeing him)

A further very significant pattern in Wordsworth and Thomas is the metaphorical transformation of a basically relational process into a material one, which we refer to as activation of tokens or existents. Some quite common verbs like *surround, lie* are half material half relational, and these proportions may vary with the subject of the verb (Martin and Matthiessen 1991). For example 'the moat surrounds the castle' pushes in the direction of a relational process, whereas 'the soldiers surrounded the castle' pushes towards the material. Exploiting such vocabulary is a widespread tendency in Wordsworth, so nature becomes more active than static:

> The visionary dreariness . . .
> **Invested** moorland waste, and naked pool,
> The beacon **crowning** the lone eminence

> The garden **lay**
> Upon a slope **surmounted** by <u>a plain</u>
> Of a small <u>bowling-green</u>; beneath us *****stood**
> <u>A grove</u>

> There **rose** <u>a crag</u>,
> That, from the meeting-point of two highways
> Ascending, *****overlooked** them both

Instead of 'being at the top of' an eminence or slope or two highways, the plain or beacon or crag 'surmounts' or 'crowns' or 'overlooks' them. In this environment of active existence and relations, even the quite normal *stood* seems to take on more energy than usual. The high percentage (16 per cent) of landscape as affected in *The Prelude* (Table 9.6) is partly due to those activated material processes, which represent the positions of one part of the landscape in relation to another.

Similarly in Thomas, we find the following examples of activation of tokens:

> The fields beyond that league **close in** together/And **merge** [cf. 'are together and indistinguishable']
> the road, the wood that **overhangs** [cf. 'is above']/And *****under-yawns** [cf. 'is below'] it,
> A white house *****crouched** ['was in a low position'] at the foot of a great tree.

Typically paths and roads are not just positioned next to a place or between two places but *run, mount* or *take* you from one to the other:

> Where the firm soaked road/*****Mounts** beneath pines
> On all sides then, as now, paths *****ran** to the inn;/And now a farm-track *****takes you** from a gate.

Personification, co-ordination dissolving the human–nature distinction

Some examples of the activation of experiences and tokens/existents above have been asterisked, to indicate personification or at least animation. This is one way of problematising the human–nature boundary. LANDSCAPE IS HUMAN BODY, discussed earlier, is a specific sub-set of such personification. Personification is particularly common in Thomas, whether of light:

> When mist has been **forgiven**/And the sun **has stolen out,**/**Peered, and resolved** to shine at seven

or plants

> Harebell and scabious and tormentil,/That blackberry and gorse, in dew and sun,/**Bow down to**;
> On the prone roof and walls the nettle **reigns**

or weather

> All day the air triumphs with its two **voices**/Of wind and rain:/As loud as if in anger it **rejoices**.

Sometimes the personification is used very subtly, as in 'Aspens':

> Over all sorts of weather, men, and times,
> Aspens must shake their leaves and men may hear
> But need not listen, more than to my rhymes.
> Whatever wind blows, while they and I **have leaves**
> We cannot other than an **aspen** be

That ceaselessly, unreasonably **grieves,**
Or so men think who like a different tree.

These lines confuse the literal with the personifying metaphor by co-ordinating the trees with the poet, 'they and I' and 'we', and using predicates that apply metaphorically to one and literally to the other, as follows:

LITERAL	They have leaves/I have	
METAPHORICAL		leaves ('sheets of paper')
LITERAL	They [we] cannot other than an aspen be/I	
METAPHORICAL		cannot other than an aspen be
LITERAL	An aspen	/I unreasonably grieve
METAPHORICAL	unreasonably grieves	

A further technique for such blurring is co-ordination of the human and natural elements, particularly common in Thomas. In earlier lines from 'Aspens' we have:

- And **trees and us** – imperfect friends, **we men/And trees** since time began; and nevertheless/Between us still we breed a mystery.

Other examples are:

- so that I seem a king/Among man, beast, machine, bird, child,
- kind as it can be, this world being made so,/To stones and men and beasts and birds and flies,/To all things

Summary

We can now summarise what we have found in Section 9.5. In terms of a comparison between *SOTW* and Thomas/Wordsworth:

- Nature is more frequently an actor/sayer than an affected in Thomas/Wordsworth than in *SOTW*.
- In Thomas and Wordsworth there are a large number of natural sayers, whereas there are none in *SOTW*.
- Among the natural actors, Thomas and Wordsworth have a higher ratio of intransitive to transitive, and *SOTW* the reverse, though landscape and weather are important transitive actors in Wordsworth.
- Nature as experience is much more common in Thomas and Wordsworth than in *SOTW*.

In addition, we noted the following pro-ecological techniques in Wordsworth and Thomas:

- frequent use of the ergative middle in Wordsworth;
- widespread activation of experiences, tokens and existents;
- personification and co-ordination to blur the human–nature divide.

9.6 CASE STUDY 3: ANALYSING INDIVIDUAL POEMS BY EDWARD THOMAS AND ALICE OSWALD

The poet Shelley claimed 'poets are the unacknowledged legislators of the world'. It would indeed be a more hopeful world if poetry were more widely read than reports like *SOTW*. But we can best appreciate the ways in which poetry uses language to legislate an alternative representation of nature by looking at whole poems.

July (Edward Thomas)

Naught **moves** but clouds, and in the glassy lake	(1) Intransitive actors – ergative middle
Their doubles and the shadow of my boat.	
The boat itself stirs only when I break	
This drowse of heat and solitude afloat	(2) Nominalisation of nature as transitive actor
To prove if what I **see** be bird or mote,	(3) Experience
Or **learn** if yet the shore woods be **awake**.	(4) Experience (5) Personification
Long hours since dawn **grew**, – **spread**, – and **passed**	(6) Activation of existents
on high	
And deep below, – I have **watched** the cool reeds hung	(7) Experience
Over images more cool in imaged sky:	
Nothing there was worth **thinking** of so long;	(8) Experience
All that the ring-doves **say**, far leaves among,	(9) Sayer
Brims my mind with content thus still to lie.	(10) Verbiage of birds as transitive actor/ instigator – verb made ergative
	(11) Dis-personification

Some of the notes on the grammar of the poem need little discussion – the ergative middle (1), the common occurrence of nature as experience (3, 7, 8) and the personification (5). But (2), 'the drowse of heat', is worth considering further. One likely interpretation would make 'heat' an actor/instigator and 'drowse' a nominalisation of the verb *to drowse*. This verb is normally simply intransitive, but this interpretation would make the equivalent un-nominalised clause ergative effective – 'the heat/solitude causes me to drowse'. It is certainly the case that the verb *brim* (10), normally simply intransitive, is turned into an ergative effective verb. Compare the more normal grammar of 'My mind brims with all that the ring doves say.' Moreover, (11) 'brim' applies a verb literally used of water to the mind, and through this metaphor blurs the distinction between human persona and the lake on which he is floating, literally brimming at its edges. (6) is also worth discussing. We might think of the verbs 'grew', 'spread' and 'passed' as a kind of activation of existents, rather than tokens, equivalent to 'came into existence', 'established its existence' and 'ceased to exist', respectively.

Sonnet (Alice Oswald)

towards winter flowers, forms of *ecstatic* water,	(1) Personification passim
chalk **lies** dry with all its *throats* open.	(2) Activation of token
winter flowers **last** maybe one frost	(3) Activation of existent?
chalk **drifts** its heap through billions of slow sea years;	(4) Intransitive → ergative effective
rains and **pools** and **opens** its *wombs*,	(5) Actor intransitive and self-directed transitive
bows its *back*, **shows** its *bone*.	
both **closing** towards each other	(6) Activation of token
at the *dead* end of the year – one	
woken through, the others **thrown** into flower,	(7) Past participles
holding their wings **at the ready** in an increasing	(8) Present participles
state of crisis.	
burrowed into and **crumbled**, **carrying**	(7) Past participles
these small *supernumerary* powers **founded** on *breath*:	
chalk with all its *pits* and *pores*,	
winter flowers, **smelling** of a sudden entering elsewhere	(9) Experience
	(10) Nominalisation

The first obvious feature of this poem is its exploitation of the metaphor theme LANDSCAPE/EARTH IS HUMAN BODY. All the italicised vocabulary personifies the chalk in this way (1). 'Pits' is a conventional metaphor for small depressions in the skin, but here the direction of metaphorical application is reversed. Even 'supernumerary' could be part of this personifying pattern as it usually refers to a temporary employee or extra member of a social group. The chalk/body is often sexualised. So 'breath' is ambiguous – is it the heavy breathing of the chalk through its open throats waiting for the penetration by flowers? Or, less of a personification, is it the carbon dioxide which forms the basis of the calcium carbonate of the chalk; and also the gas which the flowers take in and photosynthesise into oxygen?

Turning to the grammar of processes, in the context of so much sexualised personification 'lies' (2) activates 'chalk' from a token into an intransitive actor, as though lying on a bed. 'Last' (3) might be seen as an activation of an existent – "continues to exist". Straightforwardly we note chalk as an intransitive actor of the verbs 'rains' and 'pools' (5). When it is a transitive actor subject of 'opens', 'bows', 'shows' and 'drifts' (5, 4) chalk is not acting on anything beyond itself, rather like the patterns of intransitive actors we saw in

Wordsworth's representation of animals and birds. 'Drifts' (4) is a further instance of the conversion of an intransitive verb into an ergative effective verb, as we saw with 'brims' in 'July'. As we perceive the chalk and its shapes and formations it is static. But from the perspective of billions of years of geological processes these verbs make us see the shapes of the chalk as active. This is a kind of radical activation of nature. A more familiar candidate for activation of tokens is 'closing' (6), equivalent to the less active meaning that the flowers and the chalk 'are close to each other'.

The past participles 'woken', 'thrown', 'burrowed', 'crumbled', 'founded' (7) are worth discussing. It may be that the actors here can be inferred from the context in most cases – it is probably the flowers that have woken, burrowed and crumbled the chalk. But the actor who threw the flowers and founded the chalk is less certain. This conforms to the pattern common in Thomas where the frequent use of passives and past participles suggests a (divine?) force behind the natural world (Goatly in press). With the present participles 'holding' and 'carrying' (8) we do have transitive verbs with presumably the flowers and chalk as the transitive actors, though the flowers' action of holding their wings only affects themselves. We have, too, winter flowers as an experience of the process 'smelling' (9). However, this clause is ambiguous – could the flowers also be an experiencer sensing a sudden entering or penetration elsewhere? We are not sure, and it is unclear what is doing this entering – water entering the chalk perhaps, or flowers the chalk? Paradoxically, it seems to be the flowers, traditionally seen as female, that are more like males entering the throat or womb of the chalk. This ambiguity is caused by the nominalisation 'entering' (10). The fact that we cannot easily attach a specific actor to it perhaps hints at the primacy of process, as in quantum mechanics.

Birdsong for Two Voices (Alice Oswald)
a spiral ascending the morning,
climbing by means of a song into the sun,
to be **sung** reciprocally by two birds at intervals   (1) Sayer
in the same tree but not quite in time.

a song that **assembles** the earth   (2) Nominalisation as transitive actor –
out of nine notes and silence.   creative process
out of the unformed gloom before dawn
where every tree is a problem to be **solved** by birdsong.   (3) Nominalisation as transitive actor

Crex Crex Corcorovado,
letting the pieces fall where they may,   (4) Transitive actor
every dawn **divides** into the distinct   (5) Ergative middle
misgiving between alternate voices   (6) Nominalisation

sung repeatedly by <u>two birds</u> at intervals	(7) Sayer
out of nine notes and silence.	
while the sun, with its **fingers** to the earth,	(8) Personification
<u>as the sun</u> **proceeds** so it **gathers** instruments:	(9) Intransitive actor
	(10) Transitive actor...
it **gathers** the yard with its **echoes** and **scaffolding** sounds,	(11) Nominalisations
it **gathers** the **swerving** away sound of the road,	(12) Nominalisation
it **gathers** the river **shivering** in a wet field,	(13) Personification
it **gathers** the three small bones in the dark of the eardrum;	
it **gathers** the <u>big bass silence of clouds</u>	... (10) Transitive actor
<u>and the</u> mind **whispering** in its **shell**	(14) Sayer (15) Dispersonification
and <u>all trees</u>, with their **ears** to the air,	(16) Personification/literalisation
seeking a steady state and **singing** it over till it **settles**	(17) Actor and sayer

As with Thomas, and to a lesser extent Wordsworth, this poem celebrates the power of birds as sayers, birdsong. As transitive actor birdsong 'assembles the earth' at dawn, solves the problems of the tree and lets 'the pieces fall' (2, 3, 4). But notice that this powerful actor is itself a process, a nominalisation of *(birds) sing*. And there is an extra emphasis on process if you *sing a song*, because the song does not exist independent of the process in the verb *sing*. The poem blends this song with the sun, phonologically, of course, 'by means of a song into the sun to be sung', and because the sun ends up 'singing' as well (17), but also because the sun too is a powerful transitive actor or instigator (10): it 'gathers ... instruments ... the yard ... the sound of the road ... the river ... silence of clouds ... the mind ... all trees ... bones ... in the eardrum', with this latter emphasising nature's power over humans. It also seeks a steady state (17) – a state that does not change over time 'not quite in time', unlike the 'dawn'. The gathering is done with the sun's 'fingers' (8) an obvious personification, just as the river is personified as 'shivering' (13) and the trees by having 'ears' (16). Notice how this latter metaphor echoes the literal 'eardrum', suggesting a deliberate confusion between humans and nature as in Thomas, in this case humans and trees. Conversely, 'shell' (15) referring to the skull or brain, by dis-personification, blurs the human–nature distinction in the opposite direction.

There are other nominalisations which emphasise process – 'scaffolding' (11) could be the actual metal bars but it only produces sounds in the process of assembly/disassembly. Though 'sound/s' refer to processes or the results of processes this is not an obvious nominalisation, but 'echoes' (11) and 'swerving' (12) clearly are. The effect of the nominalisation 'misgiving' (6), rather than emphasis on process, might be the removal of an explicit experiencer. 'Eardrum' and 'misgiving' and 'mind' hint at an experiencer, but human presence is downplayed, and the trees with 'their ears to the air' are just as likely the experiencers. In any case, 'misgiving' is ambiguous and might be the nominalisation of a material process, meaning the giving of the birdsong which is faulty because it is not quite in time. So the absent experiencer is also possibly a hidden recipient.

The only place where human consciousness is obviously present is in 'the mind whispering' (14). But this inner verbal process is comparatively weak, soft and uncommunicative compared with the all-powerful creative song of the birds and the sun.

Besides the nominalisations of the form *–ing*, we have several present participles: 'shivering', 'whispering', 'seeking' and 'singing', suggesting ongoing and repeated processes.

This poem, more than any others we have analysed, uses nominalisation to emphasise the process basis, the vibrations as of instruments producing sounds, of being and becoming, reflecting the theory of quantum mechanics or superstring theory. Moreover, by the use of the phrase 'steady state' and the emphasis on repetition ('sung', 'singing', 'sung repeatedly') it may hint that this steady state can be achieved by the repetitive processes behind the dynamic equilibrium that *Gaia* theory celebrates.

Though the data from just three poems is limited, we can observe patterns, some of which we found more generally in Thomas and Wordsworth – the emphasis on nature as experience, sayer and actor; the activation of tokens and existents; and personification. In addition we have noted the upgrading of intransitive verbs into ergative effective clauses; dis-personification; using metaphors taken from the literal natural context to apply to humans, and vice versa; and the use of nominalisation to emphasise process. These appear to be some common grammatical and lexical strategies for representing our inclusion within nature, nature's power to act and communicate and our need to respond to it as experience and recognise it as process. In this latter respect, poetry and science seem in accord with each other and to resist representing nature in a common-sense way as a passive resource.

9.7 SUMMARY AND POSTSCRIPT

We have seen that Wordsworth, Thomas and Oswald use some grammatical techniques to mitigate the effects of a "Newtonian" grammar.

- Ergative verbs are used to construct natural landscape as possessing its own energy.
- Experiences are activated into actors making the experience of nature very powerful.
- Tokens and existents are activated into actors: nature *does* rather than *is*.

- Nominalisations emphasise the process-basis of nature, and these processes become powerful actors.

And in addition Thomas and Oswald blur the human–nature distinction through:

- personification (and dis-personification);
- using metaphors from the literal context;
- co-ordination of the human and non-human;
- passives suggesting a powerful natural (or divine) force.

In brief, nature is seen as equal to humans in its power to communicate and act.

We would like to suggest, as a parting thought-provoking comment, that the view of the natural world represented by these poets, along with aspects of their grammar, provides a much better model for our survival than that represented by *SOTW 2012*. We had better take note of Wordsworth, Thomas and Oswald, the physicists and the ecologists, rethink and re-speak our participation in nature, before it rethinks or rejects our participation in it.

ACTIVITY 53

Please refer to the companion website for the activity material.

FURTHER READING

Please refer to the companion website for the list of further reading.

10 THE POWER OF FICTION AND COMEDY

The aim of this chapter
- to illustrate whether humour operates as liberation or control;
- to introduce the interpersonal aspects of humour;
- to demonstrate the use of parody as means of challenging existing ideologies;
- to critically evaluate the deployment of visual parody (to show how parody, although subversive, may end up reinforcing a separate set of values);
- to suggest how fan fiction subverts power or authority.

Contents

10.0 Introduction: humour as liberation or control
suggests that humour is ambiguous between being a force for liberation and resistance or as a means of domination, relating this to selective theories of humour.

10.1 Shared ideologies and interpersonal aspects of humour
explains how the interpersonal relationships between the humourist and audience and social group targeted will affect the success of humour.

10.2 Parody
introduces three models of parody, showing how the source expression and contents of the parody texts may interact with contrasting expression and content; it illustrates the models with two examples, parodies of a children's beginning reader and the Red Riding Hood story (the language of political correctness).

10.3 Visual parody
looks at how visual parodies, especially in public spaces, function to debunk dominant societal discourses or ideologies while at the same end up promoting a particular kind of ideology.

> **10.4 Fan fiction**
> surveys the different kinds of fan fiction and the ways they resist the legal authority of copyright, and how they challenge the dominance of the original by transgressing for example, its dominant (a)sexual ideology, and how they may make fun of the famous and powerful.

10.0 INTRODUCTION: HUMOUR AS LIBERATION OR CONTROL

In Chapters 7 and 8 we have looked at ways of challenging the authority of transnational corporations and their advertising through critical discourse analysis (CDA) and of challenging the authority of the corporate news media through social media and alternative news sources. In Chapter 9 we explored the ways in which the authority of climate science is challenged by business interests. More subtly we explored the ways in which the language of environmental texts under the influence of the Natural Capital Agenda can represent nature in ways unhelpful to ecology and how poetry might challenge this representation. This final chapter of the book considers another potential weapon for challenging authority: humour. We look at humour's role in psychological, social and linguistic liberation, and the role of parody or fan fiction in writing back against the power of dominant fictional texts or existing discourses.

Nineteenth- and twentieth-century theories of humour often centred on the idea that humour is a psychological liberation. Herbert Spencer (1864) thought of it as a form of release and regulation of nervous energy. Freud (1905/1963) saw jokes as liberating us from the psychological tension between our subconscious desires (the id) and the need to control them (the superego). For him, humour countered the repression of feelings about the sacred, the taboo and the disgusting, and was a temporary carnival, a rebellion against normal prohibitions. Since prohibitions and taboos are imposed by society, humour was theorised as social liberation, too. It may be seen as a rebellion against the rules of society and the powerful people who enforce them and benefit from them. Bain (1865) identified the associated pleasure in degrading persons of dignity: this frees us from the normal constraints which force us to honour and respect them. For example, the German poet Heine told a joke about a poor lottery agent boasting that the super-rich Baron Rothschild treated him as an equal – quite "famillionairely". Freud (1905/1963) interprets this joke as a criticism of the Baron's patronising condescension. Or consider this joke: 'President Obama recently came under fire over the lack of diversity in his cabinet. Then Obama said, "You guys know I'll be there, too, right?"' (Jimmy Fallon). The possible implication of the joke is that Obama as president is a kind of tokenism – that because he is (half) black he doesn't have to represent black, minority or diverse interests.

However, humour can also be used in the exercise of power. For instance, Holmes (2000) investigates how bosses use joking discourse as a means of social control, especially in "egalitarian" societies. And Billig (2005) has developed a theory of humour as a means of socialisation. Parents laugh at and "tease" their children, embarrassing them in order to signal their inappropriate behaviour (Scheff 1997). Freud gives an example of "little Hans", who was looking obsessively at a pretty eight-year-old girl in a hotel restaurant. His parents laughed at him and thereby embarrassed him as a form of discipline (Billig 2005: 230ff.).

This ambivalent nature of humour, like environmental discourse, means that humorous texts are caught up in the struggle for power. Anti-political correctness (p.c.) jokes are an example. From the 1960s onwards in Western societies campaigns have been waged, with some success, against discrimination on the basis of race, gender, sexual orientation, religion and disability. These attempts to give a voice and power to previously marginalised and weak groups obviously threaten the power of white, male, straight, Christian, able-bodied elites, who criticise discourse and social practices which reflect the success of these campaigns as "political correctness". The result has been a slew of anti-p.c. jokes. For a taste of these one only has to look at the British comedian Jimmy Carr in his "Telling Jokes" series (e.g. www.youtube.com/watch?v=wFjimNe2HJM). He routinely makes jokes about women looking old, gays and the sick and disabled. Making this latter group the butt of his jokes matches well the current UK government's anti-welfare policies, where the sick and disabled are often identified as "scroungers". The great humour theorist Bergson said that humour induced a temporary anaesthesia of the heart (Bergson 1900). Such anti-p.c. humour could be seen as an attempt to make lack of sympathy permanent.

Perhaps the greatest social control we experience is in learning our first language. Language, according to Barthes, is fascist (Billig 2005: 238). The control is over our bodies – our vocal apparatus is disciplined to conform to the phonological standard of our parents' speech community. Learning a language controls our minds – we noted in Chapter 2, when discussing Whorf's linguistic relativity hypothesis and kinship terms, how the language one speaks makes it easier to think in some ways and more difficult to think in alternative ways. Learning the norms of discourse and appropriate generic structure (Chapter 1) also controls our social behaviour.

Linguistic humour can be seen as a resistance to this straitjacket of linguistic convention. Word play, the use of puns, false analysis of meaningful linguistic units or pseudo-morphology, are all an attempt at liberation from the language code. Consider this pun:

A philosophy professor and a sociologist are holidaying at a nudist camp. The philosopher turns to his colleague and asks, "I assume you've read Marx". "Yes," replies the sociologist, "I think it's these metal chairs."

(Carr and Greeves 2007: 121)

Or these examples of pseudo-morphology:

"What's a baby pig called?" "A piglet."
"So what's a baby toy called?" "A toilet."

– What do you do with a wombat?
– Play wom.

So we laugh sympathetically at intentional attempts to liberate us from the inconsistencies and ambiguities of the code. But we also target people who are unable to adapt their vocal apparatus (or minds) to its demands, or who are ignorant of register and genre. Take the joke:

VICAR: I hereby pronounce you man and wife.
BRIDE: And you pwonounce it vewy nicely, vicar.

The bride is the target/victim of the joke for three reasons: first, her inability to pronounce *r*, her failure to adequately control her vocal apparatus; second, her ignorance that in this generic context 'pronounce' is more likely to mean "announce that you are"; third, her unawareness that a compliment by the bride on the vicar's speech fails to conform to the generic structure of the wedding service.

Let's sum up by considering this joke:

Japanese PM Shinzo Abe comes to Singapore to deliver the keynote speech at a security conference, the Shangri-la Dialogue. Abe arrives at Changi Airport and it is his turn to go up to the immigration counter.
'Name?'
'Abe. Shinzo Abe.'
'Nationality?'
'Japanese.'
'Occupation?'
'No, I'm here for just a few days.'

It demonstrates a rejection of power and authority first by targeting Abe for not understanding the likely meaning of 'occupation' in this context, and implicitly attacking a rising Japanese militarism. Moreover, it exploits, even if it does not explicitly criticise, the absurdity of ambiguity in language by punning on the word *occupation*.

From a wider perspective, though humour might be a coping mechanism or a means of dealing with repression/oppression, it stops short of challenging the (unjust) social systems which cause the repression/ oppression in the first place. We might express our aggression towards powerful politicians through humour (rather than, say, throwing shoes or grenades at them) but this will not remove them from power. Humour might even reduce the pressure for real social or regime change. Telling jokes about Japanese militarism will not by itself reduce it.

An additional argument against humour as a form of liberation is the fact that to make the required inferences to get the joke we often resort to stereotypes. And these stereotypes are often created by those in power or fighting for power in society. We saw this in our discussion of an Irish joke in Chapter 4. Irishmen are stereotypically represented as stupid because the English working classes in the nineteenth century wished to enhance their own employment power by spreading this myth. But the unfair stereotype persists, now perhaps reinterpreted in terms of power – the supposed superior intelligence of the English.

10.1 SHARED IDEOLOGIES AND THE INTERPERSONAL ASPECTS OF HUMOUR

Humour has important consequences for interpersonal relationships. Paul Simpson (2003: 86) developed a framework for these in the context of satire, as diagrammed in Figure 10.1. Humour can create a closer relationship between satirist (joke-teller) and satiree (audience), for example, and, in aggressive satire, distance both satirist and satiree from the satirised (target). However, if there is little cultural or ideological gap between the audience for the joke and the target of the joke, then the

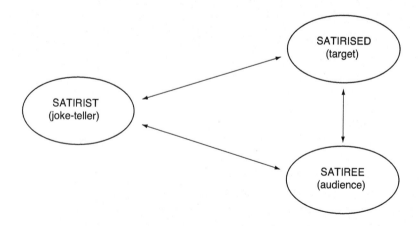

Figure 10.1
The satirical triad

joke may fail and the distance between joke-teller and audience increase (Simpson 2003: 86–87, 154–157). For example, readers who are Japanese and supporters of Abe may not appreciate the joke above and telling it may alienate them from the joke-teller. Joke websites therefore become a way of declaring and promoting one's own identity (Oring 2003: chapter 10).

There is an added complication if we consider the distinction between outsider and insider humour. Negative jokes with particular social groups as the targets may be rejected as discriminatory if the satirist/joke-teller is not a member of the satirised social group, but be perfectly acceptable if they are. Black comedians can get away with anti-black jokes that would be thought racist in a white person's mouth, especially if the audience are also black (Simpson and Mayr 2010: 194). And if a Japanese person told the joke about Abe, then this might be more acceptable to a Japanese audience than if a Chinese person told it.

10.2 PARODY

We briefly introduced parody in Chapter 6 in the context of intertextuality. We will discuss it in more depth here, as parody can often be seen as a form of humour that attempts to undermine the authority of an existing well-known text, although it may sometimes be affectionate towards those texts rather than hostile. The discussion of parody also prepares for a discussion of fan fiction, much of which is parodic.

Walter Nash (1990) developed an interesting theoretical framework for discussing parody. There is not the space to illustrate all of his models but we can look at three, one simple and two more complex. The first and simplest is style parody, where we take the style of a particular text or author, a **source expression**, and imitate it to give us a **derived expression**, but introduce an incongruous or **displacing content** (Figure 10.2).

We saw an example of this in the parody of the Heinz ad in Chapter 6, where the can of beans is displaced by the spray paint can, the picking up is displaced by the putting down, the Beanz are displaced by Deanz, and Heinz is displaced by Finez. The rhythmical structure is preserved as is the unconventional spelling of the plurals in the last line. So much of the original expression is derived here, that it is not a very sophisticated parody. More interesting are parodies that derive aspects of style, rather

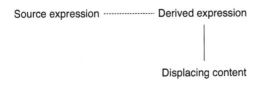

Source expression ⸱⸱⸱⸱⸱⸱⸱⸱⸱⸱⸱⸱⸱⸱⸱⸱⸱ Derived expression

Displacing content

Figure 10.2
Simple style
parody

than just repeating words and expressions wholesale, which is the case with our second example, by Wendy Cope (2010).

As young children, not only do we learn our language, but we also have stories read to us and are taught to read. We have little choice over what books we read at a young age, as we are at the mercy of our parents. One popular reading scheme, the Jane and Peter books, published by Ladybird, was commonly used in the second half of the last century. Typical extracts from these books were as follows:

> Here is Peter. Here is Jane. Peter is here and Jane is here. Here is the dog. Here is Jane. Here is Jane and here is the dog. Jane likes the dog. Peter likes the dog. Jane and Peter like the dog. The dog likes Jane and Jane likes the dog. This is the ball. Peter has the ball. Peter likes the ball.

> Here is Peter. Look at Peter! Here is the ball. Look at the ball! Here is the dog. Look at the dog!

> Peter kicks the ball. The dog chases the ball. Look, Jane! Look at Peter! See him kick the ball. Look, Peter! Look at the dog! See him chase the ball!

Wendy Cope's parody is as follows:

Reading Scheme by Wendy Cope

Here is Peter. Here is Jane. They like fun.
Jane has a big doll. Peter has a ball.
Look, Jane, look! Look at the dog! See him run.

Here is Mummy. She has baked a bun.
Here is the milkman. He has come to call.
Here is Peter. Here is Jane. They like fun.

Go, Peter! Go, Jane! Come, milkman, come!
The milkman likes Mummy. She likes them all.
Look, Jane, look! Look at the dog! See him run!

Here are the curtains. They shut out the sun.
Let us peep! On tiptoe, Jane! You are small!
Here is Peter. Here is Jane. They like fun.

I hear a car, Jane. The milkman looks glum.
Here is Daddy in his car. Daddy is tall.
Look, Jane, look! Look at the dog! See him run!

Daddy looks very cross. He has a gun?
Up milkman! Up milkman! Over the wall.
Here is Peter. Here is Jane. They like fun.
Look, Jane, look. Look at the dog! See him run!

Some of the sentences are repeated word for word from the source texts. Others simply imitate aspects of grammatical style: the short sentences; imperatives followed by exclamation marks; the simple present tense in most cases; the vocatives addressing the characters by name; the general repetitiveness. The displacing content, the implied sex between Mummy and the milkman interrupted by an angry Daddy who, with the dog (?) chases him over the wall, necessitates a change of vocabulary, but preserves these stylistic features: 'Here is the milkman'; 'The milkman likes Mummy'; 'Here are the curtains. They shut out the sun'; 'The milkman looks glum. Here is Daddy in his car'; 'Daddy looks very cross. He has a gun? Up milkman! Up milkman! Over the wall.'

However, in terms of large stylistic structures there is a secondary source expression, as the poem is in the form of a villanelle. This is a 19-line form of verse consisting of five stanzas of three lines followed by a stanza of four lines. It has two repeating rhymes in alternate lines (*-un/-um* and *–all*). The first and third line of the first stanza ('Here is Peter. Here is Jane. They like fun') and ('Look, Jane, look! Look at the dog! See him run') are repeated alternately as the last lines of the first five stanzas. But the last stanza includes both repeated lines.

So this parody might be diagrammed as in Figure 10.3. In fact, the Peter and Jane readers (source expression 1), and the villanelle (source expression 2) share a repetitiveness which makes them similar.

Our third example is a parody of another text that we might have had introduced to us by our powerful parents when we were young children – *Little Red Riding Hood*. Let's look at one original version of the story followed by the parody. (I have attempted to label the speech acts occurring in both texts in brackets, to facilitate later analysis).

Little Red Riding Hood (original)
Little Red Riding Hood's mother was packing a basket with eggs and butter and home-made bread.
　　'Who is that for?' asked Little Red Riding Hood. [*Question*]

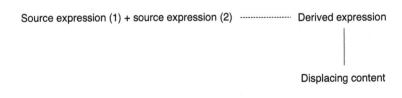

Source expression (1) + source expression (2) ------------ Derived expression

Displacing content

Figure 10.3
Complex parody

'For Grandma,' [*Reply*] said Mother. 'She has not been feeling well.' [*Statement (Sympathising)*]

Grandma lived alone in a cottage in the middle of a wood.

'I will take it to her,' [*Offer/Undertaking*] said Little Red Riding Hood.

'Make sure you go straight to the cottage,' [*Command/Advice*] said Mother as she waved good-bye, 'and do not talk to any strangers.' [*Command/Prohibition*]

Little Red Riding Hood meant to go straight to the cottage but there were so many wild flowers growing in the wood, she decided to stop and pick some for Grandma. Grandma liked flowers. They would cheer her up.

'Good morning!' [*Greeting*] said a voice near her elbow. It was a wolf. 'Where are you taking these goodies?' [*Question*]

'I'm taking them to my Grandma,' [*Reply*] said Little Red Riding Hood, quite forgetting what her mother had said about talking to strangers.

'Lucky Grandma,' [*Appreciation*] said the wolf. 'Where does she live?' [*Question*]

"In the cottage in the middle of the wood,' [*Reply*] said Little Red Riding Hood.

'Be sure to pick her a nice BIG bunch of flowers,' [*Advice*] said the wolf and hurried away.

The wolf went straight to Grandma's cottage and knocked at the door.

'Who is there?' [*Question*] called Grandma.

'It is I, Little Red Riding Hood,' [*Reply (Lie)*] replied the wolf in a "little girl" voice.

'Then lift up the latch and come in,' [*Invitation*] called Grandma.

Grandma screamed loudly when she saw the wolf's face peering around the door. He was licking his lips. She jumped out of bed and tried to hide in the cupboard, but the wolf, who was very hungry, caught her and in three gulps ate her all up. Then he picked up her frilly bedcap that had fallen to the floor and put it on his own head. He pushed his ears inside her cap, climbed into Grandma's bed, pulled up the bedclothes and waited for Red Riding Hood to come. Presently there was a knock on the door.

'Who is there?' [*Question*] he called, in a voice that sounded like Grandma's.

'It is I, Little Red Riding Hood.' [*Reply*]

'Then lift up the latch and come in.' [*Invitation*]

She opened the door and went in.

'Are you feeling better, Grandma?' [*Question (Sympathising)*] she asked.

'Yes dear, I am. [*Reply*] Let me see what you have in the basket.' [*Request*]

As the wolf leaned forward the bedcap slipped and one of his ears popped out.

'What big ears you have,' [*Exclamation*] said Little Red Riding Hood.

'All the better to hear you with,' [*Self-praise*] said the wolf, turning towards her.

'What big eyes you have Grandma!' [*Exclamation*]

'All the better to see you with,' [*Self-praise*] said the wolf with a big grin.

'What big teeth you have!' [*Exclamation*]

'All the better to eat you with!' [*Self-praise/Threat*] said the wolf and threw back the covers and jumped out of bed.

'You are not my Grandma!' [*Blame/Recognition*] she screamed.

'No I'm not. [*Confirmation*] I'm the big bad wolf', [*Identification*] growled the wolf in his own voice, 'and I'm going to eat you up.' [*Threat*]

'Help! Help!' [*Appeal*] shouted Little Red Riding Hood as the wolf chased her out of the cottage and into the wood.

The woodcutter heard her screams and came to the rescue. As soon as the wolf saw the woodcutter's big wood-cutting axe, he put his tail between his legs and ran away as fast as he could.

'What a lucky escape I had,' [*Exclamation (Relief)*] said Red Riding Hood to the woodcutter.

What a lucky escape indeed.

Little Red Riding Hood (Parody)

There once was a young person named Red Riding Hood who lived with her mother on the edge of a large wood. One day her mother asked her to take a basket of fresh fruit and **mineral water** to her grandmother's house [*Request*] –**not because this was womyn's work, mind you, but because the deed was generous and helped engender a feeling of community**. Furthermore, **her grandmother was not sick, but rather was in full physical and mental health and was fully capable of taking care of herself as a mature adult**.

So Red Riding Hood set out with her basket of food through the woods. Many people she knew believed that the forest was a foreboding and dangerous place and never set foot in it. Red Riding Hood, however, **was confident enough in her own budding sexuality that such obvious Freudian imagery** did not hinder her.

On her way to Grandma's house, Red Riding Hood was accosted by a Wolf, who asked her what was in her basket.

[*Question*] She replied, 'Some **healthful snacks** for my grandmother, [*Reply*] who **is certainly capable of taking care of herself as a mature adult**.' [*Praise* (deflect implied criticism)]

The Wolf said, 'You know; my dear, it isn't safe for a little girl to walk through these woods alone.' [*Warning*]

Red Riding Hood said, '**I find your sexist remark offensive in the extreme,** [*Objection*] but I will ignore it [*Undertaking*] **because of your traditional status as an outcast from society,** [*Sympathising*] **the stress of which has caused you to develop your own, entirely valid worldview.** [*Acceptance*] Now, if you'll excuse me, I must be on my way.' [*Apology*]

Red Riding Hood walked on along the main path. But, because **his status outside society had freed him from slavish adherence to linear, Western-style thought,** the Wolf knew of a quicker route to Grandma's house. He burst into the house and ate Grandma, **an entirely valid course of action for a carnivore such as himself.** Then, **unhampered by rigid, traditionalist notions of what was masculine or feminine,** he put on Grandma's nightclothes and crawled into bed.

Red Riding Hood entered the cottage and said, 'Grandma, I have brought you some **fat-free sodium-free snacks** [*Offer*] to **salute you in your role of a wise and nurturing matriarch**.' [*Affirmation*]

From the bed, the Wolf said softly, 'Come closer, child, so that I might see you.' [*Command/Request*]

Red Riding Hood said, 'Oh, I forgot you are as **optically challenged** as a bat. [*Criticism* (downgraded by euphemism)] Grandma, what big eyes you have!' [*Exclamation/Criticism*]

'They have seen much, and forgiven much, my dear.' [*Statement/Self-exoneration*]

'Grandma, what a big nose you have [*Exclamation/Criticism*] – **only relatively**, of course [*Mitigation*], and **certainly attractive in its own way**.' [*Praise*]

'It has smelled much, and forgiven much, my dear.' [*Statement/Self-exoneration*]

'Grandma, what big teeth you have!' [*Exclamation/Criticism*]

The Wolf said, '**I am happy with who I am and what I am**', [*Self-affirmation of identity*] and leaped out of bed. He grabbed Red Riding Hood in his claws, intent on devouring her. Red Riding Hood screamed, not out of alarm at **the Wolf's apparent tendency toward cross-dressing, but because of his wilful invasion of her personal space.**

Her screams were heard by a passing woodchopper-**person (or log-fuel technician**, as he preferred to be called). When he burst into the cottage, he saw the melée and tried to intervene.

But as he raised his ax, Red Riding Hood and the Wolf both stopped.

'And what do you think you're doing?' [*Objection*] asked Red Riding Hood.

The woodchopper-person blinked and tried to answer, but no words came to him.

'Bursting in here like a Neanderthal, trusting your weapon to do your thinking for you!' [*Criticism*] she said. '**Sexist! Speciesist!** [*Insult*] How dare you assume that **womyn** and wolves **can't solve their own problems without a man's help**!' [*Objection*]

When she heard Red Riding Hood's speech, Grandma jumped out of the Wolf's mouth, took the **woodchopper-person's** axe, and cut his head off. After this ordeal, Red Riding Hood, Grandma, and the Wolf felt **a certain commonality of purpose**. They decided to set up **an alternative household based on mutual respect and coopera-tion**, and they lived together in the woods happily ever after.

(From *Politically Correct Bedtime Stories* by Jim Garner)

This parody can be modelled as in Figure 10.4. Source expression (1) is the feminist and otherwise "politically correct" language which we have emboldened in the text of the parody. Source expression (2) is the expression of the original story. The most obvious displacement of content in plot terms is the reversal of killer and victim roles – grandma becomes killer not victim, and woodcutter becomes victim rather than powerful rescuer. The anti-ageist, anti-sexist, anti-imperialist, anti-speciesist, anti-militarist displacing content is for the most part expressed in the p.c. language (1), though Red Riding Hood's objections to the woodchopper and the cutting off of the woodcutter's head is not mark-edly in this style. Indeed, it seems to be the source expression (1) that is the main target of the humour here, rather than the original story. This includes the (perhaps mythical) insistence on renaming of occupations, e.g. 'log fuel technician', the removal of –*man* as part of *woman* by 'womyn', and the use of *challenged* as part of a euphemism. So this is not the kind of parody, like Wendy Cope's, that makes fun of the original text in order to undermine its authority.

The two (or more) source expressions which are mixed in this story tend to achieve their humour by having different levels of formal-ity, implying different degrees of contact. The last sentence is a good

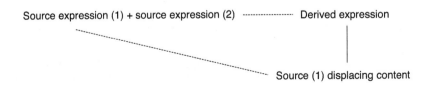

Source expression (1) + source expression (2) ⋯⋯⋯⋯ Derived expression

Source (1) displacing content

Figure 10.4
More complex parody

example. The "p.c." formal style 'an alternative household based on mutual respect and cooperation' where all of the lexical items except *household* are from French and Latin, contrasts with the exclusively Old English vocabulary 'and they lived together in the woods happily ever after', itself the traditional way of ending a fairy tale bedtime story. At the other extreme of informality we have the colloquial 'And what do you think you're doing?', and the idiomatic slang 'Bursting in here like a Neanderthal, trusting your weapon to do your thinking for you!'

Another aspect of the parodic content/source expression concerns the displacement of the kinds of speech act in the original and how these position the characters as subjects. First of all, and central to p.c. discourse, is the way in which speech acts are used to celebrate the identity of previously marginalised social groups – females, the young, the elderly, wolves. I have used the label *affirmation* for such speech acts in the parody. In a similar way we notice *acceptance* of diversity, *sympathising* and *praise* for these groups and *mitigation* of any (implied) *criticism*. Second, we notice that Red Riding Hood is more often the subject of *commands (prohibitions)* and *advice* in the original than in the parody, especially from her mother (one interpretation of the original could be as a cautionary tale, reminding children to take their parents' commands and advice seriously). However, when the wolf in the parody subjects her to *warning* about the dangers of the woods, Red Riding Hood adopts the assertive role of a stereotypical feminist, by her *objection*. But her greatest anger is directed towards the woodcutter, when he prepares to kill the wolf. This powerful male figure, originally the hero from the dominant social group, who saves the helpless girl, invites *objections, criticism* and *insult*, before Grandma kills him so that the members of marginalised groups can establish their own community.

This example illustrates the way in which anti-p.c. humour operates by exaggeration and caricature within the parody. Let's look, for example, at the term 'speciesist', which the parody invites us to laugh at. Actually, speciesism against wolves is a serious problem. The best-selling Chinese novel, translated into English as *Wolf Totem*, shows the disastrous environmental consequences of the demonisation of wolves and later attempts to eradicate them from the pasture lands of Mongolia. The overgrazing that results causes desertification and is a major cause of the severe sandstorms that plague Beijing every spring.

10.3 VISUAL PARODY

So far, we've looked at how parody in linguistic texts becomes a means of writing back against the authority of dominant texts and expressions of ideology. In its strong form, it challenges a given representation by subverting or reversing its intended message. The same can be achieved by visual parodies. These, especially in public spaces, usually take the form of advertisements or campaigns promoting a particular cause by commenting on a dominant discourse. They often draw attention to manipulative claims or promises of institutions such as governments and corporations. Let's illustrate this by looking at an example.

The example we discuss is an ad from the brand Amul, the largest milk producer in the world. This company is a producers' co-operative, which grew out of protests against the exploitation of farmers by middlemen, taking inspiration from the 1946 freedom movement in India. (For the detailed story of this milk-producing co-operative movement, see www.amul.com/m/about-us). In keeping with the spirit of the co-operative, the ads for its products are social commentaries, humorous takes on topical issues employing parody. Over the years, the parodic Amul ads and the Amul mascot girl have become symbols of humorous critiques of dominant societal discourses. Let's analyse an example.

At an Asia-Pacific Economic Cooperation (APEC) summit, President Putin of Russia wrapped a shawl around Peng Liyuan, the wife of Chinese Premier Xi Jinping. A photograph of the incident can be seen in Image 10.1.

The visual parody in the Amul butter ad (Image 10.2) makes fun of the reaction of state media and authorities in China to video footage of this incident. Putin's act was first broadcast on Chinese state TV, but as soon as it went viral on social media the footage and all its associated commentary were hastily removed from the Chinese internet. This reaction by the state media reflected the kind of control that authorities exert over any material about the country's leaders. It may also have been

Image 10.1
Putin and Peng Liyuan: the content for parody

Image 10.2
Visual parody of the Putin and Peng incident in an Amul butter ad

prompted by cultural differences over what is considered acceptable behaviour in public. The Amul butter ad parodies the incident and its consequent reaction.

In this ad, Putin and Peng, and Putin's action on Peng – the source content – have been parodied through an expression derived from the source of cartoon-style caricature (source expression 1). Slightly differently, the cartoon-style Amul girl has substituted for the APEC aide as displacing content, though both are onlookers. The slab of butter is also displacing content for one of the tea mugs in the photo.

The headline of the ad 'You shawl not do that' draws from the well-established source expression of the Ten Commandments in the Bible. The sentence formula 'Thou shalt not…' or in modern Bible versions 'You shall not' (for instance, 'you shall not commit adultery') acts as source expression (2). The content 'shawl' is displacing content for 'shall', referring to the shawl being placed around Peng's shoulders by Putin. As state authorities removed the footage of the incident from the internet, a clear message (commandment) went out: putting a shawl on the Premier's wife is clearly not considered appropriate or acceptable behaviour in public. This is reflected through the integration of the visual caricatures co-deployed with the verbal headline.

In visual representational terms the ad realises two narrative transactional processes. The first is the actional process with the vector extending from Putin's hands towards Peng's shoulders, and the second is the reactional process as the gaze from the Amul mascot is extended towards Putin and Peng. In interpersonal terms, the ad makes a visual offer, as none of the participants' gazes are directed towards the viewer. The viewer is expected to look at the represented participants as objects of contemplation. This is also mirrored in the subjective perspective of the oblique angle at the same level used to suggest that the participants are not part of the viewer's world. As a result the ad is expected to be contemplated from a distance with a social relation of equality or neutral power, as a humorous take on the reaction of the authorities towards Putin's gesture. In a sense, the ad not only parodies the knee-jerk reaction of authorities, but also comments on the notion of censorship by the state. So we can see how the visual parody here becomes a vehicle of questioning, commenting or getting back at power in a light-hearted manner.

We have been discussing how this visual parody resists the ideology of Chinese state control. However, ironically, these ads end up furthering consumerist ideology. The Amul mascot displacing the content of the onlooking aide, and the butter displacing the content of the tea mug, work in conjunction with the headline and by-line of the ad 'Amul Strengthens ties!' Together these serve as a reminder of the brand and how Amul butter can be used instead of the shawl as a means of improving relations between the two countries. The reaction and consequent censorship by the government is made laughable through the visual parody. At the same time the ad promotes private consumer choice of its product as an alternative to government control of public behaviour.

This brings us back to the first question raised in Section 10.0 as to whether humour is a liberating factor or a means of control. While the humour used in the visual parody acts as a form of resistance to power, it simultaneously functions as a mechanism of exercising power through capitalistic control. So, by critically analysing these visual parodies, we can notice a doubling effect through simultaneous resistance and promotion. This might be evidence, as demonstrated in Chapter 9, that it is literary texts, rather than parodic ads or environmental reports, that can protest existing ideologies in the least compromising way.

ACTIVITY 54

Please refer to the companion website for the activity material.

10.4 FAN FICTION

Parody is a commonly used technique in fan fiction. **Fan fiction** has been defined in two ways: 'the work of amateurs retelling existing stories', which applies to most literary works within an oral tradition, where the sense of a single author never really applied in the first place; or 'the reworking of another author's characters', which is a more modern concept associated with the notion of a single author and their copyright (Morrison 2012). I do not think the relationship between fan fiction and parody has been theorised, though these definitions might be related to Nash's concepts of source expression, derived expression and displacing content. 'Retelling existing stories' suggests only minor changes of expression and content, if the aim of the speaker writer is to reproduce faithfully what they heard. The second definition suggests a radical displacing of content in terms of the actions and relationships of characters, though some aspects of the characters (at least their names) remain constant.

In what ways can fan fiction be seen as subversive of power or authority? First, there is the general sense that it represents a challenge to copyright laws. Authors whose works are the sources of fan fiction have differing views on copyright infringement. Anne Rice, author of *Interview with the Vampire*, took a strong stand over fan fiction, feeling upset that her copyrighted characters could be violated. By contrast, Douglas Adams, author of *the Hitchhikers Guide to the Galaxy*, welcomed fan fiction as enhancing his understanding of the parallel worlds created in that novel. J.K. Rowling initially thought of taking legal action against George Lippert's *James Potter and the Hall of Elders' Crossing*, whose hero was the son of Harry Potter (HP), but later allowed publication. She is reasonably relaxed about fan fiction, providing it does not contain racism or pornography. However, such is the nature of the internet that HP pornographic fan fiction is beyond control and one of its most popular forms.

We can explore the transgressive and subversive aspects of fan fiction as we consider various subgenres. **Slash fiction** is a kind of fan fiction that originally featured characters from the source text in homosexual relationships. For instance, Holmes/Watson from Sherlock Holmes, Spock/Kirk from *Star Trek*, Harry Potter/Ron Weasley from the HP series or Jesus/Judas from the gospels. Introducing gay relationships can be seen as an attempt to undermine the power of heterosexual ideology, sometimes apparent in the original text. For instance, there is plenty of HP lesbian porn fan fiction, known as **femslash**. Later, the term *slash fiction* was used for any pornographic fan fiction. It includes **chanslash**, originally a Japanese subgenre that involves sex with minors, also observable in some of the 16,000 or more Justin Bieber fan fiction stories. Chanslash might be a rather disturbing attempt to transgress the cultural norms that outlaw paedophilia. The transgressive eroticism of slash fiction may have its origins in a need for psychological liberation:

> There is a dark sexual undercurrent to the majority of fanfic, as if on a subconscious level the fan actually resents the control that their idol or idealised character has over their life. Through the act of writing fanfic, and subjecting characters to compulsive or vengeful love, sex, S&M or rape, the fan then regains control.
>
> (Morrison 2012)

It is worth mentioning Jane Austen in this context. She has been the source for 200,000 fan-fiction works, and nearly 250 published books.

Many, if not most of these, are pornographic. We see here another aspect of resistance against authority. Austen not only has the authority of a canonical writer, but by avoiding any explicit description of sex might be felt to be prudishly distorting reality. After all, the main themes and climaxes of her books are about courtship and eventual marriage. She therefore invites resistance in the form of fan fiction with sexually explicit displacing content. This is quite similar to the BBC film of Austen's *Mansfield Park*, which highlights the horrors of slavery that remain unmentioned in the novel, despite Sir Bertram's business interests in the West Indies.

Some slash merges with **self-insert fan fiction**. The latter is a sub-genre in which the author appears as a character. When the two merge the author makes love to a famous fictional character. This sub-genre can be thought of as an attempt to raise the status of the author in terms of fame and physical attractiveness. Indeed a dominant version of insert fiction is known as Mary Sue fic, where the thinly disguised author becomes an exemplary character superior to the famous people with whom she interacts. Paula Smith in 1973 wrote the short story 'A Trekkies Tale' in which she visits the *Starship Enterprise* and is the centre of sexual attraction for the whole crew. The superiority of these self-insert characters may show the contempt of the writer for the characters to which he/she is superior.

Other sub-genres of fan fiction have a less obvious tendency towards subversiveness or enhancing self-worth. These include **cross-over** or **mash fiction**, where the characters from different works or genres appear in the same text. An example would be *Abraham Lincoln Vampire Hunter*. This particular case might seem iconoclastic of a major US statesman. In terms of Nash's model, crossover fiction involves displacing content from two or more texts or text types. **Alternative universe (AU) fiction**, which now seems to dominate fan fiction, imagines hypothetical situations involving familiar fictional characters. The *Twilight*-based AU pursues the possibilities of Bella being engaged to Jasper not Edward, Edward and Bella meeting in kindergarten, Jacob and Edward as gay lovers or Bella on *The Titanic*. Crossover or mash or AU fan fiction could generally be seen as resistance against the authority of the original text by deconstructing it.

In some ways we have come full circle to the situation where fan fiction represents a democratisation of literary production rather like the multiple authorship or lack of individual authorship of medieval literature, before the age of legal copyright. The hugely successful *Fifty Shades of Grey*, for example, has its origins in the *Twilight* AU slash fan fiction. The novel is derivative of the 60,000 existing *Twilight* fan fiction productions that were circulating well before E.L. James wrote the book.

It is in a sense a collective creation. Ironically, it commercialises the fan fiction that was on the web, and is thereby co-opted into the economic sphere of publishing for economic gain.

 PROJECT 5

Please refer to the companion website for the activity material.

10.5 SUMMARY

We hope we have shown in this chapter the potential for humour to resist power, even though it may equally be used to reinforce or cement existing power structures. The language we are taught, the books that are chosen for us or read to us as children, the canonical texts that are held up to us as highly respected cultural objects during our education, and the bestselling texts of popular culture can all provide source expression (and content) which can be resisted through parody and fan fiction. Moreover, the powers exerted by government and corporations can themselves be ridiculed, if not weakened by satirical parody.

Along with the critical analysis of ads (Chapter 7), participation in citizen journalism to give alternative representations of the social, economic and political world (Chapter 8) and poetic attempts to create an alternative representation of nature (Chapter 9), humour can take its place as a tool in resisting power.

 FURTHER READING

Please refer to the companion website for the list of further reading.

GLOSSARY OF TERMS

Listed below are the main key terms used in this book, together with brief definitions. These key terms include those which appear in bold on their first appearance in the hard copy book.

This is not a full list of linguistic terms, and often the definitions are simplified. For students who are majoring in English Language or Linguistics dictionaries or encyclopaedias such as David Crystal's comprehensive *A Dictionary of Linguistics and Phonetics* (6th edition, 2008, Oxford: Blackwell), Rob Pope's *English Studies Book* (2nd edition 2002, London: Routledge), or Ronald Carter's *Keywords in Language and Literacy* (1995, London: Routledge) are recommended.

Abstract
A short summary of the story provided before a narrative begins, capturing the 'point' of the story. It signals that a narrative is about to commence and is a bridge to make the narrative relevant to the preceding conversation.
Actional process (see **narrative process**)
Activation of existents (see **existential process**)
Activation of experiences (see **mental process**)
Activation of tokens (see **relational process**)
Active
One kind of grammatical voice. Clauses can differ according to whether they are in the active or the **passive** voice. In the active voice the subject of the sentence is the participant who acts or speaks or experiences. In the equivalent passive sentence this participant, if mentioned at all, will be in a *by* phrase, and the subject will be the participant affected or what is experienced. For example:

the dog bit the man	active
the man was bitten by the dog	passive
I noticed the bird first	active
the bird was noticed by me first	passive

Actor (see **material process**)

Adjective

The part of speech which describes, modifies or gives extra meaning to a noun or noun phrase, for instance (1) 'the *green* bottles' (2) 'the bottles are *green*'. Most adjectives can have *very* in front of them. They can usually be used attributively, before the noun, as in (1), and predicatively following the noun as in (2).

Adverbial

A word or phrase (or sometimes a clause) which gives information about the process described in the rest of the clause (or another clause). It gives information about the time, manner/attitude, position/direction, accompaniment, beneficiary or purpose of the process. For example 'Yesterday (time) I reluctantly (manner/attitude) went to a football match (direction) with my children (accompaniment) for my wife's sake (beneficiary), to give her a break from the kids (purpose).' The first two of these adverbials are words, the next three are phrases, and the last one is a clause. They all give us extra information about 'I went'.

Affected (see **material process**)

Affective words

We use this phrase to mean words which are empty or drained of conceptual meaning and simply convey emotion, e.g. swear words, which show negative emotion, and empty subjective words like *nice, fine, cool, good, great, wonderful, smashing, fabulous*, much used in advertising copy.

Agreement maxim

An aspect of the politeness principle which says it is more polite to agree than disagree (see also **preferred seconds**).

Analytical process (see **conceptual process**)

Animation

Using a verb, adjective or noun normally associated with an animal or living thing for an insentient or non-living entity, e.g. the mountain *breathed* on my face, the *shivering* trees, the *blind* building.

Anthropocentricism

The ideology that humans are central or most important. This view tends to marginalise nature as a resource rather than something existing and acting in its own right.

Approbation maxim

An aspect of the politeness principle which says it is more polite to show approval or give praise than to voice disapproval or criticise.

Assertive

A kind of speech act in which the speaker describes and gives information about the world. Speech act verbs which describe assertives include *state, swear, inform, remind, tell*.

Assured readers

Readers who are highly motivated to read or continue reading a text. **Non-assured readers** are reluctant or show little interest in the text. Texts for assured readers need to be less visually informative than those for non-assured readers.

Attribution

The element of the generic structure of news reports that indicates the source of the information in the report, for example a news agency such as Reuters.

Attributive clauses (see **relational clauses**)

Background

One of the elements in the generic structure of news reports. It includes references to previous events, even those stretching back into history, and details of the physical circumstances in which the event took place. It resembles Labov's **orientation**.

Balance

One basic design for paragraphs or texts, in which there is a weighing-up of descriptive facts, or arguments for and against a proposition, giving equal proportion to each side.

Behavioural process

An intermediate process between a mental process and a material process, which describes the outward manifestation of an inner feeling or condition, or an intentional perception. Here we find verbs describing facial expressions, gestures, etc., and verbs like *watch* and *look at*, which contrast with the mental perception verbs like *see* and *notice*.

Carrier

The thing or participant in a relational clause to which some quality is attributed (see also **relational process**).

Chain

A paragraph design where the sentences appearing in succession are linked most obviously only to the sentence before. Cohesive links are achieved by repeating vocabulary, or using pronouns to refer 'back' to something which has come in the previous sentence.

Change of state presupposition

When a text mentions a change of state and thereby assumes that the thing or person that changes is or was in a different or opposite state. For example 'Your food will get cold' presupposes that the food is not cold, i.e. it is hot or warm.

Classificational process (see **conceptual process**)

Cluster

A basic means of visual organisation of texts, consisting of a local grouping of verbal or visual items next to each other on a printed or web-page, and separated from other clusters by space or other graphic means. **Cluster hopping** means reading one cluster followed by another cluster (and then perhaps going back to the first cluster), in a modular rather than a progressive reading style.

Coda

An element of generic structure by which a narrative is completed. It is a bridge out of the narrative and often uses changes of tenses and time adverbs to bring us back to the present.

Cohesion

The patterns of language in a text which help it to hang together across sentence boundaries to form larger units like paragraphs. Cohesion can be lexical or grammatical. Lexically, chains of words related in meaning across sentences make a text cohere; grammatically, words like *this, the, it, the latter* can establish cohesion.

Comments

Part of the episode in the generic structure of news reports. It comprises evaluations of the other elements and speculations about what might happen next.

Commissive

A kind of speech act in which the speaker/writer commits to some future action by the speaker/writer. Speech act verbs which describe commissives include *promise, threaten, vow, volunteer, undertake, agree to*.

Complicating action

The most essential generic element in a narrative. It contains clauses describing linked events or actions, in past or present tense, ordered chronologically. If the order of clauses is reversed we have a different narrative. For instance, 'He went to Harvard and got a bachelor's degree' is a different story from 'He got a bachelor's degree and went to Harvard'.

Conceptual process

In visual communication this is a process that represent the identities, qualities and essence of things/people, rather like relational or existential processes in the grammar. Conceptual processes are classificational, analytical or symbolic. The classificational assign to classes, the analytical assign possessive attributes to a thing or person, and the symbolic suggest an extra meaning to what is represented.

Conjunction

A word which is used to link two clauses into a larger clause. Examples would be *and, but, although, unless, if, when, so that*.

Consequences

An element in the generic structure of news reports. The consequences are anything which was caused by the main event, namely another event, or a human physical reaction or verbal reaction.

Contact

The degree of intimacy or solidarity in social relationships. Frequency of meeting, variety of contexts in which we meet, and the time period over which our meetings last are all factors in determining contact.

Contested terms

Words which provoke an emotional or other reaction because of the ideology recognised in their use, and the fact that some people deliberately object to their use, e.g. *poetess, chairman*.

Core vocabulary

The most basic vocabulary in a language: the most frequently used, most accessible and that first learned by a child.

Dateline

In the generic structure of news reports, the place (not time) from which the news story was filed by the reporter.

Declaration

A kind of speech act in which the speaker/writer brings about an institutional change by the mere act of speaking/writing. The speaker/writer has to be ratified by society and its institutions and has to be in the correct institutional context. Speech act verbs which describe declarations include *christening, marrying, declaring war, sentencing, pleading (guilty or not guilty), signing (a contract)*.

Declarative mood

The grammatical mood usually used to make statements (rather than issue commands or ask questions). The test for declarative mood is whether subject precedes the finite verb. For example:

Subject	Finite	
He	took	the chestnuts.
He	did	look a fool.

Deductive structure

The structure of a paragraph or text where the main point or idea comes first. In **inductive structures** the point comes last. Deductive structures allow skimming or abandoning reading half-way through the text. Inductive structures emphasise the process of reading rather than simply the information as a product.

Degrees of involvement (see **perspective**)

Degrees of power (see **perspective**)

Derived expression (see **parody**)

Direct speech

A form of reporting speech in which the words actually spoken are included within quotation marks, and in which there is a reporting clause preceding or following the quote. For instance 'John said, "I will come tomorrow."' Or '"I did not have a sexual relationship with Monica Lewinsky," Clinton said.'

Directive

A type of speech act in which the writer/speaker attempts to make the reader/hearer do something, e.g. 'Could you type out the agenda?'. Examples of directive verbs would be *ask, command, request, suggest, plead, beg.*

Discourse

As we use the term, the interpersonal act of communication in which the writer intends to affect a reader and the reader attempts to work out the writer's intentions. The writer may encode some of her meaning in text as part of this act of communication. *But beware, there are many conflicting definitions of this term in the literature.*

Discussion

A genre which presents information and opinions about more than one side of an issue: it may end with a recommendation based on the evidence presented. It is associated with the kind of text organisation known as a balance.

Dispersonification

Describing humans in terms that are normally used for animals, plants or inanimate objects, for example *furrow* referring to lines on a human face, or *eruption* to refer to a pimple or boil on human skin.

Displacing content (see **parody**)

Dispreferred second (see **preferred second**)

Effective

A term used to describe ergative material process clauses in which there are two participants. When there is only one participant the clause is called **middle**. The terms *effective* and *middle* are roughly equivalent to the more traditional *transitive* and *intransitive*.

Emotion

An aspect of interpersonal relationships in which affect or feeling is expressed. It can be positive or negative, and fleeting or permanent.

Emotive spin

Words may share the same conceptual meaning but differ in emotive meaning, and this difference could be called 'spin'. A famous trio are *slim, thin* and *skinny. Slim* spins positively, *skinny* negatively and *thin* doesn't spin at all.

Episode

An element of the generic structure of news reports comprised of events and consequences.

Ergative

A specific kind of verb (or language). The difference between ergative verbs and other verbs can be seen when we add a second participant to the clause. With non-ergatives the clause is extended to the right, with ergatives to the left.

	non-ergative	ergative
1 participant	John ate	The boat sailed
2 participants	John ate a grape	Paul sailed the boat
	⟶	⟵

Euphemism

A word used to avoid a direct reference to something considered impolite. For example *comfort woman* for *sex slave*. Sex, urination and excretion, and death are the commonest topics for euphemism, though politically contested terms are also avoided by this technique.

Evaluation

An element in the generic structure of narrative. Labov identified evaluation with those clauses which don't belong to the narrative action, but which delay its forward movement. These comprise comments by narrator or character, emotive devices, comparatives, *if* clauses, negatives, questions, exclamations and future tense clauses.

Event

An element of the generic structure of news reports comprising the main event and the background.

Exclusive *we* (see **pronoun**)

Existential presupposition

The assumption that a (definite) noun phrase must refer to something that exists. If a new word or phrase is invented, such as *shopaholic*, then we assume that some people exist in the world who belong to this class.

Existential process

In the transitivity system of grammar existential clauses are those which represent the existence of a thing/person. This participant is known as the existent, e.g. 'there is an elephant in my garden'. Existents in existential processes can be grammatically re-encoded as actors in material processes. For example 'There is a grave in the valley' ⟶ 'A grave sits in the valley', giving rise to what we call the **activation of existents**.

Experience (see **mental process**)

Experiencer (see **mental process**)

Explanation

The endpoint or aim of critical discourse analysis, showing what social and ideological forces underlie or determine text and discourse meanings.

Exposition

A genre whose purpose is to advance or justify an argument or put forward a particular point of view.

Expository questions

A question which the writer herself goes on to answer. It is a way of introducing or stimulating interest in an issue or discourse topic, or of providing a frame for the discourse which follows.

Expressive

A kind of speech act in which the speaker expresses an inner feeling. Speech act verbs which describe expressives include *thank, congratulate, lament, complain, apologise.*

Face

An aspect of interpersonal relationships. It has two aspects, **positive face** and **negative face**. Negative face is the basic claim to territories, personal preserves, rights to non-distraction, freedom of action and freedom from imposition. Positive face is the positive consistent self-image or 'personality', crucially including the desire that this self-image be appreciated and approved of.

Fan fiction

This has been defined in two ways: 'the work of amateurs retelling existing stories', or 'the reworking of another author's characters'. It might be regarded as a kind of parody, reacting, humorously, to a source text and displacing its content. There are various sub-genres. **Slash fiction** is a kind of fan fiction that originally featured characters from the source text in homosexual relationships but is now used to label any pornographic fan fiction. **Chanslash** involves sex with minors. **Femslash** is lesbian porn fan fiction. **Alternative Universe (AU) fiction** imagines hypothetical situations involving familiar fictional characters. In **crossover** or **mash fiction** characters from different works or genres appear in the same text. In **self-insert fan fiction** the author appears as a character.

Free direct speech

A way of representing speech in which the words actually spoken are quoted, but without a reporting clause, e.g. ' "I will resign on Monday." '

Free indirect speech

A way of representing speech in which there is no reporting clause, the lexical words actually spoken remain the same, but some of the grammatical words known as **shifters** change. For example if the actual words spoken were ' "I will visit you tomorrow" ' in free indirect speech this would become 'He would visit him the next day'.

Gaze (see **vector**)

Generic structure

The stereotypical structure of a particular genre, also known as a discourse schema. It provides a kind of template into which an author can fit her text. For example, the generic structure for each entry in a telephone directory is:

SURNAME followed by GIVEN NAME followed by ADDRESS followed by NUMBER

Grammatical metaphor

A way of encoding meanings in grammar which is not the most direct, simple or acquired first in learning a language. For example the use of a noun to refer to a process rather than a thing as in nominalisation 'She made a change to the cast rather than 'she changed the cast', or the encoding of a circumstance as an experiencer 'Tuesday saw us climbing the Eiffel Tower' rather than 'We climbed the Eiffel Tower on Tuesday'.

Heteroglossic texts (see **monoglossic texts**)

Ideational meaning

Conceptual meaning, which represents, sorts and classifies the outside world and the mental world.

Identifying clauses (see **relational clauses**)

Ideology

As I use the term it means the ways of thinking which (re)produce and reflect the power structures of society, or, more briefly, 'meaning in the service of power'. *This term has many different definitions in different political philosophies.*

Imperative

The grammatical mood most obviously associated with commands. Imperative mood uses the bare or base form of the verb without any subject before or after it. For example: 'fill in the form'; 'have a drink'; 'take a break'; 'see me on Tuesday morning'.

Implying, implication

The unstated message the writer wishes to convey beyond what is encoded in the text. The reader is expected to make **inferences** about the writer's implications. If someone says 'I can't open this briefcase' and you reply 'Here's a key' you are implying that the person should use the key to open the briefcase and expecting the person to infer this. The process depends on familiarity with a schema in which keys are used for opening locks and in which suitcases have locks.

Indirect speech

A way of reporting speech where there is a reporting clause, no change to the lexical words, but changes to some words to bring them into line with the time, place and person of the reporting clause. E.g. 'John said "I will come here tomorrow"' becomes, in indirect speech 'John said that he would go there the following day'.

Indirect speech act

Using one kind of grammatical mood structure to indirectly perform a speech act associated with another mood. For instance, using the declarative mood, instead of interrogative, as a question, e.g. 'You went to Starbucks' last night?'. Or the declarative mood, instead of imperative, as an indirect command, e.g. 'The dog needs to be fed' instead of the direct 'Feed the dog'. Indirect commands/requests are considered more polite than direct ones in imperative mood.

Inclusive _we_ (see **pronoun**)

Inductive structure (see **deductive structure**)

Inference (see **implying, implication**)

Instigator (see **ergative**)

In effective ergative clauses, those where the verb has an object, the participant who causes the process, e.g. 'Paul' in 'Paul cooked the rice'.

Interpersonal meaning

The aspect of (textual) meaning which creates or reflects the roles and relationships between reader and writer (or speaker and hearer).

Interrogative mood

The grammatical mood associated with questioning. The grammatical test for the interrogative is that the finite verb precedes the subject

	Finite	_Subject_	
	Did	you	eat the plums?
What	were	you	doing?

The only exception to this rule is with _wh-_ interrogatives when the _wh-_ word is the subject, e.g.:

Subject	_Finite_	
Who	ate	the plums?

Intertextual chains

The process by which one text is passed on through a series of readers/writers and may be modified in the process. There are particularly long intertextual chains in the news-gathering process and on multiply-edited entries on Wikipedia.

Intertextuality

The way in which one text impinges on other later texts, or, to put it another way, how texts feed off and relate to each other. Examples are quotation, paraphrase, fan fiction and parody.

Irony

Saying or writing something very different or opposite from what one knows to be true, with the intention that the hearer/reader will realise that it is not true. (If you intend them not to realise this falsity it is lying rather than irony). Irony often involves echoing or quoting what another speaker actually said or might have said and which turns out not to be true, as a way of showing dissatisfaction with or scorn for that person or their message.

Latent ideology

The ideology which we accept in our everyday life and discourse without being aware of it. Ideology very often becomes hidden through a process of **naturalisation** in which we come to accept that the texts we encounter and their language are the only natural way of representing experience. It is only because ideology is so well hidden that people can believe in the ideal of 'objective' or 'unbiased' reporting. Learning an exotic language or doing critical discourse analysis are good ways of becoming aware of latent ideologies.

Lead

The element of the generic structure of news which comprises the first paragraph of the news report. Along with the headline it gives a summary. It usually contains information about who did what, when, where, and how.

Linguistic relativity

The claim that the language we speak determines the way we think about the world and ourselves. The weak version claims that speaking one language makes it difficult to think as the speakers of another language do, the strong version that it makes it impossible.

Localised or modular texts

Texts using graphic or visual devices to create easily perceptible sections which can be read selectively and in any order. By contrast, texts that are not sectionalised by visual or graphic information tend to be **progressive**, and are read in linear order from start to finish.

Location circumstance

An adverbial of place, telling where a process took place. It is possible to 'promote' a location circumstance into an actor, a strategy which might give more syntactic prominence to the 'environment'. For example 'snakes slithered over the rocks' could become 'the rocks are slithering with snakes'.

Main event

The event in a news story which is referred to most prominently in the headline and the lead (see also **lead**).

Material process

A process which is an action or event and answers the question 'What happened?' The thing responsible for causing the action/event is called the **actor**. The thing that the action or event affects is called the **affected**.

Medium (see **ergative**)

In ergative clauses the participant that is the subject in middle clauses, i.e. when the clause has no object, or the object in effective when the clause has an object, e.g. 'rice' in 'the rice cooked' or 'Paul cooked the rice'.

Mental process

A process of perception, cognition or emotion. In grammatical analysis the 'person' who experiences these perceptions, thoughts or emotions we can call the **experiencer**, and these perceptions, thoughts or emotions are called the **experience**. Experiences in mental process can be coded in the grammar as though they were actors in material processes. For example 'I noticed the river' ⟶ 'the river arrested my gaze', 'we love the forest' ⟶ 'the forest touches our hearts', and we refer to this as **activation of experiences**.

Metaphor

A figure of speech or tool of thought in which one thing is experienced in terms of another. Like irony, a metaphor often states something which the writer does not believe but depends on for its interpretation on similarities between what is stated and the actual state of affairs, not, as with irony, on dissimilarities.

Middle (see **ergative**)

Middle clauses are ergative clauses which have no object, in contrast with effective clauses which have an object, e.g. 'the rice cooked' is a middle clause, 'John cooked the rice' is an effective clause.

Minor sentences

Stretches of text punctuated as sentences but which are incomplete either because the main finite verb or subject has been missed out, e.g. on a postcard 'Went to Venice yesterday. Lovely weather, but too crowded.' In dialogue such utterances or 'sentences' occur quite naturally, for example in response to questions.

Modal constructions

Verbs, adjectives or adverbs which express obligation/permission, probability, inclination or usuality. Modal verbs are the following auxiliary verbs: *may, might, can, could, will, would, shall, should, must, have to, ought to, need*. Examples of modal adjectives and adverbs are *permitted, allowed, expected, required, possible, possibly, inclined to, determined to, usually, sometimes, always*.

Modesty maxim

The aspect of the politeness principle which says that in order to be polite one should be modest, criticise oneself or underplay one's achievement rather than praise oneself or boast.

Modular texts (see **localised or modular texts**)

Monoglossic/monologic texts

Texts in which only one voice is heard, one opinion or point of view is apparent. These contrast with **heteroglossic texts**, which are many-voiced and dialogic with diverging opinions and points of view.

Multimodality

Texts are multimodal if they combine more than one mode of communication. For example, TV ads will often combine the visual mode in the film, the language mode in the speech, and the musical mode as background or in jingles.

Narrative, narrative structure

A genre in which one tells a story as a means of making sense of events and happenings in the world. It can both entertain and inform. The generic structure of narrative, according to Labov, is

(Abstract) ^ (Orientation) ^ Complicating Action ^ Resolution ^ (Coda)
......................+ (Evaluation)..................

Narrative process

In visual communication this is a process that represents actions, events and changes, rather like the material processes of grammar. There are two kinds of narrative process: **actional** (which may be transactional like transitive material process verbs with an affected), or **reactional** where the direction of gaze of one participant indicates that they are reacting to another process.

Narrative report of speech act

A means of reporting speech in which none of the original words need occur. '"I will resign tomorrow"' might become in narrative report of speech act 'Jean Paul indicated his intention of relinquishing employment on the 6th May'.

Naturalisation (see **latent ideology**)

News story

The major element of the generic structure of news reports. The news story comprises the episode and comments.

News values

Aspects of news content which make it more likely to get into the news. They include reference to elite persons and nations, cultural proximity and meaningfulness to the reader, intensity such as larger numbers of casualties and fatalities cross the threshold for inclusion in the news, unexpectedness, and negativity.

Nominalisation

A grammatical transformation, or grammatical metaphor, which turns a verb or an adjective (or clause) into a noun (noun phrase). It is brought about most obviously by adding a suffix, (e.g. *rough* ⟶ *roughness*, *imply* ⟶ *implication*), but less obviously by using a noun which has the same form as a verb, e.g. *a catch*. Nominalisation allows the omission of both participants in a clause, e.g. actor and affected in material process clauses. Its other effects are to remove time or tense and to introduce existential presuppositions.

Non-assured readers (see **assured readers**)
Non-restrictive premodification (see **restrictive premodification**)
Noun
The part of speech typically used for referring to entities with dimensions in space – things, people, places etc. Structurally, nouns fit into frames like 'John noticed the...'. In terms of their form, they regularly inflect or change form to mark the plural, e.g. *ship/ships, dog/dogs, mouse/mice*.
Noun phrase
The phrase of which the noun is the head, the compulsory constituent. Noun phrases can vary in length from one word, e.g. 'dogs', to very complex structures with premodification and postmodification, e.g. 'my neighbour's scruffy black dog which you see every morning and which persists in burying bones in my garden...'.

Object (see **subject**)
Objective perspective (see **perspective**)
Old English
The form of the English language up to around 1100 AD, in contrast with Middle English, 1100–1500 AD, and Modern English, 1500 to the present.
Optionality
The choice of saying 'yes' or 'no'. It is important in making polite requests to put them in question form and even politer to put them in the form which makes it easy to say 'no', e.g. 'You couldn't drive me to the station, could you?'.
Orientation
An element of narrative structure which gives information about the time, place, persons and situation/activity type they are engaged in when the action takes place. Typically this section will include adverbials of time and place, relational verbs like *to be* and progressive *-ing* forms of the verb.
Overwording
When a phenomenon, person or thing is referred to with unnecessary frequency and with a variety of different terms. This often betrays a preoccupation or obsession due to ideological struggle.

Parody
A kind of intertextuality used for humorous purposes, in which the content is presented in an inappropriate style. For example, 'I put it to you that when you should have been washing your hair in anti-dandruff shampoo last night, you were in fact watching TV all evening, is that not so? Do you plead guilty or not guilty of having dandruff?'. This talks about hair-washing and dandruff in the style of legal cross-examination. Parody may involve three elements: the **source expression** and **derived expression** (e.g. language of the law) and **displacing content** (hairdressing, hair-washing).

Passive, passivisation (see **active**)

A tense of the verb which takes the form of *had* + past participle. It refers to an event which occurred before the past events that you are already describing. For example, 'When he returned to his flat Paul saw that the dog had chewed the carpet'. Paul's returning and seeing is already referred to in the past tense. The dog's chewing the carpet took place before he returned and saw it, so we use the past perfect *had chewed*. (Halliday calls this tense the past in past).

Past tense

The tense typically used to refer to something which happens before it is reported. Many verbs mark the past tense with *-ed*, though some change their vowel sound *see/saw, come/came, take/took*.

Periodicity

The patterns of repetition with variation of visual organisation, such as clusters, which allow multiple entry points for the same topic or meaning.

Personification

Using a verb, adjective or noun normally used to describe a human to describe an animal, plant or non-living entity, e.g. 'the hills danced for joy', 'the daffodil encouraged the tulip to bloom', 'the bald landscape'.

Perspective

An interpersonal meaning of visual communication. It may be **subjective perspective**, where the point of view is built-in and determined by the participant in the image, and where the gaze of the viewer has an entry point. Subjective perspective combines **degrees of involvement** and **degrees of power**. Involvement is conveyed by 180% angle to the viewer who is parallel to the horizontal orientation of the participant in the image. Degree of power is conveyed by the downward or upward vertical angle – if the viewer looks down on the participant the viewer is more powerful, and vice versa, and if the viewer looks up to the image, the viewer is less powerful and vice versa. **Objective perspective**, where there is no initial built-in focus for viewer gaze, is realised by a direct frontal angle or perpendicular top-down angle.

Possessive clauses (see **relational process**)

Possessive presupposition

The kind of presupposition that is made when we use *'s* to indicate possession, or the pronominal 'adjectives' *hers/his, their, my, our, your*. For instance, 'I looked under Raymond's car for your rabbit' presupposes >> 'Raymond has a car' and 'you have a rabbit'.

Power

A major element in interpersonal relationships, indicating inequality between speakers. The power takes various forms: physical strength; the authority given to a person by an institution; status depending on wealth, education, place of residence; or expertise, the possession of knowledge or skill.

Pragmatics

The branch of linguistics concerned with the production and interpretation of utterances in context. Whereas **semantics** answers the question 'how do we know what this sentence means?', pragmatics answers the question 'how do we know what X means by uttering/writing this sentence in this time and at this place?'. It studies topics like establishing the referent, the principles governing polite co-operative talk, speech acts, propositional attitude and inference.

Preferred second

The preferred second member of a pair of speech acts. For example, in the speech act pair of invitation followed by acceptance or refusal, acceptance is preferred and refusal is **dispreferred**. The dispreferred is often accompanied by delays or voiced hesitation and an account or apology, e.g. 'Mmm er sorry I can't make it then because I've got to go to a meeting'.

Premodification (see **restrictive premodification**)

Present tense

The tense of the verb which refers to habitual actions or present feelings or states. For example, 'I go to college by bus', 'I feel sick this morning', or 'The phone is dead'. With most verbs the present tense is the basic shortest form of the verb, that is the infinitive without *to*, e.g. *(to) dive*. But the third person singular of the present tense adds an *s* to this base form, e.g. *he/she/it dives*.

Presupposition

An assumption made by a speaker or writer which is not explicitly stated. Strictly speaking the presuppositions of a sentence remain unaffected when it is negated. This makes presuppositions less easy to argue against than their equivalent explicitly stated sentence. For example, 'Clinton's dishonesty was frowned on by the majority of Americans' when negated becomes 'Clinton's dishonesty was not frowned on by the majority of Americans'. But the negated sentence still presupposes, without stating it, that Clinton is dishonest.

Procedure

A genre which shows how something can be accomplished through a series or steps of actions to be taken in a certain order. Examples are instructional texts like recipes.

Progressive form of the verb

The form of the verb which has *-ing* on the end. It indicates that the process referred to by the verb is still in progress, incomplete or unfinished, e.g. 'I was *driving* to work when lightning struck my car'.

Progressive texts (see **localised or modular texts**)

Pronoun

A word which normally substitutes for a noun or noun phrase, e.g. *I, you, they, him, myself, some, these, any.* First person pronouns are *I/me* singular, *we/us* plural, second person pronoun is *you*, third person pronouns are *he/him she/her, they/them*. The general or impersonal pronoun is *one*. *We* can either be **inclusive**, including the reader, or **exclusive**, excluding the reader.

Propositional attitude

The attitude a writer or speaker has to the proposition which they have expressed, for example desirability in commands, uncertainty in questions and belief in statements. But note that in ironical or metaphorical statements the attitude is less than belief. Mood encodes some kinds of propositional attitude linguistically, but in graphic communication it is very difficult to encode.

Range

A participant in a material process clause that, though it is the object of the verb, is not much affected by the process, e.g. I entered <u>the room</u>.

Reaction

An element of the generic structure of news reports, namely, an action taking place in response to the main event.

Reactional process (see **narrative process**)

Reading position (see **subject positions**)

Receiver (see **verbal process**)

Recipient

The person or participant in a material process clause who receives the other affected participant, e.g. 'Pom' in 'We gave Pom the cigarettes'.

Register

This refers to the relationship or correlation between the social situation in which a text is processed and the linguistic features of the text. The aspects of social situation comprise field – the contents of what activity is going on, tenor – the interpersonal relations between writer and reader, and mode – the role of language in the activity. If the text is an engineering textbook, for example, the field will be engineering and education, which will be reflected in technical vocabulary and definitional sentence structures, the tenor will be reflected in fairly formal vocabulary and impersonal grammar like passives, and because the mode is exposition, there will be explanation of new technical terms in less specialised vocabulary or metaphors.

In this book's use of the term register, these linguistic features are those at the level of the sentence and below, so that genre includes register, and genre may be described as register + generic structure.

Relational process

A process which describes states of affairs, static situations. It relates two things, or a thing and a property, the **token** and the **value**, e.g. 'John (token) is a teacher (value)', 'John (token) is in the dining room (value)'. Common relational process verbs are *to be* and *to have*. Relational clauses may be **attributive**, where the token is a carrier and the value is an attribute (e.g. John is silly, Paul is a hairdresser) or **identifying**, where the token is identified and the value an identifier (Jeremy Corbyn is the Prime Minister) or **possessive**, where the token is a possessor and the value is a possession (e.g. Amelia has a piano). Tokens in relational processes can be grammatically encoded as actors in material processes. For example, 'Five trees are in the valley' ⟶ 'Five trees stand in the valley', giving rise to what we call the **activation of tokens**.

Resolution

An element of the generic structure of narrative provided by the last of the narrative clauses. It brings the sequence of actions and events to a relatively neat end, by, for example, solving a problem.

Resource integration principle

The way in which various multimodal resources are combined to create and reinforce meanings. For example, in promotional material the verbal, visual and spatial may be integrated to highlight meanings that would not otherwise be so obvious.

Restrictive premodification

When a premodifier, for example an adjective before a noun, is used to define a sub-set of the things referred to by the noun, for instance *black* in 'black cars'. Adjectives can also be used with a **non-restrictive** meaning, indicating that all of the referents of the noun share the quality referred to by the adjective, e.g. 'The warm waters of the Gulf Stream'. This restrictive/non-restrictive ambiguity can be exploited for purposes of stereotyping.

Rheme (see **theme**)

Rhetorical question

A sentence in interrogative mood that looks like a question but is in fact an indirect way of making a statement, e.g. 'who left the window open?' could convey 'someone left the window open'.

Rhythm

A regular pattern of stressed (louder) and unstressed (softer) syllables.

Sayer (see **verbal process**)

Schema

The mental organisation of stereotypical knowledge about objects, sequences of behaviour and discourse patterns. We generally rely heavily on schematic knowledge in making inferences when interpreting discourse.

Semantics (see **pragmatics**)

Shifter

A word which changes its meaning according to who utters it, when and where. For example *I, here*, and *now*. Also known as a *deictic* term.

Social distance
The relationship between a visual text and the viewer, involving degrees of closeness. Close shots, medium shots and long shots respectively convey an increasingly distant relationship.

Source expression (see **parody**)

Stack
A kind of paragraph structure common in argument or exposition which comprises lists of arguments or facts. These are often used to justify the thesis or argument stated in the topic sentence which precedes them.

Step
A kind of paragraph/text structure associated with procedural genres. Each sentence or clause of the paragraph describes one step in a process and is presented in the order in which it occurs.

Stereotyping
Assuming on the basis of some members of a class having a characteristic that other members have that characteristic.

Subject
Subjects and **objects** are major elements in a clause and are noun phrases. In the active voice in statements (declarative mood) subjects precede the verb and objects follow the verb. In 'John hit the ball', 'John' is the subject, and 'the ball', the other noun phrase, is the object. The subject, not the object determines whether the verb has the plural or singular form:

Ducks love the pond	Plural Subject + Plural Verb + Singular Object
The duck loves the ponds	Singular Subject + Singular Verb + Plural Object

Several pronouns in English have different forms according to whether they are subject or object. For example *he* (subject), *him* (object), *she* (subject) *her* (object), *they* (subject) *them* (object), *I* (subject) *me* (object), *we* (subject) *us* (object).

Subject positions
The relative roles, positions and identities created for reader and writer through texts/discourse. These positions are culturally determined through subjection to societal institutions such as the educational system, religious organisations, the family and the media. The subject position of a reader is the **reading position**. This is more likely to be consciously learned/taught, for example we might learn to read literature or a religious text according to certain conventions of interpretation.

Subjective perspective (see **perspective**)

Summary
The element of the generic structure of news reports consisting of the headline and the lead (first paragraph).

Symbolic process (see **conceptual process**)

Sympathy maxim

One of the maxims of the politeness principle. It states that one should at least take an interest in the readers' problems or successes and ideally claim your feelings match theirs. Examples of sympathising would be condolences and congratulations.

Synthetic personalisation

Treating a mass audience as though they are individuals being directly addressed. It is very common in advertising and the media and facilitated by the singular/plural ambiguity of *you*, e.g. 'Thank you for visiting our store. See you soon' above the exit to a supermarket.

Tact maxim

One aspect of Leech's politeness principle which says that to be polite when making requests one should build in indirectness and optionality, for example using statements or questions rather than commands.

Text

The physical form which the writing (speaking) takes on the page (in the air) and the meanings which this physical form encodes. We use it in contradistinction to the term *discourse*. Decoding of text depends upon semantics and answers the question 'What does the text mean?'.

Text population

The people and characters mentioned in a text.

Textual meaning

The meanings involved in the organisation of a text, for example the distribution of information within a clause and paragraph, or the overall generic structure.

Thematic development

The pattern of themes over a whole paragraph or passage.

Theme

The informational starting point in the clause. In English it corresponds to the first of the basic elements of the clause – subject, object, verb or adverbial. The remainder of the clause constitutes the **rheme**. For example:

Theme	*Rheme*
The florist shop	stocks wonderful hollyhocks

It is normal to put old or given information in the theme and new information towards the end of the rheme.

Time

In (online) news reports the date (and hour/minutes) when a news report was posted (or updated).

Token (see **relational process**)

Topic sentence
The sentence in a paragraph which encapsulates the main idea. In 'stack' paragraphs it generally appears at the beginning (and/or end).

Transitivity
The resources of the grammar devoted to ideational meaning, that is, the representation of the physical and mental worlds and what goes on in them.

Upgrading
The choice of a less common word when an ordinary one will do, in order to sensationalise or exaggerate the nature of the activity.

Value (see **relational process**)

Vector
The imaginary line in an image, which shows the path of movement or direction of gaze. The **gaze** is the vector formed by the glance of the participant/s towards the viewer. Gaze which is directed to the viewer makes a **visual demand**, while gaze directed elsewhere makes a **visual offer**.

Verb
A word-class or part of speech which refers to a process – of doing, being, experiencing or saying (see **material, relational, mental** and **verbal process**). Verbs can be inflected, that is change their form or ending to show tense. For example:

> she works hard (present tense)
> she worked hard (past tense)

Verbs can be either main verbs or **auxiliary** verbs. For example in the sentences

> I may decide to go to the match
> He did tell me to come at three.

'decide' and 'tell' are the main verbs, and 'may' and 'did' are auxiliary verbs. Auxiliary verbs cannot usually stand on their own, for example 'I open the fridge' and 'I can open the fridge' but not 'I can the fridge'. One type of auxiliary verb is a modal verb (see **modal constructions**).

Verbal process
A process of saying or writing (or other symbolic expression). In verbal process clauses the participant doing the saying or writing is the **sayer**. The person addressed is the **receiver**. What is actually said is the **verbiage**.

Verbal reaction
One element of the generic structure of news reports which refers to a spoken response to the main event.

Verbiage (see **verbal process**)

Visual contact

The connection established between the image and the viewer by looking at how images directly or indirectly address their viewers. Visual contact is realised through the resource of the gaze.

Visual informativeness

The extent to which a writer uses devices like graphics, pictures, colour, white space, bullets, asterisks, and highlighting to make a text more visually arresting than homogenous print. Visually informative texts tend to be more localised and to cater to non-assured readers.

Visual demand (see **vector**)

Visual offer (see **vector**)

REFERENCES

Althusser, L. (1984) *Essays in Ideology*. London: Verso.

Austin, J.L. (1962) *How to Do Things with Words*. Oxford: Oxford University Press.

Bain, A. (1865) *The Emotions and the Will*, 2nd edition. Harlow: Longmans.

Baldry, A. and Thibault, Paul (2006) *Multimodal Transcription and Text Analysis*. London: Equinox.

Batkiewicz, S. (2011) Does digital technology offer continuity or change in news production. Unpublished paper, School of Oriental and African Studies www.academia.edu/1160130/Does_digital_technology_offer_continuity_or_change_in_news_production, retrieved 10 June 2015.

Baudrillard, J. (1989) *America*. Trans. C. Turner. London: Verso.

Bazerman, C. (1992). *The Informed Writer: Using Sources in the Disciplines*. Boston, MA: Houghton Mifflin.

Bazerman, C. (2003). 'Intertextuality: How texts rely on other texts'. In C. Bazerman and P. Prior, *What Writing Does and How It Does It: An Introduction to Analyzing Texts and Textual Practices*. London: Routledge, 83–96.

Beck, U. (1992) *Risk Society: Towards a New Modernity*. Trans. Mark Ritter. London: Sage.

Bell, A. (1991) *The Language of News Media*. Oxford: Blackwell.

'Benefits in Britain: separating the facts from the fiction', *Observer*, 6 April 2013, www.theguardian.com/politics/2013/apr/06/welfare-britain-facts-myths, retrieved 12 May 2014.

Bergson, H. (1900) *Le rire: essai sur la signification du comique*. Paris: Felix Alcan.

Bernhardt, S. (1985) 'Text structure and graphic design: the visible design'. In D. Benson and J. Greaves (eds), *Systemic Perspectives on Discourse*, vol. 2. Norwood, NJ: Ablex.

Billig, Michael (2005) *Laughter and Ridicule: Towards a Social Critique of Humour*. London: Sage.

Bimber, B. (2003) *Information and American Democracy: Technology in the Evolution of Political Power*. Cambridge: Cambridge University Press.

Bohm, D. (1980) *Wholeness and the Implicate Order*. London: Routledge.

Carr, J. and Greeves, L. (2007) *The Naked Jape: Uncovering the Hidden World of Jokes*. Harmondsworth: Penguin.

'China's tragic crackdown on social media activism', *Fortune*, 12 September 2013, http://management.fortune.cnn.com/2013/09/12/china-social-media, retrieved 12 May 2014.

Cixous, H. (1981) 'Sorties'. In E. Marks and I. De Courtivron (eds) *New French Feminins*. Brighton: Harvester, 90–99.

Colomb, G.G. and Williams, J. (1985) 'Perceiving structure in professional prose'. In L Odell and D. Goswami *Writing in Non-Academic Settings*. New York: Guilford, 87–112.

Cope, W. (2010) *Making Cocoa for Kingsley Amis*. London: Faber.

Crystal, D. (2001) *Language and the Internet*. Cambridge: Cambridge University Press.

Davis, H. and Walton, P. (1983) 'Death of a premier: consensus and closure in international news'. In H. Davis and P. Walton, *Language, Image, Media*. Oxford: Blackwell, 8–49.

Faigley, L. (1992) *Fragments of Rationality*. Pittsburgh, PA: University of Pittsburgh Press.

Fairclough, Norman. (1995) *Media Discourse*. London: Arnold.

Fairclough, Norman. (2001) *Language and power*, 2nd edition. Harlow: Longman.

Fish, S. (1980) 'Is there a text in this class'. In S. Fish, *Is There a Text in This Class?* Cambridge, MA: Harvard University Press, 303–321.

Fowler, R. (1991) *Language in the News*. London: Routledge.

Freud, S. (1905/1963) *Jokes and their Relation to the Unconscious*. Trans. J. Strachey. London: Routledge.

Friedan, B. (1964) *The Feminine Mystique*. New York: Dell.

Frith, S. (1981) *Sound Effects*. New York: Pantheon.

Galtung, J. and Ruge, M. (1973) 'Structuring and selecting news'. In S. Cohen and J. Young (eds) *The Manufacture of News: Social Problems, Deviance and the Mass Media*. London: Constable.

Garner, J. (2011) *Politically Correct Bedtime Stories*. London: Souvenir Press.

Geis, M.L. (1987) *The Language of Politics*. New York: Springer-Verlag.

Glasgow University Media Group (1980) *More Bad News*. London: Routledge.

Goatly, A. (2007) *Washing the Brain: Metaphor and Hidden Ideology*. Amsterdam: Benjamins.

Goatly, A. (2011) *The Language of Metaphors* (2nd edition). Abingdon: Routledge.

Goatly, A. (in press) 'The poems of Edward Thomas: a case study in Ecostylistics'.

Greenslade, R. (2009) 'Controlling interest', *Guardian* 27 July 2009, www.theguardian.com/media/2009/jul/27/newspaper-owners-editorial-control, retrieved 26 March 2014.

Halliday, M. (1994) *An Introduction to Functional Grammar*, 2nd edition. London: Arnold.

Halliday, M. and Matthiessen, C. (2004) *An Introduction to Functional Grammar*, London: Hodder.

Hanlon, J. (1999) 'A pound of flesh', *New Internationalist* 310: 26–27.

Harvey, D. (1996) *Justice, Nature and the Geography of Difference*. Cambridge, MA: Oxford.

Hiraga, M. (1991) 'Metaphors Japanese women live by', *Working Papers on Language, Gender and Sexism*, vol. 1, no. 1, AILA Commission on Language and Gender, 38–57.

Hoey, M. (1973) *On the Surface of Discourse*. London: Allen and Unwin.

Holmes, J. (2000) 'Politeness, power and provocation: how humour functions in the workplace', *Discourse Studies* 2(2): 159–185.

Horgan, J. (1998) *The End of Science*. London: Abacus.

Jones, J. (1991) 'Grammatical metaphor and technicality in academic writing', in F. Christie (ed.), *Literacy in Social Processes*, Darwin: Centre for Studies in Language and Education, 178–198

Kress, G. (1985) *Linguistic Processes in Sociocultural Practice*. Oxford: Oxford University Press.

Kress, G. (2014) 'Reading, learning, and "texts" in their interaction with the digital media'. NCRM Working Paper (unpublished). Retrieved from: http://eprints.ncrm.ac.uk/3597.

Kress, G. and Van Leeuwen, T. (1996) *Reading Images: The Grammar of Visual Design*. London: Routledge (2nd edition in press).

Labov, W. (1972) *Language in the Inner City*. Philadelphia, PA: University of Pennsylvania Press.

Lakoff, G. and Johnson, M. (1980) *Metaphors We Live By*. Chicago, IL: Chicago University Press.

Larkin, P. (1955) 'Toads'. In P. Larkin, *The Less Deceived*, London: The Marvell Press, 32–33.

Leech, G. (1983) *Principles of Pragmatics*. Harlow: Longman.

Leech, G. and Short, M. (1973) *Style in Fiction*. Harlow: Longman.

Lemke, J.L. (2002) 'Travels in hypermobility', *Visual Communication* 1(3): 299–325.

Levinson, S. (1983) *Pragmatics*. Cambridge: Cambridge University Press.

Lovelock, J. (1988) *The Ages of Gaia*. Oxford: Oxford University Press.

Lovelock, J. (1995) *Gaia: A New Look at Life on Earth*, new edition. Oxford: Oxford University Press.

MacRobbie, A. (1991) *Feminism and Youth Culture: From Jackie to Just Seventeen*. London: Macmillan.

Martin, J.R. and Matthiessen, C. (1991) 'Systemic typology and topology'. In F. Christie (ed.) *Literacy in Social Processes*. Darwin: Centre for Studies of Language in Education, Northern Territories University.

Miller, A. (1958) *Collected Plays*. London: Cresset Press.

Mills, S. (1995) *Feminist Stylistics*. London: Routledge.

Monbiot, G. (2014a) 'Cleansing the stock', www.monbiot.com/2014/10/21/cleansing-the-stock, retrieved 26 July 2014.

Monbiot, G. (2014b) 'The pricing of everything', www.monbiot.com/2014/07/24/the-pricing-of-everything, retrieved 26 July 2014.

Montgomery, M., Durant, A., Fabb, N., Furniss, T. and Mills, S. (1992) *Ways of Reading*. London: Routledge.

Morrison, E. (2012) 'In the beginning, there was fan fiction: from the four gospels to *Fifty Shades*', *Guardian*, 13 August 2012.

Muhlhäusler, P. (1996) 'Linguistic adaptation to changed environmental conditions'. In A. Fill (ed.) *Sprachokologie und Okolinguistik*, Tubingen: Stauffenburg Verlag.

Nash, W. (1980) *Designs in Prose*. Harlow: Longman.

Nataf, Z.I. (1998) 'Whatever I feel....', *New Internationalist* 300(4/98): 22–25.

Oring, E. (2003) *Engaging Humor*, Urbana and Chicago, IL: University of Illinois Press.

Orr, D.W. (1992) *Ecological Literacy: Education and the Transition to a Postmodern World*. New York: State University of New York Press.

Oswald, A. (2005) *Woods etc.* London: Faber and Faber.

Pound, L. (1936) 'American euphemisms for dying, death and burial', *American Speech* 11(3): 195–202.

Poynton, C. (1989) *Language and Gender: Making the Difference*. Oxford: Oxford University Press.

Prigogine, I. and Stengers, I. (1985) *Order out of Chaos*. London: Flamingo.

Rifkin, J. (1987) *Time Wars*. New York: Touchstone/Simon and Schuster.

Rong, J. (2008) *Wolf Totem*. Harmondsworth: Penguin.

Ross, A. (1998) *The Language of Humour*. London: Rouledge.

Saville-Troike, M. (1982) *The Ethnography of Communication*. Oxford: Blackwell.

Schank, R. and Abelson, R. (1979) *Scripts, Plans, Goals and Understanding*. Hillsdale, NJ: Erlbaum.

Scheff, T.J. (1997) *Emotion, the Social Bond and Human Reality*. Cambridge: Cambridge University Press.

Schleppegrell, M.J. (1996) 'Abstraction and agency in middle school environmental education'. In J.C. Bang, J. Door, Richard J.

Alexander, Alwin Fill and Frans Verhagen (eds) *Language and Ecology: Proceedings of the Symposium on Ecolinguistics of AILA '96, Jyvaskala.* Odense: Odense University Press, 27–42.

Scott, K. (2013) 'Pragmatically motivated null subjects in English: a relevance theory perspective', *Journal of Pragmatics*, 53: 68–83.

Searle, J.R. (1969) *Speech Acts: An Essay in the Philosophy of Language*, Cambridge: Cambridge University Press.

Searle, J.R. (1979) *Expression and Meaning*. Cambridge: Cambridge University Press.

Shieh, Yee Bing (1994/1995) *Language in the Singapore News: Constructs of China and the United States.* Singapore: National University of Singapore.

Short, M. (1988) 'Speech presentation, the novel and the press'. In W. Van Peer (ed.) *The Taming of the Text: Explorations in Language, Literature and Culture.* London: Routledge, 61–81.

Simpson, P. (1993) *Language, Ideology and Point of View.* London: Routledge.

Simpson, P. (2003) *On the Discourse of Satire.* Amsterdam: Benjamins.

Simpson, P. and Mayr, A. (2010) *Language and Power: A Resource Book for Students.* London: Routledge.

Spencer, H. (1864) 'The physiology of laughter'. In H. Spencer, *Essays: Scientific, Political and Speculative*, second series. New York: D. Appleton.

Spengler, O. (1922) *The Decline of the West.* London: Allen and Unwin.

Sperber, D. and Wilson, D. (1995) *Relevance: Communication and Cognition*, 2nd edition. Oxford: Blackwell.

Talbot, M. (1992) 'The construction of gender in a teen-age magazine'. In N. Fairclough (ed.) *Critical Language Awareness.* Harlow: Longman, 174–199.

Tan, Kim Luan (1993) Describing students' literature test essays using systemic linguistics. Unpublished MA dissertation, National University of Singapore.

Tanaka, K. (1994) *Advertising Language: A Pragmatic Approach to Advertisements in Britain and Japan.* London: Routledge.

Tewksbury, D. and Rittenberg, J. (2012) *News on the Internet: Information and Citizenship in the 21st Century.* Oxford: Oxford University Press.

Thomas, E. (1949) *Collected Poems.* London: Faber and Faber.

Thomas, J. (1995) *Meaning in Interaction.* Harlow: Longman.

Thomson, J.B. (1984) *Studies in the Theory of Ideology.* London: Polity Press.

Van Dijk, T.A. (1986) 'News schemata'. In C.R. Cooper and S. Greenbaum, *Studying Writing: Linguistic Approaches.* London: Sage, 151–185.

Van Dijk, T.A. (1988a) *News Analysis: Case Studies of International and National News in the Press.* Hillsdale, NJ: Lawrence Erlbaum.

Van Dijk, T.A. (1998b) *News as Discourse*. Hillsdale, NJ: Lawrence Erlbaum.

Van Leeuwen, T. (1987) 'Generic strategies in press journalism', *Australian Review of Applied Linguistics* 10(2): 199–220.

Volosinov, V.N/Bakhtin, M. (1973) *Marxism and the Philosophy of Language*. Trans. L. Matejka and I.R. Titunik. Cambridge, MA: Harvard University Press.

Whorf, B.L. (1956) *Language, Thought and Reality*, edited by J.B. Carroll. Cambridge MA: MIT Press.

Wignell, P., Martin, J.R. and Eggins, S. (1993) 'The discourse of geography: ordering and explaining the experiential world.' In M.A.K. Halliday and J.R. Martin (eds) *Writing Science: Literacy and Discursive Power*. Pittsburgh, PA: University of Pittsburgh Press, 136–165.

Williams, R. (1977) *Marxism and Literature*, Oxford: Oxford University Press.

Williamson, J. (1978) *Decoding Advertisements: Ideology and Meaning in Advertising*. London: Marion Boyars.

Wolfson, N. (1989) *Perspectives: Sociolinguistics and TESOL*, Rowley, MA: Newbury House.

Wordsworth, W. (1933/1960, first published 1805) *The Prelude*. Oxford: Oxford University Press.

Worldwatch Institute (2012) *State of the World 2012: Creating Sustainable Prosperity*. Washington, DC: Island Press.

INDEX

Bolding indicates the place where the term is first introduced and explained
Please also refer to the glossary on the website.

Taylor & Francis eBooks

Helping you to choose the right eBooks for your Library

Add Routledge titles to your library's digital collection today. Taylor and Francis ebooks contains over 50,000 titles in the Humanities, Social Sciences, Behavioural Sciences, Built Environment and Law.

Choose from a range of subject packages or create your own!

Benefits for you

>> Free MARC records
>> COUNTER-compliant usage statistics
>> Flexible purchase and pricing options
>> All titles DRM-free.

Benefits for your user

>> Off-site, anytime access via Athens or referring URL
>> Print or copy pages or chapters
>> Full content search
>> Bookmark, highlight and annotate text
>> Access to thousands of pages of quality research at the click of a button.

REQUEST YOUR **FREE** INSTITUTIONAL TRIAL TODAY

Free Trials Available
We offer free trials to qualifying academic, corporate and government customers.

eCollections – Choose from over 30 subject eCollections, including:

Archaeology	Language Learning
Architecture	Law
Asian Studies	Literature
Business & Management	Media & Communication
Classical Studies	Middle East Studies
Construction	Music
Creative & Media Arts	Philosophy
Criminology & Criminal Justice	Planning
Economics	Politics
Education	Psychology & Mental Health
Energy	Religion
Engineering	Security
English Language & Linguistics	Social Work
Environment & Sustainability	Sociology
Geography	Sport
Health Studies	Theatre & Performance
History	Tourism, Hospitality & Events

For more information, pricing enquiries or to order a free trial, please contact your local sales team:
www.tandfebooks.com/page/sales